NON-SUNNI MUSLIMS IN THE
LATE OTTOMAN EMPIRE

Gözümün Nurlarına...
For Duygu, Idál, Ediz & Noya

'The difference between Orthodoxy or My-doxy and Heterodoxy or Thy-doxy.'
— Thomas Carlyle (1837)

NON-SUNNI MUSLIMS IN THE LATE OTTOMAN EMPIRE

State and Missionary Perceptions of the Alawis

Necati Alkan

I.B. TAURIS
LONDON • NEW YORK • OXFORD • NEW DELHI • SYDNEY

I.B. TAURIS
Bloomsbury Publishing Plc
50 Bedford Square, London, WC1B 3DP, UK
1385 Broadway, New York, NY 10018, USA
29 Earlsfort Terrace, Dublin 2, Ireland

BLOOMSBURY, I.B. TAURIS and the I.B. Tauris logo are trademarks of Bloomsbury Publishing Plc

First published in Great Britain 2022
This paperback edition published 2023

Copyright © Necati Alkan, 2022

Necati Alkan has asserted his right under the Copyright, Designs and Patents Act, 1988, to be identified as Author of this work.

For legal purposes the Acknowledgements on p. vii constitute an extension of this copyright page.

Series design by Adriana Brioso
Cover image: Alouite women and children from Diary in Photos Vol. III., by Whiting, John D., and G. Eric Matson, 1938. Library of Congress (LC-DIG-ppmsca-17414-00190).:

All rights reserved. No part of this publication may be reproduced or transmitted in any form or by any means, electronic or mechanical, including photocopying, recording, or any information storage or retrieval system, without prior permission in writing from the publishers.

Bloomsbury Publishing Plc does not have any control over, or responsibility for, any third-party websites referred to or in this book. All internet addresses given in this book were correct at the time of going to press. The author and publisher regret any inconvenience caused if addresses have changed or sites have ceased to exist, but can accept no responsibility for any such changes.

A catalogue record for this book is available from the British Library.

A catalog record for this book is available from the Library of Congress.

ISBN:	HB:	978-0-7556-1684-8
	PB:	978-0-7556-4474-2
	ePDF:	978-0-7556-1685-5
	eBook:	978-0-7556-1686-2

Typeset by RefineCatch Limited, Bungay, Suffolk

To find out more about our authors and books visit www.bloomsbury.com and sign up for our newsletters.

CONTENTS

List of figures	ix
Acknowledgements	x
A note on transliteration	xii

Introduction 1
    State of research about the Alawis and other non-Sunni groups based
        on Ottoman sources 2
    Sources and research questions 9

Chapter 1
THE NUSAYRIS IN THE OTTOMAN EMPIRE: A 'HETERODOX'
TRIBAL COMMUNITY AND THE STATE 15
    1.1. The Nusayri-Alawis: Beliefs and history 15
    1.2. The Ottoman Nusayris: Geography, Social Structure and Authority ... 25
    1.3. The status of the Nusayris in the Ottoman political system 34

Chapter 2
'APPROPRIATE OBJECTS OF CHRISTIAN BENEVOLENCE': PROTESTANT
MISSIONARIES AND THE NUSAYRIS 41
    2.1. Protestant American millenarian dreams in the nineteenth century ... 41
    2.2. Mission among heterodox groups: the Alevis and Druze 45
    2.3. Harvesting the souls of the Nusayris 51

Chapter 3
ABDÜLHAMID II'S CIVILIZING MISSION AND THE POLICY OF
'CORRECTION OF BELIEF(S)' 81
    3.1. The roots of 'correction of belief(s)' and conversion campaigns
        until the nineteenth century 82
    3.2. Correcting the beliefs of the Bektaşis after 1826 86
    3.3. The 'fine tuning' of the state during the Tanzimat and the reign
        of Abdülhamid II 94
    3.4. Fighting for the Nusayri soul in the Hamidian era 107

Chapter 4
THE NUSAYRIS UNDER YOUNG TURK RULE (1908–1918) 117
    4.1. The double-edged sword of the Young Turk Revolution 118
    4.2. Protestant missionary efforts among the Nusayris 121
    4.3. Muslim responses to Protestant missionary work 133

4.4. Late Ottoman official perceptions of non-Sunnis: the case of the Beirut province	146
4.5. The Nusayris in the Province of Beirut	150
Conclusion	159
Notes	163
Bibliography	203
Index	227

FIGURES

1.1	*Waterwheel, Antioch, Turkey*, by G. Eric and Edith Matson, between 1898–1930, Library of Congress.	26
1.2	*Antioch (Antakiyeh) and environs. Interested natives*, by G. Eric and Edith Matson, 1707, Library of Congress.	39
2.1	Yusuf Jadid and his wife Mariam. James McKinnis Balph, *Fifty Years of Mission Work in Syria* (Latakia, 1913), frontispiece.	54
2.2	Suleiman Hassan Makhloof, 'Daoud'. *Olive Trees*, August 1899, p. 255.	55
2.3	Telgie Ibrahim. *Herald of Mission News*, May 1892, p. 96.	68
2.4	Telgie's sisters Zahra and Safiya seated in the middle row, left and right. *Herald of Mission News*, February 1895, p. 30.	69
2.5	Dr. David Metheny and his family. *Herald of Mission News*, May 1892, p. 93.	71
3.1	*A Nosairiyeh of Antioch*, by G. Eric and Edith Matson, 1936, Library of Congress.	95
4.1	*Alouite women and children gleaning*, by John D. Whiting and G. Eric Matson, 1938, Library of Congress.	157

ACKNOWLEDGEMENTS

The focus of this book, the Alawis, has been my focus since my MA study at university. I have been collecting and reading materials about them in an attempt to write something in the future. This did not materialize until many years after I had finished my PhD. From 2008–2009 I was senior fellow at Koç University's Research Center for Anatolian Civilizations (Istanbul) and officially embarked on the project with a research grant. The next attempt to get moral and financial assistance for this project at the University of Erfurt (Germany) was, unfortunately, frustrated. I nevertheless managed to publish my article 'Fighting for the Nuṣayrī Soul: State, Protestant Missionaries and the 'Alawīs in the Late Ottoman Empire'.[1] What followed was a period of anxieties about my professional career and the future of my then small family. A glimmer of hope appeared when one of my unsolicited applications was answered by a generous person.

The genesis of this book, then, was at the University of Bamberg in Germany. I would like to express my sincerest gratitude to Patrick Franke, Chair of the Department of Islamic Studies, who sent my proposal 'The Nusayri-Alawis in the late Ottoman State' to the *Deutsche Forschungsgemeinschaft* (DFG, German Research Foundation) and secured a temporary position for me as principal investigator from January 2016 to April 2019. I was able to do my research through the generous funding of the DFG (Project ID: FR 1536/5-1). In this process Patrick was always supportive, and attentively and critically read my research and offered many insights in our meetings.

I am also grateful to the *Gerda Henkel Stiftung* that financed my research with a scholarship from January 2015 to January 2016. Many thanks are due to Thomas Podranski (Head of Research Scholarships and Special Programmes) for tackling administrative issues then. During this period, I was visiting researcher at the University of Bamberg, where Patrick provided an office for me. Again, I am indebted to him for his kindness, and to his secretary Iga Seemann for the time she spent solving administrative issues over the years.

Although working on this book has been a lonely experience, research is not the product of a single person. My thanks go to the staff of the Ottoman Archives in Istanbul (former *Başbakanlık Osmanlı Arşivi*, BOA) for its assistance and helpfulness in digitizing and making easily available the relevant documents when I was physically on the spot. The Archives made it eventually possible to access and download many documents from its website. However, as this was not possible to do from abroad in Germany, I am grateful for my friend Ufuk Celme for downloading and sending electronically additional documents during the last phase of the completion of the book when I was unable to be in Istanbul.

I also should like to thank all those colleagues and friends who contributed intellectually to this work. Firstly and foremost, I am indebted to Abdulhamit Kırmızı (formerly at Şehir University, Istanbul), visiting lecturer at the University of Bamberg's MA programme Cultural Studies of the Middle East (2020–2021), who thoroughly read my final manuscript and shifted my attention to aspects that had not occurred to me previously. Owen Miller (Bilkent University) and Rıza Yıldırım (Emory University) showed curiosity in my work and willingness to read my manuscript and made valuable suggestions. I am also grateful to Rossitsa Gradeva (American University in Bulgaria), and Baki Tezcan (University of California, Davis) who read earlier versions of parts of this book and commented. I also thank Vefa Erginbaş (Providence College), who kindly included my paper 'The Ottoman Policy of "Correction of Belief(s)"', integrated in this book, in his *Ottoman Sunnism: New Perspectives*[2] and made critical remarks together with John Curry (University of Nevada, Las Vegas).

At Bloomsbury Publishing, my thanks go first to senior commissioning editor Sophie Rudland, who showed sincere interest in my book proposal. Rory Gormley, commissioning editor, displayed all the expertise, enthusiasm and patience an author could hope for. Yasmin Garcha, editorial assistant, has been very helpful with many details of the book. Finally, yet importantly, the two anonymous readers were kind enough to give a positive report about my proposal, made many critical suggestions about the contents of my manuscript and helped turning it to a book. It is impossible to write a complete and accurate work. Just as we try to make up the deficiencies of those before us, those after us will correct our shortcomings and correct our mistakes. 'Over every knowledgeable person is one more knowing.' All errors of fact and judgement are mine.

To Birgit Asbeck I owe dearest thanks for being on the spot whenever we needed her, especially for taking care of our children and staying with them until late at night when my wife and I went out for a movie or a dinner to maintain relative sanity. My thanks are also due to my friend and colleague Johannes Rosenbaum for occasional relaxing chats over a Turkish lunch and tea at *Buhara*, also for his and Samira's support with our children. Thank you also to my colleague and friend Andreas Wilde for his wit and 'positive pessimism' while enjoying our quiche and coffee at *Zuckerbrot*.

My family has been supportive in many ways over the years: I thank my dearest father Necmettin Alkan, with whom I had many conversations about the Alawis over the years before he left this world, my dearest mother Sakine for her constant prayers, and my siblings Nevin, Meryem, Necdet and Esin for their good wishes. My parents-in-law Ayhan and Hüseyin Ayranlı and my brother-in-law Seçkin have been of immense help in Turkey (and in Germany) helping with the children when I was absent for conferences, research or writing. I am also grateful for their occasional financial support. To both my families: *Sağ olun, var olun!*

Most importantly, there are no words whatsoever to thank you, my beloved Duygu, who has been my companion in this long and at times uncertain and stressful journey. You have been *very* supportive, patient, self-sacrificing and bearing with my mood swings. I do not know how to recompense you. *Hakkın ödenemez!* You and our three daughters have been the light of my eyes, my joy and my haven when I was distressed. I hope that you all are now convinced that it was not a waste of time after all.

Bamberg/Germany, 29 February 2020

A NOTE ON TRANSLITERATION

Ottoman Turkish proper names and terms are rendered in modern Turkish. The following letters of the Turkish alphabet have these equivalents in English: c = j; ç = ch; ğ = lengthens the preceding and following vowel; ı = similar to 'u' in *millennium*; j = as in the French *journal*; ö = as in 'her' (without the 'r' sound); ş = 'sh'; and ü = as in 'pure'. Arabic and Persian proper names, unless they appear in quotes from secondary literature, have been rendered without diacritical marks for the sake of simplicity.

INTRODUCTION

Based on extensive use of empirical sources, this book is a discussion of the fate of non-Sunni 'nominal' Muslims in the perception of American Protestant missionaries and the Ottoman state, with a focus on the nineteenth through to the beginning of the twentieth century, and the fate of the Alawis in this period. The *Alawis*, also known as *Nusayris*, belong to an early branch of the so-called 'heterodox' Shi'a, who are centred in North-Western Syria – part of modern Syria and the Turkish province of Hatay – and South Anatolia ('Cilicia') with its centres Adana, Mersin and Tarsus. The main focus of the book lies in the interaction between the Alawis, the late Ottoman state and Protestant missionaries. Throughout the centuries the Alawis, who had been living in Ottoman Syria, are thought to have kept their faith secret by living in seclusion owing to fear of persecution by the Sunni Orthodoxy. The religious beliefs of the Nusayris have been studied since the nineteenth century, based on their writings that are now extant in European libraries. For example, the work by the most famous Alawi convert to Protestantism, Sulayman al-Adhani, *Kitab al-Bakura as-Sulaymaniyya fi Kashf Asrar ad-Diyana an-Nusayriyya*[1] (*The Book of Sulaimân's First Ripe Fruit, Disclosing the Mysteries of the Nusairian Religion*), published in 1863/1864 by American Protestant missionaries, is a detailed exposition of the Alawi belief system and rituals and was for a long time the basis of Western knowledge about the religious tenets of Alawism. As he publicly disclosed the secrets of the Alawi religion in the book, al-Adhani is said to have been killed by Alawi sheikhs.[2] Most of his book was translated into English and published with a brief introduction in 1866.[3] The famous American Presbyterian missionary Henry H. Jessup recounted his meeting with al-Adhani and his life story, describing him as 'as repulsive a man as I have ever met in the East' but he soon learned (also from an Arabic letter of introduction) that 'he was a man of learning and wide reading' and found him to be 'an authorized expounder of that weird system of diabolical mysteries'. Jessup added that he and fellow missionaries encouraged al-Adhani to write a book about the tenets and mysteries of Nusayrism, which was ultimately published in Beirut: 'His book attracted wide attention. The Syrians bought and read it eagerly and copies were sent into Nusairi districts where it made a sensation.'[4]

Another book written by an Alawi is the Arabic *Ta'rikh al-'Alawiyyin*. The author of this 'landmark' book Muhammad Amin Ghalib at-Tawil (d. 1932) was an Ottoman official from Adana who had served at several posts.[5] He wrote his book first in Turkish (it seems not to be extant) and later translated it into Arabic and published it in 1924 in Latakia/Syria (with later editions and Turkish translations). Even though it contains many historical flaws and is an apologetic work, his book is historically important and probably the first of its kind to construct an Alawi identity. Since sources such as these about Alawi history and beliefs are rare, I will use Ottoman and missionary sources here to convey perceptions of this religious community.

Historical knowledge and information about the Nusayris in the nineteenth century, based on Ottoman and missionary sources, has been rather meagre. Only in recent years has this kind of research intensified.[6] These are listed in the previous footnote and discussed in the following paragraphs. There also various studies about the Alawis in Turkish that do not use Ottoman sources.[7]

State of research about the Alawis and other non-Sunni groups based on Ottoman sources

To date, there are a few historical studies of the Alawis in the specified period and of these few have used Ottoman archival materials. Dick Douwes gives a useful overview of the subject in his article 'Knowledge and Oppression: The Nusayriyya in the late Ottoman Period',[8] but does not use Ottoman sources. Based on Arabic primary sources in Syria, French primary sources in Beirut, and English, French and Arabic secondary literature, he analyses the religious and secular leadership of the Nusayris and their relationship to the community of believers and the state authorities from 1840 to around 1890. He focuses on the change in the status of the Nusayris in the provincial administration, which results from the fact that the Ottoman officials based their decisions in the late nineteenth century less on religious than on political motives and made religion a tool of politics. The Ottoman attitude towards this community changed in this context from a tacit tolerance of 'schismatic faith' to a policy of 'correction of belief(s)'.

In two short articles, '19. Yüzyılda Heterodox Dinî Gruplar ve Osmanlı İdaresi' ('Heterodox Religious Groups and the Ottoman Administration in the 19th Century') and 'Alevilik, Nusayrîlik ve Bâbıâli' ('Alevism, Nusayrism and the Sublime Porte'), İlber Ortaylı examines the relationship between Anatolian Alevis and Nusayris as heterodox religious groups on the one hand and the late Ottoman government on the other. He contrasts the Nusayris with other heterodox groups such as the Druze, crypto-Christians and Sabbatians (or *Dönme*, followers of the Jewish 'messiah' Shabbatai Zwi, seventeenth century). Ortaylı comes to the conclusion that in the late nineteenth century heterodox groups were reintegrated into society by the Ottomans – despite their ambivalent attitudes – in contrast to the reign of Mahmud II (reigned 1808–1839), in which the Alevis and Bektaşis in particular were allies of the Janissaries and were persecuted and had to go underground. In both periods, however, these groups came under state control.

Stefan Winter's early contribution to the topic of the Alawis in the late Ottoman period can be read in two articles, 'La révolte alaouite de 1834 contre l'occupation égyptienne: perceptions alaouites et lecture ottomane' and 'The *Nusayris* before the Tanzimat in the Eyes of Ottoman Provincial Administrators, 1804–1834'. In both articles he deals with the Alawis before the Tanzimat ('reform') period, using only a few Ottoman documents. The first aspect of his research is the Alawi uprising of 1834 and the Ottoman response to the occupation of Syria by Muhammad Ali, the Egyptian governor who endeavoured to reform Egypt and the occupied territories. The Alawis, who lived as farmers in the mountains, rebelled against Muhammad Ali's centralization policy, in particular the military service that was imposed on them, while the Alawis living on the coast of Syria expressed their satisfaction at Muhammad Ali's efforts to level expression of religious differences in society. In his second article Winter deals with the attitude of the Ottoman governors in the province towards the Nusayris. Winter shows that the Ottoman attitude towards the Tanzimat was not only characterized by hostility. On the one hand, the Ottomans allied themselves with the Nusayris against common enemies, e.g. Muhammad Ali; on the other hand, some members of this community managed to rise in the Ottoman hierarchy and hold important offices.

Selim Deringil has researched the heterodox groups in the Ottoman Empire in connection with the politicization of Sunni Islam in the late Ottoman era. Towards the end of the nineteenth century, tension between the Ottomans and Europeans increased due to Christian missionary activities on Ottoman soil. The fear of infiltration of the Muslims on the part of the Europeans and Americans, who increasingly made it their business to free non-Muslims and non-Sunnis from the 'yoke' of the Ottomans, led Sultan Abdülhamid II (reigned 1876–1909) to the spread of the 'official' Hanafi Sunni version of Islam. During the last decades of the nineteenth century, the Hamidian regime pursued a policy of 'Sunnitization' in eastern Anatolia, Syria and Iraq. This policy aimed at the centralization and unity of the Ottoman state and at introduction of 'heretical' groups to the teachings of the Hanafi school. As part of an education campaign, schools (sg. *medrese*) and mosques were built in the provinces concerned and trained teachers and missionaries were sent out to teach and instruct in religious matters. The aim was to 'civilize' the population in these areas and make them 'good Muslims' in order to immunize them against Christian and, especially, Protestant, missionary propaganda. Through such efforts the government hoped to avert the threat posed by these heterodox groups, which appeared to threaten the integrity of the Ottoman Empire. In his recently published book *Conversion and Apostasy in the Late Ottoman Empire*,[9] Deringil analyses the changes that nationalism, national identity and belonging went through in the multi-religious milieu of the late Ottoman Empire and how the social and political function of religious conversion changed.

Yvette Talhamy's Hebrew dissertation 'Mridot ha-Nusayrim bi-Suriya ba-mi'ah ha-tish'ah 'israh' (The Nusairi Revolts in Syria in the Nineteenth Century) has been, until 2016, the only monograph on the history of the Nusayris in the late Ottoman Empire based on Ottoman sources in the Ottoman Archives in Istanbul (Başbakanlık Osmanlı Arşivi, BOA). This work was only accessible to me through an English summary. Accordingly, she analyses the circumstances of the Nusayri revolts following an overview of their history up to the nineteen century. In a second study, her essay 'The Nusayri Leader Isma'il Khayr Bey and the Ottomans (1854–58)', Talhamy deals with the rise and fall of Isma'il Khayr Bey, who was influential in the 1850s in the Alawi Mountains in Syria. Talhamy examines why there was no group solidarity, unity and cooperation among the Nusayris when Isma'il Bey rebelled against the Ottomans and how his uprising affected the Nusayris. The essay draws on secondary literature as well as British and French archival material, but only on two documents from the aforementioned Ottoman archives, although there are at least a dozen or more documents on Isma'il Bey and his relationship with the Ottoman authorities. In another article, Talhamy examines American Protestant missionary activity and Ottoman conscription among the Nusayris in Syria and in the nineteenth century. Talhamy examine the aims, methods and results of the Protestant missionary activity among the Nusayris and the impact of their presence and work in these districts upon the Ottoman authorities and their dealings with the Nusayris. She concludes that the investment of the missionaries in the Alawi Mountain did not pay off, and that despite the many schools that were opened there and which functioned for decades, at the turn of the twentieth century the number of the Alawi intellectuals was still minimal and they remained the most illiterate of all the local population of Syria.[10]

In her doctoral dissertation 'Anxieties of Conversion: Missionaries, State and Heterodox communities in the Late Ottoman Empire' (University of California/LA, 2009), Zeynep Türkyılmaz deals with the triangular relationship between evangelical missionaries, the Ottoman state and heterodox groups, concentrating on the question of 'anxieties of conversion' among the Crypto-Christians, Nusayris and Kızılbaş (Anatolian Alevis). She sees the conversion missions of the evangelical missionaries and the Sunni missionaries and teachers from Istanbul as an arena for competition for alternative modernization projects. While the Protestant missionaries took advantage of the unexplained politico-religious status of the heterodox groups in the Ottoman state to bring about the rebirth of Christianity in the biblical regions through conversions, the Ottoman central administration saw religious heterodoxy as treason and therefore a danger ideologically as well as for the physical wholeness of religion and state. Türkyılmaz also examines the redefinition of the socio-religious subjectivity of heterodox groups towards the state and global networks that resulted from the above-mentioned clash. In summary, her work is a study of the tension between modernity, religion and state administration in the late Ottoman Empire.

Most recently, in 2016, Stefan Winter published his ground-breaking and revisionist book *A History of the 'Alawis*. In this excellent and well-researched study Stefan Winter aims to prove that this 'metanarrative' or notion of 'historical persecution' is not borne out by the historical evidence. Without discrediting the relevance of Alawi religious identity and the sectarian community as a subject of analysis, he bases his study on secular rather than religious sources in order to show the broad mutual relationship of the Alawis with their neighbours, rulers and supposed oppressors. What makes Winter's book outstanding is his use of sources that have not previously been made use of. By scrutinizing Mamluk administration manuals, Ottoman and Turkish archival documents in Istanbul and Tripoli, and the Alawi prosopographical literature, he challenges the notion that they had been always an isolated community, different from other rural populations, or were subjected to systematic discrimination. Winter's aim is to provide a less essentializing, more material account of Alawi history by not focusing on the religious character of the community but by employing a secular approach to their history. He does so by highlighting locality and privileging the socioeconomic, political and administrative context of modern Alawism's development over its purely religious traits. And he provides a perspective throughout the centuries in order to form an opinion of the necessarily profound transformation of Alawi communal identity over time.[11]

In a similar fashion, there have been studies about similar non-Suni 'non-conformist' religious groups such as the Yezidis and the Alevis. Edip Gölbaşı has written extensively about the Yezidis in his MA thesis and other articles.[12] These deal with the political order and the new power regime of the Ottoman Empire in the nineteenth century and the policy of 'taming' under Sultan Abdülhamid II for groups at the margins and those who were considered 'heretical', 'uncivilized' or 'nomadic'. One of the main problems between the state and the Yezidis was military service/conscription, which the Yezidis allegedly opposed in accordance with their religious beliefs, and the conversion policy of the Hamid period, which was initially introduced with 'persuasion' tactics where applicable, but were later also implemented through pressure and violence. In addition to the aspects of the state's perception of Yezidi identity, these studies also focus on the question of their status, which is closely linked to their position in the political structure.

Most recently Yalçın Çakmak published his revised doctoral thesis about the Kızılbaş-Alevis with the title *Sultanın Kızılbaşları: II. Abdülhamid Dönemi Alevi Algısı ve Siyaseti* ('Sultan's Red Heads: Alevi Perceptions and Politics during the Era of Abdülhamid II', Istanbul 2019). Anxiety over issues of security of the empire, centralization, the politics of Islamic unity of Sultan Abdülhamid II and the relations of the Alevi community with the Armenians and Western missionaries played a significant role during his reign. The Alevi community became a current issue of the empire due to their central role both in domestic issues and regional dynamics. Consequently, these developments led the empire to certain mandatory implementations against the Alevis. The most efficient method Abdülhamid II resorted to was the politics of enforced 'correction of the beliefs' (*tashih-i akaid*) of the community members. The primary aim of his book is to analyse the dynamics which brought the Alevis to the agenda during the reign of Abdülhamid II. In relation to this aim, Çakmak discusses Abdülhamid II's Alevi politics in the history of the Ottoman Empire within the context of continuity and disengagements. Another aim is to deal with the place of the empire's approach towards Alevism throughout the period within the context of the non-Sunni politics from a comparative perspective. Furthermore, he illustrated the representations of Kızılbaş-Alevi communities by Western missionaries, travellers, researchers and officers.

Mention must be also made of a very recent revisionist study about the Kızılbaş-Alevis before the nineteenth century. The history of the Kızılbaş-Alevis in the

Ottoman Empire has so far mostly been remembered and described in the context of persecution and oppression. Benjamin Weineck's study *Zwischen Verfolgung und Eingliederung Kızılbaş-Aleviten im osmanischen Staat (16.–18. Jahrhundert)* ('Between Persecution and Inclusion: Kızılbaş-Alevis in the Ottoman State (16th–18th centuries)', Baden-Baden 2020) provides such dominant and essentialist narratives with a perspective that analyses the complexity of the relationship between the state and the Kızılbaş-Alevis. The author explores the question of how this relationship developed from the 16th to the 18th century: After the persecution of the Kızılbaş, who were regarded as dissidents and 'heretics', a relationship was established that aimed primarily at the appropriate integration of these groups into the Ottoman rule. On the basis of Ottoman sources previously unused for research about Alevism, Weineck shows that the Kızılbaş-Alevis regularly interacted with agents of the state in different contexts. Thus, this work contributes to a re-evaluation of the history of the Kızılbaş-Alevis in Ottoman times.

The last addition here to this literature about non-Sunni groups is Cem Kara's recent book *Grenzen überschreitende Derwische: Kulturbeziehungen des Bektaschi-Ordens 1826–1925* ('Dervishes Crossing Borders: Cultural Relationships of the Bektashi Order 1826–1925', Göttingen 2019) which is about the cultural relations of the Bektaşis in and outside the Ottoman Empire. With the investigation of horizontal cultural contacts in the Ottoman state, Kara worked on a desideratum, since previous research only focused on vertical relationships between the government and the religious communities. To this end, he poses the research question: in which way was the religious culture of the Bektaşis transformed by cultural contact. This question encompasses types of contact and their limits, mutual perceptions of those involved and (im)material cultural assets exchanged in contact with each other. At its core, Kara's case study offers a bird's eye view of the Bektashi order from the nineteenth to the beginning of the twentieth century. The balanced presentation of the examined cultural relationships testifies to the relevance of the research on interweaving of religious subgroups. Nevertheless, the work leaves room for further studies on the cultural relations of the Bektaşis. This also includes the relationship with the Kızılbaş-Alevis, as the discipline of Alevi studies is still relatively early.

Finally, it is necessary to briefly dwell on the work *A History of Muslims, Christians, and Jews in the Middle East* (2017) by Heather J. Sharkey.[13] She deals with the diverse relationships between Muslims, Christians and Jews in the Ottoman Empire. In the context of changes and reforms in the nineteenth century, she emphasizes that on the one hand the Ottoman state began to regard its subjects as individuals at times – theoretical freedom of conscience, responsibility for taxation or military conscription; on the other hand, they continued to be classified and treated as members of older collectives and above all as members of religious communities of Muslims, Christians and Jews. Sharkey notes that this tension between the older strategy of seeing people as members of a collective and the newer, albeit uneven, strategy of recognizing people as individuals was an integral part of the modern age. The Alevis, the Druze, the Yezidis and the Nusayris/Alawis fell into this ambiguous category. Over the course of the nineteenth century, this ambivalence found expression in a number of strategies that were irregular. This was particularly obvious with the Yezidis, who were periodically taxed by the Ottomans with the Islamic 'poll tax' (*jizya*) but this was demanded neither from the Druze, nor the Alawis. At times, the Ottomans did not draft the Yezidis into the military, but they were then forced back to military service and conversion to Sunni Islam at other times.

Knowledge of the Nusayris and similar groups such as above in modern times began with Western travellers, orientalists and missionaries, from the early nineteenth century. These groups with secret and nonconformist religious beliefs were studied for learning purposes, sometimes to bring them into the fold of Christianity but also to find ways of exploiting them against the Ottomans politically. In the Ottoman Empire real interest in the Nusayris started during the reign of Sultan Abdülhamid II. The fear of infiltration of heterodox Muslims by foreigners, especially by American and English Protestant missionaries, pressed the Sultan to attract them by educative means to the official Hanafi-Sunni school. In the process, the status of the Nusayris changed during the late nineteenth century as a result of the missionary attempt to convert them and the Ottoman fear that they would become another 'European problem' for them to deal with. A fight for the Nusayri soul began that left them changed.

In spite of the large amount of Ottoman official documents and other sources, the history of the Nusayris in the late Ottoman Empire is still very little researched. The aim of this study and attempt to fill this gap is based on the hypothesis that the change in the self-designation of the Nusayris was part of a broader socio-political process dissociating them from the Ottoman Empire and preceding the final collapse of this state for some decades. While taking internal differences within the Nusayri community into account, the book will elucidate this process and put it into historical context, by comparing it with similar transformation processes within other heterodox communities of the Ottoman Empire, especially Alevis Yezidis, and Druze.

Chapter 1 begins with a discussion of what is regarded as 'heretical' and 'heretics' based on the Qur'an and hadith (oral Islamic traditions) and ties this to the Sunnis' perception of groups such as the Alawis. An overview of the history and the beliefs of the Nusayris/Alawis from its inception in ninth/tenth century Iraq until today introduces to the reader this much talked-about 'secretive' religious community in the Islamic world. This is done in the light of secondary literature based on various sources in Arabic, Ottoman/Turkish and European languages. Next, I discuss the importance of geography, social structure and authority among the Alawis. While the geography of the so-called 'Alawi/Nusayri Mountains', their heartland in the hinterland of Latakia, has been described and discussed since the nineteenth century as being their 'mountain refuge' where they supposedly hid since the Crusades due to their 'heretical' beliefs, there is not much written about their social structure and, to a lesser extent, about Alawi religious and secular authority in European languages. This chapter attempts to give an appraisal of these, followed by an outline of the Alawis' status in the Ottoman political system.

The proselytizing efforts of Protestant missionaries, mostly American, in Ottoman Syria among heterodox non-Sunni groups and in particular their conversion efforts among the Nusayris, are the subjects of Chapter 2. Inspired by millenarian beliefs, since the eighteenth century Protestant missionaries in North America – and also in Europe – anticipated and worked for a new social order. This religious zeal targeted the Jews in the Holy Land, the native Christians (Greek and Arab) and eventually, since missions among the Jews and native Christians proved difficult and proselytizing Sunni Muslims was forbidden, communities such as the Nusayris ('Alawis), who were heretics in the eyes of the Sunnis and regarded as pagans by the missionaries themselves. Two hitherto, rather unexplored cases of conversion from Nusayrism to Protestantism serve as examples for discussing the role of the late Ottoman state regarding centralization, state and missionary education and religious conversion and how the relationship between the Ottomans and the USA/Europe worsened during these times.

Chapter 3 analyses the policy of 'correction of belief(s)', the ideological and political background of the Hanafi-Sunni 'civilizing mission' and accordingly the conversion strategies of the administration of Sultan Abdülhamid II. I argue that Mahmud II's administration used this concept in the context of the persecution of Bektaşis during the first half of the nineteenth century, and I compare the application of this policy with the similar strategy of Abdülhamid II, who applied it to non-Sunni Islamic sects such as the Turkish or Kurdish Alevis, the Nusayris in Syria, the Shi'is in Iraq, and the Yezidis in eastern Anatolia. The motivation of the Hamidian regime was to 'civilize' these non-conformist groups and bring them into the Sunni fold by fine-tuning their beliefs. I demonstrate how this concept evolved, beginning in the eighteenth century when it was invoked in the context of taming groups such as the Abkhaz and Circassians, and, later, Caucasian tribes. During the tumultuous reign of Mahmud II, Ottoman administrators and scholars made use of this term as an official policy to correct the beliefs of the Bektaşis both before and after the prohibition of their order.

Lastly, Chapter 4 investigates whether and what changes occurred during the Young Turk rule (1908–1918), particularly with regard to the Nusayris. After providing an outline of the Young Turk Revolution in 1908 and its repercussions among ethnic and religious groups, I consciously follow and leave room for the narratives of Protestant missionaries about their activities among the Nusayris in Ottoman Syria in the wake of the Revolution. I attempt to illustrate the missionaries' response to the promise of freedom in the Empire, analyse whether the circumstances for proselytizing improved and how the Nusayris in turn responded to the missionary efforts. A key issue that has not been dealt with sufficiently in my opinion is how Muslims, especially intellectuals of the Young Turk era, have viewed missionary work, especially that of American Protestants. This subchapter reveals the role of Islam during the supposedly 'secular' Young Turk rule and how the Nusayris were perceived. I complete this chapter with a very late Ottoman official text about various ethnic and religious groups in Syria and Palestine, a publication that was commissioned as a 'scientific and civilizational guide' in search for solutions of the ailing Empire and which sought to create modern identities among those peoples and instil hope for a 'bright' future.

Sources and research questions

Among the primary sources used in this study are first the documents belonging to various funds in the *Başbakanlık Osmanlı Arşivi* (BOA, Prime Ministry Ottoman Archive) in Istanbul.[14] These documents are among the primary objectives of the book since the bureaucracy had its own internal correspondence and these constitute sources of reference for understanding the state policy towards the Nusayris/Alawis and similar groups. They are from the Ottoman capital Istanbul to provincial and local governors especially in Syria, and vice versa, and also central in understanding the attitude and politics of the Ottoman state, the officials and, as reflected there, of the common people towards the Nusayris in the first place and also vis-à-vis the missionaries, especially the American Protestants, who are one of the main focuses of the book. BOA documents from the pre-Tanzimat period, roughly from 1826 to 1839 during the reign of Sultan Mahmud II, deal mainly with the aftermath of the abolition of the Janissaries, namely the prohibition and persecution of the Bektaşis. While the Janissaries and their allies the Bektaşis were regarded as the arch-enemies of the state, which aimed at centralization and modernization, and are depicted negatively and described as degenerate, the original Bektaşi creed and its founder, Hacı Bektaş, deserved praise.

The Tanzimat period (1839–1876), comprising the reigns of Sultan Abdülmecid (1839–1861) and Abdülaziz (1861–1876), describes Nusayri uprisings, struggles between Nusayris and Sunnis, and Nusayri tribes among themselves. This period also includes records of the conscription of Nusayris to military service. In general, the policies towards groups of nominal Muslims were broader in application and not necessarily negative in nature. The main question for Ottoman officials and intellectuals was rather how they could accommodate them as potential allies into the mainstream 'orthodox' position.

The majority of the Ottoman documents date from the later reign of Sultan Abdülhamid II and deal with the conversion policy that was carried out in Syria and South-eastern Anatolia. What is striking here is the network of Hanafi-Sunni missionaries and teachers who were active everywhere in these areas, sent by the Ministry of Education (*Maarif Nezareti*) in order to convert the population through education in medreses and mosques and to make them 'good' Muslims. Ottoman documents on the Alevis, Yezidis and the Druze from the same archive are analysed for a comparative approach. The Ottomans' attitude to these non-Sunnis is similar to that of the Nusayris. The more rigid policy of Abdülhamid II towards sectarian groups, as reflected in official communications, must be seen as a result of catastrophic military defeats, especially in the Balkans; instead of winning them over they needed to be suppressed as potential enemies. Those who were willing to comply with the state's policies were worthy of cooperation. It must be stated that there is a scarcity of Ottoman archival sources from the Young Turk period about the official view towards the Nusayris, which leaves us with a gap. I have integrated some documents from that period and, though very few in number, we can observe in them that the Young Turk rulers were concerned about missionary activities as much as officials in the Hamidian period were. This is also expressed in publications by Islamist thinkers of that period, which I used in order to fill the gap.

My research was facilitated by a compilation of Ottoman archival documents about the Nusayris: Ali Sinan Bilgili et al. (eds.), *Osmanlı Arşiv Belgelerinde Nusayrîler ve Nusayrîlik (1745–1920)* (Ankara, 2010; henceforth referred to as *OABNN*); it includes many of the documents in my possession and has the images of the documents and their transliterations in Latin letters. Ranging from the eighteenth century (for which there only one document) until the War of Independence by Mustafa Kemal Paşa (later Atatürk), this volume includes topics about diverse aspects of the Nusayri community vis-à-vis the Ottoman state. Written by the Prime Ministry, the ministries of Foreign and Internal Affairs, of Education, of Justice or of War to governor generals, local governors, directors of education etc., the documents also include communication with representatives of foreign states, such as the American Embassy in Istanbul and regional consulates. The topics range from Protestant missionary activities, the relations of the Nusayris with other groups, foremost Sunnis, within the regions they inhabited, the efforts to include the Nusayris into the Sunni majority and the Nusayris' wish to become Sunnis, the construction of mosques and schools in Nusayri villages and towns, the education of children, the revolts and banditry by Nusayris, the injustices committed by Ottoman regional/local officials towards the Nusayris, the rewarding of Nusayris who served well the Ottoman state, and the Nusayris' behaviour during the French occupation of South Turkey and Syria.

In all periods, it is possible to follow the attitudes and policies of the central state policy, towards the Nusayris and similar groups, which includes statements, reports and journals presented by a number of major and minor officials. These documents also reflect their rather negative picture of those communities, and reflect the biased nature of the documents as they reflect the subjective view of the officials. Another type of Ottoman archival document are reports that the central government in Istanbul asked to be sent from the provinces; these provide hints as to the policies Istanbul applied or would apply regarding the Nusayris. Ottoman archival documents are also important because they contribute significantly to the clarification of specific events through which the community came to the fore. Among these are, firstly, the cases of the two Nusayri converts to Protestantism, Suleiman Hassan Makhloof ('Daoud') and Telgie Ibrahim.

Other contemporary Ottoman sources such as newspapers and works by Ottoman historians are also to be consulted. The latter includes, for example, *Tarih-i Cevdet* by Ahmed Cevdet Paşa (2nd ed., 1892), the then official historian who dealt with the Nusayris and the Druze in a derogatory fashion; we must also mention another, rather unknown, short handwritten treatise by him regarding socialists in which he traces the origin of the Nusayris back to ancient 'proto-socialist' and 'rebellious' movements in ancient Persia, such as Mazdakism out of which, according to the Paşa, emerged the 'secret, heretical' (*batini*) religious groups such as the Isma'ilis, Kızılbaş-Alevis, Freemasons etc.[15]

Another, very late Ottoman, contemporary but hitherto ignored source about the various religious and ethnic communities that is used here is the yearbook

Beyrut Vilayeti on the province of Beirut from 1917–1918. In two volumes, the two authors deal with different religions and sects in what is now Syria, Lebanon and Israel, including the Nusayris. In addition to the general history and geography of the region, the work also deals with the history, beliefs, number and conditions of the different religious communities and the places where they live. Though biased and written from what seems to be an 'Ottoman orientalist' viewpoint, this source provides interesting details about the tour of the two authors who I would call 'missionaries of modernity'.

Letters and reports from missionaries who worked in Syria form another source for the book. Of great importance is the five-volume work *The Missionary Herald: Reports from Ottoman Syria* edited by Kamal Salibi and Yusuf K. Khoury,[16] in which letters and personal diaries of missionaries working in Syria are reproduced, which were published by the ABCFM (American Board of Commissioners for Foreign Missions) in its periodical *The Missionary Herald* from 1819 to 1870. The ABCFM was the institution that sent the missionaries to the Ottoman Empire from 1819 and also financed them. The representations in the *Missionary Herald* reflect the experiences that the missionaries had with 'heterodox' religious groups such as the Nusayris, Yezidis and Druze and with the Ottoman administration in Syria. They give us fascinating details about the work and daily life of the missionaries and provide information about the missionaries' view of these communities. While these offer interesting details about the daily life of the missionaries and the people, they are limited in that they do not always offer correct historical information. This stems from the fact that knowledge on Nusayris was sometimes acquired from biased sources. Nevertheless, in the later decades of the nineteenth century missionaries and other Europeans or Westerners were able to travel and live among Nusayris and so wrote about their experiences in letters or books. Such sources are among the primary sources here. And in 1870 the ABCFM mission in Syria was handed over to the *Reformed Presbyterian Church of North America* that was administered by the *Board of Foreign Missions of the Presbyterian Church*.[17] Its reports and results are available in various journals (e.g. *Herald of Mission News*, and *Olive Trees*) at the Reformed Presbyterian History Archives at http://rparchives.org and constitute an important source for Protestant missionary activities. Together with the Ottoman archival sources they provide a clearer picture of specific events in the Nusayri community, such as the above mentioned two converts.

As far as possible, texts from Catholic missionaries who worked among the Nusayris and from the Nusayris themselves are also utilized for my research. On the part of the Catholic missionaries, this includes in particular the writings of the Jesuit and orientalist Henri Lammens, who had personal contacts with Nusayris around 1900 and published his impressions of it in at least five treatises.[18] Alawi texts, such as Ghalib at-Tawil's *Tarikh al-Alawiyyin* ('History of the Alawis') revolve around initiatives for rapprochement by Ottoman statesmen such as Midhat Paşa, who was governor of Syria from 1878 to 1880.

A gap in this study is that there is a lack of Alawi sources in general, except for at-Tawil's and al-Adhani's book, but these also do not provide Alawi perspectives on the result of Ottoman and missionary propaganda among their community.

It is crucial to state that both the Ottoman and missionary sources are biased and have their pitfalls in that they present their own specific view of the Nusayris and the other similar groups discussed in this book. Both sides approach the Nusayris (and similar groups) as being outside 'civilization' and deprived of religion, that is to say, 'true' faith: for the Ottomans they were Muslims off-limits and the Protestant missionaries thought that the Nusayris were 'pagans', nor did they think they were Christians even though some of their beliefs resembled Christian ones. Due to these very particular perspectives Ottoman and Protestant missionary sources need to be reflected on openly and critically.

Based on the sources mentioned above, the following questions will be answered in the book: What was the result of Christian and Ottoman propaganda among non-Sunnis and, in particular, the Nusayris? How did the Christian missionaries integrate them into their new social order inspired by millenarian beliefs? What role did these 'heterodox' and marginalized groups play in the 'civilizing mission' of the regime of Sultan Abdülhamid II? What was the reaction of these groups to the Ottoman educational and civilizing efforts? What was the attitude of the Young Turks and of Muslim intellectuals towards the missionaries and Nusayris after their revolution in 1908? The main goal of the book is to describe the change in the relationship between missionaries, Ottoman state actors and the Nusayris in the late Ottoman Empire. In particular, aspects such as conversion, resistance, assimilation, integration and military conscription will be examined. Furthermore, to what extent did the tribal and religious fragmentation of the Nusayris affect their relationship with the Ottoman Administration?

From the analysis of the sources the impression emerges that the Alawis underwent a collective transformation process between 1840 and 1918. In the book this process is compared to processes taking place at the same time in other 'heterodox' groups of the Ottoman Empire. Markus Dressler showed in a study how Turkish and Kurdish Shi'i-heterodox groups, which were previously contemptuously referred to as 'Kızılbaş', were renamed and re-signified as 'Alevis' (Aleviler) in the late nineteenth century in response to their being researched by Western orientalists and the discourses of Turkish nationalists.[19] This book is based on the hypothesis that the Nusayris' transition to the self-designation *Alawiyyun* ('Alawis', 'Alawites') was part of an analogous socio-political identity formation and demarcation process that needs to be examined. The situation is similar with the Yezidis, where identity politics was closely linked to discourses on origin. A search for the Yezidi's ethnic and religious origins began with the development of modern concepts of nationalism and racial identity from the nineteenth century. On the religious level, there has been a predominantly Iranian–Zoroastrian and an Arab–Muslim approach. Theories based on ethnicity ranged from purely Kurdish origins to descent from the Assyrians or Sabians.[20] In my study, such identity formation processes in other 'heterodox' communities will be used for comparison.

I am aware that the word 'Nusayri' has a negative connotation, I nevertheless use it as it appears in Ottoman documents and other sources before 1920 for ease of reference. It is widely accepted that it was only from that date onwards that the

Nusayris named themselves 'Alawis' (followers of Imam Ali) to shake off any hint of heresy and to prove that they belong to Shi'a Islam, as the fifth Islamic legal school. I am also, however, challenging the widely accepted view that the name 'Alawī' was only used after 1920. A study of Ottoman archival documents of the late nineteenth century reveals the opposite.

Chapter 1

THE NUSAYRIS IN THE OTTOMAN EMPIRE: A 'HETERODOX' TRIBAL COMMUNITY AND THE STATE

1.1. *The Nusayri-Alawis: Beliefs and history*

In his book about 'heretics' in the Ottoman Empire in the fifteen to seventeenth centuries the Turkish scholar Ahmet Yaşar Ocak quotes Xenophon,[1] a student of Socrates, asking himself by what arguments his teacher was indicted and why the Athenians believed that he had to die for the good of the state: 'For the indictment against him was something like the following: Socrates commits an injustice by not believing in the gods in which the city believes and by bringing in new and different divine things *(daimonia)*; he commits an injustice also by corrupting the young.'[2]

This being just one example, throughout history followers of various religions and groups within religions accused each other of being deviant from what was perceived as the 'true' or 'sound faith'; those who were labelled as 'heretics' were blamed for misleading or corrupting the people. Looking at the statement just quoted, we can infer that states that have an official religion can force people to follow it with all its obligations. Anything else introduced from outside is regarded as blasphemy and heresy.

There are differences in all religious traditions due to several factors, such as theological, socio-political, cultural, economic and ethnic. As a result, each group tends to label those who are different from them as 'the other', despite the fact that they belong to the same religion. Such is the case not only in Islam.

> While divergence from the mainstream does not *ipso facto* create a need for a formal split into factions, there will always be groups who use opposition to the dominant tradition as a means of affirming their separateness; and similarly, the mainstream understanding of a tradition can be strengthened by criticising alternative understandings.[3]

Within Islam, the groups outside the mainstream, 'the other among us' or the 'internal others', are called *al-firaq ad-dalla* ('misguided sects') or *ahl al-bid'a* ('people of innovation', sectarians); labels that refer to 'deviant' conceptual trends or sects within Islam. Their conflicting viewpoints are perceived as the origin of *fitna* ('sedition') and hence as a threat to the unity of Islam. And whereas these sects accuse the mainstream of being insufficient and heretical, they are themselves called 'outsiders' (*khawarij*) in the mainstream traditions. Another term that has been used pejoratively by Sunnis for 'internal others' who refuse legitimate Islamic leadership and authority is *rafida/rawafid*, meaning 'rejecter(s)'. This has been especially applied to the mainstream Twelver Shi'a and any of the Shi'i groups.[4] In the Ottoman Empire followers of Shi'a Islam and various of its off-shoots such as the Isma'ilis, Nusayris, Alevis, Bektaşis, etc., were called *râfizî/revâfız*, or *ehl-i rafz*.[5] Yet, interestingly, the Ottoman state also called sedentary Sunni tribes and the ultra-Sunni Wahhabi movement as of the eighteenth century *râfizî* due to their opposition to the state.[6] Another widely used term for 'heresy, heretical', borrowed from Persian, is *zindiq* (Arab.) or *zındık* (Turk.).[7] *dalal* (and its variants), i.e. 'error; going astray' (cf. Q 1:7) is a term mentioned in many places in the Qur'an and needs to be seen in combination with *al-firaq ad-dalla* for sects deemed as 'misguided'.

Looking from this 'orthodox' viewpoint, we may argue that Islam bases its beliefs primarily on the Qur'an as a revealed holy text; hence the Word of God is the 'true belief' and the foundation. 'Guide us in the straight path (*ihdina as-sirat al-mustaqim*)' (Q 1:6)[8] is the middle way; anything else outside it is excess (*ifrat*) or deficiency (*tafrit* or *taqsir*). The recipients of the Prophet Muhammad's (d. 632) message were, firstly, the polytheistic Arabs who had to be brought back to the true belief in the one God (*Allah*) and so abandoned all other deities, and secondly the Jews and Christians who had corrupted their teachings. They all had strayed from the 'straight path', not obeying the real commandments of Allah and so not submitting to His will (*islam*). They needed to be reminded of the true religion, named *islam* in the Qur'an, and receive guidance (*huda*) to it. The third recipient of the Quran's message is, of course, the Muslims. The first Sura (1:7) stresses at the end that God may preserve the believers from the path of 'those who are astray' (*ad-dallin*).

According to Islam's message, the previous confessions or religions, such as Arab Paganism, Zoroastrianism, Judaism and Christianity, were subverted and so made a new divine message necessary, which in turn needed to abrogate their administrations, laws and excesses. As is expressed in Qur'an 5:48, 'To every one of you We have appointed a right way and an open road (*li-kullin ja'alna minkum shir'at^{an} wa minhaj^{an}*)', we can say that each prophet abrogates the laws of his predecessor.[9] Islam replaces difficulties or hardships in previous dispensations; in other words, it restores the 'deterioration of the pristine, easy-going relationship between God and His creatures (sometimes characterized in the sources by the term *fiṭra*) into a series of abstruse and arduous legal systems'.[10] In the words of Ze'ev Maghen:

> Islamic tradition on the whole envisions what amounts to only two *über*-phases in the forward march of humankind: (1) the world under the spiritual sovereignty of a wide range of sinfully innovative and harmfully excessive doctrines; (2) the world under the spiritual sovereignty of the restorative and moderating doctrine of Islam. . . To the extent that the pristine, *fiṭra*-based faith of Adam - and its later reincarnation, the *millat Ibrāhīm* [religion of Abraham] – are included in this

legendary historical process, we might better speak of a bell-curve in three stages: (1) the reign of right religion, (2) doctrinal deviation/innovation across the board, and (3) return to Truth with Islam.[11]

Harmfully excessive doctrines or 'wrong beliefs' in pre-Islamic dispensations, then, needed to be replaced. One of the concepts that is central to Islamic belief and has been used to this day in discourses about 'right' and 'wrong' belief is *ghuluww* or 'transgression' with regard to religious beliefs. Apart from oral traditions (sg. *hadith*), the *ghuluww* concept occurs twice in the Qur'an; in 4:171 and 5:72–77 in the context of the 'corrupted' beliefs of the Christians calling Jesus 'son of God', and in 9:30 – though in this latter verse *ghuluww* is not mentioned but implied – the Jews are condemned for calling the prophet 'Uzayr/Ezra 'son of God':

> People of the Book, go not beyond the bounds in your religion (*la taghlu fi dinikum*), and say not as to God but the truth. The Messiah, Jesus son of Mary, was only the Messenger of God, and His Word that He committed to Mary, and a Spirit from Him. So believe in God and His Messengers, and say not, 'Three.' Refrain; better is it for you. God is only One God. Glory be to Him – That He should have a son! To Him belongs all that is in the heavens and in the earth; God suffices for a guardian.
>
> 4:171

> They are unbelievers who say, 'God is the Messiah, Mary's son.' For the Messiah said, 'Children of Israel, serve God, my Lord and your Lord. Verily whoso associates with God anything, God shall prohibit him entrance to Paradise, and his refuge shall be the Fire; and wrongdoers shall have no helpers.' They are unbelievers who say, 'God is the Third of Three.' No god is there but One God. If they refrain not from what they say, there shall afflict those of them that disbelieve a painful chastisement. ... The Messiah, son of Mary, was only a Messenger; Messengers before him passed away; his mother was a just woman; they both ate food. Behold, how We make clear the signs to them; then behold, how they perverted are! ... Say: 'People of the Book, go not beyond the bounds in your religion (*la taghlu fi dinikum*), other than the truth, and follow not the caprices of a people who went astray (*dallu*) before, and led astray (*adallu*) many, and now again have gone astray from the right way.'
>
> 5:72–77

> The Jews say, 'Ezra is the Son of God'; the Christians say, 'The Messiah is the Son of God.' That is the utterance of their mouths, conforming with the unbelievers before them. God assail them! How they are perverted!
>
> 9:30

Thus Jews and Christians were criticized for overstating the roles of 'Uzayr and Jesus, by referring to them as 'God' or as 'the son of God'. The Christians were also criticized for the 'monasticism they invented – We did not prescribe it for them' (57:27). The Jews in turn were also castigated for their defamation of Jesus as being an 'illegimate' child; as well as for sanctioning marriage between half-siblings.[12] Owing to such extremes in religious beliefs, Muhammad is reported to have admonished his followers not to be excessive in their beliefs: 'Those who went before you came to ruin because of extremism in their religion (*halaka man qablakum bi'l-ghuluwwi fi'l-dīn*)' and 'beware of exaggeration in religion (*iyyākum wa'l-ghuluww fi'l-dīn*).'[13]

A further central concept to which Muslims must adhere is the injunction 'commanding right and forbidding wrong' (*al-amr bi al-maʻrūf wa an-nahy ʻan al-munkar*), a central and vital concept, mentioned in various places in the Qur'an (3:104, 110, 114; 7:157; 9:71, 112; 22:41, and 31:17).[14] Within these directives, for example, the followers of Muhammad are called the 'best nation' (*khayr umma*), and they are 'commanding right and forbidding wrong' (3:110). It is a religious obligation that also concerns Muslim rulers and can be summarized as follows:

> The principal function of government is to enable the individual to lead a good Muslim life. This is, in the last analysis, the purpose of the state, for which alone it is established by God, and for which alone statesmen are given authority over others.... The basic rule for Muslim social life and political life, commonly formulated as 'to enjoin good and forbid evil,' is thus a shared responsibility of the ruler and the subject, or in modern terms, of the state and the individual.[15]

Apart from the believers' active engagement in 'commanding right and forbidding wrong', 'disorder' or 'chaos' (*fitna*) should be prevented in any event because it runs counter to the just, peaceful and law-abiding society that the Qur'an foresees for humanity.[16]

In Qur'an 2:143 God appoints the Muslims as the 'midmost/moderate nation' or 'community in the middle' (*umma wasat*) and Muhammad affirmed, 'The best of things is their middle.'[17] 'The true religion of God', as it was expressed by a medieval Muslim scholar, 'is midway between the slack and the fanatic (*dīn Allāhi bayna al-muqaṣṣir wa'l-ghāly*[sic]).'[18] On the one hand, the Qur'an tells the believers to 'forbid not such good things as God has permitted you' but at the same time cautions them 'transgress not' (5:87).[19] At-Tabari (d. 923), chronicler and commentator of the Qur'an, argues that *wasat* stands for the middle of two extremes and describes the moderation of the Muslim believers thus: 'They are neither exaggerators (*ahl al-ghuluww*) in respect to religion, (...) nor those who reduce something (*ahl al-taqsir*).' He interprets *wasat* as 'justice' or 'equity' ('*adl*), thereby implying that the Muslims are a 'just community'.[20] In the words of the classical Qur'an commentator al-Qurtubi, excess and deficiency are two evils, the good is between the two evils,[21] and 'the middle shuns exaggeration and deficiency (*al-wasat mujanib^an li al-ghuluww wa at-taqsir*).'[22]

Yet, there are examples of people within the Islamic community who have been accused of drifting away from the middle and exceeding the limits of their beliefs. Here we are concerned with accusations brought forward against groups within

Shi'a Islam called *ghulat* or 'exaggerators'.²³ These were factions whose leaders ascribed divinity to the imams ('leaders'), starting from Imam Ali ibn Abi Talib up to the 11th Imam Hasan al-Askari. Alternately, *ghulat* leaders saw the imams as divine manifestations in terms of Docetism, the Christian doctrine stating that Christ did not have a real body but an apparent one, and also that he did not die; this concept was also applied to the imams.²⁴ Imam Ali is said to have cast out Ibn Saba',²⁵ the first who had venerated him excessively, and supposedly let his followers (*Saba'iyya*) burn. It seems that this was a later innovation to show Ali in the role of the foremost enemy of the *ghulat*.²⁶

We have many recorded statements from the Shi'i imams opposing *ghulat* ideas and refuting the claim to divinity. Imam Ali is said to have stated: 'Do not exaggerate concerning us as to worship us (*lā tatajāwazū binā al-'ubūdiyya*)... Beware of exaggerating as the Christians do, for I dissociate from exaggerators (*wa iyyākum wa'l-ghuluwwa ka-ghuluwwi al-naṣārā, fa-'innī barī'un min al-ghālīn*).'²⁷ And: 'I dissociate from the exaggerators as Jesus son of Mary dissociates from the Christians. O God, forsake them forever and do not help anyone of them.'²⁸ Later the 8th Imam, ar-Rida, is reported to have said about the deification of Imam Ali: 'Whoever exceeds [the limit] to the point of worshipping the commander of the faithful [= 'Alī] [as God], is among those with whom God is angry and those who are astray.'²⁹ A man told ar-Rida that some people attribute to Ali God's attributes, whereupon the Imam trembled with fear and replied: 'God is beyond what the transgressors and unbelievers say.'³⁰

The 4th Imam Ali Ibn al-Husayn (Zayn al-'Abidin) is recorded as having said: 'A group of the Shi'a loves us so much that they attribute what the Jews said about 'Uzayr and what the Christians said about Jesus to us; therefore, they are not our followers, nor are we from [sic; of] them.'³¹ The 6th Imam Ja'far as-Sadiq stated:

> Warn your youth about the exaggerators, lest they ruin their religious beliefs, for truly the exaggerators are the worst of God's creatures; they try and belittle the majesty of God while claiming lordship for the slaves of God. Indeed, the exaggerators are worse than the Jews, the Christians, the Zoroastrians, and those who associate partners with God.³²

And Hasan al-'Askari is reported to have cast off Muhammad ibn Nusayr,³³ the eponymous founder of Nusayrism ('Alawism), for his extreme beliefs. He regarded the imam as a divine manifestation, for which the imam is said to have sought refuge in God from Ibn Nusayr and wished God to curse (*la'nat Allāh*) him.³⁴

Mainstream Sunnis and Twelver Shi'is refer to those excesses of glorification of the Imams which entailed going beyond the limits of certain basic Islamic norms and principles. Sheikh Mufid (d. 1022), an early influential Shi'i theologian, stated: 'The *ghāliyān* [Persian for *ghulat*] are those who pretend to profess Islam, but who regard Imam 'Alī and his children as having the properties of divinity and prophecy, and presenting them as having qualities which go beyond the bounds of the truth.'³⁵ And al-Majlisi (d. 1699, compiler of Shi'i hadiths, see above) explained:³⁶

Ghulūw in regard to the Prophet and the [religious] leaders applies if we name them God, or that in our prayers and our worship we see them as partners with God, or that we see creation or our daily sustenance as being from them, or that we believe that God has incarnated Himself (*ḥulūl*) in them, or that we say that they know the secrets of the unseen without [needing] inspiration from God, or that we think of the Imams as [having the same rank as the] Prophet, or that we presume that knowledge and recognition of the Imams renders us beyond the need for any kind of worship and absolves us of all religious responsibilities.[37]

As referred to above, the imams sought 'refuge in God' from the *ghulat* and declared them disbelievers and ordered their death. On the other hand, the scholar Amir-Moezzi argues that the imams were not really denying the ideas of the *ghulat* as such but condemned men such as Ibn Nusayr for declaiming them publicly instead of keeping them secret:

> The act of condemning does not necessarily prove a divergence from doctrine, especially since certain remarks by the imams tend to suggest that the imams did not curse some of their disciples for what they said, but rather because they said it, in other words, because they did not respect the rule of the Secret. Ja'far said: 'I sometimes teach a tradition to someone, and then he leaves me and reports the tradition exactly as he heard it from my mouth; because of this, I declare that it is licit to condemn and to hate him.'[38]

Traditions ascribed to Imam Ja'far may have been invented later because of the widespread acceptability of *ghuluww* views; it is difficult to find Shi'i figures of that time who don't show similar thought processes. It seems that he made doctrinal changes in the sphere of beliefs regarding the imams being incarnations of the Divinity, for after him this particular doctrine appears to have died out and classified as extreme. Hence, the name *ghulat* probably dates to a time after Imam Ja'far.[39]

Nusayrism as a *ghulat* group emerged in Iraq in the ninth century and was shaped by several sheikhs over a period of 200 years. The common name 'Alawiyya ('Alawism') is derived from the Arabic term 'Alawi, and can be translated as 'follower of Ali'. It thus reflects the worship of the Alawis of Ali ibn Abi Talib, the cousin and son-in-law of Muhammad. The common opinion is that the designation 'Alawi for *Nusayri*, however, is a relatively young term and was not widely used until the beginning of the twentieth century. The name most commonly used in the previous millennium in both Islamic and Western sources for this group was *Nusayri*.[40]

The origins of Alawism date back to Iraq in the ninth century AD. The Arabs who conquered the territory of present-day Iraq after the death of the Prophet Muhammad (531–623) encountered ancient cultures with sophisticated belief systems against which Islam was still very young and undeveloped. Thus, Islamized followers of ancient Babylonian religions, Zoroastrianism, Mazdakism, Manichaeism, Judaism, and various Christian denominations infused diverse ideas into the Islamic community and caused religious debates on concepts such as 'transmigration of the soul' (*tanasukh*), 'occultation' (*ghayba*), 'return' (*raj'a*), 'descent of the Spirit of God into Man' (*hulul*), the 'divinely inspired leadership' of the Imamate (*imama*) or 'anthropomorphism' (*tashbih*). People who dealt with 'heterodox' issues from the standpoint of orthodox Sunni Islam were called 'transgressors' (*ghulat*). They were described as needing a 'priest-god figure' to project these ideas onto.[41]

They chose Imam Ali and later his descendants for the following reason: shortly before the Arab conquest, Byzantine Syria and Iraq, part of Zoroastrian Iran, had been enemies. After the dynasty of the Umayyad caliphs (661–750), who in the view of the Shi'is were unlawful rulers of Islam, established their caliphate in Syria, Imam Ali chose Iraq as his residence. When the Umayyads dominated Iraq after Ali's death, the Shi'a opposed them.[42] Nothing was more appropriate than to project this opposition onto the person of Ali, who would defeat the usurpers and restore justice. Ali's return, however, became more and more remote, and the concept of the occultation was transferred to the succeeding Imams.[43] Most likely, non-Arab followers of ancient religions in Kufa, the city Imam Ali had chosen as his capital had a significant influence in the development of the later religious beliefs of the Shi'a.[44] At the time when non-Arabs wanted to convert to Islam, they became 'clients' (Arab. *mawali*, sg. *mawla*) of individual companions of Muhammad or one of the Arab tribes. They had inferior social status, but subsequently gained significant economic and political influence.[45] They are said to have shaped the Shi'a in its beginnings with their teachings.[46] They went so far as to attribute to Imam Ali and the later Imams not only immortality but also divinity. The moderate Shi'is accused them of 'exaggeration' (*ghuluww*). Conversely, the *ghulat* called the moderates 'shorteners' (*muqassira*), meaning, that they 'fell short of' fully acknowledging the divine nature of the Imams.[47]

Among the diverse currents of 'extreme' Shi'ism arose the *Nusayriyya/'Alawiyya*. They go back to Muhammad Ibn Nusayr, who was a close companion of the 10th Imam Ali al-Hadi (also Ali an-Naqi), and his son Hasan al-'Askari, the 11th Imam of the Twelver Shi'is. His teachings were similar to other Shi'i groups who preached the divinity of Ali and the other imams and were called 'exaggerators' by their adversaries and by Muslim heresiographers. According to his own writings, Ibn Nusayr was the intimate messenger of those imams from whom he claimed to have received secret knowledge, thus posing as the 'gate' (*bab*) to them. After Ibn Nusayr's death in about 864, Ibn Jundab and al-Junbulani led the community and transmitted his mystical traditions; little is known about them.[48] Of particular importance, however, is the fourth leader, al-Husayn Ibn Hamdan al-Khasibi (died 969),[49] who not only contributed to the survival of the community, but was actually the most influential scholar, the true founder of Nusayrism. He was convinced that he was the leader of the 'real Shi'a',[50] and began to openly preach a mystical Shi'ism in Sunni Baghdad, whereupon he was arrested. After escaping from prison, he went to the city of Harran (now in south-eastern Turkey), where he is said to have gathered around him a group of men who called themselves 'the monotheists'. The political turn in favour of the Shi'i dynasty of the Buyids[51] allowed al-Khasibi to return to Baghdad. Soon after he settled in Aleppo where he was supported by the

Shi'i Hamdanid ruler Sayfu'd-Dawla.[52] His experience in Iraq led al-Khasibi to practice *taqiyya* in Syria. Al-Khasibi was a prolific intellectual, author and poet, whose collection of poems (*Diwan al-Khasibi*) was expanded by later authors;[53] his works are an important source for the early development of Nusayrism. He died in Aleppo and was buried there.

The Byzantine conquest of large parts of Syria and the collapse of the Hamdanids were large setbacks for the Nusayris. Nevertheless, in the tenth and eleventh centuries they managed to form new communities in Aleppo, Beirut, Tiberias, and especially in the mountains in the hinterland of the coast. Rural Christian, pagan, members of the more superficially Islamized communities from this region are said to have converted to Nusayrism. The eleventh century brought with it some charismatic and educated Nusayri leaders, among them Abu Sa'id at-Tabarani[54] (died 1035), who wrote most of the essential works of the Alawi tradition, notably the *Majmu' al-A'yad*, the 'Book of Festivals'.[55] At the turn of the twelfth century, both the great missionary work and the unified leadership of the community ended. From now on, the transmission and development of the Nusayri doctrine was in the hands of local, semi-learned sheikhs, who often opposed one another. This transformation from a predominantly urban and intellectual to a rural tribal society had a large impact on the quality of the teachings and religious works. In addition, the twelfth century brought unstable conditions to the region, and the Nusayris suffered at the hands of the Ismailis, the Crusaders and later the Ayyubids under Salahu'd-Din al-Ayyubi, who defeated the Crusaders; they saw themselves after the Shi'i Fatimid rule as the innovators of the true Sunni faith.[56]

The situation of the Nusayris improved in the early thirteenth century with the arrival of Emir Makzun as-Sinjari, who consolidated the rule of the Nusayris over the mountains with the help of a large Bedouin army from the mountains of Sinjar in Iraq. These soldiers remained in the country, and their descendants form part of the local population.[57] Only a few decades later, the region of the Nusayris was conquered by the Mamluk Sultan Baybars; he is said to have severely persecuted all Shi'i groups, but his efforts to force the Alawis to accept Sunni Islam were unsuccessful. In 1318, a Nusairi uprising with social as well as religious roots began when a Nusayri declared himself the 'Mahdi', the expected saviour of the Muslim community. This uprising shook the region around the city of Jabala (or Jabla), but it seems that economic reasons in particular prevented the Mamluks from completely destroying the Alawis. The cause of the Mamluks' punitive campaign against the Nusayris in 1318, which was often presented as a general policy of the Mamluks, was a tax revolt and it was later portrayed by pious Sunnis as a purely religious conflict; but this is not to say that it did not also have religious causes.[58] What followed was a process of 'turning inward' on the part of the Nusayris. This was not caused by a supposed conflict with Sunnis or Shi'is, but by internal debates about the limits of religious authority and orthodoxy within the community. The attitude of the Sunni dynasties of the Ayyubids and Mamluks towards the Nusayris was more tolerant than indifferent or hostile.[59]

Contrary to the common belief that the Nusayris have been an offshoot of the 'mainstream' Twelver Shi'a since their beginnings in the tenth century, most recent research says that the Nusayris were branded as heretics only after the institutionalization of the Twelver Shi'a in the eleventh century. It should also be noted that the community spread from Iraq to Syria not because of persecution, but as a result of missionary zeal in competition with the Isma'ili and other Shi'i subgroups. During this period, the Nusayris were supported by local Shi'i-inclined dynasties like the Hamdanids or Fatimids.[60] Thus, until the eleventh century, the Nusayris were active in disseminating their teachings and not a marginal Islamic group. The Nusayri mission was interrupted after the First Crusades, and only later did the followers retreat to the mountains in north-western Syria and organized themselves into various tribes for military needs against the Crusaders, Isma'ilis and representatives of resurgent Sunni Islam. It was only after that the Nusayris became a 'minority', so to speak, for the rest of their existence.[61]

At the beginning of the fourteenth century, the conservative Sunni scholar Ibn Taymiyya (died 1328) issued formal legal opinions (sg. *fatwa*) declaring the Nusayris 'infidels'. In research and popular belief to date, even among the Alawis in Syria, the *fatwa*s of Ibn Taymiyya and others from the Ottoman period had a great influence on how the Nusayris/'Alawis were seen and are still seen by the Sunni majority. Because the Alawis were considered infidels, the Sunnis were allowed to confiscate their properties, sell them as slaves, and even kill them. Stefan Winter notes that for centuries the famous and oft-cited *fatwa* of Ibn Taymiyya was misused as the only official Muslim orthodox view. It seems that, in fact, the views of Ibn Taymiyya did not have much influence either during the Mamluk rule or later in the Ottoman Empire until the eighteenth century.[62] But to verify this statement a comprehensive study which would make use of a variety of sources from the thirteenth until the eighteenth century would be required. Winter adds that Sunni rulers were more anxious to systematically levy taxes than to deal with the divergent teachings of the Nusayris.

After the conquest of Syria by the Ottomans in 1516, Sultan Selim I (r. 1512–1520) began to 'Islamize' the Nusayris, but had no success. On the whole, however, the four hundred years of Ottoman rule over the territory of the Alawis can be described as ambivalent. Contrary to the traditional view among the Alawis that the Ottomans tried to wipe them out after the conquest of Syria at the beginning of the sixteenth century, Ottoman tax registers show that the rulers tried to increase their tax revenues and maintain specific Alawi levies.[63] One phenomenon that strained the relationship between the Ottomans and the Nusayris at the time was the banditry of the Nusayris. Ottoman legal documents show that this was considered a social problem and not a religious one. The Ottomans believed that banditry was due to the manipulation of 'ignorant' Nusayris by powerful people. And unlike historians of the twentieth century and the present, who claim that there were no reliable sources for the period between the sixteenth until the nineteenth centuries, we have evidence that there exist credible sources about the social, administrative and political Situation of the Alawis.[64]

With the decentralization of the state and the independence of the Ottoman provincial elite in the eightwwnth century, well-known families among the Alawis were employed by the authorities as tax farmers. This, in turn, helped these families to become a landed gentry and gain wealth and prestige through tobacco cultivation and commerce as never before. Another development that had far-reaching implications for the Nusayris was the division of the community into different tribes and clans (tribalization) due to increasing social inequalities within the community. While some families became wealthy and influential, the rest remained destitute and financially dependent on the former. Impoverishment of Alawis was less a consequence of external factors than of internal tribal rivalry and religious fragmentation.[65] The latter was the result of the splitting of the Alawis into two great factions: the *Haydariyya*, named after Sheikh Ali Haydar (15th c.) also known as the *Shimaliyya* ('The Northerners') or the *Shamsiyya* ('sun-worshippers'), and the *Kalaziyya*, named after Sheikh Kalazu (d. 1602/1603), also called *Qibliyya* ('The Southerners') or *Qamariyya*, ('moon- worshippers').[66] All this fuelled mutual looting and raiding, which then provoked the Ottomans to take military action against the mountain Nusayris. 'Alawi communities on the coast from Syria to Cilicia were not confronted with these problems and suffered less from state-sponsored repression than from social discrimination by the surrounding Sunni majority.[67]

As a result of the unequal social situation, migrations of groups of disadvantaged Nusayris into various regions on the Syrian coast, inland and into the Antakya area, Hatay in present-day Turkey, followed. The increasing classification of the Nusayris as a uniform 'sect' or tribal faction with a political goal at the end of the eighteenth and the beginning of the nineteenth century can be traced back to the penetration of the European powers and general instability. Local Ottoman officials in particular, rather than the central administration in Istanbul, were worried that the Nusayris were now tools of foreign powers. As enemies of the state, the Nusayris were exposed to religious and social disciplinary measures.[68]

Since the end of the eighteenth century, the Ottoman central administrations in the provinces were weakened by semi-autonomous local rulers. These came into conflict with Nusayri notables, whereupon their community, according to Winter's argument, was branded for the first time in Ottoman society as heretics and outcasts. Despite increasing discrimination and exploitation by provincial officials, Nusairi leaders supported the spread of Ottoman rule in Syria and resisted the reign of the Egyptian governor Mehmed Ali, who occupied Syria from 1831 to 1841.[69] In the ensuing decades of the centralization of power during the Tanzimat and the reign of Sultan Abdülhamid II, the Nusayris were subjected to measures aimed at bringing them to the fold of Sunni Islam and thus the 'right path'. Another measure to control the Nusayris and subordinate them to the central authority was the conscription to military service. In the Nusayri regions and places where similar groups lived, mosques and medreses (schools) were built with the aim of transforming 'heretics' into loyal subjects. Despite the fact that official Ottoman documents attest to conversions of tens of thousands of 'heretics' to Sunni Islam, Abdülhamid's 'civilizing mission' failed. Even the American Protestant missionaries, who had tried to create a new social order based on their millenarian faith, had little success in converting 'heterodox' Muslims. The Nusayris, on the other hand, were experiencing a process of collective transformation at that time, and they chose for themselves the name 'Alawis' (Turk. *Aleviler*, Arab. *'Alawiyyun*). The change in self-designation was part of a socio-political process of demarcation from the Ottoman Empire, which began in the last decades of the 19th century before its final collapse.[70]

Despite all efforts of the Ottomans to assimilate them, the Nusayris made use of the modern school system and had representatives in the local councils, which were introduced as part of the reforms. Thus, the Nusayris probably gained a voice as a political group for the first time. We can say that the attitude of the Ottomans towards the Nusayris was ambivalent. On the one hand, the Alawis appeared in census lists as Muslims, and the men were drafted into the Ottoman army. In the nineteenth century, some Alawis had even occupied high offices.[71] On the other hand, the Alawis were under suspicion as the largest 'non-Orthodox' group in the region, especially local officials. However, there is no evidence of systematic persecution for religious reasons by the Ottoman authorities. The numerous military attacks on Alawi villages were mostly reactions to local uprisings, which in turn were often the result of ruthless tax collection.[72]

A turning point in the modern history of the Alawis was the end of the First World War and the collapse of the Ottoman Empire. After the collapse of the Ottoman Empire at the end of the First World War in 1918, its enemies fought for control of its provinces. In 1920, France took over the province of Syria (today's Syria, Lebanon and Alexandretta/Iskenderun in the Turkish province of Hatay) and in the same year the League of Nations gave France the mandate over this region, which also included the hinterland of Latakia at the eastern Mediterranean coast, which for centuries had been the main settlement area of the Alawis. The name *Alaouite* was accepted after the First World War in the wake of the short-lived 'Alawi State' (*État des Alaouites*, Arab. *Dawlat al-'Alawiyyin*) under French rule in Syria as a semi-autonomous region and later as one of the states of the Syrian Federation. The Alawis were made into a dominant religious community by the French in opposing Sunni hegemony in Syria.

Ottoman rule ended with the defeat of the Empire and its final dissolution at the end of the First World War. The victors, Britain and France, divided the Arab provinces according to their respective interests. The territories of present-day Syria, Lebanon, Jordan, Palestine and Israel were geographically known as 'Greater Syria', the borders of which were created and imposed by the two European powers. The aim was to benefit from religious and ethnic diversity by applying the principle of *divide et impera* – 'divide and rule'.[73]

1.2. The Ottoman Nusayris: Geography, Social Structure and Authority

The Alawis occupy the area of the most eastern Mediterranean coast in Syria and Turkey including the area around the Asi (Orontes) River. Other Alawi settlements are scattered east of the Asi at Homs and Hama. A major Alawi settlement in Syria until today is Latakia, an important port city, as are Baniyas, Tartous and Jabla

Figure 1.1 Old Antakya (Antioch)

(Jableh, Jabala). In the nineteenth century other cities such as Safita and Sahyun (modern al-Haffah) figure prominently as major Alawi settlements of which the latter seems to be mostly Sunni now. Turkey's Alawis inhabit many places in the modern Hatay province around Antakya (Antioch), which includes the port city of Iskenderun, and the neighbouring Çukurova Plain (Cilicia) around Adana and Mersin.

As discussed previously, throughout their long history, the Alawis have been considered by their Sunni neighbours to belong to a heretical 'sect' or even as 'unbelievers' outside the Islamic community. And for many centuries, the Alawis lived mainly in the hinterland of Latakia at the eastern Mediterranean, the coastal mountains of Syria called the 'Mountains of the Alawis' (*Jibal al-'Alawiyyin*), which protected them from persecution. The Alawis have been known as an isolated group, a tribal and agrarian society bound by tradition. This isolation has been significantly enhanced by their endogamy, which still prevails today among them. During the nineteenth century, many Alawis immigrated to the region of Antakya and the plain of Cilicia and settled between and in the Turkish cities of Adana and Mersin. At about the same time, larger Alawi groups moved from the mountains to the fertile lands around Hama and Homs. Only during the second half of the twentieth century did many, especially educated Alawis, move to the major cities of Syria, especially to Damascus, Latakia and Homs, where they often live in separate neighbourhoods. Due to the harsh economic conditions in the mountains, significant emigration from the Alawis to North and South America occurred in the late nineteenth and early twentieth centuries.[74] Since the 1970s, a large number of Alawis left Turkey for Europe, especially Germany.[75] Basically all Alawis speak Arabic as their mother tongue. Until recently, this also applied to the Alawi communities in southern Turkey. Only among the younger generations is a tendency to Turkish monolingualism recognizable.[76]

As regards their so-called 'isolation' in the face of 'persecution' still used by historians, this paradigm is according to Stefan Winter one of the most persistent stereotypes of Alawi history. The 'mountain refuge', often portrayed as a clear geographical fact, states that the inaccessible coastal highlands of Syria and Lebanon have served since the beginning of time as a refuge for minority sects fleeing religious oppression in the cities and plains of the interior. However, this view is not confirmed in such simple terms by the available evidence: neither the Druze, Isma'ili, Shi'i or Alawi populations came to the region to actually escape persecution elsewhere, nor were the Islamic states really unable to maintain dominance over the mountains. The Alawis were concentrated in the coastal highlands, often inaccurately called in the literature 'Ansa(i)riyya' Mountains (corrupted from the local dialectic pronunciation of 'an-Nusayriyya', not because they had to flee there as refugees, but because the Ayyubids and Mamluks were successful in institutionalizing Sunnism elsewhere by building mosques, equipping madrasas and promoting Sunni jurisprudence, rather than chasing after minor rural 'heresies.[77]

The Alawis were a segmented society divided by tribe, factions and class; this fact had a significant influence on the internal solidarity within this religious community. The Nusayris were divided into four large tribes or tribal confederations ('asha'ir); the Khayyatin, Haddadin, Kalbiyya and Matawira, and each confederation comprised several small clans or sub-tribes. Each clan in the tribal confederation also had its own chief, a fact that made cooperation and unity difficult. The Nusayris also suffered severely from the internal quarrels of the tribal chiefs.[78]

Nusayri society can be described as composed of the following classes: 1) religious leaders, 2) landowners, and 3) ploughmen/peasants (Arab. sg. *fallah*/pl. *fallahun*, corrupted: *fellahin*, *fellaheen*) or the general population that constituted the majority of the Nusayri society. Chieftaincy was hereditary and so was succession to religious office. Until the twentieth century the above-mentioned differences within Nusayri society invited disturbances and bloody clashes. The lack of distinctive religious or secular leadership prevented the Nusayris from achieving internal solidarity and forming an ethnic group. From the beginning of the nineteenth century the Nusayris were in a state of mutiny but they never acted as one united group.[79] The absence of internal cooperation between the Nusayris disadvantaged them in any conflict. The Ottomans were aware of the problems in Nusayri society and had often tried to use these to their advantage, following the policy of 'divide and rule'.

Despite the fact that the heads of the tribes and clans, being of the highest class, came from rich families and mostly inherited this position, some poor *fellahin* could also rise up and become head of a clan. The life of the chiefs was different from the life of the common people and they mostly had more agricultural possessions; they obtained revenues from the peasants and collected taxes. The *fellahin* possessed some small lands in the mountains and lived on them, with the exception of some who worked on lands of other Alawis who were landowners in exchange for shares; some also possessed land on the plains.[80]

The general division in the Alawi community is typical of other esoteric groups such as the Druze which also consists of nobles/elites (*al-khassa*) and ordinary or common people (*al-'amma*). But unlike the Druze, Alawi common men were not excluded from being taught their religion.[81] The sheikhs ('elders') were religious figures (*rijal ad-din*) who held religious authority and secular officials (*muqaddams*, 'headmen') mediated between their community and the Ottoman administration.

Of the religious figures, Nusayri texts speak of the imam or leading sheikh, and his two assistants in religious ceremonies, the *najib* (noble) and *naqib* (chief), all of whom form a triad. The imam leads the community of believers, who believe that he has utmost spiritual, inborn and intellectual qualities; on his shoulders rest the instruction of the religion; he is in charge of religious matters, keeps the religious secrets and teaches the religious obligations; followers believe that the imam is the 'best of creation', who excels all in character and religion; therefore all tribal chiefs and the common people revere him to the utmost degree and pay him full respect. He receives money and gifts for religious services, e.g. for the ceremony of initiation, for writing amulets/charms and prayers or if asked, for foretelling the best time to marry, for instance, or mediating between two parties when there is a quarrel or other issues.[82] Sometimes sheikhs attain reputations for solving quarrels and if a sheikh is known for his fear of God, his good character, benevolent activities and the like, he is a candidate for being treated like a saint after his death – after which people visit his grave to pray, expecting blessings and make offerings and leave gifts. These places, usually located on a hill, became sacred tombs, a 'place of visitation', *mazar* or *ziyara* in Arabic (Turk. *mezar/ziyaret*).

Gertrude Bell (1868–1926), English writer, traveller and influential political administrator, who helped create modern Iraq,[83] observed at the beginning of the twentieth century the 'funeral feast of a great sheikh much renowned for piety' in Syria and remarked: 'To have a reputation for holiness in the Jebel Noṣairiyyeh is as good as a life insurance with us.'[84] With poetic words she talked about a grave of a Nusayri saint at 'the top of the Noṣairiyyeh hills':

> The Noṣairis have neither mosque nor church, but on every mountain top they build a shrine that marks a burial-ground. These high-throned dead, though they have left the world of men, have not ceased from their good offices, for they are the protectors of the trees rooted among their bones, trees which, alone among their kind, are allowed to grow untouched.[85]

Another account speaks about those 'characteristic structures which are prominent landmarks all over the Nussairyeh country'. The Nusayris visited these holy places on hilltops, often near a grove of trees, 'with the hope of securing some special blessings'. The grove itself was also considered sacred, and no Nusayri would dare to break a twig from the branches of those trees. Usually the 'Zeyarats' were built over the graves of 'specially holy persons, although most of the stories told of them properly fall within the category of fabled lore'.[86] Talking about the veneration of *ziyara*s and the role of the sheikhs who are their keepers, Samuel Lyde (1825–1860), the famous English missionary who lived during the 1850s among the Nusayris, noted: 'The sheikh was a venerable old man, with a manner as if he had been accustomed to receive the great ones of the earth, probably acquired from his central position, and his intercourse with men. I have found some others of the Ansairee sheikhs possessing an air of simple dignity; in fact, a feeling of pre-eminence and authority communicates this even among barbarous nations.'[87]

There is an extensive corpus of research about religious authority in Islam, focusing on diverse aspects involving the interplay of religion, law, politics and society, relating it to the *shari'a* (Islamic law) and *fiqh* (Islamic jurisprudence) and providing comparative cases.[88] As essential as it is to discuss religious authority, it is also crucial to study those who wield authority. While religious authorities in mainstream Islam, Sunni and Twelver Shi'a, have been discussed at length,[89] sufficient studies about religious authority/authorities in the theological fringes of the Islamic world do not exist, particularly in the case of the Nusayris/Alawis, at least not in European languages.

What follows then is an attempt to define religious authority and its meaning in Islam in order to provide a background and discussion about what religious and secular authority looked like in Nusayri/Alawi society with its tribal structure consisting of clans, social classes and religious leadership. Secular authority among the Alawis in the Ottoman Empire was represented by the *mukaddem* (Arab. *Muqaddam*, village head), and the religious class consisted of the sheikhs or *meşayih*/*mashayikh* ('elders, religious heads'). We will also look at how religious authority was passed among the founders of the religious community, how it later was passed on by the sheikhs and through which symbolic acts and rituals they maintained it. I place my discussion of religious authority among the Alawis in the theoretical framework of French sociologist Pierre Bourdieu of 'charismatic/symbolic capital'. I also deal with some Alawi writers in the twentieth century who challenged this hereditary sheikh institution and wrote that after the founding of the religion, sheikhs engaged in corrupt practices for monetary gain. Finally, I will try to show in the context of dynamics of religion how the religious authority of Alawi sheikhs has changed or been undermined in modern times.

'Authority', according to Max Weber, consists of three types of authority, which are but 'ideal types': charismatic, traditional and legal-rational. Charismatic authority rests on the devotion of an exemplary character of a 'superhuman' individual who possesses a specific/exceptional sanctity and/or distinguishes himself through heroism and has an established order revealed by him; traditional authority bases itself on an established belief in the sanctity of ancient traditions and the legitimacy of those exercising this authority under them; and rational authority is grounded on a belief in the 'legality' of patterns of normative rules and on the right of those who are elevated to authority under such rules to issue commands. These are reference points which are to be found in any given society, and there are also sub-types of mixed types of authority.[90]

These definitions are applicable to secular (state) and religious settings. Religious authority in Islam can be deduced from the Qur'an itself, though the concept of authority is conveyed by different expressions. Probably the most disputed and manipulated verse with regard to authority is 4:59, the 'obedience verse': 'O believers, obey God, and obey the Messenger and those in authority among you (*ati'u Allah wa ati'u ar-rasul wa uli'l-amr minkum*). If you should quarrel on anything, refer it to God and the Messenger.' In fact, obedience to the Prophet is equal with obedience to God: 'Whosoever obeys the Messenger, thereby obeys God' (*man yuti' ar-rasul fa-qad ata'a Allah*, 4:80). Only the Messenger speaks for God, he is His mouthpiece: 'And obey God and obey the Messenger, and beware; but if you turn your backs, then know that it is only for Our Messenger to deliver the Message Manifest' (5:92). While the authority of God and Muhammad are clear, the question remains as to who is meant by 'those in authority (*uli'l-amr*) among you'. This is interpreted differently by Sunnis and Shi'is: 'The ambiguity of Q 4:59, as well as its potential political significance, made it subject to numerous interpretations, most of which reflect the opinions of the various theological and political groups in early Islamic society.'[91]

Classical Sunni interpreters of the Qur'an such as at-Tabari and al-Qurtubi defined Muslim leaders such as sultans, caliphs, amirs (commanders) and the 'ulama (scholars of religion) as being 'those in authority' (*ulu'l-amr*).[92] Thus, not only political leaders but also religious guides and scholars are suggested as persons with authority. Some classical Sunni exegetes say that only some companions and commanders during the lifetime of Muhammad are intended by 'those in authority'.[93] For the Shi'is *ulu'l-amr* are the infallible twelve imams, the rightly guided and legitimate successors after Muhammad.[94]

Gudrun Krämer and Sabine Schmidtke have provided a useful critical overview of religious authority and authorities – 'men and women claiming, projecting and exerting religious authority within a given context' – in Muslim societies and ask the following questions that are useful for our discussion here: 'Who speaks for Islam? Who do Muslims turn to when they look for guidance? To what extent do individual scholars and preachers exert religious authority, and how can it be assessed?' and they also state that 'Religious authority is an elusive concept and notoriously difficult to define'.[95] Following Max Weber's definition of authority, it is the 'chance' or ability to obey or follow one's rules and rulings without coercion. Even though Weber distinguishes between authority (*Autorität*) and power (*Macht*) – the latter involves coercion – sometimes the differences between the two are blurred:

> *Religious* authority can assume a number of forms and functions: the ability (chance, power, or right) to define correct belief and practice, or orthodoxy and orthopraxy, respectively; to shape and influence the views and conduct of others accordingly; to identify, marginalize, punish or exclude deviance, heresy and apostasy and their agents and advocates. In the monotheistic religions founded

on revealed scripture, religious authority further involves the ability (chance, power, or right) to compose and define the canon of 'authoritative' texts and the legitimate methods of interpretation.[96]

Religious authority also implies legitimacy and trust; it can manifest itself in individuals, a group of people and institutions that have inherited or acquired qualifications. It is effective when others are willing to credit a person, group or institution with religious authority. As with other kinds of authority, religious authority is not 'a fixed attribute, but is premised on recognition and acquiescence'.[97] It is therefore an interactive concept in which the person who wields authority and those who obey are interdependent.

Defining religious authority in Islam is particularly difficult because Islam is not uniform. Sunnis and mainstream Twelver Shi'is have a difference of opinion when it comes to authority. The major difference and bone of contention is the rightful succession after Muhammad, i.e. the caliphate and imamate. Within Sunni and Shi'a Islam there are countless divisions, Sufi orders and movements whose views about authority differ. This appears even more complex when we consider notions of authority among so-called heterodox or non-conformist non-Sunni groups, such as that of the Nusayris. The closest type of authority that applies to the Nusayri leadership as defined by Weber is the traditional one mixed with charismatic authority.

The most important task of the leading Nusayri sheikh of a locality is the instruction of religious tenets or the initiation.[98] This sheikh must be from a family of sheikhs who are specialized in the ceremony of initiation. The initiation into Nusayri secrets is confined to men who are at least 15 years old. Women are excluded because they are not regarded as reliable to keep the secrets. Dogmatically, they are not regarded as spiritual beings, to say the least; some Nusayri texts say that women are created from the sins of the devils.[99] The initiation is only for boys from Nusayri parents; if a Nusayri man marries a non-Nusayri woman, the boys are not instructed. The initiation usually takes nine months for sons of common people and seven for sons of nobles, which is equivalent to the length of a pregnancy; at the end the novice is reborn spiritually after learning the esoteric (*batini*) teachings that non-Alawis do not possess.

The length of the initiation is different in theory and in practice; for Turkey, especially the Hatay province around Antakya, we can say that the initiation of the Nusayri adept occurs in one phase in the Kalazi faction; and in three ritual phases in the Haydari faction. In theory and based on Nusayri writings, in the beginning the religious instructor or 'uncle', *al-'amm as-sayyid* (Arab.), is chosen. In former times this was a sheikh; more recently it can be a man who is grounded in Nusayri theology, is reliable, popular and of upright character. He introduces the novice to the religious ceremony led by the three sheikhs, the imam, the *najib* and the *naqib*. In the first phase the novice is led to the place of ceremony and introduced to the imam; after being confirmed as capable for receiving the secrets, the imam tells the adept to put on the shoes of those who carry out the initiation in order to show his humility.[100]

In the second phase, after forty days the family of the novice holds a big feast during which the new candidate is taught the titles of the sixteen chapters of the Nusayri holy book *Kitab al-Majmu'*, a testimony of faith. After seven or nine months, the third phase of the initiation begins and the novice is taught the secrets of the Nusayri belief. For this, a second instructor, the 'uncle of the introduction' (*'amm ad-dukhul*), is chosen. He ushers or introduces the novice to the community of chosen Nusayris. The novice lives in the house of the uncle, who is his spiritual father, and usually cannot come of the house until he finishes his instruction. At this stage the novice testifies that he will not disclose the secrets to anyone and guarantees this with his life.[101]

The details of the Alawi initiation are too long to be described here. What is important is the symbolic value of the initiation. Apart from the spiritual aspect of the initiation, it is also a profitable business for the sheikhs, who receive animals for sacrifice, are invited to meals by the family of the adept and receive money in the form of *zakat*, the alms-giving tax.[102] The uncle also receives gifts from the family of the adept. If the family of the adept is not wealthy, the initiation ceremony is reduced to one stage only because they cannot afford to pay much money, bestow gifts or hold big meals. For this reason, sheikh families are usually wealthy in terms of economic capital. Based on the theoretical framework of the Pierre Bourdieu,[103] they achieve this through symbolic acts and so accumulate symbolic and charismatic capital that increases their prestige and power/authority.

Bourdieu proposes four types of capital: economic, cultural, social and symbolic. Like economic capital, the other three are also accumulated. He offers a sociology of symbolic power in which he addresses the important topic of relations between culture, stratification and power. He contends that the struggle for social recognition is a fundamental dimension of all social life. In that struggle, cultural resources, processes and institutions hold individuals and groups in competitive and self-perpetuating hierarchies of domination. He advances the bold claim that all cultural symbols and practices, ranging from artistic tastes, style in dress and eating habits to religion, science and philosophy – indeed to language itself – embody interests and function to enhance social distinctions. Bourdieu focuses on how these social struggles are refracted through symbolic classifications, how cultural practices place individuals and groups into competitive class and status hierarchies, how relatively autonomous fields of conflict link individuals and groups in struggle over valued resources, how actors struggle and pursue strategies to achieve their interests within such fields, and how in doing so actors unwittingly reproduce the social stratification order.

Symbolic capital is the sum of economic, cultural and social capital. According to this theory, Alawi sheikhs gain religious authority, reputation and privileges through the accumulation of economic, cultural and social capitals that express themselves in symbolic acts. Religious authority is one of the distinguishing features of the sheikhs; it is linked with their heritage and they strongly adhere to it.

As all religion is subject to change and evolution, so the religious authority of the Alawi sheikhs has faced opposition. Syrian Alawi writers in the twentieth century challenged the hereditary institution of the sheikh and wrote that, after the founders of early Alawism died, the local sheikhs corrupted the religion and abused it for private gain by misleading the believers. One of these 'Alawi authors is Hashim Uthman, a lawyer from Latakia. Even though he was not from a family of sheikhs, he belonged to a lay religious movement that aimed at reforming 'Alawism. Uthman apparently also acted as one of the apologists unofficially representing the Ba'th regime in Syria.[104]

Uthman writes that, after the time of the great masters, the Alawis reclined to the mountains and lived in seclusion. They split into two factions, the Haydariyya and Kalaziyya, and only one other group remained faithful to the religious duties of the Islamic shari'a. Later, the sheikhs gained hegemony within their society and corrupted the sayings of their ancestors, interpreted them incorrectly and made the common people believe that the Alawi faith was a separate 'school' (*madhhab*), neither related to the Sunni nor the Shi'a.[105]

Declarations such as *al-'Alawiyyun Shi'a Ahl al-Bayt* from 1972–73,[106] in which eighty Alawi sheikhs and scholars in Syria and Lebanon declared that they are Shi'is and the words 'Alawis' and 'Shi'is' are interchangeable, are according to Uthman only lip service (*iqrar bi al-lisan*). He argues that 90 per cent of those who signed this do not fulfil their religious duties such as obligatory prayer (*salat*), fasting and pilgrimage. The reason for this, as Uthman continues to explain, is that those leaders maintain that the obligations only hint at spiritual truths and need to be interpreted in esoteric terms and they say that some Shi'i hadiths about being faithful to the family of Muhammad is ranked higher than the fulfilment of the five pillars of Islam. Uthman further points out that it is the sheikhs' fault that the teachings of the early Alawis, which are consistent with the shari'a, were corrupted. Here Uthman makes reference to the reformist thinker Muhammad Ali Isbar, who heavily criticized the Alawi sheikhs for keeping the *zakat* incomes for themselves; they do not go to the Friday and holy day prayers but perform Sufi-like prayer meetings; they tell people not to fast during Ramadan and that God did not prohibit alcohol (e.g. wine is used in religious ceremonies). Uthman says about Isbar that his book *'Adatuna wa Taqaliduna* caused considerable repercussions and was widely disseminated, as it was published in three editions in 1976, 1978 and 1980. Uthman remarks: 'It was indeed like an earthquake under the feet of the sheikhs. Therefore, the sheikhs declared Muhammad Ali Isbar a renegade and wrote a refutation.'[107]

Like Hashim Uthman, there were other Alawi authors writing in the twentieth century that early Alawism always belonged to Twelver Shi'ism and followed thus the Ja'fari *madhhab* in its beliefs and rulings. This is, as far as I know, the case in Syria but not in Turkey. In Turkey Alawi people also do not hesitate to refer to themselves as Nusayris. Even though the interest of young Turkish Alawis in their religion has been declining, the Alawi people still broadly show respect to the sheikhs and observe religious feasts or participate in acts of worship, such as visiting the tombs of saints and sheikhs.

Dynamics and change within the Alawi community and in the context of relations with Sunnis, non-Sunnis and non-Muslims is what concerns us in the book. Their status changed throughout the centuries through internal and external factors, as we will see in the following pages.

1.3. The status of the Nusayris in the Ottoman political system

The Ottoman Empire was a conglomerate of officially recognized religions as well as secretive and officially unrecognized factions within and outside Judaism, Christianity and Islam. These not only concealed their beliefs but sometimes did not accept the official religion or mainstream beliefs. Even though non-Sunni religious groups within Islam were regarded as Muslims, they were labelled 'heretical' (*rafızi*) and largely ostracized by the Sunni clergy and people. Within the Muslim community, such 'heretics' were the Shi'is, Alevis, Yezidis and the Nusayris. These were creeds seen as divergent from the caliphal Hanafi-Sunni dynasty and had no official status as autonomous religious communities (*millet*).

1.3.1. The early nineteenth century

In the first three decades of the nineteenth century we see efforts by the Ottoman administration to treat the Nusayris, alongside the Yezidis and the Shi'is of Lebanon, as political scapegoats. They were linked with rebellions incited by local governors in Syria or accused of collaboration with the Greeks, who during their nationalist revolt in the 1820s, supposedly tried to unite 'heterodox' groups against the Muslims. At the same time, governors in Syria, who were hostile towards each other, showed leniency towards the Nusayris and similar groups and proposed their pacification in an attempt to win them as allies.[108] Some decades later, in 1855, when the Crimean War between the Ottomans and Russians (1854–1856) raged, it was reported that the 'mountain tribes of Syria', i.e. the Nusayris, were not indifferent observers of the current crisis and thought that any change would lead to the betterment of their situation; they would be happy about the defeat and overthrow of the Ottomans and celebrate this almost like a 'national triumph'. When some Nusayri chiefs were imprisoned in Latakia after an internal feud, some Greeks, who were agents of Russia, approached and told the angry Nusayri people how unfaithful their Turkish overlords were and that Russia would help them if they wished. The Greeks also distributed money among them, incited them to rebel against the Turks and to free their chiefs.[109]

Despite this rebellious image of the Nusayris, individuals from northern Syria, in and around Antakya, were regarded as loyal citizens who did not engage in banditry but pursued their living as farmers or townsmen. It appears that the Nusayris of this region are almost completely unmentioned in official Ottoman documentation until after the second half of the nineteenth century. This may have been a way of the Ottomans choosing to allow these people to exist and contribute to society while officially not recognizing their religious preferences, as a way to overcome political dissonances in their realm. But even the Nusayris of the south, living in the Nusayriyya Mountains near the coast city Latakia (Lazkiye), people who supported their insufficient agricultural income with brigandage, could also appear as loyal subjects. In fact, in this period these Nusayris are described by European travellers mostly as hard-working and peaceful people.[110]

This image of peace-loving people gradually changed as a result of the Egyptian occupation of Ottoman Syria by Mehmed Ali Paşa. His son Ibrahim Paşa became governor of Syria and inaugurated economic, administrative and military reforms with the aim of integrating the province into a new Egypt. As part of his programme, he began to collect the arms of the local population and enforced general conscription.[111] Consequently, insurrections occurred, and the Nusayris, alongside the Druze, incited the first revolt against the Egyptians in 1834;[112] they not only refused to disarm and send recruits to the army but attacked the troops in Latakia and destroyed government buildings. Around the same time the peasants of Palestine also began a rebellion against the Egyptians.[113]

It was reported in an annual register of events in 1835 that the whole of Syria was in revolt against Mehmed Ali and his son Ibrahim. The former subjugated Syria when Albanian and Kurdish insurrections, said to have been promoted and supported by Mehmed Ali, employed the Sultan's military resources and saved him from Ottoman attack. 'Men and money for his works and armies were exacted from the Syrians with merciless brutality.'[114] Men capable of bearing arms were carried off by the Egyptian soldiers, and these arrested every Muslim man who was fit for military service. The maltreatment and arrests were extended to Turks, Jews and Christians alike. The following description of Mehmed Ali's campaign of forced conscriptions from 1856 serves to illustrate the conditions in Syria:

> These conscriptions, and the equally oppressive rigour of the pecuniary exactions, produced insurrections in various parts of the country. They were partial and uncombined movements, therefore easily suppressed; but they demonstrated the hatred the Syrians had conceived to the rule of Mehemet Ali. At one time the mountaineers of Prayaz[?] and the Druses, instigated, it was said, by the Porte, raised the standard of revolt. The latter had already been decimated, and their villages burned; but, urged by despair, they rose again, interrupting communications, plundering the caravans, and assassinating travellers. Ibrahim himself marched against them at the head of 12,000 men, dispersed and disarmed them. The Ansaries next appeared in arms. They were overthrown at the first encounter: they implored forgiveness, but Ibrahim ordered them all to be slaughtered, except those capable of acting as soldiers, and burned down their villages. Similar measures exasperated the people more and more, but all their insurrectionary movements only ended in discomfiture and greater severity. Ibrahim became doubtful of the fidelity of Aleppo; he therefore resolved to disarm its population. His mode of carrying his resolution into effect was a refinement upon his former cruelties. He assumed that every man was possessed of arms: every inhabitant, therefore, without exception, was ordered to deliver up a musket. Those who had none, and were too poor to comply with the order, were subjected to the bastinado.[115]

A US journal speculated in 1839 that: 'One cause why these violent conscriptions took place in Syria may probably be found in the fact that, in the early part of 1835, the plague had nearly depopulated Egypt.'[116] There were at least four conscriptions between 1833 and 1836. As was reported in a German newspaper in 1835, the Christians were not spared because Egypt was depopulated, i.e., there were not enough men and mostly women worked on the fields and in the factories, and the number of the Muslims in Syria was not sufficient. There were two Coptic regiments and Syria's Christians were also targeted for recruitment. Enlisting Christian men into the army was a heavy blow for the agriculture in Syria because, as deficient as it was, it was dependent on the 'diligent' Christian fieldworkers. Syrians on all sides were bitterly exasperated, and Ibrahim openly declared that he wanted to 'degrade' them to the rank of the Egyptian *Fellahs* (poor fieldworkers).[117]

During this decade of Egyptian rule in Syria from 1832 until 1841, the Ottomans supported and armed the Nusayris against Ibrahim Paşa.[118] After Ibrahim Paşa and his troops left Syria, the Nusayris used their army experience to turn against the Ottomans. However, Ibrahim had managed to break the independence of the Nusayris and fractured their solidarity. He ensured that the different Nusayri tribes were in strife with each other; his gold had turned Nusayri against Nusayri. Later, the Ottomans did not hesitate to use this disunity to their advantage.[119]

Even though the Nusayris were defeated in their 1834 revolt, the event was reported by a local Ottoman official to the Sublime Porte in favourable and exaggerated terms, stating that the 'numerous and powerful' Nusayris were strategically successful. Obviously, the writer wanted to further local interests and emphasized that the people in Syria wanted the Ottomans to end Egyptian occupation. The reality was different: whereas the traditional feudal Nusayris in their mountains were against the Egyptian modernizing reforms and sided with the Ottomans, the Nusayris at the Syrian coastal plain appreciated Mehmed Ali's efforts that promised religious equality too.[120] An Ottoman campaign in Syria against Egypt, which parts of the Syrian population hoped for, did not happen. The discriminatory behaviour towards the Nusayris after the Egyptians left Syria implies that the Ottomans did not care about their loyalty.

The pre-Tanzimat period was not wholly negative for the Nusayris. There are cases of a few Nusayris who served as state functionaries, some attaining high positions. A Nusayri who Kara Mehmed Paşa (d. 1828–29), also called *Kara Cehennem* ('Black Hell') was a celebrated Nusayri Ottoman military official. A native of Antakya, he was acting as master general of the imperial artillery (among other functions) and is said to have bombed the Janissary barracks in 1826 during Sultan Mahmud II's 'Auspicious Event' (*Vaka-yı Hayriyye*). While this latter attribution seems to be incorrect, it is certain that Kara Mehmed rose to the rank of full vizier as grand admiral (*kapudan-ı derya*), 'the first and only Nusayri ever to achieve that distinction.' He is regarded as having been 'foresighted' (*tedbirli*) and was a source of pride for his townsmen and apparently encouraged the migration of Nusayris to Istanbul and Bursa.[121] Kara Mehmed had failed to defend a port in Morea during the Greek rebellion (1822) but nevertheless was seen by Mahmud II. as 'illustrious and capable from among my vezirs, and experienced, hard-working and decorated from among my splendid ministers, in every way deserving of favour and worthy of benevolence' and appointed as governor of the rich province of Ankara and Çankırı.[122] He was married to the daughter of Halil Hamid Paşa, a former grand vizier. This family connection helped Kara Mehmed's son Mahmud Bey (d. 1841) to serve at the imperial chancery of state.[123]

Another noted official who is recorded as a Nusayri was Mehmed Emin Vahid Efendi, born in Kilis (South-eastern Anatolia) and taken as a child to Istanbul by his mother, appointed to high office as ambassador to France by Sultan Selim III (reigned 1789–1807) in 1806. Vahid Efendi later became chief accountant (*defter emini*) at the Imperial Council (*Divan-ı Hümayun*) and was appointed governor of Hanya (1819–1820) and Aleppo (1826–1827). He was known as Vahid Mehmed Paşa, the title Paşa given to him because he was made vizier. He held the position of vizier four times but it was taken from him three times due to laxity or mismanagement. Vahid Mehmed Paşa died in 1828 before he set out to Bosnia as new governor.[124] Among the noteworthy events during Vahid Efendi's ambassadorship in Paris was his encounter with Napoleon Bonaparte. He describes this in his Embassy Diary (*Sefaretname-i Fransa*).[125]

Kara Mehmed and Vahid Mehmed Paşa are identified by Mehmed Süreyya (d. 1909), a biographer of Ottoman officials, as Nusayris without any negative connotation. Of course, one cannot be sure whether the above-mentioned Nusayris became important officials due to the tolerance of the Ottomans or simply because they hid their Nusayri identity. The most important question in this regard is how Vahid Efendi could have been a Nusayri since historically there were no Nusayris/Alawis in Kilis. *Sicill-i Osmani* mentions, however, that Vahid Efendi built his father's grave at the Nusayri cemetery in Kilis.

In contrast to this official Ottoman stance is the attitude of the famous statesman and historian Ahmed Cevdet Paşa (1822–1895) as an example of the opinions about 'heretical' groups among conservative Muslim statesmen in the Tanzimat period. He made derogatory remarks about his rival Fuad Paşa's wife's family from Antakya, writing that although Fuad knew about her family's too lax moral behaviours he would remain blind to this because his wife and his father-in-law were Nusayris and this group (*taife*) did not care about morals.[126] Cevdet Paşa writes in the same vein about the Nusayris in his *Tarih-i Cevdet*, sometimes based on hearsay. After a lengthy exposition about the history and beliefs of the Druze who he also regarded as misguided, he says that the Nusayris live in the mountains of Syria and Tripoli, talks about their 'fallacious' (*bâtıl*) creed, accuses them of libertinism and promiscuity, states that they adore Imam Ali and the other imams and are therefore similar to the 'rejecters (of proper Islam)' (*revâfız*). He ends the discussion with the Arabic expression *Hafazna Allah min shurur 'aqa'idihim* ('God save us from the evils of their beliefs').[127]

In a rather unknown short article in manuscript form with the title *Sosyalistlere Dair Bir Makale* ('An Article Regarding the Socialists')[128] Ahmed Cevdet Paşa traces the origin of 'secret' (*batini*) religious groups such the Nusayris, Isma'ilis, Kızılbaş-Alevis, and even Freemasons, back to proto-socialist and rebellious movements in ancient Persia such as Mazdakism, a socially radical movement of religious sectarians that dominated ancient Persia in the late CE fifth and sixth centuries, the leader of which was a certain Mazdak. He says that similar modern ideologies such as Socialism, Communism and Nihilism[129] emerged in Asia and later developed in Europe. In the Islamic world, Cevdet Paşa further argues, the Mazdakites infiltrated Islam in order to corrupt its rules and cause mischief, and that later Mazdakism evolved and appeared in the garb of Alevism.[130] With regard to the Nusayris he states that the 'fallacious religious schools' (*mezâhib-i bâtıla*) in Syria such as the Nusayris that are within the extreme Shi'a (*gulât-ı Şia*) belong to the esoterics (*Bâtıniyye*). They would interpret Quranic verses wrongly in order to promote their fallacious beliefs and mislead ignorant people. The Mazdakite rite that was still inherent in their hearts they would support with the Quranic verse 'It is He who created for you all that is in the earth' (Q 2:29),[131] meaning that they made lawful everything in the world to be shared by everyone, whatever it is, including women, accusing them again of libertinism.[132]

1.3.2. The Tanzimat and its aftermath

Being regarded as nominal Muslims, the Nusayris were subject to different Ottoman policies. From 1840 until 1880 conflicts and banditry increased in the Nusayriyya (Ansariyya) Mountains.[133] Disagreements between Nusayri tribes were not the only cause for this. Almost every year Ottoman troops carried out punitive expeditions in the Mountains in order to collect taxes, disarm villagers and recruit soldiers. The mountaineers usually refused to pay taxes and to send their sons to the army.[134] Resistance to paying taxes is recorded as early as 1757 when it is reported that Nusayri tribes chased the tax officers (*mübaşir*) and sent a letter of warning to the governor Abdurrahman Paşa, saying that he should not oppress the people.[135]

As observed by the Austrian(-Hungarian) consul in Beirut in 1877, 'the authorities are powerless against this wild commotion of the Nasairians' (*Gegen dieses wüste Treiben der Nasairier sind die Behörden machtlos*). Even in older times, when the Ottomans had enough military personnel, they could do nothing against the Nusayris. Those 'daring mountain tribes' always knew how to avoid military service and payment of dues; they always found in their difficult mountain districts the best protection against the advancing expeditions of the 'Turks'. Since the outbreak of the Russo–Turkish war, their raids expanded and their 'impudence' increased and probably would not be stopped soon.[136]

There were many Nusayris who were identified as bandits roaming the country for loot throughout the nineteenth century and we find them in mutiny against the Ottoman state from time to time, again for refusing to pay taxes and send their sons to the army. There appeared armed Nusayri brigands that attacked troops and defied the local Ottoman administration but also attacked other Nusayri clans or raided villages of Muslims and Christians which sometimes entailed murder. Ottoman official records offer a good documentation about the unexplored research topic of Nusayri banditry, their activities. It remains to be explored whether these brigands had a social function and to what extent they fit into the model of 'social bandits' by Eric Hobsbawm, who extended Fernand Braudel's analysis of bandits.[137]

Nusayris living in the coastal plain were integrated into the provincial administration and tied to local notables but the increasing number of raids by

Figure 1.2 Old Antakya (Antioch), interested natives

Ottoman troops forced many of them to move northwards or to the plains of Hums and Hama where they cultivated the lands.[138] Emigration of Nusayris from south to north to the Adana-Çukurova region seems to have commenced in the beginning of the nineteenth century, due to better economic prospects and religious discrimination.[139]

Although the Nusayris were not seen as Muslims in terms of creed and denied official legal status, they were included in the Muslim *millet* in the formal censuses, not treated as non-Muslims and did not pay the poll-tax (*jizya*). In the early Ottoman period in Syria they had to pay a capital tax (*dirham al-rijal*).[140] In our period under discussion no documents could be found confirming the payment of this tax but the fact that the Nusayris were considered apostates, may have influenced the tax assessment. The Ottomans levied heavy taxes from the lands where Nusayris worked as farmers, even though it is unclear whether this occurred based on religious grounds. Theoretically, albeit Islamic law did not tolerate apostates, it did not have a basis for an unfair fiscal burden.[141]

Despite that the Nusayris constituted two-thirds of the population in the region of Latakia and elsewhere, they did not have representatives in the regional council. Both Muslims and Christians opposed the idea of their official representation. In some places such as Hama the Nusayris were allowed by the authorities to make use of the shari'a courts for legal matters.[142] The same was true for Adana and Mersin but not for Antakya. In Adana and Tarsus the Nusayris were allowed by the authorities to make use of the shariʿa courts for legal matters (*Nusayriler ehl-i İslam'ın hukuk-i şer'iyyesinden tamamıyla hissedar olarak*).¹⁴³ But overall this issue remains vague. As apostates the Nusayris had no legal rights; they could not claim any right at the Islamic and secular regulation courts and their testimony there was not heeded (*işbu taifenin mahkeme-i şer'iyye ve nizamiyyede öteden beri şehadetleri istima ettirilmediğinden*).¹⁴⁴ It seems that only in some cases they were allowed to be witnesses against Muslims and Christians.¹⁴⁵ Halil Kemal Bey, the Ottoman director of education in Aleppo (1886–1889),¹⁴⁶ who wrote the words above in a memorandum in November 1892¹⁴⁷ during his second term as director of education in Syria, described the situation of the Nusayris in Antakya. He remarks that his motivation to write the memorandum was that since he had served as director of education he was experienced and knowledgeable enough to share his observations. His intention was also to present his findings and solutions regarding the prohibition of Nusayris from entering Mosques and the issue of their education, which have been continuing for a long time in relation to the 'people of Islam' (Sunnis).

With the reform period and the secularization of the civil code of laws in the Ottoman Empire, the Nusayris had a more secure legal status. Owing to increasing European intervention, for example in the Balkans and with the Armenians in Anatolia, and the fear that the Great Powers could also 'protect' the Nusayris, the authorities were more inclined to include them in the Muslim *millet*. Another factor in this context was the increase in missionary efforts of American Protestants among the Nusayris and similar groups, especially after the 1850s.

The Protestant *American Board of Commissioners for Foreign Missions* (ABCFM) was actively proselytizing in Ottoman Syria and Cilicia (South Anatolia) from 1819 on and after 1870 so was its successor, the *Reformed Presbyterian Church of North America* (RPCNA). The missions tried to reach the native Christians and Jews but especially heterodox groups such as the Nusayris (Alawis), who were considered 'heretical' by the Sunni Ottomans and 'pagan' by the missionaries. Both vied to win the hearts and minds of the Nusayris and similar heterodox groups. As we will see in the next chapter, this resulted in conversion campaigns and an ideological and political battle between the Ottoman Empire on one side and the USA, European nations and Protestant missionaries on the other. Sultan Abdülhamid II (r. 1876–1909) and his civil servants tried to convert groups perceived as 'heretical' (heterodox). Shiʿis, Yezidis, Nusayris, Alevis and other groups were targeted in order to win them over to the Ottoman version of Sunni Islam so as to turn them into 'good' subjects in a centralized state and to 'immunise' them against the Christian threat.

Chapter 2

'APPROPRIATE OBJECTS OF CHRISTIAN BENEVOLENCE': PROTESTANT MISSIONARIES AND THE NUSAYRIS

In this chapter I will provide a history of conversions of Nusayris and similar 'heterodox' groups to Protestantism based on Ottoman archival and missionary sources. Preceding this I discuss the activities of Protestant missionaries, especially American, in the Ottoman Empire, including how they perceived the Islamic realm; and with what expectations they approached the issue of proselytizing, and who they targeted.

In order to highlight this, two cases of Nusayris who converted to Protestantism are at the core of this chapter. The first is Suleiman Hassan 'Daoud' Makhloof, one of the first converts in Syria, who suffered at the hands of the Ottomans for his conversion. The second is Telgie Ibrahim, a Nusayri girl from Tarsus near Mersin, whose family had converted to Christianity and who was ultimately taken to Philadelphia (USA) by a Protestant missionary in 1889. Daoud's and Telgie's cases caused tremendous uproar and diplomatic crises between the Ottomans and some European countries and the USA in the 1870s and 1890s concerning the activities of Christian missionaries in the Ottoman Empire and the legitimacy of their schools. Whereas Daoud converted, lived and died in the Ottoman Empire, Telgie's story shows how she was Christianised and how later she and her descendants were integrated into and assimilated by American society.

2.1. Protestant American millenarian dreams in the nineteenth century

Speaking of the 'revival of Christianity', Isabel Burton, the wife of the famed British explorer and orientalist Richard Burton (1821–1890), had remarked: 'Christianity was born and grew in Syria. She gave the light of the Gospel to the world. The grace of God has returned to Syria.'[1] She further wrote that Syria has been 'cursed with races, tribes, creeds and tongues enough to split up the country, and cause all manner of confusion':

> These various religions and sects live together more or less, and practise their conflicting worships in close proximity. Outwardly you do not see much, but in

their hearts they hate one another. The Sunnites excommunicate the Shiahs, and both hate the Druze; all detest the Ansariyyehs [Nusayris]; the Maronites do not love anybody but themselves, and are duly abhorred by all; the Greek Orthodox abominate the Greek Catholics and the Latins; all despise the Jews. It is a fine levelling school, and teaches one, whatever one's fanatical origin or bigoted early training may have been, to respect all religions, and to be true to one's own.[2]

In 1877 an Austrian(-Hungarian) diplomat in Beirut remarked that the events of 1860 in Mount Lebanon when the Druze had slaughtered the Christian Maronites were an example of the hostility between various religious groups. He hoped that Istanbul would always remember that 'the province of Syria harbours a great mixture of the most diverse and restless nations, lurking only for the moment when, driven by the centuries-old religious and national hatred, they should attack one another' (*getrieben von dem Jahrhunderte alten Religions- und Nationalhasse, übereinander herzufallen*). He was sure that without the support of a commanding military force, the authorities would never be able to contain 'these wild elements' (*diese wilden Elemente*). He believed that security was becoming more and more endangered and that brigandage would grow. He observed that in Syria there was no danger that the people would oppose the government in a hostile way, that there would be an insurrection to forcibly separate Syria from the existing state. Aspirations of this kind were unknown there. It was quite understandable according to him, if one looked a little closer to the ethnographic conditions of this province. However, the one thing that was always to be feared in Syria was 'the clashing of the various religious collectives that hated each other to death' (*ist ein Aufeinanderstossen der sich gegenseitig in den Tod hassenden verschiedenen Religionsgenossenschaften*).[3]

Lady Burton, as others have done, sketched a rather gloomy picture of the religious landscape of Ottoman Syria. This disorder served well the missionary worldview of a corrupt Islamic world that would be brought to an end by the power of the Gospel distributed by the missionaries. What is more, 'the Word', when spread all over the world, would usher in the Second Coming of Jesus.

After the emergence of the United States of America as an independent state after 1776, it established international relations for economic purposes.[4] American ships cruised the Mediterranean where the USA came into contact with the Ottoman Empire beginning with the Barbary Wars.[5] When the USA and the Ottomans signed an economic treaty in 1830 capitulations were granted to the Americans and economic and political relations developed.[6] Before an American Legation, represented by David Porter as chargé d'affaires, was established in 1831,[7] activities conducted by American citizens including missionaries were patronized through the British embassy in Istanbul and its consulates throughout the Empire.[8] After that Americans lost their privilege of being British subjects before Ottoman law, and as the British legation was more powerful American missionaries continued to seek close relations with British diplomats and hoped to secure their presence in the Ottoman domains.[9] As the international relations and economic power of the USA increased in the second half of the nineteenth century and its missionary activities grew, this required a considerable American naval presence in the eastern Mediterranean with occasional visits of battleships to Ottoman port cities.[10] This was one method to intimidate the Ottomans in a time when the influence of the USA deepened. The other, humane, method was the missions being established in the Ottoman Empire.

The Protestant missionary movement commenced for religious purposes first, i.e. the evangelization of the world, or 'illuminating and emancipating the world'.[11] As Michael Oren states in his book about the relationship of the history of America with the Middle East, there existed from the Pilgrims onwards within American Protestantism a strong emotional attachment to the Israelites of the Hebrew Bible. Parallels were drawn by the Pilgrims between their experiences and those narrated in the Bible, such as the crossing of the Israelites of the Red Sea to escape from the oppression of the Pharaoh in Egypt; likewise did the Pilgrims cross the Atlantic to be far away from King George III's England, who fought the American colonists and was labelled a tyrant 'Pharaoh'.[12] This respect for the ancient Israelites led to a desire to convert contemporary Jews in order to bring them into the 'correct' fold and hasten the Second Coming:

> Many educated American Protestants believed that their new nation had a providential mission to help redeem the world and bring about the millennium, the thousand-year reign of Christian peace.... If the United States was to contribute to the establishment of the New Jerusalem, it would have to export Christian purity to the actual Holy Land and be instrumental in the conversion of its present inhabitants.... The fact that the Holy Land was in the hands of the Turkish 'empire of sin' remained one of the major obstacles and therefore one of the central themes of early American eschatological interest.[13]

Proselytizing was the original and immediate aim of the missionary project, albeit not the only one. In the mid-nineteenth century 'the utopia of the Protestant missionaries in Turkey consisted of an almost millenarian belief in a new social and symbolic order, promoted by their own evangelistic, educative, and civilizing efforts, and linking their modern belief in progress with evangelical spirituality'.[14] It was inspired by the teachings of their religion and by their patriotism for their young country, and this in turn led to a belief that American ideals should be spread throughout the world. It formed the basis of the Second Awakening (1800–1830), the revivalist or millenarian religious movement that launched the ABCFM.[15] It stressed both a return to religion and a glorification of American democracy and values all over the world. It was a project that started for religious (evangelical) purposes but ended being a civilizing one, meaning that it brought secular education and modernity in form of schools and universities in Anatolia and Ottoman Syria.[16]

When the first two missionaries, the young reverends Levi Parsons (1792–1821)[17] and Pliny Fisk (1792–1825)[18] were sent to the Ottoman Empire, their chosen aim was to convert the people to Protestant Christianity.[19] They believed that '[w]hile conversions might be made elsewhere in the world, only in Palestine

... would they have an immediate and millennial impact. Only there would the Protestant's [sic] longing to reunite with their spiritual forebears, the Jews, converge with their yearning for the Messiah's reappearance.'[20]

Even though proselytizing the Jews in the Ottoman Empire may have been the real aim, the missionaries were not unconscious of Islam as the dominant religion in the Ottoman Empire[21] and that a substantial number of non-Protestant Christian communities also lived there. The ABCFM's representatives also hoped to convert the non-Protestant Christians, the Muslims and the other non-Sunni groups living in the different provinces. Considering their eschalatogical view of history in the early nineteenth century, they had four great expectations with regard to the Middle East: '(1) the global spread of the gospel; (2) the return of the Jews to Palestine and their 'restoration' (acceptance of Jesus Christ); (3) the fall of the Pope; and (4) the collapse of Islam.'[22]

One way to achieve the last goal was through the conversion of Muslims, whereby the foundation of Islam would be sapped. But owing to the lack of a formal relationship between the USA and the Ottoman Empire, the missionaries set out without knowing one important thing: proselytizing Muslims was illegal in the Ottoman Empire.[23] This fact probably shocked the missionaries upon their first arrival in the Empire:

> The nature of the Turkish government may be considered unfavourable to Christian missionaries. Once Mahomedans were engaged in disseminating their religion by the sword. Then conversion or death was the only alternative offered to those under their power. Now death is the penalty of apostasy from their religion.[24]

The mere existence of so many non-Muslims living rather peacefully under Ottoman rule should have showed the missionaries that their statement could not hold true. But this was less problematic than the fact that any Muslim who converted would be executed by the state. Despite this disturbing situation, the missionaries remained optimistic about their new field of labour and understood that they would only have to adjust to the new situation and change their priorities. Fisk and Parsons wrote:

> All who are not Mahomedans are allowed to change their religion as they please, and to make what efforts they please to convert each other. The government never interferes [...] As to any molestation from the government, we feel almost as safe as we should in Boston. Should a Christian mission acquire considerable influence, it may attract notice; nor is it easy to predict what would be the consequences [...] There is reason to believe, that American missionaries will enjoy as much safety as merchants and other Christians who reside here and think of no danger.[25]

The two missionaries understood that on foreign soil they could be well protected by British consuls throughout the Empire. They respected Ottoman law significantly enough not to work against the ban on preaching to Muslims. Also did they not recognize the degree to which their mission would be changed because of this prohibition and that their target population would become the non-Protestant Christians living in 'Greater Syria' (modern-day Syria, Lebanon, Jordan, Palestine and Israel). At first their religious goals for the 'reconquest' of the Holy Land were expressed in apocalyptic terms; they 'used a plainly militant language'.[26] It was a 'spiritual crusade to the land of promise' where the 'strongest fortresses of error and sin' could be taken.[27] The 'influx of light' caused by the missions in Syria would alarm the 'Prince of Darkness' and lead 'the Man of Sin' to double his efforts. Therefore 'the Beast and the False Prophet occasionally unite' for opposing missionary efforts but this opposition would only be 'a prelude to the battle of the great day' when Islam would be overthrown.[28] The 'crescent' would be pulled down and the 'standard of the cross' lifted up.[29] The prospect for Parsons, after he and Fisk had entered the Ottoman Empire in Izmir, was 'that Turkey must be drenched in blood'.[30] By using 'metaphors of war', 'the world is seen as a battleground between the Kingdom of God and the kingdom of Satan. This conflict is regarded as spiritual warfare.' At the end of this the Kingdom of God will be victorious.[31] Despite all this imagery, the missionaries were careful to distinguish between the historical Crusades, which they associated with Catholicism and whose physical violence they condemned. Both Catholicism and Islam were considered violent and intolerant by them.[32]

As early as the 1820s these missionaries targeted Syria (including Palestine) as Lands of the Bible[33] that they reclaimed and gave attention to socially marginalized heterodox Muslim groups such as the 'Metawalies' (Shi'is), Druze and the 'Anseiries' (Nusayris), who were not accepted by the Sunni 'Turks'. These groups who lived in the region stretching from Antioch to Palestine, a 'hiding place of schism and heresy',[34] 'though nominal Mohammedans, have scarcely any religion at all; and when the day comes, as it certainly will before long, that Mohammedans shall be converted to God, they will furnish a most interesting field of labor.' By establishing the necessary missions also among Muslim marginals, especially the Druze and 'the pagan Ansarrea' (Nusayris), God would 'hasten the downfall of Satan's empire throughout this land and the whole world'.[35] The missionaries integrated non-Sunni groups in their version of salvation and the fact that converting Jews and Muslims was difficult and was met with resistance caused them to use oriental Christians and heterodox groups as agents for 'leavening the Levant'.[36]

The Christian missions became more active and effective in their work among non-Sunni groups after the Ottoman state initiated political, social and religious reforms that would grant non-Muslims more rights than they previously had. A cursory look at the reform period is in order here.

2.2. Mission among heterodox groups: the Alevis and Druze

Even though attempts to modernize the empire had already taken place in the late eighteenth century, the Ottomans administration was more fully transformed after the Tanzimat ('reorganization') reforms were introduced. The years 1839–1876 are known as the *Tanzimat-ı Hayriyye* ('Benevolent Reordering' or 'reform')[37] period in the history of the Ottoman Empire. Successive sultans and their high-ranking ministers aimed to reform the Ottoman state so as to compete with the European Powers and to prevent their infringement upon internal Ottoman matters. The reforms were proclaimed through three imperial edicts: the *Gülhâne Hatt-ı Şerîf* ('Noble Edict of Gülhane') of 1839, the *Islâhat Fermânı* ('Reform Edict') of 1856 and the *Kânûn-i Esâsî* ('Substantial Law') of 1876.[38] While an overview of the Tanzimat is provided below, a detailed account is beyond the scope of this study.

It must be noted here, however, that in classical European and Turkish historiography on the Ottoman Empire, the overall purpose of the Tanzimat is presented as having entailed the secularization and marginalization of religion. In reference to the first reform edict, previous historiography stressed that it was written under Western influence and that its ideas were borrowed from Western political theory. The drafting of the Gülhane Rescript was mainly attributed to Mustafa Reşid Paşa and Sultan Abdülmecid did not seem to be involved in its creation. In a pioneering article Butrus Abu-Manneh provides ample evidence that contradicts this classical view. He demonstrates that the impact of orthodox Islamic principles of the Naqshbandiyya-Mujaddidiyya, an Islamic Sufi order, taught to Sultan Abdülmecid by his mother Bezmiâlem, and the contribution of several high-ranking political and mostly religious leaders are evident in its drafting. This research indicates that this reform was written as a response to the neglect of the shari'a among representatives in government and religious circles, the prevailing misconduct and injustice by local governors and by the sultans themselves since the eighteenth century. Furthermore, it appears not only that members of the royal family were influenced by the teachings of the Naqshbandiyya-Mujaddidiyya but also several Palace functionaries at the *Bâb-ı Âli* (the Sublime Porte) and upper echelons of society.[39]

Three points were stressed in the first edict: firstly, guaranteeing and securing the safety of the life, honour and property of all subjects; secondly, the introduction of a tax system; and thirdly, conscription into the army and the limitation of military service to a certain period. Another innovation was provincial cabinets, including leaders of the Muslim and non-Muslim communities. The second edict of 1856 that was again proclaimed by Abdülmecid reiterated the equality of all Ottoman subjects and went beyond it. Here the impact of European Powers is evident, for the equality of Muslims and all non-Muslims, especially Christians, comprised every aspect of society and even gave the latter some advantages over the Muslims. This second imperial decree opened the second stage of the Tanzimat, which lasted until the end of the reign of Sultan Abdülaziz and paved the way for the proclamation of the *Kanûn-i Esasî*, first Ottoman constitution on 28 December 1876. Following Mustafa Reşid Paşa, three men left their imprint on the period between 1856 and 1876: Âli Paşa, Fuad Paşa and Midhat Paşa who was the patron of the 'Young Ottoman' reformers in the late 1870s. Together they drafted the 1876 *Kanûn-i Esasî*.

The principal concern of the *Kânûn-i Esâsî* was the introduction of the first constitution *(meşrutiyet)* in Turkish history and it was drafted under the auspices of Midhat Paşa. Accordingly, the period starting from 1876 is known as the 'First Constitution' *(Birinci Meşrutiyet)*. Its main aim was to restrict to some extent the exercise of the powers of the sultan and for the first time it accepted a parliamentary system. Among other things, the terms of this constitution covered basic rights and privileges, the independence of courts and the safety of judges. The reform decrees were partially directed towards winning the support of European powers and re-emphasized the equality of all subjects under the law. It allowed civil and political rights to Christian subjects. The main goal of the reforms was to preserve the Ottoman state. After Sultan Abdülaziz was deposed in 1876 under the leadership of Midhat Paşa and the short ineffective interregnum of Sultan Murad V (three months), Abdülhamid II reigned from 1876-1909.[40] Though he initially accepted the constitution and a parliament, in 1878 he dissolved it and strengthened his position as an absolute ruler for 33 years until he was overthrown by the Young Turk revolution (1908-1909) and the constitution and parliament were again put into effect. This began the period called *İkinci Meşrutiyet*, 'Second Constitution'.

The religious and social changes after the proclamation of the first Tanzimat edict in 1839 gave advantages to the Protestants too, and they were granted the status of *millet* in 1850 with help from British influence.[41] The year before the Ottoman government had decided that Protestant Ottoman subjects should appoint a representative among them as mediator between the government and the Protestant community.[42] The Protestant Armenians, who had previously been excommunicated by the Gregorian Armenian patriarchate, were officially accepted as a *millet* in 1850 under the pressure of the American and British governments. Following this the American Protestants intensified their activities, especially among the Armenians of Anatolia.[43]

The second *Islahat* ('reforms') Edict of 1856 granted more rights to non-Muslims; Protestants had the right to establish their educational institutions through which their activities among Eastern Christian, especially the Armenians in Eastern Anatolia, accelerated. Parallel to these efforts the Protestant missionaries became more active among religious groups outside the mainstream Sunni Muslims, such as the Alevis, the Druze, the Yezidis and the Nusayris. Before the American Protestants became more active and successful in the last quarter of the nineteenth century and the number of students in their schools and of their congregations in the Ottoman realms increased, there had been other, Catholic, missionaries, Jesuit, or Dominicans, who acted under French protection.[44] The general attitude of the Protestant missionaries was that without reaching the Muslims the Kingdom of Jesus would not be established. And heterodox Muslim groups seemed to be 'the long-searched-for open door to Islam'.[45]

The Alevis, also known as Kızılbaş, are the biggest and most important religious group in Anatolia. Alevism,[46] a mystical and 'heterodox'[47] branch of Shi'a Islam, worships Imam Ali, the fourth caliph and the first Shi'i imam and teaches that he is the source of divine knowledge. Different religious groups with Shi'i were marginalized under successive Sunni sultans. They lived in remote corners in the east of the Empire, and were looked upon with contempt by Sunni ulema (religious scholars), who described them as immoral unbelievers without holy books. Their villages were without mosques and recognizable as Alevi settlements; Abdülhamid II and his successors constructed mosques for them. Alevis held an inferior status within the system and to some extent still do in the Republic of Turkey.[48]

The Protestant missionaries approached the Alevis after the Ottoman state had granted the formation of the Protestant *millet* in 1850. 'It was one of mutual sympathy, some shared values, and common hope for a new age. The reality, however, fell far short of the great expectations.'[49] The 'universal Kingdom of Jesus', the ultimate goal of the American Protestants, was motivated by the hope that there would be no limits, authentic encounters and sympathy beyond the differences of doctrine. Surprisingly, the Alevis declared to the missionaries that their faith was the same as theirs, and willingly participated in Bible lessons. The Alevis allowed them to participate in their secret religious *cem* (assembly) sessions; probably the first time that foreigners were allowed to do so.[50]

Another shared factor was that the missionaries and the Alevis both had ambivalent attitudes towards Ottoman state authorities. Whereas for the Protestants he was the anti-Christ, the Alevis looked the sultan-caliph as unbelieving Ummayyad caliph Yezid who let Imam Husayn be killed in Karbala in 680. Yet, for the Alevis, criticizing the political system and Sunni Islam did not mean excluding Muhammad and Islam per se, and the missionaries needed to realize this. The ABCFM discovered that the Alevis were nominal Muslims in search of fundamental reform because they had suffered for centuries, even more than Christians had. Once they were evangelized, they would be an 'ideal agent' for the change the missionaries hoped to promote in the wider Ottoman Empire. When Alevi chiefs began to identify themselves as Protestants and Kızılbaş groups tried to redefine their identity and social role, the Ottoman authorities felt that this touched vital interests of the state. When a missionary suggested a charter for the Kızılbaş based on the *Islahat* Edict of 1856, the state authorities opposed extending a *millet* status to the Alevis and rejected the offer of protection. Even though the Alevis were seen as heretics, they were nominal Muslims, and their conversion to Protestantism was unacceptable and panicked the authorities. Despite the Protestants' wish for the protection of the Alevis, the states from which they came were disinclined to pressurize the Ottoman state.[51]

Henceforth the Protestants reduced their contacts with the Alevis after the 1860s and 1870s. The ABCFM proved powerless to assist them in improving their social position; the Alevis faced repression from the local authorities and Sunnis in general. The missionary work among them was not successful but many Alevis continued to see themselves as Protestants, which meant 'social and scientific progress in accordance with the precepts of their own religion of the heart'. Despite good relations between the Protestants and the Alevis, the latter were left to their own devices.[52]

A crucial aspect that concerned the Ottoman central and provincial administrations was the relations and supposed alliance between Alevis and Armenians in Eastern Anatolia. After the Ottomans' defeat at the war with Russia (1877–1878), the Treaty of Berlin stipulated the better treatment of the Armenians in Anatolia; with this, the independence of the Armenians came also to the fore among the Armenians and in Europe. Yet, owing to the Empire's territorial losses in the Balkans because of said war, the Ottomans focused on the Anatolian heartland and were keen to keep the equilibrium among the people there. The question of the Western missionaries' relations with and their activities among the Armenians and the relations of the latter with other 'suspect' groups especially outside the Sunni fold became a cause of concern. In fact, the Ottomans who were always prejudiced towards the Alevis/Kızılbaş, now targeted them alongside the Armenians who had also become a threat. The Ottoman perception of the Alevis was that they were supporting the independence of the Armenians. There were two reasons for this: the Kızılbaş supported the Safavis back in the sixteenth century and were thus long seen as traitors, and the Armenians and the Alevis often lived together in the same places in Anatolia. Despite the fact that they did not always live in peace together and, for instance, Kızılbaş Kurds sporadically attacked and killed Armenians, non-Sunni groups were usually friendly towards each other and their relations were more positive than that with the Sunnis. Alliances between 'traitors', as the Ottomans perceived it, was dangerous.[53]

The accusation of a so-called 'cooperation' between the Armenians and the Alevis was especially evident among Ottoman officials after 1890 when the Armenian Question was reaching its peak during the Hamidian era. Mehmed Memduh Paşa who was governor in Ankara and Sivas and known for his anti-Armenian stance, was among the officials who were convinced of a political alliance between the two groups.[54]

As much as this and the missionaries' activities among the Alevis troubled Abdülhamid and his state, the relationship between the Protestants and the Yezidis in Eastern Anatolia after the 1870s was also disturbing, even though the results were not favourable to the missionaries. The more the ABCFM extended its contacts with the Alevis and Yezidis, whose beliefs and practices were diametrically opposed to that of Sunni Islam, the Hamidian regime realized that this was a serious threat to its authority and made efforts to prevent these relations. The mission of the ABCFM was active in the city of Mardin from where they evangelized the Yezidis, however this work did not have as exciting a dynamic as the one among the Alevis. Still, the sultan and his administration were concerned enough to weaken the relationship between the Yezidis and the Protestants.[55] The Hamidian reaction to the missionaries and the counter propaganda regarding the Yezidis will be discussed in the next chapter.[56]

In Syria, Protestant missionaries exerted efforts to establish the 'evangelical Truth' among the Druze and the Nusayris. 'In no part of Asia Minor are the racial and religious conditions more complicated than in Syria.' This observation by the German missionary Julius Richter in 1910 repeats what Lady Burton (above) and others have remarked about the complicated diversity of religious and ethnic groups in Ottoman Syria. The Christian population was large but there was 'hardly any possibility of united progress' due to many divisions among the different denominations. The Muslims, too, were not united, and there existed 'a number of peculiar religious bodies of a national character with hardly any Muhammadan characteristics'. He provides the numbers of all religious groups, among which is that of the Druze (80,000–100,000) and the Nusayris and Isma'ilis (150,000–200,000 but the former 'probably not more than 75,000'),[57] and then goes on describing the Druze, Nusayris and Isma'ilis.[58]

The ABCFM was engaged in missionary work among the native Oriental Christians but as time passed by, it realized that it proved difficult to convert them. There was a 'spirit of patriotism' among the local Christian communities that preserved the integrity of their old and venerated institutions against foreign influence. The Roman Catholic Maronites were, initially, especially bitter opponents of the American Protestants. And the enmity of the Maronites towards the Druze reached its climax from the 1840s on and resulted in the massacre of the Maronites by the Druze in 1860, later known as the Mount Lebanon civil war.[59] In Safita near Tartus, the Protestants faced persecution from the Greek Orthodox Church, who drove them out. The Ottoman authorities in Damascus and Tripoli did not assist the Protestants.[60]

After less success among the Oriental Christians the ABCFM missionaries shifted their focus to the Druze and had high hopes of their conversion. This was also induced by the friendly approach of the Druze community to the Protestants.[61] This interest in the Protestant Mission from 1835 to 1842, however, arose out of practical reasons: during the reign of the Egyptian viceroy Ibrahim Paşa in Syria the Druze, regarded as part of the Muslim community, opposed conscription into the military and sought to become Christians to escape military service,[62] because at that time only Muslims were permitted to enter the army. In 1836, many Druze converted to Protestantism to avoid conscription in Ibrahim Paşa's army. In 1841–1842 Protestant missionaries in the USA reported that the Druze community, consisting of 100,000 members, 'has formally resolved to embrace Protestant Christianity'. They asked the American Board in Beirut to 'take charge of their spiritual interests' and send them teachers, wanted schools and missionary labour in their villages. The Board saw this as 'probably the most important opening for missionary labour which Divine Providence ever presented'. For the American mission 'all Syria is laid open', and it hoped that this would provide access to the whole Druze nation and that the Nusayris, with similar religious and civil conditions, would follow suit. The American missionaries thought that 'a breach is made in the wall of Mohammedan despotism, through which Christian teachers may pass and repass with their coverts'. They reported that the Druze chiefs requested a high school in their capital Dair al-Qamar near Beirut in which their young nobility would be educated.[63] The missionaries were very enthusiastic but this did not last long. Later, the Druze reverted to their original faith.

In his memoirs of 1910 Henry H. Jessup discusses the failure of mass conversions to Protestantism, saying that the Protestant movement in Syria consisted mainly of individuals. According to him, the only successful mass conversion was that of the Armenians of Antep ('Ayntab) and Maraş (Marash) in the year 1851.[64] Richter had observed that many Druze sheikhs sent deputations to the American Protestants or sought to be visited; others asked for schools in their villages. These efforts by the Druze for conversion to Protestantism grew each day but the missionaries did not comply with all the requests. They were sceptical about mass conversions, which had allowed the Druze to become Protestants in name at least. The Americans 'would not barter the sacredness of their religion for a mere increase in numbers'. Even if they only carried out missionary work cautiously among the Druze, the Ottoman army put an end to this, and under threat of punishment, took promises from the sheikhs not to abandon Islam for Protestantism. The Ottomans, too, had an interest in having 'these tall and robust mountaineers' in the army.[65]

In the end the ABCFM had to abandon its mission among the Druze. It had proved to be a 'road map to nowhere'. During the 1860 civil war the reputation of the Druze in the USA was negative due to media coverage and sympathetic towards the native Christians, so much so that the conversion project was not financially supported. Another, not less important, factor was the administrative change regarding public education in 1869 by the Ottoman state. All schools in Ottoman domains, including foreign ones, were included in a legal framework with the aim of modernizing and secularizing primary education. The effects of this were felt in Syria only after 1885 when the educational administrations in the provinces enforced the new regulations. The missionaries could not agree with the new curricular regulations or justify their existence: henceforth Muslims were prohibited from sending their children to foreign schools when a Muslim private or state school was available. As a result, many missionary schools among the Druze and the Nusairis were closed.[66]

2.3. Harvesting the souls of the Nusayris

The ill-treatment of the Nusayris by the majority of the population and the authorities had aroused the compassion of Christian missionaries who tried to 'win their souls'. Here we will restrict ourselves to the views and experiences of American Protestant Missionaries towards the Nusayris written in the 1830s and 1840s. For the American Protestant missionaries, the Nusayris were 'a wretched and degraded people... for whom no evangelical exertions have been made'[67] who were constantly oppressed by an unjust Ottoman government.[68] What the Nusayris needed was 'the word of life'.[69] They were 'appropriate objects of christian [sic] benevolence' because

> their religion, whatever it be, exerted no good influence upon them. It is in fact no better than paganism. Some of their ideas and many of their practices are truly abominable. Their women are in a most degraded condition, being regarded as incapable of religion, and treated almost like irrational creatures. Of course the ignorance and wretchedness of the people is very great. The way of peace they have not known.[70]

Initially the missionaries did not have much knowledge about the Nusayris, in particular about their beliefs, except rumours. There are some reports by Westerners about how Nusayris kept their secrets. We have missionary reports about encounters with Nusayris about whom they wanted to learn more in order to proselytize them. They regarded the Nusayri people as hospitable and sociable but when it came to talk about their faith they were 'much more willing to sip coffee and smoke tobacco, than to impart information about their country or their faith'. The Nusayris had 'hermetically sealed' their mouths due to fear of being hated and watched by the Muslims.[71] One missionary neatly sums up this attitude with an Arabic proverb: 'I talked to him to the east, and he answered to the west'.[72]

Gertrude Bell, for instance, recounts at a much later time (1905) what she had heard in Syria from a certain soldier called Hajji Mahmud:

> Mahmud happened to be in the Nosairiyeh m[oun]t[ain]s [Nusayriyah, Jabal al] once at that time with 5 or 6 khayyal.[73] They were invited by the sheikh to put up at his house. Next morning, they woke and found not a man there, no one to bring them water or food. They questioned the women who knew nothing. Mahmud went to the house of the Sheikh ud Din and there found a great gathering of [Arabic] seated round on the floor. In the middle was a large bowl of wine and an empty jug by it. The Sheikh ud Din was conversing with the jug. He put questions to it which Mahmud c[oul]d not hear and it answered with a gurgling sound. Magic no doubt said Mahmud. When they saw him they were very angry and began to hustle and beat him. He defended himself as best he c[oul]d calling out that he was the dakhil[74] of the sheikh. The Sheikh held up his hand and ordered them off. They obeyed at once. The Sheikh then kissed Mahmud's hands and feet, begged his forgiveness, gave him money and entreated him not to repeat what he had seen. Mahmud though it wiser to hold his tongue.[75]

Some basic information about the Nusayris could be 'ascertained' by the missionaries at an early stage during their mission: that they numbered from 100,000 to 200,000; they were divided into different 'sects'; they did not have places or times for prayers; they had feasts; no marriage laws; they had their own religious books; they believed in the transmigration of the soul; and that they were illiterate.[76] Eventually more information could be drawn about 'this most miserable, ignorant and forsaken people', when missionaries travelled and lived among them they gathered statistics in the sixteen districts of Northern Syria with more than two thousand villages and the names of the chiefs in each district. According to another missionary in 1847, the Nusayris were the 'chief attraction' for a mission in Syria and 'would probably prove a very accessible people' because of the above mentioned and other reasons:

> For generations they have seen no strangers or foreigners among them, except insulting enemies and outrageous oppressors. This has given them a distrust and a certain dislike of all strangers; but I am convinced that this would soon give way, and that the opposite feeling would be strongly awakened towards those who should come to them as steadfast and true friends.... They spread all round the head of this sea [Mediterranean], and constitute the major part of the peasants on the great plains of Tarsus and Adana. Such a numerous, widespread,

semi-barbarous and wholly neglected population present strong claims upon our Christian compassion; and if they are accessible to the missionary of the gospel, as there is reason to hope they will prove to be, ought they not to be looked after and provided for, with as little delay as possible? It is not a new, distant, inaccessible land. They are at the door, so to speak, of the mission now in the country.[77]

The missionaries felt proximity to the Nusayris not only because of compassion but also due to religious reasons: supposedly, this people did not practice Islam ('They are not Moslems') but seemed to be nearer to Eastern Christianity.[78] When American Protestant missionaries first set foot on Ottoman soil, the two 'most fanatical, bitter and zealous' opponents of Protestantism were Islam and Eastern Christianity. The original aim was to purify the nominal 'degenerate' Christian sects, revive their spiritual faith and make them preach the pure Gospel. Thus, becoming true Christians and being united in one evangelical church, they would exert a vigorous influence on the Muslims with their righteousness.[79] For this purpose, the Nusayris were sometimes seen as lost Christians and included among Christian denominations.[80]

The missionaries were convinced that the Nusayris were receptive to the Gospel and willing to receive missionaries and send their children to Protestant schools. They needed only to be convinced that 'they [the missionaries] were sincere friends, and had come, not to rob, oppress and abuse them, but to befriend them and do them good'. Their 'ignorance and wretchedness, their utter destitution of religion, their isolation from all the rest of the world' were regarded as important factors to open missions among them. To bring 'these miserable, outcast heathen, without God and having no hope' into the fold of Jesus was urgent and overdue.[81] All over, the Protestants of the ABCFM use the word 'pagan' and 'heathen' for groups that seemed not to follow Judaism, Christianity and Islam. In the words of Rufus Anderson, a prominent minister at the Board, the word 'heathen' was descriptive and not restrictive.[82] Missionary schools were eventually established to educate those 'who are destitute of the knowledge of Christianity'.[83]

Besides nominal Christians, Jews and Christians, the Nusayris were included. Children especially needed to be taught the Bible. The main purpose of founding schools stemmed from the belief that by teaching the local youth, regardless of their religion, to read they would be able to choose the only 'true' religion, i.e., Protestant Christianity.[84] Overall, only a few Nusayris converted to Protestantism; this is also true for other American missions among Armenians, Nestorians and Assyrians in Iraq or the Jews in Anatolia and Palestine.[85] In 1845 one missionary assessed the situation by saying that 'we have had no tokens of any special influences of the Spirit. We can report no additions to the number of our communicants, and they seems to reign around us an almost universal spiritual death.'[86] By the year 1868 American missionaries admitted that the Nusayris 'have not been reached in any considerable numbers by the gospel', though some had become 'enlightened' through the existence of a Protestant community near them. The missionaries still hoped that before long the evangelists 'will have penetrated that section of the country, and that we shall begin to sap the foundations of Islam, among those who are less fanatically attached to all its precepts'.[87] From time to time the Ottoman state opposed the missionaries and their schools, and those of the Syrian mission were closed down (though reopened later) in the late 1880s until the early 1890s,[88] at the height of Sultan Abdülhamid II's power. In the remaining pages of this chapter this opposition shall be illustrated with two cases of conversions from Nusayrism to Protestantism.

2.3.1. 'Our soldier Daoud': Suleiman Hassan Makhloof

In the eyes of Christians in Europe and the USA the opposition of the Sunnis against the Nusayris manifested itself in the 1870s in the form of the Ottoman state. Some young Nusayris had converted in the 1850s through the efforts of the Anglican missionary Reverend Samuel Lyde (1825–1860) who was the first Westerner to live with the Nusayris in Syria. 'A devoted evangelical minister of the Church of England, and possessed of some means, established, some years ago, a

Figure 2.1 Yusuf Jadid and his wife Mariam

school among that people, in whose spiritual welfare he took a deep interest.'[89] He settled there in 1853 and lived in Bahamra (sometimes Bhamra) near Latakia until 1859. Lyde is the author of two books about the Nusayris, the second of which is a pioneering work and was published after his death.[90] After establishing a school in Bahamra in 1854 the Nusayris, some leading members of the community sent their children to the school and converted to Protestant Christianity. A boy named 'Hamood' (Hammud) was the first baptised Nusayri convert (1861)[91] and his friend Suleiman Hassan Makhloof, the second convert and who suffered for his new Faith, was baptised as 'Daoud' in 1865.[92] Yusuf Jadid (Yusef Jedeed) was also among the first Nusayri converts and married the first female convert Mariam (3 May 1866). They were the first Christian family organized among the Nusayris.[93]

When Daoud[94] (1844–1899) professed his faith in Christ as a boy he faced opposition from his father, and from the local sheikh who first threatened him and

Daoud in 1888.

Figure 2.2 Suleiman Hassan Makhloof, Daoud

forced him to testify that Muhammad was a prophet and apostle. When Daoud refused to comply with the sheikh's request, the latter resorted to violence. In brief, Daoud did not give up Christianity until his death in around May 1899.[95] As a man of 29 years, he was arrested by the Ottoman authorities and was harassed and imprisoned because of his conversion, on the pretext that he deserted the military.

One of the troubles the Ottoman state faced in this period was the conversion of Nusayris to Christianity as a result of missionary efforts. Once a converted person had difficulties, whether it was pressure from the state or the people, after becoming Christian, the case was highlighted by missionaries to the public and had a broad repercussion.

As documented by the Ottomans in early 1875, two Nusayris – they are unnamed but internal evidence shows that they are the above-mentioned Hamood and Hassan/Daoud – in Latakia, one of them a teacher at the missionary school, had become Christians, were transferred in 1873 to Damascus by the governor, imprisoned there and were allegedly exposed to violence. Thereupon Protestant societies in Britain, the USA, France, Belgium, Holland, Germany, Sweden, Norway, Switzerland and Greece sent a petition with 143 signatures and archbishop, bishop, priests and other clergy from Britain a petition with 117 signatures, to the Ottoman state.[96] According to the Ottomans the British protested against the 'discrimination' against Christians in the Ottoman Empire and described this in four points:

1. Four Nusayris from Latakia, two of whom were deserters from the military and two conscripted to the military by draft lottery, hid in a Protestant school. Consequently, they were arrested by soldiers. They had earlier converted to Protestantism and therefore the American consul and missionaries requested that they be sent back to their villages and exempt from military service. But since they were Ottoman subjects and deserters, this was not possible according to the effective military rules, even if they changed their religion; this was communicated to the Americans and the families of the Nusayris in clear terms.
2. Two persons from among the converts were prevented from studying at said school and it was closed eventually by the local government and the students dispersed.
3. Some years before this a certain Mustafa from the city of Maraş[97] became a Protestant and propagated his conversion in his town. The people were agitated, and in order to prevent the assassination of Mustafa, he and his wife were sent to Latakia, kept for some days at the gendarmerie and then further sent to Izmir.
4. The selling of Turkish translations of the Torah and the Gospels on the streets and bazaars in Istanbul by itinerant missionaries and the arrest of those who were involved was another issue.

The Ottomans stated that these events were exaggerated in English reports of informants (*jurnal*) as a prohibition of Protestantism and were seen as ill-treatment of Christians in the Ottoman Empire. This was done in order to excite the patriotic feelings and religious zeal of the members of the Bible Society (*Cemiyet-i İnciliye*); and these 'deceitful publications' stated that this kind of treatment was opposed to the 'freedom of religion and faith' in the Imperial decree released in the year 1855;[98] in order not to worry and oppress the Christians, 260 English notables and clergymen signed a petition together with their former ambassador Lord Redcliff in order to present it to the sultan. The British embassy informed the Porte that five representatives were sent to Istanbul for this.

The Ottomans replied to the concerns of the Europeans that the four Nusayris mentioned above were not arrested because they converted to Christianity, and the government did not intend to punish them as they stated. The main reason was, the Ottomans stated, because two of them were conscripted to the military by drawing of lots (*kur'a*) three years ago but they did not appear at the military. So, they were seen as deserters, and if their ages would be over the limit, they still would do some kind of service at the barracks. The students at the supposedly closed Protestant school were dispersed not because of the local government but the students' parents wanted so in order to prevent them from being converted by the missionaries. The man in Maraş who became Protestant was removed from his city and held at the gendarmerie in Izmir because the local government feared that he might have been killed by the people. In addition, the Imperial government did not prohibit the selling of Turkish Bible copies but allowed its publication and distribution; giving a license was not problematic – it only forbade selling it in bazaars by itinerant missionaries.

Overall, in the estimation of the Ottomans the petition presented by representatives of a religious group was unprecedented; if allowed, it would invite other groups to put forward complaints for other cases to the sultan, such as the Catholics or the Orthodox, who thought that they were not appropriately protected. The British 'exaggerated' the matter, saying that the people of England were extremely affected by the treatment of those Christians in the Ottoman Empire and that if the sultan denied the audience to the five representatives, this would not only hurt the representatives who have travelled so far but also the English people, being friends of the Ottomans and their well-wishers, and have sacrificed their lives for the independence of the Ottomans. Since the representatives were respected people their request for an audience was to be reconsidered.[99]

According to this petition converts to Christianity in the Ottoman Empire were oppressed by local officials in the provinces despite the assurance in the 1856 Tanzimat Edict that changing one's religion was not to be persecuted. Hence, the Ottoman state was accused of failing in the matter and needed to defend itself in the face of these accusations and offered the above explanation.

The release of the Nusayri converts and the convert in Maraş was discussed in the parliaments of Britain and the USA and is extensively documented from 1873 to 1875.[100] In late 1873 the British Consul-General G. Jackson Eldridge in Beirut wrote to Ambassador Sir Henry Elliot and described the case of the Nusayri converts:

> Three young men of about 30, named Yussef Jedeed, Hassan Maklouf, and Selim Khalaify, of Ansairiyeh parentage, who were educated many years ago in the

schools of the Mission founded at Lattakia by the Rev. Mr. Lyde (a British subject), and who were brought up as Christians and Protestants, a public profession of which faith they have made, and have, as I am informed, always been inscribed as Christians in the Government registers. For some years past they have been employed as teachers in the schools established by the said Mission (which has now passed into the hands of American missionaries with an English coadjutor) in the Ansairiyeh mountain.

...the Kaymakam of Lattakia, who was in the mountain village where the schools of which they had charge are situated, summoned them to appear before him and arrested them on the pretext that they were evading the conscription.

I am informed they were grievously ill-treated and made to march to Tripoli, whence they were forwarded by French steamer to Beyrout, where they arrived yesterday; and are to be sent on to Damascus to-day to be enrolled as recruits in the army, contrary to the regulations of the Empire, as I am told they have regularly paid the 'aána asharié,' [sic. *iane-i askeriye*][101] or military tax, which is exacted from all Christian subjects of the Porte.

I have, therefore, the honour (being assured of the *bona fides* of the case) to request your Excellency to take steps for the immediate release of these men, and for their return to their homes with a fair indemnity for the suffering and inconvenience they have endured, as a vindication of the liberty of conscience in Turkey, of which so much has of late been spoken and written.[102]

The fate of the Nusayri converts, who at some point were prisoners of the government in Damascus, was compared to the persecution of early Christians, even to that of St. Paul who had suffered in the same city.[103] A Protestant representative in Damascus noted that 'we are having a great battle here, to maintain the rights of converts to religious liberty.... Perfect freedom is the law of the empire for converts, and it will only be by stirring up public opinion at home, that we shall be able to maintain it for them.'[104]

The American missionary J. F. Patterson had presented the 'painfully interesting case' in November 1873 in a letter in which he recounted the heavy plight of the three Nusayri converts through the hands of Ottoman authorities. Even though the American consul general Mr Hay in Beirut had presented the case to the American representative in Istanbul and pleaded for the release of the Nusayri men from the yoke of the military service, the latter had turned a deaf ear to this. Patterson was appalled by this act in the name of the USA: 'What a spectacle! The nation which leads the world in the proclamation of religious liberty, standing like a dumb-dog before religious persecution when she has the right to demand that it shall cease!'[105]

On 12 March 1876 the British Embassy wrote that for the last two years it had been trying to remove Yussef Jedeed, Selim Khalaify and Daoud Suleiman, who had been Protestant Christians since childhood, from military service at the Fifth Army (at Syria). But fear was voiced about what would happen if everyone in the Nusayri tribe became Protestant in order to be exempted from military service. It was suggested to discharge them from military service in a way that would not set an example for those who would become Protestants.¹⁰⁶ The fact that Christians were on equal terms with Muslims and had to complete military service (after the 1856 *Islahat* edict)¹⁰⁷ remained but the British pressed for their release, probably not on grounds of their religious beliefs but in some other way. The efforts continued, when in the summer of 1874, the American missionary Joseph Beattie went to Istanbul and had an interview with the American and English ambassadors. Returning to Latakia he wrote a lengthy report about Daoud's case. The American minister, Mr Boker, told him that he could not do anything but the British ambassador Elliott could act and demand Daoud's release. After proceeding to the British embassy and Beattie's purpose of visit was explained, Elliot is said to have remarked that the Nusayri converts, whether Christian or not, must serve in the Ottoman army: 'It is a law of the empire, and they cannot get rid of it. Their conversion to Christianity does not exempt them from military service. If this were allowed, multitudes would become Christians for the sake of escaping the conscription, which would be a great injury to the gospel.' Beattie contended that the purpose of the three Nusayri men was not exemption from military service but they wished to serve in the army as Christians but in a Christian regiment because they were molested and reviled by Muslim soldiers and forced to pray with them 'Mohammadan prayers'. Elliot hinted to the fact that it was impossible for the sultan and his government to form Christian regiments and he could not interfere.¹⁰⁸

In the first half of the year 1875 Daoud was removed to Istanbul where he still suffered as a Christian and his condition, according to a missionary report, 'was rendered even more intolerable by Mohammedan hatred to the Christian religion'.¹⁰⁹ There he apparently underwent severe persecution for his faith. A returned Nusayri soldier reported that Daoud was beaten and offered a bribe if he became a Muslim: 'He said they might blow him from a cannon's mouth, but he would not forsake his religion.'¹¹⁰ There is a lengthy report of the arrest of the Nusayri converts and their conscription in the army by Dr. David Metheny, about who we will deal below in detail. In his opinion, the Nusayris were pagans who worship other things beside God and can therefore not be 'Mohammedans in any sense'. Regarding Daoud and the others, he stated:

> Mohammedans cannot justly complain of their being proselytes from Mohammedanism. The Mohammedans complain that they were not duly registered among the Ansaireyeh. This is the answer to their complaint: though born Ansaireyeh they were never initiated into their religion which is secret—but they were *registered as Protestants* when they professed Christianity, and were publicly baptised in the church, in the presence of the congregation. They could not then properly be registered as Ansaireyeh when they did not accept that religion... The Turks affirm that they became Christians to escape the conscription; but many female Ansaireyehs have become Protestants and yet this cannot be alleged of them. They had been duly registered, and had passed the local authorities in the capital of the district who recognized them as Protestants, and allowed them to pay their dues directly to the government. This they accordingly did, and were not mixed with the villagers who are Ansaireyeh.¹¹¹

Metheny referred to a letter by Daoud in which he wrote that he was not taught the drill, not allowed a gun and had not received any pay. And that he was beaten in the face so violently that it sloughed in five places after which he was confined to bed for thirteen days. Furthermore, he was reviled daily by his officers and was not allowed to attend Christian worship. News came from an American representative in Istanbul that he was told by the authorities that Daoud had been sent to Beirut to join the regiment of Christians but that he has not yet arrived there nor has anything been heard of him to date.[112]

Later in 1875 Daoud was removed to Edirne. Another missionary report states:

> He says they gave him five months' pay before he left, and on his arrival at the town, the government took it from him, saying, if he had it he would run away. They asked him if he was a Moslem. He answered, I am a Christian. They then threw him down and beat him. They offered him an office in the army if he would recant. He said he did not become a Christian for worldly profit, and he would not recant for it.[113]

In his letter referred to above Daoud asked to have a Bible sent to him, which implies that the Ottomans took his Bible from him. It appears from a telegraph that the Ottoman prime minister informed the provincial government in Edirne on 9 July 1875 (6 Cemaziyelahir 1292) that the British vice consul there had a copy of the Bible (*Tevrat nüshası*) for Davud Süleyman, who served then at the *kazak alayı* ('Cossack Cavalry'), and asked the officials to send Davud to take the Bible. The Ottomans hesitated and feared that the vice consul would have freed Davud based on what Britain thought was an unjust and illegal military service.[114]

In a Commons Sitting (Britain) on 22 July 1875 the case about 'the persecuted Christian converts who were being treated as Moslem convicts' was put forward. An MP explained that originally the Nusayri conscripts were supposed to have been discharged from the Army based on the belief of the representation of the British Embassy in Istanbul that they had been conscripted illegally and persecuted as Christians. Later the Ottoman state maintained that these were not improperly enrolled in the Army but serving in a regiment in which men belonging to all kinds of religions. Regarding the convert from Maraş the Sublime Porte stated that he was removed from his native place because he had been in danger there. The Ottoman authorities had told him that he was free to leave Izmir under the condition not to return to Maraş where he would not have been safe.[115]

The Evangelical Alliance in Britain stressed the fact that the 'Sultan's Firman' (*Islahat* edict of 1856) assured religious liberty to the extent that 'all religions are freely professed in my dominions, none of my subjects shall be hindered in the exercise of the religion he professes, nor shall he be molested in the exercise of it'. The Ottoman state having not acted in accordance with the Alliance criticized it thus:

> The Turkish Government may say, as it has said in similar cases, that these men were arrested for their own safety. Are, then, the chains for their safety? Has the

repeated beating of the Ansairyeh teachers been for their safety? It is insisted that those teachers join their fellow-soldiers in Moslem worship. Is this for their safety? Does religious liberty mean that a man may *be* a Christian only on the condition that he scrupulously *conceal* the fact? Does religious liberty mean a premium on hypocrisy?[116]

Regarding Mustafa's case, it remarked that it 'is a clear test case of the right of a Moslem to become a Christian, and should be presented as such to the Christian Powers of Europe'. The missionaries demanded that the case also be presented to France, 'and similar violations of the engagements made by the Sultan with the European Powers for the protection of the Christian subjects throughout the Turkish empire'. Based on the eye-witness account of a pastor, the Alliance recalled how the Ottomans acted in sharp contrast to Mustafa's case when two Armenians became Muslims and this was celebrated in the streets of Maraş: 'the converts being triumphantly escorted with instruments of music, and mounted upon horses gaily caparisoned, attended by bands of soldiers and multitudes of the Mohammedan population.'[117]

The deputation of the British Evangelical Alliance arrived at Istanbul and applied for an audience with Sultan Abdülaziz but his ministers were hesitant[118] and it was not granted.[119] A German Christian journal observed in 1875 that the deputation of the 'so-called Evangelical Alliance made tracks in order to personally put forward to the Sultan its views against the persecution of the Protestants' and implied that this was unheard of since no Catholic deputation ever went to the Czar of Russia in order put forward its views against the persecution of the Catholics in his empire.[120]

The British ambassador Elliot, having received an official intimation from the Ottoman Foreign Minister Saffet (Safvet) Paşa of the removal of the prohibition against the printing of the Bible, further wrote to the British Foreign Office about the four issues relating to conversion and conscription,[121] which was emphasized in the Ottoman report discussed above. He found that 'the arguments on the side of the Turks were not without their weight' because, while freedom of religion was guaranteed to each of the sultan's subjects, the right of making proselytes from among the Muslims, was never intended to be given. When the permission to disseminate the Scriptures was granted this was meant to be for the native Christians. But it soon became evident that some colporteurs circulated the Turkish versions of the Christian scriptures among Muslim Turks. Even though their employers disapproved and regretted this it caused feelings of hostility on the part of the authorities and the Muslim population. Elliot regarded the case of the family from Maraş as 'a distinct instance of persecution' inasmuch as the Ottoman authorities denied them the right to be free in every respect. Concerning the case of Nusayri conscripts raised by the Evangelical Alliance, he repeated 'the conviction that the statement in the address to the Sultan that the men had been taken because they were Christians was incorrect'. The matter was that of a general conscription that was being enforced throughout the Empire. Elliot opined that any interference by the British government 'is uncalled for and would be undesirable'. He further stressed that while there were isolated cases of ill-treatment of converts, 'it can be affirmed with confidence that nothing of a nature of a persecution of Christians is going on'. Native Protestants were complaining that they were kept in a position of inferiority by which other Christian denominations dominated and oppressed them. The issue surrounding the difficulties the Protestants had in the Ottoman Empire was also discussed at the US State Department, and an American diplomat noted that the clergy and notables of the native Christian sects, who were in the councils of local communes in which no Protestants were represented, hated Protestantism 'which they call atheism, more than the faith of Islam'. And these native Christians were using 'pliant Turks as cat's paws' against Protestants such as by inciting 'popular odium and even violence against them'.[122] For Elliot no complaints were heard from among any of the non-Muslims except in areas where foreign missionaries were causing jealousy and resistance from other Christian groups. Despite that, he valued the benefits of missionaries for the Ottoman Empire; especially their continuing efforts in the cause of education, 'the indiscreet zeal' of some of them provoked most of the grievances.

All the diplomatic efforts to solve the matter of the Nusayri conscripts were to no avail. Daoud was still kept in military service until 1880, even though he should have been released a before then. All Nusayri male members of the church were liable for conscription but they sought to protest with a petition to the government. If unsuccessful, they intended to refer it to the representatives of foreign powers resident at Istanbul. After the disappointing behaviour of the Ottoman government in this matter missionaries of the Reformed Presbyterian Church expressed their frustration in apocalyptic terms, after hearing the rumour that England has taken possession of Syria. They described the Ottomans as the 'Mohammedans' anti-Christ' who 'is as virulent and hostile as when Mohammed, under his green flag with his gory sword, forced the Koran on all the conquered provinces'. For the missionaries Islam 'cannot be reformed, hence it must be destroyed'. They were encouraged in seeing 'so many signs of its approaching end' through the interference of the worldwide community of Christian states: 'Christian civilization has made an estimate of its own responsibility to restrain this ferocious beast; indeed has broken many of its great teeth and put it within the iron grating of inter-national supervision, and thus curtailed his power to do evil.'[123]

As mentioned previously, Daoud was released from the Ottoman army in July 1880,[124] after nearly eight years of enforced military service with all its harsh realities. For the missionaries he was able to maintain his integrity and steadfastness in spite of insults and the most brutal treatment. He returned home 'not merely strengthened, but confirmed in the conviction that Christianity is the best of all religions'. Daoud was 'a living witness to the presence and sustaining grace of the Redeemer'.[125] 'Our soldier Daoud' nurtured the hope 'that God may give us many more such Christian men and women from among these ignorant semi-heathen people'.[126] Daoud played a double role in his life: he was the soldier in the spiritual sense who fought for spreading the Christian belief among his kinsmen; at the same time he was a soldier in the Ottoman army who was apparently oppressed for his belief.

After his release Daoud went back to his village Merj and became active again at the mission. Not only the local authorities but also his own people harassed him. When all the members of his family became members of the Reformed Presbyterian Church, the 'Alaouites began to resent his return.... They gathered together and plotted to kill him, as they had before betrayed him to the Turkish soldiers and had arranged for his arrest in 1873.' Eventually he was left in peace because he was resolute and assured them that he could use a weapon.[127] Daoud taught in his village for a number of years before he died in 1899; he was arrested and imprisoned again for a short time in 1893 and was forbidden to teach for the mission.[128] 'Born a pagan, saved by the blood of Christ, kept faithful through his suffering, his life furnishes encouragement to greater faithfulness in service.'[129] His wife, three sons and one daughter resided in the village and were met by a missionary in 1912. None of them were in the communion of the church anymore, though his wife claimed that she still was holding on to the faith.[130]

What began as a series of events under the initiative of a local governor in Syria turned the case of Daoud and the other Nusayri converts into an international affair. It instigated anxieties towards the religious mobility among this long-ignored sect, and also triggered the stigmatization of the American missionary activities in the Ottoman Empire.[131] The 'Daoud Affair' eventually led to another international political affair about a decade later and put converted Nusayris and Protestant missionaries again at the centre of hot debates between the USA and the Ottomans.

About the end of 1891, a decade after his release, the local governor accused Daoud of 'stealing children and selling them to the Americans, who are sending them to America' and showed him a list with the names of the children. Daoud confirmed the names of four of them taken to America but none of them from his region.[132] This accusation leads us to another crisis between the Americans and the Ottomans resulting from the activities of the famed missionary Dr. David Metheny in Ottoman Cilicia. He had been active in Latakia in the 1870s and 1880s and then moved to Mersin. As noted above, he had known and cherished Daoud[133] and came to the attention of the Ottoman authorities and the international public opinion, just as Daoud had.

2.3.2. A deaf-mute Nusayri girl defies the Ottomans: Telgie Ibrahim

Dr. David Metheny (1836–1897),[134] who after serving at the mission of the Reformed Presbyterian mission in Latakia from 1864, was transferred to Mersin (also Mersina in Western sources) in south Anatolia (Cilicia) in 1882. He and the other missionaries with him were later accused of converting and kidnapping Nusayri girls and taking them to America. As I have shown, Protestant missionaries tried to spread their beliefs in the Ottoman Empire among the Christians, such as the Catholics or the Armenians, and non-Sunni groups such as the Nusayris. Schools and orphanages were built in order to facilitate the spreading of the Gospel. Dr. Metheny ran a Protestant school originally opened by Evadna Sterett in Mersin in 1886, aimed at converting Nusayri girls. BOA documents deal with the matter of the kidnapping; in numerous letters and reports from November

1893 until June 1895 the case is described in great detail and offers information about the Ottoman stance towards missionary labour and relations with America. These years are at the height of the crisis that became known as the 'Armenian Question'[135] in the Ottoman Empire and which echoed throughout the world.

The Armenian issue took another turn between the years of 1887 and 1896; during this time the Ottoman Greek diplomat Alexandre Mavroyéni (Mavroyéni Bey) was ambassador to Washington DC and several important developments occurred with regard to Armenians about which he was actively reporting to Istanbul: American Protestant missionaries supported the emigration of Ottoman Armenians to the USA; these established a sizeable and respectable diaspora there; the two anti-Turkish Armenian revolutionary political parties, Hunchak and Dashnaktsutyun, were founded; Armenian revolutionaries who had received US citizenship returned to the Ottoman Empire and began activities under the protection of their new citizenship; the Armenians in the USA established a press that systematically made anti-Turkish propaganda; American missionaries and the US Press increased their anti-Turkish propaganda.[136] In a recent study about the impact of missionary influence on Armenian nationalism D. Emre Amasyalı argues that the impact of missionaries was much more unintended than is commonly assumed and resulted primarily from Armenian reactions to growing missionary influence. Amasyalı says that his research 'offers evidence that missionary influence spurred a backlash among the Armenian community that intensified preexisting local initiatives, increased investment in mass education in the provinces, and modernized its schooling system, all of which popularized and strengthened Armenian nationalism.'[137]

The Ottoman state authorities were highly concerned about foreign activities on Ottoman soil, especially when it came to converting Alawis and similar groups to Protestant Christianity while Armenians backed by Christian European Powers were seen as a source of mischief and other regions such as the Balkans also suffered from European intrusion and what they saw as the instigation of the Christian population. It is within this context that the following case of conversion and education of Nusayri children by American Protestants in Ottoman domains must be analysed. It is worthwhile describing in length roughly two years of communications and negotiations between the USA and the Ottoman Empire.

The Minister of Education Zühdi Paşa wrote on 16 November 1893 that Dr. Metheny had deceived three Nusayri sisters, the deaf-mute Nacide/Najida (8), Zehra/Zahra (13) and Safiye/Safiya[138] (10) – all daughters of a certain Ibrahim b. Mahmud from Latakia. Metheny is said to have sent Nacide to America three years before and had been keeping the other two at the school for six years. Their father Ibrahim applied for their release at the American Embassy but it was in vain. The Ministry of Education in Adana informed Istanbul that the other two girls would also be sent to the US. The governor of the province had written on 12 November 1893 that American missionaries deceived about 15–20 Nusayri girls and enrolled them in the missionary school; the government pointed out that taking the children to school and to the USA by force was illegal and asked for them to be sent back to their families but the missionaries refused.[139]

On 18 November 1893 the vali of Adana Nasuhi Paşa mentions that 15 girls from the 'Nusayri tribe from the sons of the Arabs' (*evlad-ı Arab'dan Nusayri kabilesi*), i.e., the Arab Nusayri tribe, had been kept for 3–5 years at the American Protestant School in Mersin. These could not be released due to the ineffectiveness of the *mutasarrıf* (district governor). Earlier in March, it was proposed to the Ministry of Education to build 15 primary and junior high schools but the letter went unanswered.[140] In another letter to the Prime Minister, Nasuhi Paşa writes that the American consulate informed him that the three daughters of Ibrahim and more than 20 other girls of the 'Nusayris of Arabia' (*Arabistan Nusayrilerinden*) could not be given back to their parents, since their personal records could not be identified. In a telegraph from the Prime minister to Adana (3 Cemaziyelahir 1311/12 December 1893) it was emphasized that it is undesirable that Muslim children were given to missionary schools and then sent to other countries. In the same vein, Muslim children should not be sent to Armenian schools in the province, otherwise officials were to be held responsible. Moreover, Metheny is reported to have said that he intended to add other girls to the 27 Muslim girls in his school and would give none of the girls back to their families.[141]

The overall investigation of Metheny's school involved the following matters: why and when the school was built; for what reason the local administrators in Mersin gave permission for the school buildings in spite of the fact that the missionaries did not apply to the director of Education; and whether girls were brought to the school from Syria. This was all asked of the *mutasarrıf* of Mersin but he did not reply. The Directorate of Education wrote that in 1882 Dr. Metheny from Pittsburgh (Pennsylvania) established a firm in Mersin with the name 'New York Reform Presbyterian Protestant' without having an imperial decree from Istanbul and built a school and dormitories without the permission of the municipality; and taking Muslim girls to the school was contrary to the government's rules. There were 13 teachers but only 7 of them had a diploma (2 Ottoman and 5 American citizens), the schools books were examined, after which some were prohibited; lastly, the government allowed only non-Muslim girls to attend that school.[142]

Metheny's school included primary and junior high schools and had 100 girls and 50 boys. In general, the Protestant schools in the Adana province administered by the Americans included one for the Anatolian Armenians, the second for Syrian Catholics and the last owned by Metheny especially for the Nusayris. He informed the US Embassy that unless the education expenses for the Nusayri girls were paid to him, he would not release them. Because the girls could not be taken back peacefully, the matter was referred to the Court. It was suggested that undercover civil servants be placed outside the school and ask the girls about their names and families; however, this was not possible because their records were needed in the first instance. Metheny did not show these. In addition, despite the fact that the Sublime Porte ordered that foreign schools need a license for education and the denomination and citizenship records be sent, this order was not heeded. Therefore, the state regarded this and other foreign schools as illegal.[143]

On 15 January 1894, the Legation of the USA in Istanbul issued a verbal note to find out the truth about the girls. It stated that it 'will at once ascertain from the

American teachers established at Mersina whether they refuse to send back girls at their schools to their parents who apply for them', adding that they have been instructed by telegram and letter to return to their parents any children whom they detain against their consent. The Legation wanted to make sure that after it received a full report, it would cooperate with the Ottoman Ministry of Foreign Affairs in preserving the authority parents; 'but as prejudices in the interior created by bad men sometimes obscure the truth, this Legation will have the truth if the accusation made plain and make known the result' to the Imperial Ministry.[144]

Moreover, on 27 January 1894 the US Legation informed the Ottoman Foreign Ministry that it would investigate why the girls were not given back to their families. The Legation asked for information from the teachers about the matter and ordered them to give back the girls who were taken without their parents' consent. It also promised that as soon as the Embassy received a report, it would do its utmost to assist the Foreign Ministry in defending the rights of the parents.[145] The Prime Ministry wrote to the Foreign Ministry and to Adana that after a meeting with the US ambassador the latter would write to his government to arrange the release of the girls and to the missionaries, not to send them to the US. He moreover promised that no compensation would be taken for the two other (Nusayri) girls at the school. The Ottoman Foreign Ministry should notify its embassy in Washington about the situation, Adana was already informed.[146] Following this, Nasuhi Paşa informed the Prime Ministry on 5 March 1894 that the US Consul Daras[147] wrote to the US President about Dr. Metheny being unwilling to give back the Nusayri girls and that because of this political crisis he would resign from his office. The consul moreover added that Metheny was trying either to get compensation from the Ottoman government for the education expenses or to exert influence on Ottoman soil. The consul lastly asked for Metheny, who was disobeying his own country's representative and the Ottoman government, to be removed from Mersin and to release the girls.[148]

Later the Ottoman embassy in Washington wrote to the Foreign Ministry on 6 April 1894 that the school director Dr. Metheny had an agreement with Ibrahim, the father of the three Nusayri girls; according to this, Metheny would pay the expenses for their education in America and their dowries when they would marry. The US ambassador in Istanbul told Metheny that as much as this was contrary to US law, it was also outside the duties of American teachers in the Ottoman Empire. According to Article 4 of the 1830 treaty between the two states,[149] in cases such as this one or: 'If litigations and disputes should arise between subjects of the Sublime Porte and citizens of the United States, the parties shall not be heard, nor shall judgment be pronounced unless the American Dragoman be present.'

The Advisory Office of the Sublime Porte evaluated the letter of 6 April 1894 from the Ottoman Embassy in Washington DC about the agreement between Dr. Metheny and the Nusayri father Ibrahim. It stated that the US Foreign Ministry informed its ambassador in Istanbul that if this agreement were contrary to Ottoman law, the US government would not protect Metheny. If this proved to be the case then Metheny could be expelled from the Ottoman Empire. However, since this would be contrary to the good relations between the two countries, the legal action against him should be postponed and the province of Adana informed about this.[150]

After receiving a verbal note from the Ottoman Foreign Ministry, the American Legation replied on 15 April 1895 that the charges made against Dr. Metheny would be investigated by the Consul and the Minister of the United States in person and that 'justice will be administered and the Sublime Porte informed of procedure'. Since Metheny was still extending the buildings of his school in Mersin, he would be compelled to cease this if a permit had not legally authorized him. 'A careful inquiry will be made into every fact showing how Dr. Metheny obtained possession of the young girls; and also, whether they are of Moslem or Christian parentage; and whether they are detained against the wishes of their parents or in violation of law; if detained illegally, he will be required to deliver them to those entitled to their custody.' The letter also stressed that the President of the United States had consented to the exclusion from Turkey of 'seditious men of American origin, who have become naturalized in the United States in violation of Turkish law but native-born American citizens claim treaty rights of domicile', which the Sublime Porte would respect. This same letter made clear that the US President did not have power to punish the humblest citizen until he has been adjudged guilty by some court of violating some law; and the American Minister in Istanbul who acted as a judge could not condemn an American arbitrarily.[151] With these statements, the US government made it clear that it would still protect its citizens despite inquiring of the legal status of the case. The letter highlighted unmistakably that the US Minister was not sent to the Ottoman Empire 'to drive his countrymen away, on a mere accusation, but to protect them until he finds them guilty of some offence and then he will punish'. The Legation hoped that the Ottoman Foreign Ministry would not support such an arbitrary procedure and 'that it would be in violation of the plainest principles of natural justice'.[152]

The communications proved futile for the Ottomans. Already on 13 April 1893 an American battleship named 'Chicago' had arrived at the port of Mersin to intimidate the Ottoman authorities; Metheny displayed the American flag on the school's rooftop. He did not heed his embassy's instruction to remove the flag. So far, there was no progress regarding the return of the Nusayri girls and the situation of the school. The governor of Adana was advised that Nusayri girls not be sent to foreign schools. The Ottoman Prime Ministry wrote to its Ministry of Foreign Affairs that Ibrahim, the father of the girls, had written to the latter ministry that a letter should be send to the Embassy in Washington that his girl that was forcibly taken to America should be released. Yet, the deputy of the US ambassador to Mersin admitted that Metheny refused to send back the girl and continued his activities such as constructing buildings without license. Metheny also complained to the US government and asked for the dismissal of the deputy.[153]

In other reports of the same case, it is stated that Metheny kidnapped 15 Nusayri girls and took them to America, and a European newspaper mentioned in April 1894 that because Metheny would be sentenced to death according to the shari'a due to his offence, the US government refused to send back the Nusayri girls. Thereupon Metheny went to America to pursue the matter.[154] The crisis continued

Figure 2.3 Telgie Ibrahim

another year; Dr. Metheny was stubborn as regards the return of the Nusayri girls and the closing of his school in Mersin. He engaged the two governments in a diplomatic battle from 1893 to 1895.

For the Ottomans this case of the Nusayri girls was clearly illegal.[155] The Protestant missionaries, in turn, had no doubt that Dr. Metheny had only saved the poor Nusayri girls from their plight. Their case was documented in missionary journals of the *Reformed Presbyterian Church of North America*. The destiny of the youngest of the three sisters, Nacide, was described as early as 1886. Nacide, as recorded in Ottoman reports, is however never mentioned as such by the missionaries but she is called 'Telgie', which comes from *thalj*, the Arabic word 'snow'.[156] Telgie (*thaljī*),[157] then, means 'snowy' or 'frozen/icy' probably because her mother had thrown her into ice-cold water as a baby.

The first mention of Telgie was in 1886 when Mary Metheny (Dr. Metheny's second wife), describing the work of the mission in Mersin and Tarsus and some converted Muslim girls, noted that:

2. 'Appropriate Objects of Christian Benevolence' 69

Figure 2.4 Telgie's sisters sitting in the middle row left (Zahra) and right (Safiya)

We have a little deaf and dumb girl in school, and the other girls are very good to her. ... Nahive [converted girl] said to me, 'Telgie knows how to flatter. If she sees any one with something nice to eat, she will smell their clothes and smooth them, as if to tell them they are very nice, so that she may get some. Poor thing!'[158]

Her sisters 'Zahara and Sophia' (Zahra and Safiya) were regarded as 'quite bright, and Sophia, the younger, is thoughtful and interesting'.[159]

The story of the three Nusayri sisters is narrated quite differently in those missionary journals. While the Ottomans saw it as a matter of the conversion of Muslims being educated in an unlicensed missionary school, the Presbyterian missionaries, foremost Dr. Metheny, described it as a matter of compassion, of proper education, and taking Telgie to America with the consent of her father.[160]

In the year 1886, Ibraheem Mohammed, an 'Ansairee', who was educated in one of the mountain schools of the Reformed Presbyterian Church in the Latakia district, had brought his two little girls and asked the missionaries to take charge of them, as their mother was dead. His sister 'Nyesi' was then a teacher at the school and came to the mountains where they and others spent the summer with the missionaries. He sent with her his youngest daughter who was 'deaf and dumb'. Her mother had caused her infirmity because, in a fit of anger, she had plunged her daughter into a cold stream when she was just beginning to talk. The missionaries accepted her for that summer because her aunt was there to help to care for her. Later the missionaries sent her back to her father. Sometime afterwards, she ran after them begging by signs to be taken back to school, and showing marks of ill-usage. Her father had married a second time. Telgie came back, and her father did not ask for his other children either.

As there were no institutions for the deaf and mute in the Ottoman Empire, Dr. Metheny went specially to see her father and asked him if he was willing to give her to the missionaries and put her in a school in America. The father said that he had given the girls to the doctor and he could do as he wished. Dr. Metheny then placed Telgie in a school near Philadelphia, where she learned to read and write. The missionaries hoped that she would return to Turkey and teach unfortunates like herself. In the meantime, her sisters remained at school and no one said anything about them. The eldest, when she became old enough to understand, asked and received baptism, and was a communicant in the church. The second also applied to be and was baptized.

In 1893, the aunt was discharged from the missionary employ because her school was not large enough to justify her salary. The trouble began after this. Her husband, enraged at the loss of her income, determined to revenge himself. He and the father went to the missionaries and asked that the eldest girl should be sent back to them in Tarsus. The girl herself, who was old enough in their eyes, said she did not want to go. The father said he did not wish her to go unless Miss Sterrett, the missionary who took care of her, was willing. The uncle said that if she went with him, he would bring her back in a week or two, but if not, he would complain to the government. Accordingly, he issued a complaint stating that when Dr. Metheny put the children in school he refused to release them because the father had agreed to give them four Turkish dollars per month for their services but as this had not been paid the girls stayed at the school. This complaint was sent to the US Consul, who sent it to the missionaries. However, Dr. Metheny said that he had not seen the father at all. After this, the father came to the mountains where the missionaries were spending the summer and stated that he wanted the girls to stay where they were.

Later, Dr. Metheny went to Adana and had an interview with the governor Nasuhi Paşa, telling him the facts of the case and stating that they were at liberty to go if they chose, but he did not feel that he must turn them out. He said that in the complaint sent to the government the uncle had purposely falsified the ages of the girls and the time they had been in school, in order to make them appear too young to choose for themselves. Metheny also stated that the Ottoman authorities accused the missionaries of intending to marry the eldest girl to an Armenian in town, which the missionaries said was false. The provincial government transferred the case to the Ottoman central government in Istanbul. The US minister there, A.W. Terrell, wrote a telegram, saying, 'Are you keeping Moslem children in school against the will of their parents? If so, deliver them up, and write me the facts.' Metheny thought it would have been more proper to inquire about the facts first rather than send this message openly, and he sent a copy of it to President Cleveland.[161]

The contention of the Ottomans was at first that Metheny was detaining minor children without the consent of their parents. Then they challenged the right of Christians to have Moslem children in their schools at all. The missionaries replied

Figure 2.5 Dr. David Metheny and his family.

that there were no written contracts and it was only a question between the veracity of Turks and missionaries. The former insisted that Metheny had twenty Moslem girls and intended to send these other girls out of the country.

The missionaries asked whether a Muslim of any age was at liberty to choose for himself/herself in religious matters; if not, of what use was the famous religious liberty clause? They could not understand why the Ottoman government deemed it right when a Christian of any sect wished to become a Muslim, but declared it wrong when a Muslim became a Christian. For more than thirty years, missionary work was done among the Nusayris, 'classed as Mohammedans, but really Pagans, and many of them have become Christians.' Yet in no case has this injured the Turkish government, for they have never claimed exemption from the army as Christians have a right to do. From the early 1890s the government interfered in the missionary work. In the eyes of Metheny, 'it then began a systematic course of intimidation, bribery and persecution which has resulted in the closing of some thirty-five schools.' Then an attempt was made by the local authorities here to force Metheny to sign an agreement that he would not receive pupils who were Muslims. He declined to do so. Neither was Metheny's government inclined to be of help.[162]

The matter of the Ibrahim girls escalated further as time went on. Terrell wrote a highly provocative letter to Metheny, showing that the word of the Turkish government was above the missionaries' own. Thus, the already complicated situation grew more complicated. Terrell reminded Metheny that:

> the parents of the children held by you under contract, whether really Turks or Christians, were subjects of the Sultan, and their children could not, without the consent of the government, be sent to the United States.... If you had official

authority to send the youngest child away, please procure and send me a copy of it, that I may avert from your institution the prejudice that would otherwise exist, by showing it to the Minister of Foreign Affairs ...

... I stated the facts frankly to the Grand Vizier. He expressed the utmost astonishment, and desired that the mute girl be brought back at once to the Ottoman Empire. You need not be told of the great horror felt by the Turks at an act of apostasy, and their objections to having their children raised under Christian auspices. I therefore suggest that in order to prevent those annoyances to your school that would otherwise follow, you cause the mute child to be brought back from the United States. As to the older sisters, if you will transmit a statement of the religious faith of their father, as recognized by the Turks, with their ages and a copy of your contract, I will instruct the Consul in regard to them.... The outlook now for a more kindly feeling toward American missionaries is far better than it has been since my arrival, and I need not to advise the utmost caution to avoid exciting the suspicions and fanaticism of Mohammedans.[163]

In two letters David Metheny stated the matter as he experienced it in 'clear terms' to the US Minister Terrell. In the first, Metheny stated that the uncle of the girls wanted to 'increase his harem by marrying one or both of them'. But as they had been eight years under instruction at the missionary school and accepted Christianity, they were baptized and received into membership of the Mission Church at Mersin. And being old enough, they declined to be delivered to the government to be pushed into this 'incestuous relationship, a thing abhorrent to them'. They demanded that their Christian liberty was stipulated in the Paris (1856) and Berlin Treaty (1878) and so should not be molested. The girls had already asked the British Cabinet through the Evangelical Alliance of Britain to sustain them in their rights.

In a letter to Rüstem Paşa,[164] the Ottoman ambassador at London, Rev. G. D. Mathews, the general secretary of the Alliance of Reformed Churches, holding the Presbyterian System, wrote in July 1894 that the father of the girls had asked Dr. Metheny to take the girls into his school and care for them, 'giving him the very "right of dower"'. Referring to Telgie, Mathews stated that Dr. Metheny, 'with the father's knowledge and consent', took her to Philadelphia and placed her at a school for the 'deaf and dumb' with the prospect that after her education she would return to Mersin and teach children as afflicted as herself. Mathews then added something which is not mentioned in other reports: that Metheny had 'applied to the Government official at Mersine for a passport, but was told that for a child so young and afflicted, no passport was necessary. He therefore took her without obtaining such document'.[165] Mathews continued stating that after the refusal of one of the girls to marry her aunt's husband he was angered and accused Metheny before the local authorities. The Ottoman authorities at Istanbul 'were ignorant of these facts' and so ordered Metheny to bring back Telgie from the USA 'and at present he has gone to that country for the purpose of doing so'.[166] Despite this assertion, there is no evidence that Metheny really intended to bring Telgie back.

Metheny thought that since there was no institution for the deaf and mute in the Ottoman Empire where Telgie could be taught and 'saved from the most wretched misery', he discharged his duty towards the Turkish Government in her case. He said that 'my act of kindness towards the poor, helpless, dumb child entitles me not to the blame, but to the commendation of every humane man, even to that of the Turkish officials. She was taken to the United States with the knowledge and consent of her father.' Metheny believed that 'her case was brought up at such a late date by the Adana authorities in order to forestall a number of instances of the maladministration which they rightly expect we would take up against them when the American consul would come to Mersin.'[167]

In the second letter to Terrell, Metheny wrote that he hoped to soon present formally for Terrell's official action several important questions bearing on Mission work, and especially the irregularities of Turkish officials, who, in his opinion, have been acting independent of the Sultan's will. He was unwilling to think that Abdülhamid would sanction, despite his own declarations and the Berlin treaty, the acts of repression and violence apparently systematically committed by those officials. Metheny was sure that the sultan had 'no better friends ... who labor more devotedly for the best interests and welfare of his empire and the peoples among whom we have lived and labored—some of us for near 30 years—in strict compliance with the laws and treaties.' Moreover, Metheny made some other interesting points with regard to the Nusayris. He maintained that the previous Prime Minister Kamil Paşa (1833–1913) had visited (he does not provide the year) the missionary schools in the Nusayri Mountains, 'and made a report highly commending the beneficent and civilizing influence of our schools among the Ansairiyeh, a fierce and warlike people, often in rebellion then, but now for many years at peace with the authorities.'[168]

In another report Metheny stated that when Kamil Paşa had visited the schools of the Reformed Presbyterians among the 'warlike and rebellious' Nusayris of North Lebanon, he declared in his report to Istanbul[169] that the Ottomans have never been able to civilize 'this people with fire and sword, and never could'. Kamil is quoted as having remarked: 'It is significant that an officer of the government must have a military escort in order to visit these regions, but the missionaries go alone wherever they wish, and are unmolested. The American schools are the only civilizing influences ever brought to bear on these peoples.' Metheny added that the missionaries never intended to excite sedition and that through their influence the Nusayris ceased to rebel against the Ottomans.[170]

In the eyes of Metheny and other missionaries the Nusayris were not Muslims and not allowed to worship in the mosques of various cities in Syria and Cilicia. The ones who had accepted Christianity had been 'carefully instructed to be loyal citizens'. He assured Terrell that none of them joined in rebellion against the Government but had acted as 'peacemakers'. On the contrary,

> by their peaceful character they have averted and prevented open outbreak and uprising. They are faithful soldiers. Indeed, in the disturbance a few years ago with Greece, they served with distinguished faithfulness and some of them were

promoted from the ranks and publicly commended. Had the sultan acquainted himself with these facts, he would have speedily put an end to such acts of repression.[171]

Metheny argued that there always had been Nusayri children at many schools run by the British and US missionaries, and not only Nusayri but also Muslim and Druze children in schools along the coast of the Mediterranean. In his estimation all this was within the provisions of the Imperial school law to which the missionaries had always conformed.[172] However, Metheny continued, through one pretext or another, the Ottoman government closed about 40 schools conducted by British and American missionaries, sent away teachers, and forbade them to return to their homes. Police intercepted students returning from school; their parents' names were taken down; they have been called before the authorities and threatened if they continued to send them to the school in Adana. In Tarsus the names of the Nusayri children were taken down and they were ordered into the Muslim school. Metheny added: 'We are about to present these facts to the Evangelical Alliance,[173] who will ask the signatory powers to act in the matter. . . . I am anxious for a peaceful solution of these questions, if at all practicable, but we shall demand every right guaranteed to us by the Imperial law and the treaty of Berlin.'[174]

The diplomatic crisis continued. The governor of Adana ordered Metheny to give up the girls. If not, he promised to go to Mersin and 'with a military force break open his house and take them out'. The governor gave as a reason for his demands that they would not allow Muslims to be in Christian schools. The US Minister at Istanbul stated that he would send instructions in order to restrain the Ottoman governor from the execution of his threat and ordered the girls, 'if Turkish subjects, to be delivered up to the proper authorities'. Metheny confirmed that the girls were Christians and old enough to decide for themselves. Telgie's two sisters were baptized and members of the Church. The governor made the case of Metheny and his school an exceptional case:

> The French have Moslems in their school across the street from us, and also in Adana. For over thirty years there have been Moslem children in our schools all the time, and latterly (till within six years) many hundreds of them here, in Latakia, and the mountains. Then, too, the Beirut schools have Moslems, and many are in the Mission schools in Egypt. . . . Why single us out for an attack?

Many complaints were made to and about the US Minister. He did not represent the missionaries' interests. He was looking at 'our work through Moslem glasses'. Metheny contended that the word 'Moslem' did not occur in the school law and their schools were official and legal. He expected the US Minister to say that he did not approve of the closing of the school. In his view that would end the trouble instantly.[175]

Earlier, the wife of David Metheny had complained that the religious liberty clause of the Ottomans did not mean anything. She had hoped that all the Christians would unite in order to pray for the defeat of the 'enemy'. She highlighted what she perceived as unjust, i.e., that the Muslims were allowed to perform their worship in America but the Christians were not free to do so in the Ottoman Empire: 'Shame that the votaries of the false prophet, whose religion blasts all that it touches, should have full liberty to carry on *their* worship, and build their mosque in Chicago, and yet Christians do nothing for their fellow Christians, in order to secure *them* freedom of worship here!'[176]

In late 1895 things continued much the same for the Syrian and Asia Minor missionaries. The schools among the Nusayris were closed, with only a little evangelical work possible. The question of the three Nusayri sisters and of the right of missionary schools to allow Muslims in as pupils still stood unanswered. According to Metheny, Minister Terrell was not doing his job and the source of all the troubles was Terrell, who should have been recalled as he appeared to be 'utterly unqualified for so responsible a position'.[177] A detailed letter was earlier sent to the Minister and President Cleveland: 'the Turkish officials in closing so many of our schools, [are] disturbing all our work for a generation.'[178] Metheny was sure about one thing, and that was 'the coming of the day of reckoning for Turkey', that no one could prevent: 'These times will come to an end. I am sure that the moment religious liberty is established, which is not by any means the case, multitudes will flock to our Church.'[179]

Earlier in December 1894 Jennie B. Dodds, a teacher at the Mersin mission school, had described the situation in a letter. She notes that the Ottoman governor sent word that he was coming down with soldiers, to forcibly enter the house and take out four girls; the two sisters, who had caused so much trouble, and two others. The missionaries had appealed to the American Consul in Beirut for protection. Then a representative went to Adana to let the Governor know that they have sent word to 'Uncle Sam' of his threat. She believed 'we are in the beginning of troublesome times in Turkey'. Referring to the 'the dreadful Armenian slaughter', she adds that in Adana 'they are persecuting them at a terrible rate. The Armenians some of these times will rise against the Turks. We all pray for the overthrow of the government, and yet if our prayers were answered many a missionary's life would pay the penalty.'[180]

That Dodds' letter was read by the Ottoman authorities and translated shows how concerned they were about the activities of the missionaries in the midst of the Armenian Question. According to Dodds, and in fact many other missionaries, the Muslim population and troops were attacking Armenians, other Christians and missionary schools without reason. In order to intimidate the Ottoman authorities America had been resorting to naval force, i.e., it was sending cruisers to the Mediterranean since the 1880s.[181] Metheny's plea to the US president was effective, and the US cruiser Marblehead was sent in August 1895 to the port of Tarsus to protect Americans there.[182] After arriving there in October of the same year, the missionaries felt that 'the Marblehead has been in God's hands the instrument to prevent much bloodshed here', for the Christians were in constant fear of outraged Muslims.[183]

Meanwhile, in Maraş the mission college was burned, fifteen hundred Christians killed and the missionaries confined to their houses with supplies running low, according to the missionaries. 'Massacres the order of the day... Burning and plundering going on all around. Plenty of warships of all kinds in the Mediterranean, but no stop put to these barbarities. What will the end be?'[184] Yet, in Metheny's case, the presence of Marblehead was effective: the position of the governor was refuted, the application for the Nusayri girls was denied, and in the matter of the boundaries of the mission grounds, it was found that Metheny was within his rights rather than having encroached upon others. In addition, a native Protestant church which had been closed earlier, was reopened, and a teacher of the mission who had been in prison, was released. The coming of the two ships, *San Francisco* and *Marblehead*, was seen as 'a great boon to the Christian population of that section, not because of threats or any aggressive action taken, but because it became evident that oppressive action against the Christians would be examined by foreign powers and their rights secured.' This kind of action was in the estimation of the US government 'the last resort' and for the purpose of counteracting any unjust official action on the part of the local Ottoman authorities.[185]

In the end, Metheny's school was not closed. But it seems that Safiya and Zahra were arrested or handed over to the Ottoman authorities. The illness of David Metheny and the Armenian massacres that took place in Anatolia during 1896 forced Zahra and Safiya's affairs out of the spotlight. This must have happened sometime between February 1895 and December 1896 since there is no mention about the case in the missionary journals. Jennie Dodds mentions the two girls who appear in a photograph in 1895[186] and then again in January 1897 when she refers to further hardships: 'Zahra and Sophia have stood out against beating and imprisonment, and are now banished to Constantinople, and, the last word we had from them, they are still true to Christ. They told Sophia they would torture her if she did not turn Moslem. Her answer was: "You may kill me, but I will stay in the Christian religion."'[187]

According to the missionaries, the two sisters were arrested and taken to Istanbul after they had left school and were working in a factory in Tarsus. In Istanbul, each of them was placed in a Paşa's family. There they 'also had a taste of what prison life in Turkey means'. The last the missionaries heard of them was that they were both faithful Christians. After months, they had no word of them. All the efforts to communicate with them were in vain.[188]

The deaf and mute sister Telgie remained in Pennsylvania at the school for the deaf, under the supervision of Dr. Metheny's cousin Mary Sterett. In the March 1896 issue of the *Herald of Mission News*, the editors suggested that the Ladies' Missionary Societies of the various congregations help to support Telgie. This advice was followed, as is shown in various notices in later issues of the *Herald of Mission News*.[189] In March 1898, mention is again made of the sisters. Meanwhile Zahra had returned to Tarsus but Safiya was still in Istanbul. Mary Sterett wrote:

> Among the communicants was Zahra Ibraheem, Telgie's sister. 'When she was taken away,' says Miss Sterett, 'I never expected to see her again. Poor Sophia, her sister, is still kept at Constantinople, and Zahra says she is so timid that she is afraid to do anything that might displease the Paşa's household. Recently I read a letter from her to her aunt, and I remember there was a sentence like this:

'As I write my eyes are dimmed with tears, and I pray the Lord that He will return me to Tarsus.' May the Lord keep the poor girl from faltering in her faith.'[190]

In July 1898, two missionaries stated that Sophia was 'still detained as a prisoner in Istanbul. They heard that she remained faithful to Christ and 'her letters are written in tears'.[191] And in an excerpt of a letter from a missionary dated 14 April 1898,[192] we find that Zahra has returned to Tarsus, as she is described as absent from church but present in the town. After Zahra married in 1899, she was 'prevented by the Fellaheen from attending religious services, and feels it a great deprivation'. The missionaries could visit her, though. She and the missionaries were not able to correspond with Safiya in Istanbul but her aunt received letters from her.[193] Later Zahra received a letter from Safiya, dated 4 April 1900. It was translated by R. J. Dodds Jr., who said 'there is some hope she may be permitted to return to Tarsus'. Zahra spoke of her sorrows and reprimanded Safiya about why she never wrote.[194]

Until 1902, again there seemed to be no news about Zahra and Safiya. The latter had finally returned to Tarsus. Zahra's husband was sent to the army for six years, and she was alone and desperate with her children. She was trying 'to let her light shine, although feebly, in the midst of much darkness'. Though she did not have and want any contact with Muslim women, Safiya was married to a Muslim who was very kind to her and entrusted her to the care of the Protestants when he was away. Safiya had decided to go to America to spare her children a life as Muslims.[195] She seems to have left for America in 1905.[196] Towards the end of 1904 Zahra died after a troublesome life during which two of her children also died.

The youngest sister Telgie[197] was never handed over to the Ottomans. She entered the Pennsylvania School for Deaf and Mute in 1889. Telgie's record is at the archives of that school, now Gallaudet University.[198] It is kept with the name 'Telgie Ibraheem' and mentions that she was admitted to the School for the Deaf on 22 November 1889. Her father's name is given as Yusuph Ibraheem. The document further writes: 'Born on 1 February 1881 in Asia Minor. Lost hearing at 1 y[ea]r from falling in water. Had measles, mumps and whooping cough. Good eye sight.' It is further mentioned that her foster is David Metheny of Pittsburgh and that she 'went to Perkasie, Bucks Co[unty] (Mr. Henry Deetz) at the close of school June, 1900, having been honourably discharged'.[199]

Telgie learned to read and write, and sign language. She completed her ten years of school in Pennsylvania in the summer of 1900 and required some assistance until she could obtain suitable work to support herself. For this, Mary Sterett asked her fellow missionaries to contribute.[200] Telgie married Gilbert Price, also a deaf-mute, on 24 April 1901.[201] After this, Telgie is not mentioned in the Reformed Presbyterians' journals. When she was placed in the school for the deaf, the missionaries hoped that she would return to Mersin and 'teach unfortunates like herself'.[202] This did not happen. Telgie died on 5 July 1944 in Easton, Pennsylvania. According to census records and her obituary Telgie and Gilbert had four daughters and a son, seven grandchildren; a sister named 'Mrs. Joseph Nourie' is also mentioned.[203] Telgie has many descendants today.

The stories of Daoud and Telgie are among the rare lasting successes of Nusayri conversion to Protestantism. Their life started with suffering, poverty, ignorance, illiteracy and religious conversion. It continued within diplomatic crises and international politics. Both cases ended as victories in the estimation of the missionaries: Daoud and Telgie died as Christians. Telgie was fully integrated and naturalized in the USA. From the Ottoman perspective this, of course, was a disaster.

The story of Telgie is reminiscent of the stories of numerous other 'invisible' and 'voiceless' orphans and destitute children in the late Ottoman Empire, who can be regarded as actors of social and political history. Their role can be linked to centralization and modernization projects of a modern state apparatus in Europe and the Ottoman Empire. 'Child anxiety', as Nazan Maksudyan states, became 'a general trend of modernity' in societies that began to see themselves as 'modern and civilized'. It is worthwhile quoting her analysis:

> The latter half of the nineteenth century witnessed the partial transformation of a communally segregated Ottoman society into a centrally administered polity. The multinational and decentralized empire was approximating to a centralized modern state. The attempts to 'modernize' established regulations concerning population control with new administrative designs of governmentality challenged the customary autonomy of communal authorities. The central state could now penetrate into communal affairs and have a presence in its workings. Non-Muslim religious authorities felt threatened, for they were losing their right to self-governance ....
>
> Different interested parties, the state, non-Muslim communities, missionaries, and the bourgeois public started to see orphaned and destitute children through different lenses. The motivation and discourse, on the one hand, was based on the desire to save unfortunate children from the dangers to which they were prey. These dangers included losing or being alienated from one's ethnoreligious identity, being sold into slavery, sexual abuse and exploitation, juvenile criminality, prostitution, health problems, death, conversion, and apostasy.[204]

Maksudyan adds with regard to 'foundlings', and this can certainly be applied in our case to Telgie, her sisters and other children at missionary schools, that their religious and civil status became a realm of rivalry for the state, non-Muslim communities and missionaries, among others. 'Less obvious actors' are generally not included in studies about Ottoman reform, yet, in Maksudyan's interpretation, despite the neglect by present-day historians Ottoman adults of the nineteenth century were aware of the importance of children and reassessed their role within adult male politics. The reason was that the children acquired new meanings and identities in their relations with the state, provincial/municipal authorities, religious and civil leaders of communities and foreign missionaries.[205] Christian missionaries, especially the zealous Protestants, were a threat to the Ottoman system.

In 1899 the governor of Diyarbakır described those missionaries as 'dispersed in these areas like a herd of locusts' (*cerad-ı münteşir gibi bu havaliye dağılan misyonerler*).²⁰⁶ In the words of Maksudyan, 'This description is priceless in understanding the perception of the Ottoman administration. Missionaries were numerous, they were hard workers, they were essentially harmful to the country, and they were bypassing the jurisdiction of the state. The missionaries were actually limiting the reach of Ottoman rule in some areas thanks to their success in fields of education and health.'²⁰⁷

The ABCFM could be best fought with the same weapons. Sultan Abdülhamid II and his officials, and in fact already before his time, the Ottoman state envisaged a Sunni 'Missionary Society' that would, and later did, encounter Christian missionaries. The Society would fight Protestant missionary zeal with Sunni missionary zeal. In this time of active foreign presence in Ottoman domains, the state authorities, foremost Abdülhamid II, were anxious and felt threatened, because incidents in other regions, especially the Balkans, were alarming and territories were being lost and the integrity of the Empire was at stake. It is for this reason that Abdülhamid turned his attention to fortifying the Islamic basis of his empire and endorsing the policy 'Pan-Islam' (*İttihad-ı İslam*), by which he hoped to unite the Muslims in his empire and beyond, and rectify the beliefs of 'nominal' Muslims by attracting them to the 'official' Hanafi version of Sunni Islam, and so keep it safe from dissolution.

Chapter 3

ABDÜLHAMID II'S CIVILIZING MISSION AND THE POLICY OF 'CORRECTION OF BELIEF(S)'

We have seen that the American Protestant missionaries of the ABCFM targeted various non-Sunni groups in the Ottoman Empire in an organized way which entailed the establishment of schools in various regions to educate the members of those communities according to their missionary worldview. Their efforts were more successful with respect to the Nusayris, who they regarded as forsaken and oppressed 'lost Christians'. Some cases of conversions of Nusayris to Protestantism, such as that of Daoud and Telgie went so far as to cause diplomatic crises between the Ottoman administration and Europe/USA. This all occurred at a time when the Ottoman domains were lost in the Balkans and the Armenian question was turning into a serious problem that resulted in massacres in Anatolia. Facing these problems, the Hamidian government turned its attention to consolidating and centralizing its power in regions where non-Sunnis lived and trying to bring them into the Ottoman Sunni congregation. It also tried to prevent alliances between Western powers and the Armenians.

Studies of so-called 'heterodox' religious groups in the late Ottoman period of Sultan Abdülhamid II discuss the application of the official policy of 'correction of the belief(s)' (*tashih-i itikad/akaid*) to non-Sunni Islamic groups such as the Alevis (Turkish and Kurdish), the Nusayris in Syria or the Shi'is in Iraq and the Yezidis in Eastern Anatolia. The Hamidian administration attempted to 'civilize' and turn them into obedient 'good' Muslims, thereby applying a 'fine tuning' of their beliefs. I will compare these policies with those of Mahmud II who had applied 'correction of the belief(s)' to the Bektaşi Sufi Order, which he persecuted as allies of the Janissaries (elite military troops) after their elimination in 1826. This chapter explores the evolution of the use of the neglected concept of *tashih-i itikad/akaid* from the late eighteenth century until the late nineteenth century, a period that stands out with its centralizing policies. Conversion campaigns were carried out to enforce the 'true' Sunni belief as it was understood by the Ottoman administration in order to preserve or restore order in the face of threat by groups accused of heresy and disobedience. Whenever designations and terms such as 'heretical', 'heterodox' etc., are used in this chapter, they stem from the view of the mainstream 'orthodox' Sunnis as used in the sources.

In the following pages, I will explore the evolution of the use of the concept of 'correction of the belief(s)' during the reign of Mahmud II and in the centralizing policies of the nineteenth-century sultans who followed him. The central theme here is to try to define roots of the concept of *tashih-i itikad/akaid*. This Islamic concept (Arab. *tashih al-i'tiqad*) is not mentioned in the Qur'an but discussed in books about the principles of Islam. It is linked to the Qur'anic 'commanding right and forbidding wrong', and concerns the rectification of the religious beliefs of the Muslim individual in relation to social and political life in which the ruler was commissioned to maintain the order. We shall also outline how conversion campaigns were carried out in Ottoman history to enforce the 'true' Sunni belief (orthodoxy) in order to preserve or restore order in the face of the threat of 'heretical' and disobedient elements inside and outside Sunni Islam (heterodoxy).

3.1. The roots of 'correction of belief(s)' and conversion campaigns until the nineteenth century

The concern of the Ottoman state was to stabilize the state of affairs of the population, and there was the dichotomy of 'good' and 'evil' or the 'right' and the 'wrong' in society, or what we can name as 'orthodox' and 'heterodox' way of life. One of the factors that had an impact on the transition from a 'heterodox' to an 'orthodox' Ottoman Empire emerged during the reign of Selim I[1] when the Ottomans consolidated Sunni orthodoxy in the wake of the campaign against the 'heretical' Safavi dynasty of Iran. Shah Isma'il I (r. 1501–1524)[2] and his Kızılbaş tried to win over nomadic tribes in Anatolia.[3] Anyone who did not abide by the rules of the Ottoman 'world order' (*nizam-ı âlem*) and disturbed it was a dissenter who was fiercely persecuted.[4] In the wake of this, Ottoman jurisconsults who were affiliated with the state, elaborated on *tecdid-i iman* or 'renewal of faith',[5] a term that has similar connotations to *tashih-i itikad/akaid*.

Throughout the sixteenth century the clash between Sunni Ottomans and the Kızılbaş continued. In a letter that Sultan Süleyman I 'Kanuni' (r. 1520–1566) wrote to Isma'il's son and successor Shah Tahmasb I (r. 1524–1576), he calls him and his followers 'unbelieving and irreligious people (*ashab-ı rafz ve ilhad*)' and their Shi'i creed as a 'false doctrine and useless belief (*mezheb-i batıl ve itikad-ı âtıl*)'. Based on decrees of religious scholars he declared their blood and property as lawful, meaning that they could be killed and looted. He summons the Iranian shah to repent and return to the religious principles (*akaid-i diniyye*) of Islam.[6] When the political conjuncture changed, Süleyman was favourable toward Tahmasb, as is expressed in another letter.[7] Rather than being a theological clash, this approach was pragmatic and had political motives, in that it was a defence against the Safavi propaganda in order to save the state and territory.[8] Even after Isma'il I had died and Tahmasb I was occupied with a civil war in Iran when the Safavi threat calmed down, Anatolian Kızılbaş staged an uprising independent from the Safavis.[9]

During the reign of Süleyman I and later, 'Sunna-minded trends'[10] in the form of movements of fanatic Sunni ulema (religious scholars) appeared and influenced public opinion and endangered the order.[11] There had been preachers who incited the people to oppose and attack what they deemed as impious innovations (*bid'at*), namely any belief or practice that was outside the scope of the Qur'an, the prophetic traditions and did not exist in the time of the 'pious forefathers' (*as-salaf as-salihin*). One of these was Birgivî (Birgili) Mehmed Efendi (d. 1573)[12] who came to prominence with his fundamentalist views on Islam in the 1550s and 1560s. In his major book *at-Tariqa al-Muhammadiyya*[13] that he wrote in Arabic, a section is devoted to *tashih al-i'tiqad*.[14] This is the earliest evidence in Ottoman sources I found about *tashih-i itikad/akaid*. Birgivi puts forth the fundamental beliefs of the Sunnis: that God is one and independent of everything (time and place), He cannot be described, that the Qur'an is God's word, that the universe created by God, he puts forth the belief in the prophets from Adam to Muhammad, elaborates the importance of saints, praises the first four caliphs Abu Bakr, Umar, Uthman and Ali as the best saints, and talks about other tenets regarding belief and behaviour.[15]

At the end of Birgivi's argument of the 'practical applications of piety', he exhorts his readers to remember the following:

> three things are enjoined upon you: (i) the rectification of doctrine (*taṣḥīḥ al-i'tiqād*, i.e. correct belief), (ii) an 'understanding of the situation' (*'ilm al-ḥāl*) and (iii) piety (*taqwā*). In his estimation these three things bring together everything that is necessary and are sufficient for a believer to attain salvation and obtaining God's satisfaction and thus entering Paradise. He explains further that the three must be understood as concentric circles embracing each other: 'Correct doctrine is included (*dākhil*) in understanding of a situation [...], which in itself is included in piety.[16]

Birgivi's book has been a religious primer for Sunni Muslim preachers and believers alike and has been used to this day.[17] Later in the seventeenth century, the revivalist *Kadızadeli* movement[18] that took its name from Kadızade Mehmed Efendi (d. 1635), challenged public life in Istanbul and other provinces.[19] Its views were based on that of Birgivî Mehmed and also influenced the sultans' policies. Based on the central tenet of 'commanding right and forbidding wrong' a large-scale, sometimes violent, campaign of piety or correcting the beliefs of the Muslims ensued, though the term *tashih-i itikad/akaid* does not seem to occur in contemporary sources. Another development were the efforts to convert Jews and Christians in Istanbul and to Islamize the city by converting a Jewish landscape into a Muslim landscape, as in the case of the mosque at Eminönü in the heart of the city's main Jewish district. As Marc Baer puts it: 'The most visible and symbolic manifestation of the conversion of the landscape in Ottoman territories in the wake of conquest had always been the transformation of churches and synagogues into mosques and the construction of grand royal mosques to mark the hegemony of the new rulers.'[20] These efforts of 'commanding right and forbidding wrong' and 'conversion to piety' by the Kadızadelis with regard to the Muslims had the intention of admonishing them to turn, come back to or stay in the way of the Sunni congregation (*ahl as-sunna wa al-jama'a*).[21] Later efforts at correcting the beliefs of the Muslims and non-Muslims by the Ottoman state and ulema in the eighteenth and nineteenth centuries need to be seen in the context of the centralization of the state and 'civilizing' people outside the scope of official Ottoman Islam, i.e. Hanafi-Sunnism.

Overall, the role of the ulema was crucial in watching over Ottoman society. The ideal expectation for the ulema that was rooted within Ottoman political thought was to guide the society along the right path and to prevent it from wrongdoing. The government and the ruler were included, and it was the duty of 'commanding right and forbidding wrong', to be implemented in three ways: the ulema were charged to perform the duty by word, the ruler by hand, and the public by heart.[22] The sultan was advised that he should ask and instruct the *şeyhülislam* (grand mufti, head of the ulema) to warn him of injustices occurring in the realm. Authorized by this canonized division of labour, the principal ulema stood in many cases before the sultan and protested decisions they deemed contrary to the shari'a (Islamic law) or public interest. The moral duty of 'commanding right and forbidding wrong' gained an institutional basis in Ottoman polity, as a constitutional check within the government.[23] From that time on we see the ulema also acting as agents of change for the state for the sake of centralization. This is true from the beginning of the reign of Sultan Mahmud II until the genesis of the Turkish Republic.[24]

Although we cannot say at this point when the Ottomans first used or applied *tashih-i itikad/akaid* as a political tool for the first time, the earliest reference I found in Ottoman sources and in which ulema had an active role were the educative measures to be applied to the 'disobedient' Abkhaz and Circassian tribes (*Abaza ve Çerkes*) in Soğucak/Anapa in the Caucasus toward the end of the eighteenth century. There they lived in a 'state of savagery (*hâlet-i vahşiyâne*)' according to Ottoman sources. Even though I am rather concerned here with the 'correction of belief(s)' of Islamic groups, it is worthwhile dwelling on this issue because it shows that the modern bureaucrats of the nineteenth Ottoman state interpreted the spreading of Islam in those non-Islamic regions in the eighteenth century retrospectively as the cause of 'civilization', *medeniyet* or *temeddün* in Turkish. Apparently both terms were coined in the late nineteenth century and became watchwords of the modernization attempts.[25] They were also used in conjunction with *tashih-i itikad/akaid* and education (*maarif*) among 'heretical' groups: these needed to abandon their old ways of nomadism and savagery and be brought into the 'circle of civilization'.[26] However, despite fixing the usage of the term 'civilization' to the nineteenth century, Ibrahim Müteferrika, the Ottoman who first introduced the printing press to the Empire, uses *medeniyet* and *medeni* ('civilized') already in the early eighteenth century. *Temeddün* for 'civilization' appears as early as the fifteenth century.[27]

According to the Ottoman chronicler Ahmed Lutfi most of the Circassians and Abkhaz belonged to a Zoroastrian creed called Şâsı[28] who were engaged in pillage and theft (*Şası ta'bîr olunur mecûsî âyîni üzere bulunmuş olduklarından işleri güçleri çapulculuk ve hırsızlıkdan ibâret olup*) and were 'deprived of the glory of Islam (*şeref-i islâmiyetden bî-behre olduklarından*)'. Ferah Ali Paşa (d. 1785),[29] who was assigned as governor of that region, had spread there the 'lights of Islam'.[30]

Mustafa Nuri Paşa[31] (d. 1890) notes in his chronicle that since the time Ferah Ali did this the tribes have been entering the fold of Islam and civilization (*kabâ'il-i* *mezkûre günden güne dâ'ire-i dîn-i mübîn ü medeniyyete idhâl olunmakda).*³² Despite that the Crimean rulers introduced Islam there already in the sixteenth century, many Circassians and Abhkaz were still clinging to their polytheistic beliefs or remained Christians. Later Christian Circassians also became Muslims.³³ Ahmed Cevdet Paşa,³⁴ influential Ottoman minister and official chronicler in the late nineteenth century, mentions that when the Ottoman State conscripted Circassians for the army many of the tribes were indoctrinated (*telkin*) with Islam and they all gradually left polytheism and became strong Muslims (*kavî Müslüman*).³⁵ In his *Tarih* ('History') Cevdet Paşa states that Ferah Ali Paşa was the 'spiritual conqueror' of Circassia (*fâtih-i manevîsi*). Cevdet praises his efforts for spreading Islam in those regions (*ol havâlide din-i İslam'ı neşr*) and teaching the Circassian and Abkhaz tribes what state and nation means (*devlet ve millet ne olduğunu öğretmiş*), thereby familiarized them with the Caliph of Islam, whom the Islamic law requires to be obeyed.³⁶ Like Mustafa Nuri Paşa, who retrospectively applies 'civilization' to the late eighteenth century by accrediting Ferah Ali for this, Ahmed Cevdet Paşa also uses the rhetoric of the 'mobilizational ethic' of his times for events that occurred one hundred years ago.³⁷

In the early nineteenth century, the issue of the conversion of Caucasian tribes was reiterated, and Çeçenzade Hasan Paşa (d. 1831),³⁸ governor general of Trabzon and military commander at Anapa in 1826–1827, took responsibility and went to the notables and tribal chiefs in the Crimea. He took with him imperial orders alongside manuals of faith and instructions as to 'command right and forbid wrong' and 'correct the beliefs' with and reform these people by appointing and sending a mufti and sixteen judges from among the ulema to them.³⁹ An Ottoman imperial document about Hasan Paşa from late 1826 says that some tribes have abandoned the '*şazz* innovation of the Zoroastrian custom (*mecusi adeti olan şazz bid'atini terk edüb*)', meaning that they left 'what is contrary to general rule'.⁴⁰ *Şazz* is similar to *Şası*, and Lutfî may have meant this. A contemporary English journal relates this episode by stating that 'Hassan, Paşa of Anapa, who also spent very large sums in his endeavours to convert the people to Islamism; immense crowds having, for many months, congregated daily in the valley of Anapa, to undergo conversion, and to participate in the 'largesse' distributed upon this occasion, many returning also for such *confirmation*.'⁴¹

The efforts of Hasan Paşa occurred during the reign of Mahmud II, who became sultan of the Ottomans after a violent power struggle between his predecessor Selim III and the Janissary (*Yeniçeri*) elite troops as a response to political reforms that were commenced by the sultan and intended to establish a 'new order' instead of the 'old order'. This was a time of a 'legitimacy crisis' during which the established relationship between the ruler and the ruled collapsed, when Mahmud II centralized and modernized his empire. The crisis continued well until the reign of Abdülhamid II. What is usually depicted as the decline and collapse of the empire after the late sixteenth century was rather a trend in world history during the seventeenth and eighteenth centuries.

Whereas the current view of Ottoman historiography argues that all of the old and obsolete Ottoman institutions of that period had to be destroyed or reformed, so as not to be a hindrance,⁴² Baki Tezcan has recently argued that the New Order 'either destroyed or radically weakened the central socio-political institutions of the Ottoman Empire, the ulema and the janissaries, which had been successful adversaries of absolutism in the past'. Even though this radical step made Ottoman modernization successful in terms of creating a modern centralized state, it eliminated 'the development of sociopolitical institutions that check the powers of the royal (or state) authority in a given polity'. Seen in this light, Ottoman modernization obliterated these powerful institutions of 'sociopolitical opposition in the empire that had created an indigenous model of limited government in the seventeenth and eighteenth centuries'. Tezcan sees the roots of 'the decline paradigm in Ottoman history' after the successful reign of Kanuni Süleyman 'in the historiography of the Ottoman New Order'. He argues that it makes more sense that the New Order started in 1826 with the elimination of the Janissaries, who were regarded as the guardians of the 'Old Order' (nizam-ı atîk) or ancient régime, and continued through the Tanzimat until the early Turkish Republic until 1950 because it stood for autocratic centralization.⁴³

Before, during and after the Tanzimat, the Ottoman state became a victim of its policies of centralization and attempted to face the problems with what can be called 'fine tuning'.⁴⁴ It seems that 'fine tuning' becomes important in times of crisis or emergency, the most important aspect of which is 'that it is a process through which the legitimation ideology of the state is promoted and state policy is imposed on society'. It also involves 'the process of making state policy'.⁴⁵ While Selim Deringil discusses 'correction of belief(s)' as part of the 'fine tuning' efforts or 'civilizing mission' (mission civilisatrice) of Abdülhamid II and his creation of a state ideology, we can also apply this to the centralizing policies of Mahmud II that took place earlier.

3.2. Correcting the beliefs of the Bektaşis after 1826

In the first half of the nineteenth century Sultan Mahmud II applied tashih-i itikad/akaid on a large scale to the Bektaşi Sufi order as part of his reforms. Bektaşism/Bektaşiyye⁴⁶ is a Sufi order that was established in Anatolia in the fifteenth century by Balım Sultan (d. 1519),⁴⁷ and named after Hacı Bektaş Veli (d. 1270).⁴⁸ It is one of the Muslim movements that the mainstream Sunnis, who the state also represented, eventually regarded as 'non-conformist'. Hence, Sunni clerics depicted it often as heretical. Bektaşism was widely spread among Turkish nomadic tribes of central Anatolia that originally came from Azerbaijan and Iran. Hacı Bektaş was a Sufi saint and is one of the main spiritual leaders of Alevism.⁴⁹ The Alevis, a mystical and 'heterodox'⁵⁰ or non-conformist branch of Shi'a Islam, believe that the source of knowledge is Imam Ali, the first Shi'i imam. Regardless of his Shi'i and unorthodox beliefs that are contrary to Sunni Islam, Hacı Bektaş was revered in the Ottoman Empire and still is held in high esteem in Turkey. It is said that he was a Sunni and later acquired unorthodox extremist Shi'i beliefs.⁵¹

Bektaşi dervishes had participated in the conquest and conversion to Islam of Christian domains by the early Ottomans and involved in the Ottoman army.

For unknown reasons, the elite Janissary military corps was placed under the spiritual guidance of the Bektaşis; the Janissaries were sometimes called *Ocak-ı Bektaşiyan*, 'the hearth of the Bektaşis'. Because of the association of the Bektaşis with the Janissaries and their protection by the Ottoman state, Bektaşism was considered less heretical than other similar antinomian movements of the period. As a result, they were given the mission of preventing the Kızılbaş from being extremely heretical and to unite and institutionalize the Anatolian antinomian movements in a single brotherhood. Thus, Bektaşism was domesticated by the Ottomans.[52]

As the Bektaşis were closely linked to the Janissaries, they also supported revolts against the state by the latter. The Bektaşis' involvement in opposition to Sultan Selim III in the early nineteenth century was the cause for their prohibition by Mahmud II.[53] He persecuted them as allies of the Janissaries after their elimination in 1826. His aim was to get rid of any opposition and centralize his position and the state. He began with European-style reforms for which he needed to submit different opposing groups in the empire and get rid of the Janissaries that he regarded as reactionaries.

Mahmud II continued the 'New Order' his predecessor Selim III had initiated but he was convinced that military reforms alone were not sufficient. The classical view is that since Mahmud knew that the Janissaries and other conservative groups revolted after the introduction of an innovation, he acted prudently and gathered beforehand loyal ministers, 'their natural leaders among the ulema' and soldiers around him, who could act immediately against any revolt. Mahmud pursued an unheard-of propaganda campaign against the 'degenerated' Janissaries who were seen as the enemies of the state.[54]

After the Janissaries accepted the *fetva* of the Şeyhülislam Mehmed Tahir Efendi (d. 1838)[55] regarding the creation and education of an old troop after new methods, they revolted a few days later on 15 June 1826 – for the last time – against the sultan. Mahmud II was prepared and crushed the Janissary barracks, and it is said that thousands of Janissaries were killed and many fled. This bloody campaign, called 'with typical euphemism'[56] *Vak'a-i Hayriyye* ('Auspicious Event') entailed the wiping out even of the name *Janissary* and the persecution of anyone who had associated with them, such as the Bektaşi order of dervishes.[57]

Selim III had protected the Bektaşi order and tried to win them over for their reforms, though without success. The Bektaşis in turn had supported and instigated the Janissaries in their opposition to that sultan.[58] They took part against Alemdar Mustafa Paşa, a notable from the Balkans, who marched to Istanbul with his troops to save the life of Selim. He eventually was not able to do so but installed Mahmud as sultan. The Bektaşis were persecuted due to their involvement in the revolt against the sultan and Alemdar and their supposed propagation of heresy among the people.[59] The plight of the Janissaries was more grievous: their graves were destroyed and later even a fabricated story about 'vampire Janissaries', who haunted the people but were eventually annihilated, was published in the official newspaper *Takvim-i Vekâyi* (1833).[60] Mehmed Daniş notes in his chronicle *Neticetü'l-Vekayi'*: 'There is no doubt that their hearth was abolished altogether and even a trace of the name of the Janissaries wiped off the face of the earth, and that also the Creator of the seven heavens [God] has erased the names of the hearth and the Janissaries from his Preserved Tablet.'[61]

Based on Tezcan's argument we can infer that the ensuing persecution of the Bektaşis was a political means in the wake of the centralization politics and reforms of Mahmud II. Anyone who had supported the Janissaries was punished severely. Hence, he punished with death or exiled Bektaşi leaders and followers and closed or destroyed their convents because he regarded the Bektaşis as a possible opposition to his policies of centralized modernization. In this capacity within a centralized state, the Janissaries and their allies needed to be eliminated.[62]

What is more, it appears that Mahmud II did this to appease Sunni ulema, who detested the Bektaşis, so to have their consent for his reforms concerning the military and society in general. For this Mahmud needed an ideological basis and used Sunni Islam as a means of propaganda. He was eager to win wider support for his reforms and commissioned Sahaflar Şeyhizade Esad Efendi[63] as official chronicler to write a treatise titled *Üss-i Zafer* ('The Foundation of Victory').[64]

It is an apologetic work that deals with the events of the hijri year 1241 (numerical value of the words *Üss-i Zafer*),[65] i.e. 1826 CE, surrounding the abolition of the Janissary corps. The book was published just two years after the incident. Apart from being a chronicle of the *Vak'a-i Hayriyye*, Esad Efendi digresses from his main topic in between and provides comments that he mostly calls *istitrad* ('excursion'), as to support the reasons for the elimination of the Janissaries and the prohibition of Bektaşism in the context of *Heilsgeschichte*. They constitute the core of his ideological argumentation as to why Mahmud II commenced military reforms and created a new army. Esad calls Mahmud II 'the renewer of the religion and the state' (*müceddid-i din ü devlet*) and 'the cause of repose and peace' (*bâis-i asayiş ü rahat*), who wanted to exalt the Word of God (*i'lâ-yı kelimetullah*). Esad argues that according to a hadith of the Prophet Muhammad God sends a 'renewer of religion' (Arab. *mujaddid*) at the beginning of each century, when unrest and rebellions occur and a mighty person appears to restore the order. For Esad Efendi the Janissaries were the main enemy then because they had caused problems throughout the centuries by opposing the sultans and killing the Muslim population and religious figures during their revolts.[66] He maintains (without evidence) that earlier the Janissaries had conspired with the Ottomans' chief enemy, the heretical Safavis. And as the Bektaşis were always at the side of the Janissaries and inclined to the Safavi heresy, they also were heretics. In order to convince his audience, who most probably were the ulema, Esad argues in a religious context in order to win them for Mahmud II's westernizing reforms. As a conclusion for his argumentation Esad states that there was much unrest and rebellion that heralded the coming of Mahmud II, who was born in 1199 AH, at the beginning of the thirteenth Islamic century. Around that time mischief was ripe when, e.g., the Wahhabis opposed the Ottomans and tried to prevent the pilgrims reaching Mecca, or the Janissaries who had revolted and the heretical Bektaşis supported them. Therefore Esad says that it is 'as clear and evident as the sun at midday' (*ke'ş-şems fi hevaciri's-sema zahir ü hüveyda*) that Mahmud II was the 'renewer of religion and helper of the Muslims (*müceddid-i din ve mu'in-i müslimîn*)' for that century.[67]

In a similar vein, the Ottoman statesman Mehmed Memduh Paşa (d. 1925)[68] sacralised the enthronement of Selim III as sultan and caliph in one of his chronicles about developments in the late Ottoman period. He says that Selim was essentially the manifestation of the qur'anic verse 'And We [God] strengthened with a third' (36:14; *fe-'azzeznâ bi-sâlis*).[69] Thus, Mehmed Memduh regarded Selim 'the Third' as 'the third' mentioned in this verse, and describes him as the one who decided to renew and strengthen the edifice of the state.[70] With practical steps, Selim proved to be a benefactor to the people, yet because of his mild nature he was not able to get rid of those wayward elements that incited rebellions and so lost his throne and life. As a result, the Ottoman state missed the first opportunity to revive the empire. Mehmed Memduh furthermore gives another meaning to 'the third' mentioned in that Qur'an verse. He writes that after Selim, Mahmud II was the second who continued the revival of the state but even if he destroyed the Janissaries, illnesses threatened the state and prevented its rise. That was the second time the Ottoman state missed the opportunity. Finally, and for the third time, when Mahmud's son Abdülmecid (r. 1839–1861) announced the 'Benevolent Reforms' (*Tanzimat-ı Hayriyye*), the people were happy and hopeful that the weakness of the state would be transformed into strength. Despite the beginning of the period of renewal (*teceddüd devresi*), there was no perfect progress (*terakkiyât-ı kâmile vücûd bulmamışdır*) because the regulations were not carried out based on prevalent sciences (*fünûn-i mütedâvileye tatbikan icrâ edilememesinden*) and new posts were held by men of the old system (*birer eski adam*) who acted as they wished and did not know what path they should tread in order to gain results.[71] Memduh declared the 'old order' as obsolete and asked for a 'new order' that would bring about modern progress supported by science.

As a rule, Ottoman sultans were seen in an apocalyptic light,[72] and in general, a millenarian atmosphere was widespread in the monotheistic religions from time to time, especially at the turn of a millennium or a century, particularly when there was unrest. It was a widely held belief that the Messiah would appear soon, restore religion to its pristine condition and convert the unbelievers.[73]

Mahmud II acted as a renewer, much more determined than his predecessor Selim III. After the Janissary corps was abolished, Mahmud ordered the persecution of the Bektaşis because of their proximity to the Janissaries and their 'heretic' beliefs that were contrary to Sunni Islam. The Bektaşi brotherhood was prohibited at a consultative meeting for which Mahmud II assembled the Şeyhülislam, prime minister, and leaders of Sunni Sufi orders such as the orthodox Sunni Nakşbendis.[74] An imperial decree confirmed the decision.[75] The chronicler Lutfi writes that Mahmud II abolished the Janissaries because they had lost their order that was defective like the creeds of people of error; especially some who claimed to be Bektaşis had strayed from the Islamic shari'a (*şîrâze-i nizâm ü intizâmları akaid-i ehl-i dalâl gibi halel-pezîr olup husûsiyle tarîkat-ı Bektaşîyyeye mensûb geçinen ba'zı kesân dahi şeriat ve hakîkata mugayir*). The sultan therefore reformed this 'gang' (*güruh*) of the Bektaşis in his capacity as God's representative on earth who was commissioned with commanding good (*emr-i bi'l-ma'rûf ile me'mûr halîfe-i rûy-ı zemin*).⁷⁶ In the preface of a French rendition of Esad Efendi's *Üss-i Zafer* the translator compares Mahmud II to Alexander the Great and his wall against Gog (and Magog): 'Mahmud is a terrible Alexander. The slightest sign of his face would threaten, like a wall, the efforts of a hundred thousand *Ya'juj* [Arab. for 'Gog']'.⁷⁷

Despite this harsh description, it is interesting that the imperial decree mentions that those Bektaşis who followed the Sunna would be spared and the state had always showed reverence to Hacı Bektaş, the founder of Bektaşism.⁷⁸ Mahmud II thought of original Bektaşism as an order that had followed the Sunni way and the shari'a. He differentiated between this original Bektaşism and the Bektaşism in his time, called *zamane Bektaşilik*. This 'contemporary Bektaşism' was corrupted by people who claimed to be Bektaşis but actually did not adhere to the shari'a, were lawless like the Janissaries and heretical in their beliefs.⁷⁹ According to Mahmud the decline of Bektaşism, that he spoke of as one of the 'exalted orders' (*turuk-ı aliyye*), had gone hand in hand with the decline of the Janissary corps since the two institutions had been allies. Therefore, the abolition of both was parallel; at least the Bektaşis had to be suppressed.⁸⁰

The sultan ordered that Bektaşi convents in Istanbul be either demolished, their possessions confiscated or turned into mosques or *medreses*, thus carrying out a transformation or conversion of a sacred space.⁸¹ Because of being close to the sultan, sheikhs of the Nakşbendi order were assigned to convents. Most importantly, as part of the Sunnitization of the Bektaşis, a Nakşbendi sheikh took over the central Hacı Bektaş Veli convent in central Anatolia. Nakşbendi sheikhs who also replaced other Bektaşi sheikhs in other convents, came from the Khalidiyya suborder of the revivalist and shari'a-based Müceddidi/Mujaddidi branch whose founder Sheikh Khalid had emphasized a strong fulfilment of the shari'a and revival of the Sunna. He urged his deputies in Ottoman domains who were active since the early nineteenth century that they should 'rectify the beliefs' (*tashih al-i'tiqad*) of the Muslims.⁸² The active role the Khalidiyya played during this period implies an orthodox trend in Istanbul that was utilized by Mahmud II to get support against groups that were deemed disobedient, such as the Bektaşis. The Khalidiyya and the 'orthodox trend' also played an important role later during the Tanzimat,⁸³ during which, contrary to classical historiography, religion gained importance in Empire, be they European or the Ottoman.⁸⁴

Some Bektaşi leaders who had supported the Janissaries in their last revolt were killed, others exiled to remote places where they were put under surveillance. There are archival reports about Bektaşis who were observed as having 'corrected their beliefs' and became obedient Sunnis and were released from exile. Indoctrination of Bektaşis with Sunni beliefs occurred in localities, which were 'abodes of ulema' (*makarr-ı ulema*), i.e., strongholds of the religious class, such as Kayseri, Hadim (Konya), Bursa, Manisa, Birgi and other places.⁸⁵

Whereas the main reason for the prohibition of Bektaşism was their close relationship with the Janissaries, the state based it on religious grounds, arguing that the Bektaşis were not following the shari'a.⁸⁶ In the decree prohibiting Bektaşism in Istanbul and the ones the sultan sent to the provinces he almost refrained from mentioning the name 'Bektaşi'; instead he used *gurûh-ı mekrûha* ('despised gang'), *gürûh-ı melâhide* ('gang of disbelievers'), *gürûh-ı Alevi ve revâfız* ('gang of Alevis and [Shi'i] heretics')[87], *gürûh-ı ibâhiye* ('gang of the libertines'), or *erbâb-ı rafz ve ilhad* ('people of heresy and unbelief').[88]

In Istanbul the convents were closed down by distinguished members of the *ilmiye*, the religious establishment, and officers from the Imperial Gate (*kapıcıbaşı*). They would secretly go to the convent and raid it, arrest the sheikh and his followers, and then seal the doors. The arrested persons were brought to the *Cebehane* (the Ammunition House). Each Bektaşi in Istanbul was brought to the presence of the Şeyhülislam, who would ask questions to determine their knowledge of Islam. Some passed the test and were released; others were not credible, escaped death but were exiled. Apparently, these saved their lives by resorting to *takıyye* or dissimulation as a legitimate form of defence. It was demanded that the exiled Bektaşis were put under constant surveillance in order to make them follow the shari'a rules and prevent misguided behaviour; in short, they should be sunnitized.[89] The persecution of the Bektaşis was extensive; everyone who was even accused of being a Bektaşi but actually was not was arrested and exiled. Cevdet Paşa lists in his *History* names of men who were innocent of the charge of being Bektaşis but were sent to exile.[90]

What were the measures of the 'correction of the belief(s)' (*tashih-i itikad/akaid*) or the Sunnitization of the Bektaşis? And after how many years were Bektaşi leaders and followers released because of good conduct? There are many cases based on archival evidence, what follows are just a few where we can have an idea how 'the correction of the belief(s)' worked.

In a document from January 1828 (1243) a certain İsmail and Nazif from Üsküdar (Istanbul) are mentioned as having gone astray in the path of 'contemporary Bektaşism' (*zamane Bektaşiliği yoluna saparak*) and behaved against the exalted shari'a. In order to discipline them they were sent to Güzelhisar (Aydın), which was an 'abode of the ulema' (*makarr-ı ulema*). There the mufti, various ulema, and medrese teachers taught them the glorious way of the Sunna (*tarîk-i nâciyye olan ehl-i sünnet ve cemâat*). After being indoctrinated (*telkin*) they left 'their heretic path and accepted the straight path (*tarîk-i mülhideden udûl, râh-ı müstakimi kabul*)' and so 'corrected their beliefs'. They had also performed their ritual prayers on time with the community of believers. While being on the right course, Nazif died and İsmail was affected by this and stayed behind in a bad financial condition. His wife and children lamented his wretched condition, and because it was observed that İsmail was disciplined and pulled himself together (*ıslâh-ı nefs*), they pleaded for his release. In this case we see that a Bektaşi was already released after one year or so.[91]

Another case is that of Dellâl ('broker') Ahmed who worked at the *Saraçhane* (saddlery) and Çedikçi ('slippermaker') Hafız Hüseyin from Istanbul were accused of being Bektaşis or had 'gone astray on the path of contemporary Bektaşism (*zamane Bektaşiliği yoluna saparak*)' and exiled in 1826 by imperial order to Bayındır (İzmir) and needed to be chastised, that they may 'rehabilitate themselves' (*ıslah-ı nefs*) accordingly. They had opposed the shari'a and 'tread the dark path of unbelief and heresy'. This was previously investigated by the Şeyhülislam and an imperial decree ordered their exile as a measure of discipline. According to this 'benevolent decree' the convicts were sent into exile under the supervision of a *çavuş* ('guard, sergeant') and should not be forgiven unless they 'corrected their beliefs and improved themselves'. They were cautioned, and it was advised that they should 'be caused to renounce their superstitious beliefs in word and deed (*itikadât-ı bâtıla kâlen ve kalben yed-i keff ile ve feragat etdirderek*)' according to the obligations of the shari'a. For this they had to stay in a chamber in the *Fetvahane* ('office of the mufti'), were reminded about actions contrary to the shari'a, and stayed in their place of exile for about 6–7 years performing their ritual prayers and fasting. Eventually, they heeded the cautions and gave up their previous beliefs (*itikad-i sâbıkalarından feragat etmiş*) and followed the path of Sunna and the righteous companions of the Prophet by 'correcting their beliefs'. The mufti of Bayındır, the *medrese* teachers, the ulema, the pious ones (Sunni Sufi leaders?), the imams, the preachers and other Muslims attested at a legal meeting that the two exiles disciplined themselves (*terbiye-i nefs*), followed the way of the shari'a and left their previous wretched condition. As a result, they were worthy to be forgiven and their records in the *Bab-ı Âsafî* ('the office of the prime minister') were deleted. All present in this assembly had signed and sealed the petition asking for the release of the two men.[92]

As a rule, the exiled Bektaşis were accompanied by a *çavuş* (sergeant), as mentioned above, and the officials residing in places at the exile route were advised to assure that no problems occurred. Also, local officials such as the *naib* (judges of lower ranks) and the mufti had the duty of ensuring that the exiles reached their destination. The *naib* was the first to report that this happened, and to settle the exiles and make sure that they stayed. The mufti was commissioned to ensure that the Bektaşis abandoned their old beliefs and rehabilitated themselves by word and deed. The common duty of the *naib* and the mufti was to prevent the exiles from actions contrary to religion (Islam) and not to release them until they rehabilitated themselves.[93]

It seems that Mahmud II silenced the Bektaşis as a potential source of opposition against his politics of centralization, as were the ulema, notables and the janissaries, who had come to control public opinion in Istanbul and take part in 'different agendas of order, reform, and restoration'.[94] Within this larger process of the modernization and centralization of the Ottoman state, powerful independent and semi-independent groups could not coexist.[95]

Even many decades after 1826 when Bektaşism was prohibited, there was much state-sponsored propaganda against the Bektaşis. In the same negative way as Esad Efendi spoke of them, others also reviled them, saying that the Bektaşis were heretics, did not heed the shari'a, and were immoral, womanizers or that some Bektaşis held drinking parties with women in their convents.[96] They would go among the people and spread their unbelief. As late as the 1890s and the 1910s, we have reports and accounts describing the Bektaşis as 'irreligious' and as being in need of rehabilitation.[97] This shows how rigid and long-lasting their persecution by the state was.

However, there were counter measures that the Bektaşis applied in order to escape persecution and survive. They would, for example, change their attire and headdress; Cevdet Paşa notes that because of this there remained no one who could be named 'Bektaşi'. Esad Efendi, Cevdet Paşa and other official historians write that the Bektaşis hid their beliefs and appeared as Sunnis when they were questioned by the Şeyhülislam. Others accepted to be Nakşbendis and escaped exile or came back from their exile as Nakşbendis. Yet others sought refuge in convents of other Sufi orders, mostly Mevlevi, but were cautioned not to wear their Bektaşi attire. There was also mutual influence of ideas between the Bektaşis and other orders. Also, official documents mention Bektaşis who after seeking refuge in Sunni orders, are said to have caused unrest until the beginning of the twentieth century.[98]

Despite all the persecution and propaganda against the Bektaşis, many of them were released from their exile already in the time of Mahmud II and some convents could resume their activities. In the years following the death of Mahmud II in 1839, the prohibition was not as strict as before. During the time of Sultan Abdülmecid the state was more lenient. Sultan Abdülaziz (r. 1861–1876) allowed the Bektaşis to rebuild convents or hold gatherings. Whereas immediately after 1826 Bektaşis were removed from official positions, they could serve as public servants in this period and during the reign of Abdülhamid II.[99] Apart from these developments, in the time of Abdülmecid and afterwards the Bektaşis could publish their works. This way they actively promoted themselves in order to have a positive effect on public opinion.[100] The publication of the biography or *Velayetname* of Hacı Bektaş in 1872 was even announced in a positive fashion in an Ottoman newspaper as 'elucidating the morals and rules' (*âdâb ve erkânını muvazzah*) of his 'exalted orders' [sic! *turuk-i aliyye*] for the purpose of 'dispelling the evil opinions of some ignorant people' (*bazı cehele-i nâsın sû-i zannını dâfi' olmak üzere*).[101]

The Ottoman state's attitude towards Bektaşism changed in the time of Mahmud II and later was ambivalent. While there were strict measures against them, there was also a milder approach to the Bektaşi problem. The state-sponsored 'correction of the belief(s)' of the Bektaşis during the reign of Mahmud II was also not effective because most of the Bektaşis knew how to hide verbally and physically and escape persecution. Bektaşi leaders sent petitions during the Hamidian era, asking for an official recognition of their order, which was declined on the grounds that Mahmud II had forbidden the brotherhood. For this reason, the Bektaşis reopened their convents as Nakşbendi convents.[102] The official prohibition, which had pushed the Bektaşis into hiding first, lasted until the end of the empire but the Bektaşis were visible and active again before that.

The Ottomans, as the other European empires of the time, had a long tradition of controlling or 'containing' groups for the sake of order. As we have seen above, it was about a confessional group in the heart of the empire but this was true also for groups in the peripheries. Maurus Reinkowski calls this 'ethnic containment' of tribal groups or 'ethnic-confessional groups' organized along tribal lines. And this was done through different tactics, from co-optation to brute military force:

The exertion of power was based on the idea of an eternal cycle of justice and the perception that internal eruptions of violence were perennial events, so that security and order would have to be restored again and again. The Ottoman imperial mind thus conceived of an incessant alternation between order and disorder, the ideal of security cum prosperity being always endangered by negative events and evildoers.[103]

He further states that the population was prone to 'sporadic eruptions of violence', unavoidable and to be expected to some extent, and were dealt with by admonition or, as a last resort, with physical violence. After the culprits were punished, 'the equilibrium regained'. It was a concept of imperial rule that was a combination of harshness and leniency in the individual case. In cases of expediency, the Ottoman did not hesitate to exert violence in a large scale.[104] In the next part we will see the adaption of this rule towards various 'ethnic-confessional' groups along tribal lines after the 1840s.

3.3. The 'fine tuning' of the state during the Tanzimat and the reign of Abdülhamid II

After the 1860s the eternal cyclical conception of rule of 'order-disorder-order' of the Ottoman Empire changed drastically to a new notion of order. It partially complemented and partially superseded the old order. The Ottoman state did not feel the need to restore 'an always precarious order' but instead the authorities were firmly resolved to establishing 'a new and final order.'

> The script for this fundamental transformation was written during the Tanzimat, a period of reforms that began with a sultanic proclamation in 1839 and ended officially in 1876. Its intent was to modernize and centralize Ottoman government and society. The Ottomans' attempt to regain control of their peripheral regions was motivated by the enormous financial needs of a modern state with its steadily growing bureaucracy and its array of self-imposed obligations. But it was also in part the consequence of a changing self-perception: The Ottoman Empire had to become a modern imperial nation-state.[105]

When the Ottomans lost many territories in the Balkans during the Ottoman–Russian War in 1877–1878 the attention of Sultan Abdülhamid II, in order to compensate for the losses, concentrated on the Anatolian and Arab provinces where he wanted to reinforce his authority through centralization and education of the peoples there. The educational efforts of the foreigners were therefore a threat to his position and the empire. The provinces of Beirut and Syria became stages on which Abdülhamid and Christian missionaries performed their bitter struggle over the Druze and the Nusayris. This rivalry reflected itself from time to time in diplomatic crises between France, England, America and the Ottomans.

3. Abdülhamid II's Civilizing Mission and the Policy of 'Correction of Belief(s)' 95

Despite the atmosphere of proclaimed religious tolerance in the Ottoman capital with the Tanzimat reforms, the situation in Eastern provinces was quite different. A major example for this was the conflict between the Sunni Ottomans and Shi'is in Iraq. Shi'i clerics were actively proselytizing not only among Sunni tribes but also the Ottoman officials.[106] Despite the Westernizing military and administrative reforms since the late eighteenth century, 'many of the reformers turned at the same time to what they believed to be the Ottoman heyday, the sixteenth century, and its Sunnitization of the state.'[107] The instrumentalization of Sunni Islam as an ideology continued from the Ottoman-Muslim absolutism of Mahmud II into the Tanzimat regime, in the form of an oligarchic bureaucratic absolutism. This was part of a world-wide development when, as expressed by Bayly, 'the nineteenth century saw the triumphal reemergence and expansion of "religion" in the sense in which we now use the term.' He argues that 'new, more aggressive European states and empires, alongside insurgent nationalisms, often promoted religion as their badge of identity even when they spoke of liberalism and science.'[108] The Ottoman state policies of Mahmud II need to be seen in this and the context of centralization for the sake of modernization among European states.

Although most statesmen at the time were Western-minded and moderate Muslims, they found it advisable to abandon the Muslim population to their ignorance and fanaticism. To control the masses, the state used Islam, which should fuel the superstitious beliefs of the people.[109] The aim of Sunnitization was to indoctrinate 'heretical' groups and even nominal Sunnis with the 'orthodox'

Figure 3.1 A Nusayri/Alawi of Antakya

doctrines of the Hanafi legal school. This was done through *tashih-i itikad/akaid*, the 'correction of belief(s)', in other words, a 'fine tuning' of religious beliefs of those who had inherited the idea of Islam from their ancestors and were Muslims merely by name.[110] This 'fine tuning' also concerned the conversion of non-Muslims such as tribes in the Caucasus as I tried to show above. Below I will also deal with the non-Muslim Kurdish Yezidis.

There seem to be fewer efforts with regard to 'correction of beliefs' on a large scale during the reigns of Sultan Abdülmecid and Abdülaziz (r. 1861–1876).[111] During the latter's reign a vital concern in 1870–1871 was to achieve 'alliance and unity' (*ittifak ve ittihad*) among the Muslims (Sunnis) and the Nusayris. Correspondences sent as orders from the Sublime Porte to the governors of Aleppo speak about the Antakya Nusayris' wishes to be together with the Sunnis in the mosques and contain local reactions toward this issue. Some Sunnis had opposed the idea that Nusayris should enter the mosques despite their 'superstitious beliefs'.[112] But the state refused the Sunnis' petitions in order to include the Nusayris into the Muslim community so that they would follow the 'right path'.

In March and May 1870, it was written to the Governor of Aleppo to prevent local reactions against the Nusayris and to explain the benefits of the latter's inclusion into the Muslim community, especially to the prominent and influential Sunnis of Antakya. In fact, in order to discuss the matter with the governor and find a solution, the district governor of Antakya went to Aleppo; in turn, the Mufti of Aleppo Baha Efendi was sent to Antakya to inspect the situation.[113] After these meetings, it was seen that the governor, the district governor and the mufti agreed on endeavouring to solve the issue. Accordingly and for the time being, it would be appropriate to build mosques and schools in the neighbourhoods where the Nusayris lived for the purpose of making them turn away from their own way (*meslek*) and guide them to the 'lawful path' (*tarîk-i meşru'*). And for the 'correction of the beliefs of their children (*çocuklarının dahi tashih-i akaidlerini için*)' these should be sent to the mosques and schools. Imams, preachers and teachers were to be appointed to gradually teach the Nusayris and instil them the Islamic rituals and denominational issues (*şe'air-i İslamiyye ve umûr-i mezhebiyye*) and end their seclusion and ignorance (*hâl-i uzlet ve cehalet*). The purpose of this endeavour, for which were also provided financial resources, was to see Sunnis and Nusayris together in mosques, and to teach and educate them together.[114]

Despite this strong endeavour the desired result could not be achieved in Antakya. In a letter dated 28 July 1870 (28 Rebiülahir 1287) written from the Ministry of the Interior to the Governorate of Aleppo, it was stated that the Nusayris still suffered the same treatment and complained. It was clearly stated to the governor to end this issue of not allowing the Nusayris into mosques in such a way that it should not be further reminded of.[115] Yet, the same issue was raised again by Nusayris in July 1871, and a new proposal was made. Those who sent the petition were the Nusayris residing in the village of Cilliye (Jilliya) near Antakya (wrongly called the 'Ansari tribe'). The villagers complained that they were still not admitted to mosques; they asked to be allowed to be represented by a certain Sheikh Ibrahim who they had chosen; they also wanted three mosques in their own administration.[116]

The governor was reminded that there were some contradictions between the Nusayris and the Sunnis but that the former could not be kept outside the Islamic circle and necessary measures needed to be taken. On the other hand, it is much emphasized in official documents that this region is a very important geography and a separate solution should be found in this regard. According to available documents this issue related to the Nusayris did not seem to have come up for a long time until 1892. Since then there was a continuous process of correspondence relating to finding a solution of this affair.[117]

Another concern during the reign of Abdülaziz was how to bring about reconciliation among the soldiers who belonged to different non-Sunni Islamic groups. In an article titled *İhtiyâcât-ı Askeriyye* ('Military Necessities'), published in the Ottoman newspaper *Hakayık el-Vekayi* in 1871[118] and written in the context of war (*cihad*) against 'infidels and dissenters' (*küffâr ve buğât*), the author highlights that religiously educated persons called *dâi* or 'missionary' (*misyoner*), as Europeans call them, should be sent to the regions where the followers of these divisions (*tefrika*) live. There they should teach Sunni Islam, the 'sound faith' (*akide-i sahiha*). This, in turn, would eliminate the causes for divisions within Islam and ultimately unite the soldiers:

> The Ottoman State accepts soldiers from among the Muslims in Rumelia and Anatolia. Just as the Rafızis [heretics, i.e. Alevis] have been spreading in Rumelia recently, there are different Islamic sects that are outside Sunni Islam (*haric-i ehl-i sünnet bir takım mezahib-i müteferrika-yı İslamiyye*), such as the Alevis in Anatolia who ascribe divinity to Imam Ali and are known as Kızılbaş (*Kızılbaş tabir olunan ve Hazret-i Ali'ye uluhiyet isnad eyleyen Aleviyyûn*),[119] the Yezidis in Kurdistan and the Druze, Nusayris, Metawalis [The Shi'is in Lebanon], Wahhabis, Shi'is, Zaydis, Isma'ilis, and Rafızis in the Arab regions. Although most of the members of these sects [among the soldiers] confirm and acknowledge the glorious martyrdom and holy war [for Islam], there cannot be a unity of hearts (*ittihad-ı kulûb*) due to such divisions; and because these persons will consider the other sects an enemy and look at each other with hate and animosity (*yekdiğerini düşman-ı mezheb add ederek nazar-ı nefret ve husumet ile göreceği cihetle*), it is imperative to strive to wipe out the causes for such divisions within Islam for the sake of unifying the hearts of the soldiers.

> This unity can be achieved by appointing preachers (*hoca*) who are well-versed in religious sciences and partake of the intellectual disciplines (*ulûm-i diniyede mahir ve fünûn-ı akliyeden behremend*), and are able to convince their antagonists (*hasmını ilzama muktedir*) in the regions where the followers of these sects live. And these learned personages who spread the true faith are called *dâi* in our language, which is the equivalent of 'missionary' (*misyoner*) in Europe. Even if there are found enough zealous men, who will be commissioned to spread the true faith and go to distant lands, choose of one's own accord the burden of the voyage and bear such a sacrifice for the sake of religion, the number of such volunteers will not be sufficient even under a special order.

These *dâis* should be so trained that they were acquainted with the books of the respective Islamic sects and be able to write refutations (*reddiyye*), be well versed in preliminary sciences (*mukaddemât-ı fünun*) such as geography and mathematics, should receive a salary during the two years education and schools should be built in Istanbul and other regions where they can study the 'exalted sciences' (*ulûm-i âliyye*), i.e. Islamic branches of knowledge. These missionaries should not only be active in Istanbul but be sent to Ottoman domains where these 'harmful' Islamic sects (*mezahib-i sakime*) were present and even to distant Islamic lands in order to correct the belief of the people, and safeguard Islam from weakness and to fortify its pillars. The outcome of appointing such missionaries would be the reconciliation of the hearts (*ittihad-ı kulûb*) of the Muslims in the 'well-protected' Ottoman domains.[120]

In contrast to the above mentioned rather neutral description of soldiers belonging to non-Sunni groups, a severe portrayal of the Alevi soldiers in the Ottoman army came from the late Ottoman jurist and writer Mehmed Arif (d. 1897).[121] He states in his memoirs *Başımıza Gelenler* ('What we went through')[122] about the Ottoman–Russian War of 1877–1878 (called '93 Harbi' due to the corresponding Islamic year 1293) that the reason for the corruption of the Ottoman Muslim soldiers' hearts was that they did not belong to one religious school (*mezheb*). Even if they had (typical Muslim) names such as Ahmed, Mehmed, Ali or Hüseyin, they belonged to different sects. This difference of sects (*ihtilaf-ı mezâhib*) did not mean that they belonged to the 'true Islamic schools' (*mezahib-i sahihe-i İslamiye*) such as the Shafi'i or Hanafi schools. In his opinion one fourth of the troops consisted of individuals who were on different paths, being Shi'is, Bektaşis and some akin to polytheism (*putperestliğe şebih*) far outside Sunni Islam; others were serving a 'composite and special creed' (*itikad-ı mürekkeb ve mahsus*) consisting of all these beliefs. In former times these people were political missionaries of states such as the Iranian Safavis who wanted to create disunity among the Muslims. Even if these irreligious people (*melahide*) did not exist anymore, the seeds of contention they had sewn were yielding fruit. What is more, the soldiers belonging to heretical sects were all serving the state out of fear and not owing to a sense of duty; for them, serving the Ottoman State was unjust and so they did it in a perfunctory manner (*angarya*). They cursed the Sunnis and wished the annihilation of the Empire. To them the Russians were more religious than the Sunnis; they deserted the military and escaped because their lives were precious. In Anatolia these irreligious people were sometimes called *Kızılbaş*, *Çerapof*,[123] *Vazalak*[124] or *Sofî*.[125] Mehmed Arif states that he devoted several pages to the elaboration of these creeds in his book *Binbir Hadis-i Şerif* ('One Thousand and One Hadiths') when discussing the hadith 'The believers are like a structure, each one strengthening the other (*al-mu'min li'l-mu'min ka'l-bunyan, yashuddu ba'dahu ba'dan*)'.[126]

Mehmed Arif urged the Sublime State to categorically prevent the ignorance of those ignorants with severe and effective measures (*bu cahillerin izale-i cehaletleri emrinde tedabir-i şedide ve müessire*), in order to ensure an important part of the defence against 'our enemies'. He attached utmost importance to the educative role of the officers (*zabit*) in times of war because through their staunchness the soldiers would not desert the army, even if their hearts were full of satanic delusions. Mehmed Arif's description of these 'heretics' can be seen as part of the Ottoman discourse in the nineteenth century by bureaucrats who felt the need to report them to Istanbul.

The fight against all forms of 'ignorance' was the aim of the Ottomans in later decades. During the latter part of the reign of Abdülhamid II when Sunni Islam was politicized for the imperial ideology called 'unity of Islam' (*ittihad-ı İslam*, 'Pan-Islam') in order to strengthen the position of the sultan as caliph, to preserve the empire that was falling apart, and thus stabilize the state structure.[127] Many bureaucrats composed and send *layiha*s (memorandum, formal petition) to Istanbul about political, economic, administrative or military shortcomings in the Ottoman domains and recommended solutions and reforms for these. Many of these petitions were observations in the hinterland, the *terra incognita*, about peoples who were regarded as backward. The aim of these memoranda was to 'release the people from the darkness of ignorance and bring them into the circle of civilization and happiness'. Since the reforms before and during the Tanzimat period aimed at centralizing the power of the state or the sultan, many of the memoranda were concerned with importing the central authority to the midst of peoples and tribes in the 'outback' of the Empire who were deemed 'disobedient'. This was true for tribes in the Balkans, Arab provinces, and the Kurds in the East. Not only should the tribes be settled but at the same time it was necessary to prevent alliances between tribes, weaken the position of their leaders and ultimately abolish their supremacy. According to the modern and rationalist imperial administration in the nineteenth century the *layiha*s depicted the social, cultural, economic and religious conditions of the peoples in those critical regions at the Ottoman 'frontier' and at the same time proposed that 'rebellious and savage tribes' or 'disobedient people' needed to be 'civilized' (*temdin*), their 'savagery abolished' (*izale-i vahşet*) and their superstitious and wrong 'beliefs corrected' (*tashih-i itikad*).[128]

As much as Ottoman intellectuals in Anatolia looked with disdain on the tribes there, intellectuals from southern Albania (Tosks), who played an enormous role in the Ottoman army and administration, despised the tribes of northern Albania (Ghegs). A tribal school set up there as part of the Ottoman centralization by Abdülhamid II was for the regulation of correction of 'wildness', 'ignorance' and the lack of civilization. This is aptly illustrated in a play written by the famed Ottoman Albanian intellectual Şemseddin Sami (Frasheri).[129] It describes quite vividly 'the level of social and intellectual disdain the sophisticated and highly educated aristocracy of the Empire, which included a great many southern Albanians had for the unsavory mountain Albanians'. The play shows the social contrast between the feudal North with its 'primitive' traditions such as blood feuds that did not allow the state to interfere and the South with its 'self-perceived world of civilization' as represented by the reformer Şemseddin Sami. The elimination of tribal customs of the northern Albanians and 'moral and cultural restructuring projects' were target of the Ottoman tribal schools.[130]

Hasan Bedreddin (Bedri) Paşa,[131] the military governor of İşkodra/Shkoder in Albania from 1909 to 1911, remarked with regard to the rebellion of the Albanian highlanders (Malisors) that their ancient traditional and unwritten law ('Law of

Lek') was 'definitely incompatible with modern civilization'. Bedri further stated that the Malisors 'until now have not been able to taste the pleasures of justice and civilization, just as they have been completely deprived of the good fortune of education'. Since they were not familiar with 'modern law', they would resist the state. Hence, the Ottoman state should first strengthen its gendarmerie and then, through special commissions, establish central control among them.[132] In addition to this, Bedri suggested that the state should provide scholarships to several sons of tribal leaders as a measure of indoctrination on the 'road to civilization' (*tarik-i medeniyet*).[133]

Another group in the Balkans that was in the attention of the Ottoman state were the Gypsies, a 'group in motion', who were labelled as an 'ignorant group' (*taife-i cahile*) in the 'lowest' (*esfel*) state. Despite their having been honoured with the 'glory of Islam', they were not taught Islamic morals and religious duties (*âdâb-ı İslamiyye ve ferâiz-i diniyye talim edilmemek oldukdan*). In the late nineteenth century one of the most significant concerns of the late Ottoman state was to 'reform' (*ıslah*) the Gypsies. Constant attempts were being made to deconstruct, normalize and eliminate differences of Gypsies, for instance, appointing imams to the Gypsy neighbourhoods to 'correct' their faith or opening new schools to 'save' them from ignorance and poverty they lived in. This way the late Ottoman state attempted to 'civilize' the Gypsies, i.e. make them be good Muslims, and regarded the activities of English Protestant missionaries as a threat.[134]

The late Ottoman memoranda, as in the case of the Kurdish tribes in Dersim, do not seem to be written from an objective point of view because they are based on the personal observations of the writers, statements of people who were oppressed by others or manipulative reports of notables who wanted to discredit other tribes. What is striking in the memoranda is that they do not write about the state and tribes in a generalizing manner of a dichotomy of 'good' and 'bad'. The relations between the two were too complex and multi-layered as to speak from the viewpoint of constant clash or reconciliation, and depended on time and space. In order to preserve hegemony in the region at times certain tribes allied with external powers such as the state against other tribes, following the maxim of 'my enemy's enemy is my friend'. The Ottoman state sometimes relied on tribes as potential allies for the realization of centralist reforms. In a time when the Ottoman Empire was losing territories in the Balkans, it was in need of the incomes from other regions in Anatolia, the Arab provinces and North Africa; for this the state applied its centralist policies to the unsettled people.[135] If we take into consideration the forced population movements and reform policies after the beginning of the Tanzimat period in Anatolia and the Arab provinces, the 'Dersim question' does not stand as an isolated event of this sort. 'This ethnographic curiosity', as Türkyılmaz puts it, 'was new and full of prejudices against this "heretic" [sic] community. It was not just the secular bureaucracy but the religious cadres that also thought it was their duty to help the state in its struggle against the enemies of the religion.'[136]

Among the *layiha*s sent to Istanbul there were many from Syria and Iraq. The famous Süleyman Hüsnü Paşa (d. 1892),[137] one of the main actors in the deposition of Sultan Abdülaziz in 1876, wrote an extensive and detailed report/petition (24 pages) in 1892 from his political exile in Iraq.[138] It relates to measures that he proposed to integrate diverse 'heretical' groups – these included the Wahhabis, Twelver Shi'is (Usuli, Akhbaris and Shaykhis), Aliyullahis, Yezidis, Sabians,[139] and the Babis (Baha'is) – into the official belief. He offers a breakdown of the complex ethnic (Turks, Kurds and Arabs) and religious elements in the provinces of Mosul, Basra and Baghdad and then comments as follows: 'As can be seen from the above the elements belonging to the official faith and language of the state are in a clear minority (*akalliyet*) whereas the majority (*ağlabiyet*) falls to the hordes of the opposition.'[140] He remarks that the conversion and guidance to Islam alongside the correction of the beliefs of misguided sects such as the various Shi'i branches, Wahhabis, Yezidis and Babis[141] 'is quite easy' (*ihda ve irşad ile tashih-i akideleri pek kolay*). This would be a most appropriate and utterly blessed service to the caliph of all Muslims.[142] The remedy would be a systematic propaganda and the 'correction of the beliefs' of deviant sects. Süleyman Hüsnü put forward the idea that the Ottoman state should sponsor the writing of a book called *Book of Beliefs* (*Kitabü'l-Akaid*), consisting of fifteen chapters and each dealing with one group. It should be a specific rebuttal to be used 'to correct the beliefs of misguided Islamic sects (*fırak-ı dâlle-i İslamiye'nin akidelerini tashihan*)'. For this, a 'missionary society' (*dâiyân cemiyeti, dâi-misyoner cemiyeti*) consisting of well-trained ulema should be formed, and they should scrutinize the 'unsound beliefs (*akaid-i sakime*)' of these sects. After two to three years training, they would be awarded the title *dâi ilâ'l-hak misyoner*[143] ('missionary calling to the Truth')[144] and be commissioned to correct the beliefs of misguided Islamic sects.[145] 'Religious uniformity was thus seen as a means by which normative standards of behaviour could be imposed on the population.'[146] This was an urgent necessity since those who adhered to the official Hanafi branch were in a minority among the Sunnis of Iraq. The inhabitants all together consisted of twenty different religious groups speaking one or more of the four languages: Kurdish, Turkish, Arabic and Armenian.

Another similar but much shorter petition (two pages) from May 1892 was sent to the Ottoman capital by the then prime minister Ahmed Cevad Paşa.[147] Like Süleyman Hüsnü Paşa he proposes measures in order to thwart the efforts of Shi'i ulema who tried to convert people to Shi'ism.[148] The prime minister also talks about the ethnic, religious and linguistic divisions of Iraq and highlights the importance of the publication of a *Book of Beliefs* (*Kitabü'l-Akaid*) that would be written by ten to fifteen ulema and contain chapters for each of the above-mentioned communities in order to refute the beliefs of heretics such as the Shi'is, the Babis, the Nusayris, the Bektaşis, the Yezidis, Druze, Sufis and Wahhabis. In line with Süleyman Hüsnü Paşa, Cevad Paşa was convinced that 'misguided sects' such as the Wahhabis, Yezidis and Babis could be converted and guided (*ihda ve irşad*) and their beliefs corrected (*tashih-i akide*).[149] The book would not only 'correct the beliefs (*tashih-i itikad*)' of those communities but also prevent the 'mischief' (*ifsadât*) of Protestant missionaries[150] who were active among heterodox groups (see below).

In line with other writers' proposals during that time, in Süleyman Paşa's view the cure for the problem of religious unorthodoxy was proper education. By bringing back primary and secondary schooling into the Sunni Hanafi fold all would be saved: 'The spread of education will instil the love of religion (*din*), country (*vatan*), and nationality (*milliyet*), as well as strengthening the salutary allegiance of the people to our Master the Caliph of all Muslims. While the persistence of ignorance will only increase and intensify disunity and disintegration.'[151] It is noteworthy that Süleyman Hüsnü Paşa talks here about novel ideas such loyalty to the 'country' and 'nationality' at the same time as he mentions the classical Islamic idea of allegiance to the caliph. What's more, he borrows and appreciates the European idea of missionary activity at a time when it was an aspect of political power.[152] It appears that as a result of petitions such as that of Süleyman Hüsnü it became practice after 1892 during the Hamidian reign that Sunni preachers and missionaries were allowed to practice with a diploma after a four-year period; these individuals were then ready to take their 'teaching posts' at schools (*medrese*s) in the provinces among 'marginals'.[153] They received a diploma from the Şeyhülislam. Apparently, this policy was implemented throughout the Hamidian era. In 1902 the office of Şeyhülislam wrote to the palace, reporting that the latest crop of 'missionaries' (*da'iyan*) had graduated from their special *medrese*s and were ready to take up teaching posts in the provinces. The sultan paid one thousand liras out of his own purse to be apportioned among the teachers alongside a monthly salary of 150 *kuruş* (piasters).[154]

At a time when emphasis on orthodoxy was pronounced, the Hamidian administration directed its attention to the Kızılbaş-Alevis. A local governor instructed that these people should be 'rescued from their ignorance and shown the high path of enlightenment'. For this, it should appoint preachers and distribute religious catechisms. At the same time, the imams in these villages needed to be summoned to the provincial capital where they were to be 'trained' in the local secondary school. In addition, Sunni 'advisors' (sg. *nâsih*) were to be sent to the villages for longer periods, as 'if they are left in the villages for some time they can be more effective in saving these poor pagans who have not had their share of salvation'. In keeping with official instructions, all effort was being made to establish new style schools in Alevi villages and to train *imams* as instructors. Their aim was to rescue the young 'from the pit of sin and educate them into abandoning their fathers' beliefs'.[155]

The Ottoman state was concerned with the situation of the Alevis even as late as in 1920 during the final dissolution of the Empire after WWI and its occupation by the Allied Forces. In this specific case, the overall question was how to give Islamic education to the people of seventy villages out of ninety in the district of Keban (Mamuretülaziz/Elazığ) in Eastern Anatolia that were *rafızi*, 'heretical', i.e., Alevi, and whose imams and teachers were mostly from among the 'ignorants' (*cehele*). In a letter the şeyhülislam at that time, Ibrahim Haydarizade,[156] emphasized the need for trained mobile (*seyyar*) preachers and imams who should go to those villages, stay there and 'correct the false beliefs' of the Alevis and so draw them closer to the 'path of truth'. In order to dismiss this 'calamity that emerges in some locations in Anatolia and is obviously not congruent with the religiosity and civilization of the present age' (*Anadolu'nun böyle bazı mahallerinde zuhura gelen asr-ı hâzır diyanet ve medeniyeti ile bittabi kâbil-i te'lif olmayan bu beliyyenin*), the Ministry of Education should provide the means for inculcating Islamic principles through the instruction of religious sciences by those 'able' imams and preachers.[157] As we can see from this example at a later time, the issue of inculcating Islam as an ideology was not peculiar to Abdülhamid and his officials.

The fact Alevi villages in Anatolia did not have any mosques or maybe a few is not as surprising as it seems. This was also true for Sunni villages in Syria or Palestine, as the great Arab Ottoman scholar Abd al-Ghani al-Nabulsi (1643–1731) had observed on his tour in Palestine (1690). As much as research on the Middle East has tended to argue that institutional religion prevailed everywhere, the question is how successful it was at imposing itself on the majority of the people.[158] We see this exemplified here in the case of non-Sunni groups living in rural areas.

It is worth mentioning that during his era Abdülhamid was not alone in proselytizing and 'civilizing' the subjects who were regarded as nominal Muslims or non-Sunnis. There were also the efforts of the long-standing Muslim university of al-Azhar in Cairo. According to a missionary journal, the 'great university' was the 'citadel' of Egypt, the 'stronghold of Islam', with Turkey being its political centre and Arabia its religious centre. Every year Al-Azhar drew students from all over the world and sent hundreds of 'missionaries' as propagandists of their faith. Everything from science to religion centred around, firstly, the Qur'an and secondly, Arabic, which was a dominant subject and part of the religion. The missionaries had to admit that theirs was not an easy task to face Islam but thought they would still be brave enough for this:

> Far from being a vestibule to Christianity, this study of the Koran teaches the student at Al Azhar that the Christian Gospels have been corrupted, that Christ was never crucified, and that Christianity is the great hindrance to the spread of Islam, the one true religion. Accordingly, the attack on the outworks of Islam seems comparatively fruitless, when the citadel is left untouched; and those on the spot long for the advent of a band of university men of spiritual and intellectual power, the Henry Martyns of our day, who shall study Arabic and Islam at its fountainhead, and turn upon the enemy his own weapons. The difficulties are great, but the idea and the prospect are attractive to Christian chivalry.[159]

During the Hamidian period, there was a wide range of concepts or terminology used in the Hamidian period as measures of the Islamization of marginal groups. For instance, the Yezidi tribes in Şeyhan, who 'corrected the beliefs' (*tashih-i akaid*) and the children of Shi'is in villages near Mosul who accepted the Hanafi doctrine, needed copies of the Qur'an, books to teach them the alphabet and Islamic principles.[160] The Yezidis of Mosul wanted to 'correct the belief and the doctrine' (*tashih-i itikad ve mezheb*) and convert to Sunni Islam[161] and the beliefs of 'heretical' groups in Iraq needed to be corrected (*tashih-i akide*).[162] The Nusayri population of Latakia accepted the Hanafi creed through 'correction of the religion and change of the belief' (*tashih-i din ve tebdil-i itikad*),[163] and following the 'correction of the religion and belief' (*tashih-i din ve itikad*) of the Nusayris in the Nusayriyya mountains near Latakia a mosque and a school needed to be constructed.[164] In order to prevent the 'mischief' and the 'deception' of the Kızılbaş and other 'ignorants ones' (*cehele*), some precautionary measures were proposed to 'reform the beliefs' (*ıslah-ı akaid*) of those.[165] And in order to 'purify the minds' the state spoke of *tasfiye-i ezhan*[166] and bringing 'heretics' and nomadic people back to a civilized life needed the 'wiping out of savagery' (*izale-i vahşet*),[167] describing the mentality in which these people were the officials used, e.g., 'ignorant wickedness' (*faziha-yı cahilâne*),[168] and labelled their beliefs as 'superstitious beliefs' (*itikad-ı bâtıla*)[169] or 'unlawful path' (*tarik-i gayr-ı meşru*).[170] The Ottoman state used this vocabulary to describe people who needed to be 'civilized' or whose religious beliefs required a 'fine tuning'.

As much as the Nusayri community was perceived negatively owing to a 'secrecy' and was attributed deficiency, this kind of 'gap' or 'lack' was also applied in an equal fashion to the Yezidis. This had its consequences for the way local and Western outsiders presented the Yezidis themselves. Many Westerners assumed that the Yezidis were either mentally or spiritually deficient, had 'an unbelievable slowness of mind', were 'heathen', or a 'great lewdness' was 'said to prevail within their own community'. These kinds of remarks were often a reflection of local prejudices about the Yezidis that influenced modern local discourses. 'Because of the dynamics of Orientalism, the writings of Western scholars, diplomats and travellers of the past two centuries have had a disproportionate influence on discourses of identity in the Middle East, providing both minorities and governments with some of their most powerful images.'[171]

This was in a time in which the Ottoman state tried to consolidate its power and political legitimacy in the empire's 'Wild East', and was labelled as late Ottoman 'colonialism/orientalism'[172] or 'Ottoman borrowed colonialism'.[173] It is important to point out here, however, that this concept as presented by some historians of the late Ottoman Empire has serious handicaps. As a critic of this concept remarks:

> [T]his concept is based on the presumption that the Ottoman attempts for Westernization resulted in the emergence of Western modes of thinking with regard to the concepts of civilization and the Orient. In other words, according to the defenders of the 'Ottoman Orientalism' argument, the Ottoman search for the adoption of Western civilization consolidated the perception of inevitability of Westernization. Presuming themselves as 'civilized' in Western terms, the Ottomans began to reflect their Orient as an 'uncivilized' region and tried to project their civilizational development over these backward territories in the form of a *civilizing mission*.

However, this kind of concept is generalizing and regards the East as monolithic. Even if one cannot deny the existence of a 'quasi-Orientalist' mode of thinking in the writings of some Ottoman intellectuals regarding the Ottoman Orient, these perceptions cannot be generalized in order to maintain that the Ottoman intellectual and bureaucratic elite were entirely Orientalist.[174]

Scholarship on 'Ottoman colonialism' is generally based on the conditions of the Arab provinces (Iraq, Syria and Palestine) and the Kurdish regions of the empire. Selim Deringil also provides examples from Libya, Hijaz and Yemen. He claims that 'the Ottoman elite conflated the ideas of modernity and colonialism, and applied the latter as means of survival against an increasingly hostile world', and 'adopted the mindset of their enemies, the arch-imperialists, and came to conceive of its periphery as a colonial setting'. Although suggesting the difference with the British or French experience, by arguing that the Ottoman population had a far greater negotiating power, Deringil has focused on the Ottoman elite's use of the 'civilizing motif'. He points out their attitude of 'moral superiority', leading to a position of 'moral distance', and a perception of 'them' and 'us' among the ruling elite.[175] However, there are also examples of this 'civilizing mission' and 'moral superiority' for core provinces in the heart of Anatolia, such as the large Konya and Ankara provinces or Trabzon at the Black Sea, where the population was deemed as having strayed from 'true Islam'; this shows that these elite feelings amongst the Ottoman administrative class cannot be confined to their deployment in colonialist situations in Arab lands.[176]

The implications of 'civilizing' the 'uncivilized' or 'barbarous' people at the fringes of the Empire invites comparisons with the history of Latin American states where the leaders and the urban elite depicted themselves as waging a similar struggle against the peoples in their hinterlands. As John Curry points out, in contrast to the anti-clericalism of the liberal Latin American elites, the Ottoman officials framed the dichotomy between 'civilization' and 'barbarism' in the form of religious reform, which 'just happened to intersect with the pacification and centralisation goals of the Ottoman state'. Yet, the goals of the two elites were different: whereas the Latin American elites wanted their states to get closer to European modernization, the Ottomans maintain their cultural and religious distinctiveness and avoided being swallowed up by Europe. Both the Ottoman bureaucrats and their counterparts in Latin America had the same rhetorical frameworks deriving from the Enlightenment but were prevented by the same limitations at the local level. 'One is struck by the degree to which local actors could manipulate and exploit the state's desires to arrogate resources and support to their own position.'[177] There are other ample examples for other late Ottoman contexts in which officials acted in this way.[178]

Overall, in order to supervise reforms, observe local and regional needs directly, and find solutions to problems and abuses, it was the habit of province governors to 'make a tour' in search for prosperity and progress. The reports and petitions of governors contain discussions on modernization and the 'civilizing mission' of the regime of Abdülhamid II. Education was regarded as an important tool for affecting society at the 'uncivilized' hinterland.

The same line of unrelenting criticism was picked up by Mehmet Şemsettin Günaltay (1883–1961), a conservative and nationalist/Turkist scholar (historian) and politician of the late Ottoman Empire and the early Turkish Republic, who also was prime minister in 1949–1950.[179] Günaltay had a general negative approach towards groups that originated from Shi'i Islam in Iran, including the Alevis, the

Druze, the Ismaʻilis and the Nusayris, in sum called *rafızi* ('heretics'), as opposed to 'true Islam' in Anatolia. He wrote in his book titled *Hurafâtdan Hakikate* ('From Superstitions to the Truth')[180] that the 'gang' (*güruh*) called *Ali-ilahî* (also *abede-i Ali*, 'Ali-worshippers'), had put forward a 'strange and primitive belief that is no doubt the rabble of superstitions of former centuries' (*şu garib ve ibtidai akide aʻsâr-ı maziyyeye aid hurafelerin süprüntüsü olduğuna şübhe yokdur*). These 'rogues' behaved that extremely in their 'brutishness' as to worship people like themselves (*kendileri gibi bir insanı maʻbud ittihaz edecek hayvanlıkda ileri gitmiş olan bu derbederler*) and believed that Ali had sent the prophet Muhammad.[181] His criticism of the Alevis goes as far as depicting them as 'bloodthirsty people' who would even roast their enemies, the Sunnis, alive (!).[182] Günaltay quotes in his book from the said memoirs of Mehmed Arif who regarded the Alevis as traitors deserting the military and thought that the Sunnis, foremost the Ottomans, were infidels.[183] Günaltay labels them, too, with the negative titles *Vazalak* and *Sofu* and states that the description of Arif written thirty-five years ago was still valid and exemplary for the *rafızi* in his time.[184] They were even more steeped in dark ignorance and hatred towards Sunnis, and their leaders and elders (*dede, şeyh, bey, ağa, seyyid*) persistently instigated this.[185]

To Günaltay's regret, as much as a part of the people in Anatolia belonged to the Sunni creed, these 'wretched ones were totally ignorant, inattentive of the Islamic principles, so unconscious that they regarded sloth and misery as religious necessities, and shunned innovations' (*irfanca bütün manâsıyla cahil, esasât-ı âliyye-i islamiyyeden gafil, atalet ve sefaleti icabât-ı diniyyeden add edecek kadar vukûfsuz, yeniliğe karşı son derece mütehâşi zavallılar*), the other part of the population were *rafızi* who were saturated with the superstitions of the mystics, i.e. 'heretics' (*batinîler*), even more ignorant than the Sunnis, less attached to the state and the nation (*devlet ve millet*) and, even though looking like humans, deprived of positive human traits (*şekillerinden başka insanlıklarına delâlet edecek mezayâdan mahrum*).[186] In his estimation, the Nusayris belonged to this category as well. They had 'coloured their ancient legends and superstitions with the colours of Islam and Christianity, achieved strange results', and believed that divinity and the prophetic office (*uluhiyet ve nübuvvet*) reincarnated in various figures in religious history. Among their beliefs one could find Sabian superstitions, Zoroastrian legends and Christian weirdness, which manifested itself in their extreme Shiʻi (*gulât*) creed.[187] In addition, Günaltay writes that whereas Nusayrism is akin to the Druze belief, the latter attach utmost important to chastity and the Nusayris not. He thereby uncritically adopts the notion that Nusayrism belongs to the *Ibahi* sect[188] (a sect of libertines who consider all things lawful), so much so that the Nusayri women offer themselves sexually to the Nusayri sheikhs as a sign of faith.[189] He is equally wrong by stating that the Nusayri religious mass is very much similar to that of the Anatolian *rafızi*, i.e. Alevis.[190] Overall, Günaltay's works are full of descriptions about ignorance and 'true belief' in Anatolia/Turkey. This concern extended from the nineteenth century well into the Republican era with people like Günaltay sowing the seeds of hatred towards non-Sunni groups.

3.4. Fighting for the Nusayri soul in the Hamidian era

The modernist/western educational reforms that started during the period of Mahmud II and continued during the reign of Sultan Abdülaziz, reached its peak during the reign of Abdülhamid II. During this period the state endeavoured to create a centralized system of educational affairs which had developed irregularly until then; schools were opened all over the country and efforts were made that public education would reach remote villages. On the other side, Christian missionaries of all sorts had similar efforts; from the second half of the nineteenth century there were not only Armenians and Greeks who belonged to the Eastern Churches among the target groups of the missionaries that spread rapidly in the Ottoman lands. Whether or not seen as part of the Muslim community, non-Sunni groups such as the Nusayris and Druze, who were generally disobedient towards the state authority, have also been among the target groups of the missionaries. We observe that in this period the missionaries entered into a rapid schooling activity especially in the Nusayri regions. Against this, the Ottoman State opened schools and started an educational mobilization in almost every place where the Nusayris lived.

According to an analysis of the educational facilities in Syria in a Prussian (German) newspaper, published in December 1878, the Ottoman government, even though it put less or no obstacles for the improvement of the education and teaching of its Christian subjects in Syria through foreign means, the promotion of these efforts was limited to allowing churches, monasteries and schools to import duty-free items necessary for their purposes and maintenance. These privileges dated back to ancient times. They were first given to the monasteries in the Holy Land and the Franciscan order in Syria and Palestine more than a hundred years ago, and were later demanded by all religious communities from the government as an equally due right for their pious and charitable foundations and educational institutions, which the Ottomans then granted to all of them. The government had recently begun to limit the number of foreign schools in the country, and sub-authorities received orders that have given them permission to open new schools only with the approval of the higher authority, which was difficult and time-consuming to obtain. The newspaper argued: 'Fear of proselytizing does not seem to be the reason for these measures. Rather, the opposition to the establishment of schools is particularly evident in those districts whose inhabitants only adhere to those religions that are despised by the Musselmans [sic, Muslims], such as those of Ansarians and Druze, and in which schools are completely lacking and the inhabitants live there with the greatest ignorance.'[191]

It seems that the Ottoman government did not fear the educational motivations of long-established Christian missions among Ottoman Christians but at the same time did now allow foreign missionaries on Ottoman soil to establish their schools among 'heretical' religious communities due to the fear of proselytising efforts among those. Since this estimation is from the first years of the reign of Abdülhamid II, we may infer that the sultan wanted to limit the activities of Christian missionaries among non-Sunni Islamic communities at an early stage.

The Ottoman state extended its 'civilizing mission' through education to all ethnic and religious groups in the peripheries; these needed to submit to obeying the sultan as the only authority. The Nusayris were the target of different Ottoman policies. The maltreatment of the Nusayris by the population and the authorities in the nineteenth century had aroused the compassion of Protestant missionaries who tried to convert them. As analysed above, the Protestant missionary movement was commenced for religious purposes first, i.e., the evangelization of the world. On the whole the missionary project was not successful, at least it was interrupted by the Ottoman government from time to time; a few schools of the Syrian mission were closed down in the late 1880s until the early 1890s,[192] at the height of Sultan Abdülhamid II's power.

Mehmed Ziya Bey,[193] the local governor (*mutasarrıf*) of Latakia from 1885–1892, is reported to have barred Protestant missionary work on behalf of the Ottoman government. Writing in November 1891, a missionary in Latakia stated that he 'is doing all he can to hinder our work, seizing Mission property..., turning our teachers out of doors and threatening them if they will not leave our employ.'[194] The missionaries protested the closing of the schools, saying that it was illegal because the Nusayris were 'pagans' and not Muslims.[195] What was injustice to the missionaries was justice to the Nusayris, and deviant or heretical, for the Ottomans the Nusayris were still Muslims.

After decades of Ottoman oppression by several governors until the 1880s, efforts were made later that decade to better their condition,[196] though not out of sheer benevolence but as serving the centralisation policy of Abdülhamid II. A report dated 22 September 1890[197] by a certain Hakkı stipulated that services needed to be offered to the Nusayris of Latakia who had become Hanafi-Sunnis. It is worth dwelling upon the contents of this important document since it highlights the observations of the local administration in Latakia and offers analyses of the situation in the region with regard to the Protestant missionaries. The Nusayri community, ever since wandering in the 'valley of error', accepted Islam (*minelkadim vadi-yi dalaletde bulunan Nusayri cemaatinin din-i mübin-i Muhammedi'yi kabul eylemesi*), and because of the geographic importance of the Nusayri Mountains and its people being not certain about their religious beliefs, England exerted much zeal and effort to convert them to Protestantism; previously, the English ambassador Henry Layard had asked for permission to send missionaries and so displayed his country's utmost degree of political enterprise.

Now the Nusayris were honoured with becoming Muslims and England's enterprise was made impossible but it was not enough that the Nusayris had accepted Islam; it was necessary to attract 'some irresolute religious groups (*bir takım mütereddid cemaatleri*)' to Islam through the example of the Nusayris who should be encouraged and whose faith could be consolidated through appropriate Islamic education. The Nusayris and similar communities were ruled by their sheikhs; these should be given ranks and medals and state-owned estates, as to encourage other vacillating communities to choose Islam and not Christianity and so follow the Nusayris' example.

The Nusayris should be educated and instructed by building them mosques and schools; however, since Sultan Abdülhamid II's accession to the throne the

Ministry of Education had not done substantial work, despite imperial edicts. The money from the education budget was not used, only money from 'extinct endowments' was spent (*evkaf-ı münderise*, i.e., endowments that lost their functions due to improper use and were then assigned to the Ministry of Education);[198] but since this money was usurped by many notables in the region and kept for themselves, the villages, towns and cities were deprived of schools and thus Muslim children from education. Out of more than 150 schools only four were opened and the establishment of the remainder was not even hoped. Accordingly, in order to open schools for the Nusayris the Ministry of Education was not to be asked but a special official appointed by the sultan should be sent to the region to inspect the need for schools and so facilitate the project and increase the loyalty of the Nusayris towards the sultan. In every Nusayri village a primary school (*ibtidai*) for boys should be opened, in order to be prepared for the high school (*rüşdiye*) they should be educated in the preliminary sciences, religious knowledge, the Ottoman and Arabic languages and the teachers from Beirut and other places be properly trained and be good Muslims with high ethical standard. In one or two Nusayri villages large *ibtidai* schools, attached to the sultan and paid by him, should be opened and the children there educated for free, so that their gratitude towards him will increase. The acquisition of knowledge of the pupils shall be observed and it will be seen how they will be more attached to the sultan. The expenses would not exceed the sum of one thousand liras per year. All in all, schools should be set up so that these people would not be dependent on foreigners.

Furthermore, a military school should be built in one of the towns so that the Nusayris be trained and could join the army. It would be beneficial in many ways to train some Nusayri officers and to grant to the sheikhs titles and show them respect. In order not to alarm the Nusayris, not all of them should be conscripted but in the beginning only some should be trained and educated as officers/soldiers, in order to be cautious.

It was a known fact, so the author Hakkı says, that the British were the protégées of the Druze who lived in close proximity of the Nusayris and claimed to be Muslims even though they were not, and that the Nusayris were looked upon by the British in the same way. Now that the Nusayris became Muslims, the intervention of the British was not acceptable at all, and if the Nusayris were not treated in a special way by the sultan and the officials in the Ottoman provinces did not show them the behaviour they show towards the Muslims, the Nusayris would naturally regret that they were not protected by Britain and this would also have a negative effect on the Druze. In order to prevent other communities accepting Islam, the British would instigate Ottoman officials to agitate Nusayris and so attract these to their side.

If properly treated the Nusayris would be inclined to the benevolence and protection of the sultan and show respect to some Ottoman notables, and this would cause their real love and loyalty to Islam and no doubt be an example for the Druze and similar groups in accepting Islam too.[199]

Similarly, Ismail Kemal Bey,[200] governor general of Beirut from 1890–92, writes that he was struck by the injustices done to the Nusayris when he was inspecting the hinterland of Latakia and so introduced measures to appease them. It is worthwhile to fully quote him on this issue, as it serves as an example of the centralization policy of Abdülhamid II:

> These mountaineers were as a race remarkable for their physical beauty, but, having been the objects of persistent persecution for centuries, they naturally felt but little sympathy for their neighbours. Rigorous measures had frequently to be taken against them by the Government; and every time there was need of repressive measures, these were accompanied by severity out of proportion to their misdeeds, and most of them, who took refuge in inaccessible mountains, lost their properties. When they returned after a certain length of time, these properties were returned to them, though they were no longer considered as the owners, but as tenants, and were compelled to pay rent. What was still worse was that these tenants of their own lands were forced into the bargain to pay taxes, like the actual proprietors! On learning the facts, I took steps to remedy this deplorable state of affairs by restoring their lands to them, and ordering the local authorities to treat them more justly in future, which I was sure would not only render them more contented, but would go far towards attaching them to the Government.[201]

The Latakia region was to be a 'high-profile case' for carrying out the Ottomans' 'benevolent reforms'.[202] Their 'imperial reformation' in this period was not to bring liberty to subjects but to tighten the grip on them even more and firmly attach them to the central power.[203] In order to prevent missionary work among heterodox groups Abdülhamid II pursued counter-propaganda through the establishment of Muslim schools and mosques in non-Sunni areas. These were means of a 'civilizing mission' by which 'heretics' should be converted to the Hanafi-Sunni School. A policy of reward and punishment or the 'carrot or stick' method was applied.[204] Whereas sometimes brutal methods and systematic repression were used 'to correct the ignorance and heresy of these people', often education and persuasion were applied as a 'defensive weapon' against the imminent threat to the unity and integrity of the Ottoman Empire posed by these unorthodox communities.[205]

That Sunni education as counter-propaganda was favoured instead of forceful measures is attested in the context of the conversion of Shi'is in Iraq. Broad exposure to the Sunni teachings in order to avert the spread of Shi'ism, because of 'ignorance' among the people, was seen as a remedy. Interestingly, Ottoman official documents mention that the education policy was more respectful, 'because, as a rule, enforcement for the correction of belief is not possible' (*cebren tashih-i itikad kâideten mümkün olmadığı cihetle*). Ottoman officials also added that they were inclined to favour education because 'malicious means do not behoove the Ottoman government'.[206]

As it appears, sometimes groups of these marginal elements converted to Hanafi-Sunnism willingly, as a response to Christian missionary activities. These would ask to be converted to the Hanafi School and request that schools and mosques be built in their district. Mehmed Ziya Bey warned Istanbul that if one leaves the Nusayris in a state of ignorance, this would only profit the missionaries 'who have already gone so far as to pay regular salaries to the Nusayri leaders'. Therefore, the Sultan should respond to the Nusayris' wish to become Muslims and prove to the foreigners that their government is able to take care of them.[207]

According to the Alawi author at-Tawil, one of the few Ottoman officials who seems to have cared for the Nusayris was the Midhat Paşa, governor general of Syria from 1878–1880. He had been already successful in carrying out various reforms in a brief span of time in other provinces. Suspected later by Abdülhamid of being involved in the deposition and death of his uncle Sultan Abdülaziz (1876), Midhat was removed from Istanbul and put under the yoke of organizing state affairs in the problematic province of Syria, which had seen inter-religious conflicts and several Nusayri uprisings. When Midhat set out to reform the province, he presented petitions to the Sublime Porte, which the Syrian population welcomed. One of the steps to be taken was to pacify the Nusayris. At-Tawil wrote that before Midhat Paşa, the local governor of Hama, Holo Paşa (d. 1895),[208] had befriended the Nusayris (at-Tawil uses 'Alawis' throughout). He especially had won the friendship of Hawash Bey, a Nusayri chief who was famous and loved among the Nusayris and son of Ismaʻil Khayr Bey (d. 1858), a legendary Nusayri leader who had ruled over his people in the service of the Ottomans (1854–1858).[209] After Midhat Paşa became governor general of Syria, Hawash also became his close and trusted friend and helped him in realizing his plans. But in the beginning of his governorship Midhat Paşa had not looked kindly on the Nusayris and like his predecessors gathered an army and marched to the Nusayriyya Mountain (hinterland of Latakia). He intended to subdue them to the will of the Ottomans by force, as he believed the prevalent rumours that the area was a hotbed for rebellious thinking.[210]

Yet, due to the intelligence of Midhat Paşa, 'the leader of the liberals in the East' (*as-sayyid al-ahrar fi ash-sharq*), says at-Tawil, his initial suspicion of the rebellious Nusayris soon vanished. He decided not to send troops to crush the Nusayris, as governors did before him but realized that these people also needed freedom in administrative matters. Therefore, he went to Hama and summoned Nusayri leaders (*mukaddems*) and well-known sheikhs, about five hundred from all over Syria, at a time when the region was in disarray and order needed to be restored. Addressing them as 'O my children', Midhat asked why they were rebellious and disobedient to Ottoman rule by not paying taxes and escaping conscription. Here was the highest official of the state, talking to an oppressed people, abandoned to dark ignorance and great decline by the Ottomans for centuries, asking them the biggest and most sensitive question concerning administration. The Nusayri leaders were silent and amazed at his questions and could not answer.[211] Midhat Paşa is said to have concluded his address as follows:

> O my children! I shall answer instead of you. You do not admit the government's justice because you have neither seen anything done for your favour nor came across a decision that was just.

You do not obey to the government's orders because the officials that come to you do nothing but to treat your dear selves with contempt, and in their view you are nothing but loot to be spent. You also do not find ears in the government that listen to your tragic complaints, and so your cry gets lost. You are convinced that such is the government.

As regards the Syrians, they believe that you possess morals that call for endless enmity, and they try to convince the government in this matter.

You have been in a state of rebelliousness because in your mountain you do not have schools to teach you your duties, roads that will lead you to the centre of the city, and works that will lead to civilization and welfare; you did not see anything but oppression and antagonism that force you to be in opposition and have a harsh character; therefore you remained rebellious and continued your stubbornness and opposition; this is all natural, you are not to be blamed!

O my children! I assure you that I will save you from this misrule and guarantee your self-rule similar to that of Mount Lebanon (*Jabal Lubnan*). I will open schools that will assist you in your progress, teach your duties and build roads which will allow you to participate in the universal life of society; you will become your own lord, and then you will find yourselves in the embrace of the Ottoman government that is your compassionate mother.[212]

As we can see in the account of at-Tawil, who does not specify the source of Midhat Paşa's meeting with the Nusayri leaders, he supposedly promised to save the Nusayris from their bad situation and that they would be part of a just and autonomous administration which was denied to them ever since. To further their progress and education and so let them be part of the civilized world, the governor wanted to open schools and build roads so their isolation would come to an end.

A German source gives some idea of the concerns and ideals of Midhat Paşa. It is said that he visited the German Templer Colony[213] in Haifa in May 1880. He had come for a tour of inspection in Palestine. In Haifa, Midhat inquired in detail about the affairs and needs of the community; he thanked the Templers for their efforts and for being a good example for the local population through their institutions, and wished them continued existence and success. Also, the governor showed utmost admiration for the diligence and endeavours of the colonists and said to the officials in his company that it was a shame that they (the Turks) could not achieve something similar. Midhat added that 'Turkey' had been stagnant in its development and thus turned to Europe for instructors in military institutions and the navy, industry and trade and would also need specialists in agriculture. He was not only very pleased to find a colony that met this need but promised to support its endeavours with whatever was in his power. For this he pointed out to the local governors of 'Akka and Haifa, who were with him, that it was their duty to grant all possible facilities and support to the colonists and not to complicate things, as had happened in the past. Furthermore, it is stated that Midhat Paşa was the first senior 'Turkish' official who acknowledged and appreciated the efforts and success of the Templers, and that Midhat Paşa was a man who correctly judged the situation of 'Turkey' and was eager to bring about better conditions. However, the writer asks prophetically whether the

Ottoman government in Istanbul would support the endeavours of Midhat Paşa or rather put obstacles in his way, unless he was backed up by substantial foreign aid. It was hoped that he would have sufficient time and space to take steps for the good of that underdeveloped region and would fulfil the promises of support that he had given the Templers, whose aim was the welfare of the land.²¹⁴

Midhat Paşa's plans for a more prosperous and orderly Syrian province did not materialize; whereas he had all kinds of power during his previous governorships, Abdülhamid denied this to him in Syria, thinking that his minister wanted decentralization in that region to increase his own power.²¹⁵

At-Tawil also wrote that after Midhat's meeting with the Nusayri leaders it was decided that the village of Sheikh Badr would be the centre of an autonomous Nusayri district and Midhat sent detailed petitions to Istanbul regarding this matter. Thereafter the notables, opposing his plans, complained to Abdülhamid about Midhat Paşa, writing that he wanted to declare his independence from the state.²¹⁶ On the whole, efforts by Midhat Paşa and well-intentioned officials after him to bring justice, education and welfare to the Nusayri regions were not very successful.

According to 'Alawi writers several of Nusayri religious leaders tried to reform their faith and community during the awakening (*yakza*) and renaissance (*nahda*) of the Nusayris in the nineteenth century.²¹⁷ The way they followed was to prove that the Nusayris were pious Muslims who adhered to the Islamic rules. They believed that the only cure against the lethargy of their people was knowledge/science (*'ilm*). To achieve this, one of the sheikhs succeeded in meeting Mehmed Ziya Bey, the local governor of Latakia. It is said that he was convinced to take measures in order to save the Nusayris from ignorance and illiteracy. For this the sheikh wrote a tract to the Sublime Porte, which Ziya Bey forwarded. Istanbul was pleased and agreed. Other writers say that Ziya Bey emphasized in his letter the building of Sunni schools and mosques as anti-propaganda against the Iranians who were using the Nusayris to encourage a revolt in the Ottoman Empire.

Being a functionary of the Ottoman state and a devoted servant of Abdülhamid, Mehmed Ziya's version of the story is that several religious heads and secular leaders of the Nusayris approached and told him that in early times they had been pious Muslims but in the course of time strayed far from the right path because of ignorance. Now they wanted to awake from their 'slumber of negligence' (*hâb-ı gaflet*) and see how the 'matchless' Sultan Abdülhamid, like 'a second Conqueror' (*Fatih-i sâni*),²¹⁸ had spread sciences (*ulûm*), education (*maarif*) and justice (*adalet*) in the Ottoman Empire and so 'revived the people' (*ahaliyi ihya eylemiş*). The Nusayri leaders were proud of being attached to the Sultan, wanted to return to Islam and the Hanafi School and benefit from the sciences, education and the just order. Since they had 'desired salvation' (*necat bulmak*) the governor promised them instruction in the religion of Islam, sciences and education by carrying out the necessary measures, such as the construction of schools and mosques and providing elementary textbooks about Islamic principles.²¹⁹

Towards the end of the nineteenth century another name appears to have been adopted by the Nusayris as reflected in Ottoman archival sources: *Hüdai* or 'those who are rightly guided'. Whereas Selim Deringil has misread the name as *Hıdai* and says it was 'another obscure sect',[220] Türkyılmaz argues that after the Nusayris converted to Protestantism, they 'became the magnet for the Islamization policies of the state' and thus Muslims and called themselves *Hüdai*.[221] However, this is not the case as we have cases of groups of Nusayris who converted to Protestantism and Sunni Islam in the same time period. Stefan Winter points out that the Nusayris styled themselves as *Hüdaiye*, the 'rightly-guided sect'. In 1889 they sent a petition to 'our beloved sultan' (*sevgili padişahımız*) to turn his attention to their community and condemn the constant oppression from the hands of Ottoman officials.[222]

It also appears from the memoirs of Mehmed Ali Ayni, an Ottoman official who was local governor (*mutasarrıf*) of Latakia in 1908–1909 that the Nusayris had opposed the name *Hüdai*. He recounts that a group of Nusayris 'coming down from the mountains' had approached him and said: 'We do not accept the name *Hüdai*. This word was written in the census records without our consent. Correct the records and change our name to *Haydari*, for we are the followers of Imam Ali al-Murtada, the *Haydar-ı Kerrar*.'[223] Obviously, this group of Nusayris demanding to be named *Haydari* belonged to the subsect by the same name to which I referred above. Ayni states that schools and mosques were built for the Nusayris during Abdülhamid's time and their names recorded as *Hüdai*.

Those schools and mosques were abandoned by them after the death of Mehmed Ziya.[224] According to another account, they were used as storage rooms and stables.[225] Writing in 1912 a prominent missionary reported nineteen years ago 'Zea Bey' closed the school in the village of Eldainey. After the missionaries locked up the building, the Nusayris tore it down, carried off the materials and used them with the consent of the governor, 'who gave them to understand that they would not be called to account for their actions.' 'After that the missionaries did not get back their property. Ziya Bey built a mosque instead soon after the school was closed. He attempted to instruct the children in the Qur'an, 'but it proved a failure and was long since given up, and the mosque is now in ruins, and is meeting the same fate that befell our buildings. The result has been that a generation has grown up in ignorance.'[226] And as Martin Kramer puts it, mosques had been built in Nusayri areas 'almost as talismans to ward off the foreign eye.'[227] Still, around the same time in the 1890s and later in 1904 we see reports of Nusayris in Antakya asking for conversion and for schools.[228]

On the whole, local Sunnis viewed the Nusayri conversions to Islam with suspicion, as they were allowed to hide their beliefs and appear as Muslims when forced by circumstances, meaning that they practiced *taqiyya*.[229] Despite the Ottoman official policy accepting Nusayri conversions, some meddlesome local notables and landowning families with influence in the region feared the decrease of their power and did not accept the Nusayris as Muslims and that they could enter mosques and schools. The reasons for not accepting the Nusayris as equal to the Sunnis were that they continued with their corrupt beliefs; that they become Muslims only outwardly because that way their testimony would be accepted in the courts, and being farmers working on rented fields they would lie under oath to each other and seize the fields on which they work. Moreover, the mufti of

Antakya noted that even though the Nusayris adhered to the Islamic principles (bore testimony to Islam/*şehadet,* read the Qur'an, etc.), they did this outwardly and hid their real beliefs; for this reason, they should not be allowed to enter mosques. The mufti was dismissed by the Sublime Porte, saying that even if the Nusayris became Sunnis outwardly, it did not matter, and they needed to be educated as good Muslims in order to abandon their previous corrupted beliefs. The fact that the Nusayris became Sunnis also bothered some of their sheikhs. The state ordered those sheikhs to be exiled for some time to places without Nusayri inhabitants.[230]

In these circumstances, the state's desire to include the Nusayris to the Sunni congregation brought about the opposition of the landowning Sunni notables. As would be predicted, with the beginning of the acceptance of the Nusayris to the status of the Sunnis, the rights that they would gain, especially from a legal point of view, would begin to protect them against the property owners. Therefore, the Sunni notables of the area began to provoke the people to prevent the Nusayri from entering the mosques.[231]

In fact, the issue of the Nusayris being prevented from entering the mosques by Sunnis was in the attention of the Ottoman central administration already in 1870. Orders sent from Istanbul to the governors of Aleppo include the wishes of the Nusayris to enter the mosques and pray together with the Sunnis and the local reactions against this. In February 1870 the governor Naşid Paşa had ordered Sunnis to accept Nusayris in their mosques but it was due to the long-standing enmity between the two groups that the wish of the Nusayris in Antakya was reconsidered. The fact that Islamised Nusayris had abandoned their 'old superstitious beliefs' did not count.[232] Not long after the governor reported that the case of Sunnis and Nusayris praying together was not as unfavourable as it was said, and that this was even beneficial for the unity of the state and the people. For this reason, the Sunnis who objected to the Nusayris' going to the mosques asked to explain the situation to their elders because it would be more dangerous for the Nusayris to become members of other religious groups than to live with the Sunnis. It was highlighted that the Ottoman State had not separated the Nusayris up to that point but included them among the Muslims since this was the cause of solidarity and unity for Islam.[233] This implies that the Ottoman state did consider the Nusayris as 'Muslims' in its official proceedings and treated them equally.

For the sake of unity of the Muslim community, the state deemed it politically incorrect that the Nusayris were not accepted as Sunnis and should have separate mosques and schools as a different *mezheb*. As Christians were accepted to Islam without a question, the Nusayris should also be treated equally. Some opportunist individuals in Antakya, for instance, who wanted to employ the Nusayris as 'slaves in possession' (*birkaç menfaatperestânın yani Nusayri taifesini abd-ı memluk*[234] *hükmünde taht-ı esaretine alıp istediği gibi istihdam etmekte*), prevented them entering mosques. In order to avoid this, the state sent about 70–80 soldiers to the region and ordered some of those persons to Istanbul and rebuked them. The Sublime Porte thought that if the Nusayris were not accepted as Sunnis, they would be easy targets for Protestant missionaries and eventually be converted, and so be protected by foreigners or apply to be exempted from military conscription as did non-Muslim subjects.[235] In these cases, the central administration refused the protest by the people and the notables and accepted the Nusayri conversions in order to reinforce Abdülhamid's position as Caliph of all Muslims.[236]

Whether the conversion of the Nusayris to Sunni Islam was a success or a failure is a matter of discussion. There is no doubt that it was much contested and involved the anxieties of the Protestant missionaries and the Ottoman officials.[237] One aspect of this anxiety of the Nusayris was how wives of Nusayri leaders appeared in public. Henri Lammens (1862–1937), Belgian Jesuit missionary and Orientalist, who travelled among the Nusayris in Ottoman Syria in 1900 and conversed with some of their leaders, stated that the women did not appear in public. This seclusion of the 'weak sex', however, was not a habit of the Nusayri people:

> On the contrary during the whole of our journey we have seen that women enjoy the fullest freedom. Only a few years ago an order came from Istanbul to Muslimise the Nusayris as a whole. The principal chiefs, who, in order to avoid greater extremities, said *Amen* to all the proposals of the [Sublime] Gate [Ottoman government]. In the mountains one or the other mosque was built. That was all. The Nusayris continue to practice their religion as before. Only the Sheikhs were obliged to veil their wives and lock them up, and give up drinking spirits . . . at least in public.[238]

Lammens added that in giving this order, Abdülhamid followed, without perhaps knowing it, an example given about 600 years ago by a sultan of Egypt. The result was the same in both periods, with the difference, however, that the Nusayris have not yet dared, as formerly, to transform these mosques into stables.[239]

Mehmed Behcet and Refik Temimi, two Ottoman officials who were commissioned to tour Syria in 1917 (discussed extensively in Chapter 4), made a similar statement about Nusayri women. They observed with regard to Nusayri women that they all walked around wearing their wide garments as all Muslim women do and so do not deem it necessary to veil themselves with something else. However, most of the wives of the tribe chiefs walked around covered up totally (*aşiret rüesalarının kadınları ekseriya çarşaflı olarak gezmektedirler*). The Nusayri women had a fez, which was covered with a headscarf; if they met a stranger other than a Nusayri, they covered their faces as not to show it. They even turned their heads if they met a stranger and hastily covered themselves up.[240]

The anxieties of both the Ottoman and the Nusayris continued well until the end of the Empire. Before and after the Young Turk revolution Nusayri leaders in Aleppo (1892) and Antakya and Latakia (1909) sent petitions to Istanbul and complained that despite the majority of their people, they were not represented in courts and councils.[241] Hostilities or unjust treatment by Sunnis against the Nusayris continued during the Young Turk era.[242]

Chapter 4

THE NUSAYRIS UNDER YOUNG TURK RULE (1908–1918)

The transformations in the Ottoman Empire in the nineteenth century had considerable but different effects on the various elements of the empire. As part of what is called 'defensive modernization' or 'Westernization', reforms initiated by the Ottoman state, these influenced these different groups in a way that changed power dynamics in the communities, their relations with the state, the relations between the centre and periphery, as well as the relationships between different ethnic groups. External factors also played an important role. However, sometimes these transformations proved counterproductive to achieving their goals. For instance, in the second half of the nineteenth century the Ottoman state tried to form a unified Ottoman identity under the vague label 'Ottomanism'. It is also important to note that the effects of these transformations were limited to some extent only to the elites in the central and coastal cities of the Empire, and not to the majority of the population at the margins of the empire. For example, as Der Matossian shows, the majority of Armenians in the provinces were peasants engaged in agriculture and harvesting. European ideas of liberalism, constitutionalism or nationalism were alien to them. They were more interested in the application of the concept of justice in order to find a solution to the agrarian question, which had existed for decades.[1] The same can be said about marginal groups such as the Nusayris who were trying to find their place within these changes.

Probably only a few socio-political movements in the world gave rise to hopes as great as those the Ottoman Constitutional movement gave rise to, which reached its climax in the Young Turk Revolution of 1908.[2] And likewise very few movements frustrated these hopes so quickly and decisively.[3] The revolution of the Young Turks carried out by the Committee of Union and Progress (CUP) toppled the regime of Abdülhamid under the motto 'freedom, equality, fraternity and justice', in the style of the French Revolution. Instead, the revolutionaries promised a constitutional monarchy that was ruled by law. This entailed a parliamentary democracy responsibly governed and administered by a meritocratic bureaucracy. They envisioned that political parties would replace ancient institutions such as houses of notables and religious orders as the main intermediates for political participation. They stood for a new brotherly Ottoman identity, which combined against European interference in the empire's affairs. They spoke of a free press and virtually unlimited individual freedoms. But very little of it happened, which meant that the transformations it set in motion and the changes it brought did not meet the expectations of those who truly believed in it.

In the following subchapters developments regarding Protestant missionaries' efforts among the Nusayris will be drawn from their publications. In addition to these Ottoman archival documents will throw light upon the Young Turks' observations and attitude towards the Nusayris community. Both sources are of course subjective; they have their own political agendas and cannot reveal the whole picture but are still indispensable in any attempts to understand the topic. Unfortunately, to date, there are no Nusayri/Alawi sources regarding the missionary efforts of the Protestants and the Ottomans that could paint another picture of the community.

4.1. The double-edged sword of the Young Turk Revolution

Contrary to contemporary historiography it can be said that the Young Turk Revolution was not 'a large-scale popular uprising of young Turks throughout the empire'. Neither was it a liberal reform movement. It was rather a 'well-planned military insurrection, conceived and executed in Macedonia by a conspiratorial organization whose leadership harbored a quintessentially conservative aim: to seize control of the empire and save it from collapse'.[4] Their aim was not the destruction of the ancient regime of Abdülhamid II for a new order but to restore the empire of the constitutional sultanate of 1876 that was ended by Abdülhamid in 1878. These 'saviors of the empire', as stated by Hanioğlu, were conservatives, not liberals as presumed by many Europeans then:

> the Young Turk Revolution resulted in the gradual emergence of a radically new type of regime that was to become frighteningly familiar in the twentieth century: one-party rule. The CUP retained the sultan, but reduced his stature. It reintroduced the parliament, but kept it under tight control. In the palace, in the bureaucracy, and within the military, it was the Committee that, working from behind the scenes through the existing institutions of government, came to pull the levers of imperial power.[5]

In the complex context of political, social and economic disruptions, the revolution became a fateful moment in the history of the Ottoman Empire. It was a 'double-edged sword'[6] in that it gave hope to those who staged the revolution and to the unsatisfied elements within the empire promising a new beginning and a better future but conversely it also moved the empire into the abyss of disappointment. In July 1908, many believed that the Ottoman Empire would be saved. But ten years later, in the autumn of 1918, the most prominent heads of 1908 'liberators' – Enver, Talat and Cemal Paşa – had left the country they had set fire to in 1914, and the empire was colonialized, with a Sultan who was willing to remain in his throne as the foreign states' puppet.

4. The Nusayris under Young Turk Rule (1908-1918)

The dreams of the Revolution were 'shattered' and liberty did not last long and was turned into violence between the Turks, the dominant ethnic group, and the other nondominant ethnic and religious groups, as Der Matossian shows. The Revolution of 1908 was influenced by regional and global revolutions such as the French Revolution of 1789, the slogan of which – liberty, equality and brotherhood – the Young Turks had adopted; the Russian Revolution of 1905 and the Iranian Constitutional Revolution (1905-1911). The same author states that the ideals of the Revolution came to an end because the Young Turks were reluctant to 'accommodate the political aspirations of ethnic groups', despite that those groups had adhered to the revolution's ideals. Due to the lack of negotiation between the revolutionaries and nondominant groups concerning the empire's political systems the principles of the Revolution were not realized. The failure of the Young Turk Revolution was caused by a battle of ideas: whereas the Young Turks wanted to unify all ethnic groups and assimilate them through Turkish as the official language, the abandonment of ethno-religious privileges and a centralized administrative system, the ethnic groups regarded Ottomanism as a framework for administrative decentralization in favour of their identities, languages and privileges. Through ethnic politics they contradicted the unified political system that the Revolution strove to achieve. 'The postrevolutionary period became a litmus test for the endurance of the main principle of the Revolution: the creation of an Ottoman citizenry based in equality, fraternity and liberty whose allegiance would be to the empire.'[7]

At the outset of the Revolution, all groups in the Ottoman Empire celebrated it. From every corner enthusiastic speeches were to be heard, and articles blaming the Hamidian past and praising the Young Turks were written. Aspirations and hopes such as in the quotation above were heard from many Ottomans of all religious groups once the revolution began. The Protestant missionaries were probably among those most happy that 'the great change' took place with the Young Turk Revolution.[8] They used the entreaty of the famous Dr. David Metheny who had pleaded 'O Lord, destroy this accursed government and bring it to naught' and hoped for the establishment of the 'Kingdom of the Lord'. His plea was answered now, the missionaries thought, and the Empire was promised a constitution and Parliament, yet they were cautious and hoped that the 'promise shall not die in a bewildering echo.'[9] Euphoria was experienced everywhere in the Ottoman Empire in the immediate months after the Young Turk Revolution of 24 July 1908. People were exhilarated that the oppression of Abdülhamid II had come to an end. Suddenly all were brothers and sisters, regardless of their ethnic or religious background. All kinds of events were staged to celebrate 'liberty', and everywhere exciting speeches were held emphasizing liberty of all kinds. As one missionary wrote:

> A brighter day has dawned. The prayers of God's people have been heard. If the public press can be relied upon, Turkey at last is free. On the eve of a bloody revolution when the Sultan realized that he must do something to relieve the oppression of his subjects, or be driven from the country, he has given them the

grant of a constitutional government. At night the country was in peril of an uprising, which threatened to turn its streams into rivers of blood. By the next night, the streets were thronged with happy crowds shouting 'Long live liberty'.[10]

The missionaries went as far as calling the Revolution a 'nation's sudden conversion' and even compared it to the conversion of the apostle Paul to Christianity. High and sincere expectations, the desire for reconciliation, and 'authentic potential of hope and utopia' among Muslims, Christians and Jews was shared by the Protestant missionaries and well-informed groups and individuals at the outset of the Revolution. For both sides 'It looked like the millennium',[11] implying thereby millenarist hopes for a brighter future and perhaps a 'golden age'.

In Beirut, for example, which had previously seen violent clashes between Muslims and Christians, the new regime was received favourably and witnessed now the 'sudden growth of cordial relations'. A few months after the revolution, it was impressive to observe 'the repeated reiteration of brotherhood' of Muslims and Christians, 'who were to live together in peace in this new era'. This was previously unheard of in the empire's history and anyone who spoke of such a thing before was deemed a naive visionary. Now, described a missionary, there was a gathering of many turbaned Muslim speakers, 'ringing the changes on this theme until we seemed like those standing in a dream'. According to the attending Muslims, there were cordial relations before the regime of Abdülhamid, when mothers of each religion used to nurse each other's children, and the young men called each other 'brethren'. Then, that regime came and triggered fanaticism, hatred and bloodshed. Now, with the Young Turk regime, those things were considered past and Christians and Muslims would live again as brethren. The crowds exchanged salutations of peace and blessings and verses from both the Bible and the Qur'an were seen side by side ('The beginning is from God, victory is near',[12] and 'The fear of the Lord is the beginning of wisdom'[13]). 'Then came a sentiment perhaps never written before in public – "Long live the Moslem-Christian brotherhood," and below it, "Long live liberty."'[14]

Despite these slogans at the time of the Revolution, it was not a liberal reform movement nor a popular uprising but a thoroughly planned military insurrection by a secret and conspirational organization that aimed to seize the control of the empire and stop its collapse. As mentioned previously, the revolutionaries envisioned a constitutional monarchy, a parliamentary democracy, based on the rule of law, and wished to restore the constitutional sultanate of 1876, which was suspended by Abdülhamid II two years later. Yet, very little of the freedoms the revolutionaries promised came to pass.[15] The Protestant missionaries also realized this; their sincere expectations of positive changes in 'Young Turkey' may have been due their lack of knowledge of the nature of the Young Turks until 1908.

All elements of 'a new discourse of the Ottoman nation' at the start of the Revolution such as the symbolic peace, reconciliation, the rhetoric of unanimous participation, shaking hands, solidarity and the like, later showed 'the theatricality of revolutionary brotherhood'.[16] Social and political dynamics shaped the post-revolutionary reality and the revolutionary euphoria transformed into increasing

4. *The Nusayris under Young Turk Rule (1908-1918)* 121

tensions at the local and central levels. One of these major tensions was the counter-revolution of 1909, known as the '31 March Incident' (*31 Mart Vakası*),[17] by pro-Abdülhamid reactionary students of Islamic theology (*softa*) that sought to overthrow the Young Turks but was suppressed by the latter and as its result the sultan was deposed and eventually exiled from Istanbul.[18]

4.2. Protestant missionary efforts among the Nusayris

In the euphoric atmosphere that the Young Turk Revolution had created the Protestant missionaries had high hopes for the intensification of their missions on Ottoman soil. As hopeful as everyone was, feelings of caution were also expressed. After all, Abdülhamid was still in power and was 'an emotional, cruel master whose slightest wish was law'. Hundreds had been his victims who satisfied 'his thirst for blood', and 'thousands have been massacred by his relentless soldiers and all his subjects have felt the weight of his bloody hand'.[19] After all, the sultan was 'not a ruler of paternal proclivities. He can not long continue at the head of affairs where law and order are to prevail.' Further changes were expected, and two 'adverse' factors would be 'of immense value to liberty and true enlightenment' – a free press and more freedom in school affairs. But a tendency would work against these: the 'new awakening of Islam' in deadly opposition to the Western Christianity that was represented by modern missionary enterprise. For the Muslims, 'the Western type' of Christianity was 'intensely virile as compared to the effete system of the pseudo-Christianity known during centuries to Islam'. For this reason, Protestant mission forces needed to be doubled immediately. Provided that freedom in religious affairs would be established, it was 'the time for manning our missions to the full'.[20]

The hope of the missionaries was based on the 'liberal' young men who made up the Young Turk movement who were educated either at Christian schools throughout the Empire or in the West such as in America. As the missionaries believed, the impulse of the 'liberal' Young Turk Revolution was due to the Gospel that carried that 'spirit of liberty' into the Muslim world, primarily among native Christians. This, in turn, made 'civil freedom' an important matter in Turkish affairs. Those young men who had lived in America also realized how handicapped their form of government was. 'Ignorance and its darkness born child, fanaticism, have been the bulwark of Turkish oppression. But the light of education and of demonstrated civil liberty has revealed the power of the populace.'[21] Even though the prerequisites seemed favourable, it was observed that the 'general intelligence' was not 'sufficiently diffused' among the Ottoman subjects as to make popular government possible at that present stage. There was not sufficient 'enlightenment' based on the Word of God (the Bible), 'the only basis possible to free government' – that would insure any long-lasting constitutional government. Neither could the misdeeds of the Ottoman government be overcome in one generation, nor any 'average newspaper man' think that the Protestant missionary activity was, for more than seventy years, a 'formative power in the self-governing ability that makes a constitutional monarchy possible'.[22] As we can see, whereas the missionaries were sure about the Christian influence on the one hand, they were self-critical and realistic enough to observe that the long process of their missionary activity could not change the Ottoman Empire overnight.

Thus, enthusiasm among the missionaries was widespread but at the same time they were alert. Though they were hopeful and 'matters so far seem to be progressing fairly satisfactorily', the outcome of the revolution was not predictable. The watchwords of the day were 'freedom' and 'progress', yet the reconstruction of Turkey would be 'a large and difficult problem' and it would take time to reach a solution. The overall question was whether the revolutionist leaders would be 'able to maintain a state of stable equilibrium' in spite of the almost incredible changes that were taking place: 'It goes without saying, however, that conditions will not be what they should be, but what we hope for is conditions favorable to the prosecution of our missionary work, and the spirit of the times seems to augur well for that. With freedom of the press and freedom of education, mission work would seem to have entered on a new era.'[23]

The matter of education was extremely important for the missions but was neglected in the Ottoman Empire, according to the Protestants. The Ottoman provinces were regarded as the 'most difficult fields in the world' for the missions. Ever since Abdülhamid became sultan and ruled by absolute monarchy over three continents, 'the history of the country has been written in letters of blood'. Since one-half of the population were Muslims, there was 'relentless opposition' to Christian missions in the estimation of the latter:

> Our missionaries in Syria and Asia Minor have spent much valuable time in pleading with and fighting against the Turkish government. How often have we heard returned missionaries from these fields recite the injustices of the ruling powers, and ask us to pray for the overthrow of the despotic powers of the Sultan.
>
> Let us pray that this may truly be the dawning of civil and religious liberty for the subjects of Turkey; that our missionaries may no longer be harassed by a heathen ruler; and that the people may be brought into the 'glorious liberty of the sons of God.'[24]

These sentiments were strong in Syria and Cilicia where the missions concentrated their efforts on the Nusayris. The 'the era of liberty' was seen as 'truly a novel experience' and the missionaries were enjoying a 'breathing spell'. It seemed to them that the ordinary functions of government were largely suspended and the people governing themselves. Strange enough, oppression was not rife, as it was before, and there was no fear of highway robbery. Apparently it was also a new beginning for the Nusayris: they had received permission 'to return to the profession and practice of their own religion, and they are rejoicing greatly over the fact that they are no longer to be Moslems by force'.[25] Moreover, the missionaries hoped that there would be 'perfect freedom' to work among the 'Fellahin', and they would allow the missions to preach and teach in their villages.[26]

In Tarsus, it was observed that the mission school had a larger attendance than usual – over 90 pupils had enrolled. Moreover, perhaps 'the most remarkable feature' was the interest evinced by the 'Fellahin'. On top of that, something extraordinary happened:

> One of their young(est) sheikhs, a man of great influence among them, has been very friendly, and has taken a lively interest in the welfare of the school, doing all in his power to encourage his people to send their children. He seems, too, to have a high appreciation of the benefit of gospel teaching.[27]

In March 1909 the prospects did not seem to yield fruit but the opportunity reaching the Nusayris was like never before. When a reading room was opened in Tarsus, a large number of 'Fellahin' readers, who were especially interested in religious books, came. They came to the mission 'with perfect freedom'. A few also attended the Sabbath services. A school of sixty or seventy students was two-thirds Nusayri children.[28]

In Latakia the school was in a 'very flourishing condition', attendance having reached ninety-three one day in January 1909. The Nusayris were beginning to believe 'they have some freedom', and so they were flocking in. With no interference from the government there would be still larger numbers of them. One of the members was employed in the primary department of the school, and this helped to improve Nusayri attitudes towards the Mission.[29] Also, in Syria a boys' school had 'a surprising attendance' of a larger number of 'Fellahin'. Although the officials attempted to stop them, they continued to come, and replied, 'We have our liberty now'. The attendance was close to ninety.[30] The number of Nusayris in the school had increased but recently the Governor of Latakia had given orders for them to stop.[31] Sometime later it was observed that the Nusayris were 'rather timid for a while' and did not go to the schools.[32] At another place more Nusayris were attending the school than ever in March 1909, and this was due to the new laws. Until that time they did not dare to send their children to missionary schools without suffering for it. But now with more of them attending the missionaries saw this as a 'new opening for which we have been waiting and praying'.[33]

Meanwhile, just a few days after the suppression of the counter-revolution of the '31 March Incident' and the deposition of Abdülhamid, the Ottoman (Young Turk) officials were alarmed by the activities of some European states within the empire. France assumed the protection of the Maronites, Britain that of the Druze and the USA that of the Nusayris in Syria. The missionaries of each country played a role, according to a lengthy report, trying to attract each of the religious groups in order to spread 'sciences and education' through foreign schools. It was reported that through the influence of those schools, especially French and British, there were more people in Beirut speaking French and English than Turkish, and there were sixteen foreign schools teaching sciences and only one military school, the plight of which was also unknown.[34]

The missionaries closely followed the developments in the Ottoman Empire. The 'Sick Man of the East' (the Ottoman Empire), whose death the world has been expecting, in the year 1908 recorded 'a wonderful change in his condition'. He was persuaded 'to take a dose of revolutionary medicine', and this made him able 'to sit up, look around, go out, and make all kinds of promises'. The missionaries were delighted that some of these promises were the very things they had needed. Despite their optimism, they could not know that these promises were genuine enough that that year was the marker of a new era of missions in the Empire. Hopes arose in all branches of the mission due to the promise of civil and religious liberty. They wanted to report more encouraging prospects but were realistic enough to say that they needed to be patient and not expect 'too much in one year'. Hence, even though the door was open, there was no change. It was an unsettled condition and no one knew what would happen. There had been a larger attendance from the 'Fellaheen', more than before, but other places seemed to be as afraid of working openly as before. Nevertheless, they believed that things could not return to how they were, whatever the developments might be.[35]

The attitude of the new government towards the Nusayris seemed to be ambiguous. While the above statement may have proved to be right for Latakia in 1910, where a mission school was opened in one of the villages and work was carried on long before at the request of the people, there were not as many 'Fellaheen' at the school in Suadia;[36] as they were forbidden to attend.[37] Even for the school in Latakia it was reported at some point that 'there has been a temporary decrease in the attendance of the Nusairia but this is not unusual'.[38] At the same time, since the beginning of the school year five new schools were opened, two in the villages a few hours away from Latakia, and the new government did not take action that indicated how foreign schools among the Nusayris were to be handled; it seemed that the local government was not hostile.[39]

Even towards the end of 1907, well before the Revolution, a missionary reported the intense interest of a young Nusayri sheikh of Tarsus in Christianity and the mission school there before the sheikh died. The missionaries then had contact with 'many of the most respected of the Nusairia' when they consoled them. Another 'most respectable' Nusayri sheikh asked for permission to attend a gospel service, and the missionaries' wives were visiting the Nusayri women to preach the Bible. For the missionaries there was 'apparently an awakening'. In June 1910 a missionary reported the 'prominent place' that the Nusayris held in the school in Tarsus. One of the teachers was a Nusayri sheikh and sixty-two of his pupils were Nusayris; in a Bible class by an Arab Christian teacher seventy Nusayris attended and had 'a keen interest in the study'. And to meet this 'awakened interest' among them, a woman teacher was appointed to work especially among them in Tarsus.[40] During early 1910 the attendance was over the average according to the missionaries, and there was a manifest interest especially among the Nusayris, 'which we sincerely trust may continue, and that there may be a harvest of souls as a result.'[41] In another village the headman of the village (*mukhtar*) had assured the missionaries that his people wanted a school and that 25–30 children would attend the school.[42] Then, there was another Nusayri sheikh, who taught Turkish three hours each day at the Tarsus school, with 62 of the 100 enrolled students being Nusayris.[43] The attendance of the Nusayris at the reading room in Tarsus had increased. Some who were frequenting the room said that they had previously wasted their time in the coffee houses. Even the local governor and the police chief are said to have been in favour of it.[44] Bibles were distributed to women in the surroundings of Latakia as part of house-to-house work, and 170 out of 280 were Nusayri women.[45]

One missionary regarded Tarsus as 'the most important place for the Fellaheen as to the intelligence and nobility and great sheikhs, so the Fellaheen are continually coming, increasing our opportunity and responsibility'. These 'children of the Arab' were increasingly emigrating from Syria, such as Latakia and Antioch, to Cilicia, and most of them were Nusayris. A Muslim Society tried to prevent their children from attending the missionary schools but it was of no avail in the end.[46] Overall, the Protestant missionaries were sure enough that the seeds they had sown earlier among the Nusayris in Cilicia would yield fruits. The 'subtile influence ... flows from Christian character silently and surely as fragrance from flowers, and leaves on the man it touches an impression, lasting as eternity'. Dr. Metheny had diligently worked at the mission in Mersin and apparently left an indelible imprint on the people in that region. One missionary reported an incident, which illustrates how even influential Muslims were ostensibly impressed with Metheny's work:

> Last autumn two brothers came from Mardin to Adana. For quite a while they hunted in vain for work. At last they applied to a Moslem Agha, who owns a village some hours from Adana. He asked them, 'What is your religion?' 'We are Christians.' 'Yes, but Christians are of many kinds. What kind are you?' 'We are Protestants.' 'What! Are you Metheny's kind of Christians?' 'Metheny? Who's Metheny? We never heard of him.' 'Why, Metheny of the Protestant Mission at Mersina.' 'Oh, yes, yes, we know the Mersina Protestants. That's the kind of Christians we are.' 'Well, then, you're just the kind of men I want to work for me. I would like to replace all the Moslems in my village with Christians of that brand. Bring your families and come along.' They went, and have been working there ever since, to the mutual satisfaction, we understand, of employer and employees.[47]

Still other wealthy Muslims expressed the desire to hire graduates of Protestant missionary schools because they believed that these were faithful, sincere and to be trusted.[48] Similar positive attitudes by Muslims towards Protestant missionaries apparently dominated the discourse after the Revolution. The Muslims, called by one missionary 'bigoted despisers of the disciples of the Lord', needed, according to the missionaries, to be more thoughtful and better informed and to realize that the American missionaries were disinterested and simply wished for the welfare of Turkish subjects. As conveyed by the president of Robert College (founded in 1863)[49] in Istanbul, the Ottomans were sure that the Americans were different from the Europeans and did not want to seize territory nor expected any trade advantages. Two Turkish Paşas on a ship at the Bosporus were heard to have said that Robert College, 'that splendid fortress of higher education', was 'the greatest shame to Constantinople that there is in existence,' meaning that it was a shame that there was not a single Turk who ever gave money to build a school. In contrast, 'this American who has come to Constantinople ... has put up this magnificent building to start the education of the Turkish people!' It was a disgrace that sultans and rich Paşas did not care about the education of their own people. Hence, the two above-mentioned Turkish Paşas paid 'compelling tribute' to Christianity and praised the Americans and their schools. Even a leader of the Young Turks is reported to have said in a speech after visiting the American school in Izmir: 'These American schools are the models which will be followed by our leaders in providing a system of education for our nation.' Encouraged by this liberal attitude the missionaries were sure that 'every school, from kindergarten to college, is a guide – is a moulding influence – in the future of Turkey, and will play an important part in the reconstruction of that empire'.[50] Through their schools the 'devoted soldiers of the Cross' were exhibiting the 'grace' of Jesus to all the peoples of the Empire, to Muslims, 'so-called' Christians, Jews and the Nusayris.[51]

The Protestant missionaries continued their efforts in mission work in Syria. Even during the early liberal period of the Young Turk rule, local governors or directors could be suspicious towards the missionaries but also criticize their own civil servants (*memur*) of being apathetic. In Antakya, for instance, the Director of Education (*Maarif Müdürü*) lamented that the primary schools that had been built in order to 'enlighten the thoughts of the Nusayri community' (*Nusayri taifesinin tenvir-ı efkârı*) in the villages and to 'save them from the deception of some missionaries' (*bazı misyonerlerin iğfâlâtından kurtarılmaları*), were still closed owing to the apathy of civil servants; the teachers who spent their days in Antakya in turn would get money for nothing. Even though the education of the Nusayris was important, the director deemed the empty closed schools as missing their real purpose and suggested the transfer of the teachers to other villages.[52] Around the same time, the Director of Education in Aleppo suggested the opening of an evening school in Antakya since this would have a political impact on the Nusayri community.[53] These concerns show that the Young Turks actually continued to think and act as in the previous government of Abdülhamid II regarding the Nusayris and perceived the missionaries as a threat. The missionaries thought, as we will see below, that not much had changed politically since the Hamidian era.

Despite many decades of the missionary presence and activities, they felt that most districts were untouched and that there was still much work to be done in teaching the Bible and training children for Christian life and service. According to their statistics of Syria's population of more than 3.2 million, 3 million were Muslim, Nusayri and Druze, but only one-fifth of the number of the children were being taught at Protestant missions, roughly between 16,000 and 20,000. Children were the focus because nothing had been done for them. The construction of railroads was making some of the districts easier to access. Above all, the government was taking 'more interest' and 'making more efforts' in the education of children; 'therefore, every opening should be made use of for winning them to Christ.' Another practical and crucial question was the training of workers, especially more efficient teachers.[54]

As much as the Nusayris were much beloved by the missionaries, the latter's vocabulary describing them did not change in the new twentieth century. Even in

1911 the 'heathen' Nusayris were hearing the 'truth' from Christians who were 'as a light in a dark place here' and 'let their light shine' to everyone. Usually, only a converted Nusayri was worthy of praise, such as the example of a young man near Latakia who had become Protestant after instruction at the missionary school. Being the only Christian in his village, he had endured opposition and persecution from his own people. Though eventually respected and trusted by all, he still was the 'infidel' and 'the apostate Ansaireyeh'.[55] They were a 'neglected and despised class of people', 'lost and perishing pagans' among who 'the Saviour' had found 'chosen and redeemed and consecrated followers'. In their conversion, there was 'abundant proof that the gospel is the power of God to transform character and humanize society'.[56] There are probably very few examples of neutral terms that were applied, such as by one 'missionary of wide experience', who hesitated to use the word 'natives' for the population of Syria in general because 'although strictly correct, I have a suspicion that it usually conveys the impression of NAKED SAVAGES'. At any rate, the nominal Christians and the 'Fellahin' among the natives had objections as to accepting the message of the Gospel; the Moslems and the Nusayris stated that 'the doctrine of the crucifixion is derogatory to Christ'.[57] It seemed hard but the missionaries persevered.

At the end of 1911 there were eleven village schools among the Nusayris in Latakia, and there was no opposition to them but the missionaries could not tell how long it would be until opposition came. The hope of success prevailed when a missionary wrote that the schools they established in Nusayri villages did not yield much fruit but that still few Nusayris converted to Protestantism, 'some chosen ones who have received and lived the truth, despite the withering, blighting influence of the heathenism with which they have been surrounded'. Efficient work was hindered by the 'persistent and determined opposition' of the Ottoman government over the two previous decades, and the outcome was that 'the darkness of ignorance, superstition and paganism still broods like a deadly miasma over the land, paralyzing the hearts and souls of men and casting over them the lethargy of spiritual death.'[58]

Rev. James S. Stewart, a missionary at Latakia asked around the same time in 1911, 'What shall the harvest be?' in reference to the missionary work in Syria and talked about 'the production of a good and bountiful harvest – as soil, seed, human instrumentality and divine efficiency'. Nevertheless, he was cautious and further asked whether there was any 'good soil' in Syria for propagating the Gospel. By answering his own third question whether there was 'any class or part of the mixed population in any encouraging measure responsive' to the Gospel, he admitted: 'It must be confessed that there is no such class, at least in our field ...' The only exception were the children to whom he referred with the saying of Jesus 'Out of the mouths of babes and sucklings thou hast perfected praise'.[59] But even then Stewart admitted 'that even among children much labor is spent in vain on account of unfavorable environment'.[60]

He based his conclusions on decades of experiences among various religious groups. He identified four groups, these being the Muslims ('Mohammedans'), the Nusayris ('Ansairia'), the Nominal Christians and the Armenians. The Muslims constituted the majority of the people but 'they are about as inaccessible as the North Pole'. Despite the missionaries' acquaintance and trade with them, there were no dealings in religious matters. In addition, even though the Muslims had been using the missionary clinics and schools where they read Gospels and offered prayers in Christ's name, only a very few converted because 'They are the proud enemies of the cross of Christ. How shall this enmity be overcome? Only He who sways the future can solve this problem, "What shall the harvest be?"'

The Nusayris with their 'secret' religion and 'oath-bound heathenism' were more accessible to the Protestant mission 'but as to the Gospel their hearts appear to be as hard as the nether mill-stone'. The only hope was their children, who were sent to the missionary schools to learn to read and write and recited the Scriptures. The next groups were the nominal Christians and the Armenians. The former consisted of the Maronites who were 'unfriendly toward Protestants', and the Greek Orthodox with their 'dead orthodoxy' who had no 'preaching of the Gospel, and personal, vital religion'; they were enmeshed in all kinds of practices not based on Scripture but tradition. They were, however, allowed to possess and read the Bible also in their schools and were sending their children to Protestant schools. The last group, the Armenians, were 'a sober, virile race, with a strong national spirit, proud, unscrupulous, but more responsive to the Gospel than even the Greeks'. They were the most receptive because over the previous fifty years hundreds of them became Protestants.

Though the missionaries and their native helpers were hard-working 'amid discouragements, trials and dangers', were 'praying for and expecting a glorious harvest', and did not want to abandon the field, there were many factors hampering their work. They did not see any immediate prospect of building up self-sustaining congregations, the country was not better governed than before the Revolution, the government was not more favourable to missionaries than before, and emigration (and hence loss of human resources) and intemperance were on the increase: 'We know not what the harvest shall be, but we know that He shall see of the travail of His soul and be satisfied.'[61]

When the Italo–Ottoman War (1911–1912) was raging in Tripoli (modern Libya), there was unrest among people in Syria, as elsewhere. So were the Nusayris, who hesitated to send their children to the missionary school in Latakia.[62] Others in the region were afraid for the future of the children and gave them over to a sheikh. Still other Nusayris in different villages nearby were asking for schools, and this was 'surely a bright horizon again for work among the Fellaheen'. It was in those villages that the government had shut the missionary schools fifteen years ago and 'under tyrannical rule have been kept ever since'. Even though the new regime promised changes, freedom of education remained uncertain.[63]

Only a few months later four schools were opened in those places long closed to school work. That year was 'one of promise and encouragement' in missionary work among the Nusayris, and the Protestants hoped for greater things to come in the following years. Yet their work was met with hindrances: one school was closed due to the indifference of the people to fulfil their promises, and two other schools were shut through complaints by disaffected persons to the government. The governor summoned some of the teachers but as everyone in the village agreed in favour of the schools, the government did not interfere. There were twelve schools outside Latakia with an attendance of 300 children, and all schools but one (a girls' school for Armenians) were schools for boys. Hence, an important matter for the missionaries was the education of girls but the Nusayris were hesitant, they 'have not yet waked up to the need of education for girls. (Indeed their laws prohibit it.)'[64] Neither did the Nusayris seem willing to accept the Christian message, despite their readiness for schools. It was a matter of great interest that they were requesting teachers but this had to wait because there were not the right kind of teachers to send to those villages:

> We would not like to say that all these requests for schools indicate that the Fellahin are ready to accept the gospel, or are craving for it, or that they want to give up their heathen ways; but we do know it gives an opportunity for planting the Word of God, as it is made the center of all teaching.... This sowing is surely a great privilege and the real work of the Church. To get hold of the rising generation is, in the minds of all experienced workers, far more hopeful than trying to proselytize the old. Another hopeful sign for work among this people is that they do not seem to have the fear of the government that they formerly had.[65]

The work in Tarsus in 1912 was more encouraging. In the school there was a total enrolment of sixty-three girls, twenty-four of them being Nusayris, whereas out of the forty-three boys twenty-four were Nusayris.[66] At the beginning of the year a new school was opened, at the request of village authorities, in one of the Nusayri villages, and it was hoped that it would be allowed to continue uninterrupted for some time. Only twenty-one boys could attend because there was insufficient room for more. Even though the villagers were anxious that provisions also be made for the girls and the missionaries trusted that this was the beginning of opportunities for other schools among the Nusayris, the big question was how to procure teachers. Nevertheless, the Lord would help: 'The harvest indeed is plenteous, but the laborers are few. Pray ye therefore the Lord of the harvest, that he send forth laborers into his harvest.'[67] One main reason why there was no improvement was the Italo–Ottoman War that, even though it was not directly affecting the Mersin-Tarsus region, had the effect of 'maintaining a certain uneasiness of mind and unsettled condition among the people, and it was not particularly conducive to meditation on spiritual things'. Schools of all denominations were experiencing the same difficulties. The task was not only sending missionaries from the homelands in America for the 'harvest' but also 'raising up and equipping a force of native helpers from the native converts, active and zealous for the spread of the pure gospel among their own people'. This was indispensable for the evangelization of the world.[68]

Whether people who sent their children to missionary schools cared about their ideals or not, education at their schools became 'fashionable' as time went on, as one report from Mersin stated. But people who patronized those schools did 'not value it highly enough to be willing to pay any great amount towards securing even a very common education for the daughters of their household'. When a family had a boy and a girl but the means were only enough to educate one, the boy was preferred.[69] An exception was apparently the school in Mersin, where a sewing course was set up for girls, and a Muslim girl, who was the best, served as an example to attract more. Even when the (unnamed) Ottoman government inspector visited this department, he was very interested. He then invited missionary women to the Muslims girls' school where the students had a good training. For the missionaries this was a good basis to receive the message of Christ. There were other exchanges between the Protestant and Muslim school, and the missionary women were glad that the Turkish inspector had given them the opportunity of becoming acquainted with the people. The inspector himself took 'great interest in the education of the girls'. His daughters had visited the mission school in Iskenderun, and later one of them was visiting the American mission school in Bursa and the other was at the American college for girls in Istanbul. Later the missionaries in Mersin were asked whether they could supply a teacher for a kindergarten school that the Muslims intended to establish in Adana. A missionary in Tripoli (Lebanon), who previously had sometimes trained Muslim girls for their own schools, was suggested. This was a positive development for the Protestants: 'May this new interest in the education of Moslem girls be a means toward bringing the light of the gospel to many who are sitting in darkness and the shadow of death.'[70]

Sometimes the missionaries felt that darkness loomed over their missionary work. In 1911 the war between Italy and the Ottomans, as mentioned above, and the outbreak of cholera in and around Latakia aggravated the situation.[71] In October 1912, they reported that they were in good health, the school was opened but the presence of cholera prevented the pupils from attending. Many people had left the town through fear, and there had been quite a number of deaths among Christians and Muslims.[72] Cholera and the war went hand in hand and left the country in a very troubled state: 'The war cloud looms up large, and the demand for soldiers is very great. A vigorous attempt is made to stop emigration, in the interests of the conscription.'[73] As the uncertain situation continued, in March 1913 when Nusayris, who the missionaries hoped to win over, took advantage of the weakness of the government and enriched themselves by robbery. They raided Muslim, Christian and their own people, and carried off livestock, food and household goods. The Nusayris at Bahamra did not join them but it was only a matter of time because the 'young bloods' would be hard to restrain if the unsure situation continued.[74]

Meanwhile in Tarsus there were 'unmistakable signs of an awakening among the Ansairiyeh'. This seemed to be 'one of the wholesome fruits' of the recent wars with Italy and the Balkans, which the Ottomans lost, 'demonstrating that the glory has departed from Islam'. The attendance of the Nusayris at the school in Tarsus had increased largely.[75] They were visiting the reading room at the school, and the distribution of tracts and gospels was also accelerated through a blind 'Fellah', a colporteur, who was begging and at the point of starving until an evangelist hired him. This Nusayri proved to be 'successful beyond all expectations'. He was interested in the gospel but becoming a Christian he would be 'a dispenser of the truth for the truth's sake'.[76]

The work in Cilicia was extended to villages near Adana. The people seemed delighted to read the Christian books and tracts and there was 'a manifest desire to read and investigate'. One Tarsus evangelist, a Christian Arab named 'Mallim [i.e. mu'allim/teacher] Mikhail was peculiarly fitted for the work among those villagers. He had spent much of his life among the 'Fellahin' in the villages of Latakia and had a wide acquaintance among them. Now these people in the Adana villages were almost all from the 'Ansairiyeh Mountains' in Syria, Mikhail knew the villages from where their fathers and grandfathers came. This helped him work among them.[77] The 'most encouraging portion of the field' was Tarsus, where the school attendance had increased, and most of the pupils were Nusayris; two teachers there were Nusayri converts from Latakia. The reading room was 'flourishing more than ever', through which great quantities of religious literature was sold at a low price and 'some anti-Moslem tracts' were distributed for free.[78] In a village near Latakia, there were seven girls at the school, two of whom were from the home of a Nusayri sheikh. He had visited the boarding school and asked for a place for his oldest girl. 'This may be only a glimmer that shall soon fade away, but withal it has its inspiration and its encouragements.'[79]

In all these years, the Presbyterian Church of North America felt that it had succeeded in winning converts, despite 'the combined opposition of the intolerance of the Greek Church, the paganism of the Nusairiyeh, and the enmity of Moslem officials'. A connected account of this was undertaken by Dr. Balph in his *Fifty Years of Mission Work in Syria* (see above), 'full of reliable mission facts' gleaned from official papers and from his own observations during twenty-seven years of service as a medical missionary.[80] There he summed up the mission work in Syria, the oldest foreign mission, and among many things he talked about the 'manifestations of the Divine blessing and approval', one of which was the 'gathering in of many from the darkness of superstition and paganism to the light of the gospel'. One main reason in encouraging the study of this book was evidently to throw a negative light on the Ottomans; multitudes of people had to go to America 'to be free from the oppression of a Mohammedan government, and to better their condition financially'. And this presented an opportunity to do foreign mission work at their own doors, such as in Pittsburgh where thousands of Syrians lived: 'God in his providence has brought them here.'[81] The Syrians were seen as 'good and thrifty people' but before they could be 'ideal citizens', they also, like every other people, were in need of Jesus Christ.[82]

During the War, British Presbyterian missionaries faced difficulties and some were arrested as prisoners of war, and then expelled from Syria; their wives remained among the natives and kept up the work.[83] Other limitations occurred not only in Syria but also Asia Minor occasioned by the war in Turkey. Incoming and outcoming mail was censored and so the missions could not send their reports to the Board in America.[84] In addition, many missionaries fled from Syria to Cyprus,[85] then under British rule. Later a large number of Syrian refugees from Latakia and other coastal towns came to Cyprus.[86] The British Syrian Mission reported that the American missionaries were devoting their energies to educational and medical work in Syria and that all the interventions of European Powers in Syria on behalf of the inhabitants, be they Christian or Muslim, have not done as much good as has been done by the Americans.[87]

As much as the War was of great concern, it had a higher aim to fulfil: 'This great war that gives pause to our missions in Syria, Asia Minor and Cyprus, and troubles the missionaries, their families and the converts, is God's sovereign way of preparing the field for a great harvest, and His servants for the responsible work of reaping it.'[88] The Great War had changed the circumstances, and mission work was more difficult; there were 'usual harassing obstacles in the way of work and service' and even threat of arrests of missionaries who were helping the Red Cross. A visit of two leading missionaries to Istanbul where they met the Minister of Education, did not bring change in the laws but 'a sort of armed neutrality or truce under which the schools could open' was reached. In the estimation of the missionaries, the future of Syria and the mission work there was largely dependent upon whether Germany and Turkey, who were allies, would come out as winners of the War.[89]

Since the outbreak of the War, the Syrian mission was greatly handicapped but they shifted to work 'at our door', i.e. in America, concentrating further on the Syrians in America, especially Pittsburgh.[90] Also, in the first half of 1916 the Ottoman government closed the mission schools in Mersin with no apparent reason mentioned.[91] By mid-1916 no reports or 'very meagre' reports were received from Syria and Asia Minor. There were calls to donate for the Syrian Relief Fund to relieve starvation in Syria.[92] Towards the end of WWI, the Syrian Mission struggled to meet the 'tremendous problems' it faced for its 'gigantic task'. Despite its small size 'the little army' in Syria expected to win victories. However, there was the problem of securing locations to erect church buildings – the Turkish Parliament had passed laws that made it even more difficult than in former years.

The attitude of the government hampered the work in every conceivable way: from keeping the missionaries from bringing American food such as pork, to killing the converts, among other things. Luckily for the missionaries, had the European powers not intervened not even missionary work would be allowed. Another problem that contributed to reducing the number of memberships was that new converts were immigrating to other places such as North and South America, Egypt or Europe: 'Jesus Christ makes men free and it is hard indeed to endure Turkish tyranny when once they know that freedom.' Another obstacle was the indifference of the people: 'The people in Turkey are not Gospel hungry as in many other lands... And the first thing the missionary has to do in Turkey is to teach the people that they are starving without Christ. The work is hard enough where they are hungry, but where there is no appetite, it is not an easy matter to do the cooking.' Then, there was the apparent fanaticism of the people, one of the 'greatest obstacles': 'It is begotten of the pair, Ignorance and Bigotry. And it is aggravated in the fact that it is found in different forms among different races. If it were all confined to a single race it could be more easily overcome.'[93] It is obvious from these words that not only were the Muslims not receptive to the Gospel but also other religious denominations, including the native Christians.

With an 'army' of only fifteen people in Syria, the missionaries hoped to win victories: 'What force have we to conquer territory so vast? You can't expect victories without an army. Just fifteen at the front. Not fifteen million, nor even fifteen thousand, but fifteen.' Notwithstanding this very low number, the missionaries in Turkey were seen as preparing the way for 'a great ingathering' as soon as the war ended. They counted on past victories establishing and holding outposts against 'the enemy until his power breaks'. That enemy, the Devil, representing Islam or the Ottoman Empire, 'can sit on his throne in hell and laugh at us expecting victories'. The missionaries would be supported by 'a native force on the field already trained to gather the harvest'. All these things were the 'leaven in the lump', which was more far-reaching than estimated. This would finally 'lead to Christ a vast empire'.[94]

The gap between the Young Turks and the American missionaries could not be wider. When the Ottomans entered World War I by the choice of the CUP, Ottoman Turkey developed a deep antagonism to the ABCFM and the Presbyterian Mission in Syria. The destruction of especially Armenian Christianity and its people destroyed the 'revived Christianity' of the nineteenth century, killed the American hope of a peaceful millennium and ended the American dream of a social utopia of 1908:

> Levi Parsons's somewhat forgotten apocalyptical vision of 1821, 'that Turkey must be drenched in blood,' was now fulfilled; but what would follow now, if not total hopelessness? Those cast as the principal actors of eschatological change since the 1830s, the native Christians and primarily the Armenians, had become the victims of mass murder and expulsion. Therefore, missionary America suffered serious damage between 1915 and 1923. It lost its principal friends and clients and most of its concepts.[95]

4.3. Muslim responses to Protestant missionary work

As we have seen, the approach of the Young Turk government before World War I towards Protestant missionaries was ambivalent. On the one hand, they put obstacles in their way, and, on the other, there were times when Ottoman officials and the government viewed the Christian missionary efforts positively. The positive reaction towards the missionaries and their schools was a matter of deep concern to some Muslims. An unnamed observer who happened to travel the villages of Latakia wrote about the situation of the Muslims in that region in 1914.[96] His addressees were the 'true religiously learned ones' (*hakîkî ulema*), the theological seminar of the Darülfünûn (Istanbul University) and the 'young and selfless students' of the School for Preachers in Istanbul. He was surprised to hear from the people in Türkmen towns that they were regularly visiting Armenian villages and had adapted their lifestyle. The shock was even greater when one Turkish villager reported that the Armenians had told him that the religion of Islam was a fabrication and the present government would be destroyed soon. After asking the villager whether they had received books from the Armenians, he said that a 'friend' in Kessab[97] gave him a book to read and see which religion was true. It was the New Testament (*İncil*) in Turkish translation printed in England by a 'charitable society (!)' (*cem'iyet-i hayriyye (!)*) that was given gratis to the Turkish villagers. After inquiring he learned that they all had a copy: 'I instantly started to talk and gave advice in order to discipline them and to burn the books. It seemed to be effective; after all, I am not turbaned.' Later the author went to inspect villages where he learned that each Muslim had received the New Testament, some even the Torah. In Cisr-i Şuğûr (Jisr ash-Shughur) the missionaries wielded power over the Muslims by imposing Christian ideals on them, and were 'deceiving them every day' (*adeta tahakküm etmişlerdir, her gün de bunlar kandırılmak üzere*). Somehow, the administration there did not notice this. Informing the government about the situation the author did not know what would be done but he urged the religious officials in Istanbul to come and see this, and send 'honourable' persons who would advise the Muslims.

The majority of the population in Cisr-i Şuğûr was Nusayri, and they all followed the authority of a sheikh:

> Most of them are rebellious. They give neither soldiers, nor taxes or anything. It is very easy to discipline them, and if a religious society were wholeheartedly committed, they will be honoured by the glory of Islam. I wonder why this is not an issue, or is it but not acted upon. Ah, you respected personages! Come, come, and see! Ignorance abounds. There are no learned men (*ulema*) of action here. Even if there are, some of them are corrupt (*ahlaksız*). They perpetrate the foremost evils. They are not protectors of religion, nay, they are rather traitors of religion (*hâmi-yi din değil, hâin-i din olsalar gerek*).

The author attached two Nusayri prayers[98] to his letter in which Imam Ali is extolled intended to reveal their exaggerated beliefs; the readers should then understand in what state the so-called ulema were who did not act upon this urgent matter of disciplining the Nusayris:

> Now it is your duty to leave the environs of Istanbul for the hinterland and work for the welfare of Islam. I beg your pardon but I am honoured to present to you, who are our beloved ulema, my wretched letter. And you should impose it on the true religiously learned ones, the theological seminar of the Darülfünûn and the young and selfless students of the School for Preachers that they may look with fairness and in a godfearing manner. It is hoped that they will begin to think about a remedy for Islam.

As if uninformed about decades of fruitless attempts of 'civilizing' the Nusayris, the anonymous author believed that it would be a very easy task. In his opinion, the religious authorities had failed to save Islam from evils. A few years before this an Ottoman named M. Ali Münir in Beirut, writing about the decline of the Islamic civilization in a series of articles titled 'Social Decline' (*İnhitâtât-ı İctimâiyye*), accused the ulema of being the cause of ignorance. They should be aware, he said, that hundreds of thousands of Muslims of different denominations in Syria such as the Druze, Isma'ili, Metawali or Nusayri were deprived of secular and religious education.[99] Even in Beirut, which was famous for its thriving trade due to its 'intelligent' and 'progress loving' inhabitants (*Ticâreti, ahâlîsinin zekâ ve terakkiperverliği ile şöhret-şi'âr olan Beyrut'un*), there was no primary school attached to the Ministry of Education. Here the people owed their education and civilization entirely to Catholic and Protestant missionaries: 'Unless we admit this bitter truth, we should be persuaded that we will not be able to build our enlightened future on a sound basis.' Two universities attached to the Protestants and Catholics were home for thousands of Ottoman students; on the other hand, there was only one high school attached to the Ministry of Education, which did not have a preceding primary school that was able to raise students to the level of high school education. 'If I told you that during the twenty years since the establishment of the high school only 160 *efendi*s received a diploma, you will understand how much we are interested in the level of education in Beirut.'[100]

In a similar vein, another critic of the inactive ulema was Samizade Süreyya.[101] He lamented that wherever one goes in the Islamic lands the 'confused and abandoned' (*bir tezebzüb ve harâbîde bulundukları*) Muslim 'brethren' (*ihvân*) were in a deplorable state but no one was willing to save them from their plight, even though everyone knew it. 'Each Muslim is compelled to save his correligionists from the gruesome path (*tarîk-i mezâlim*) they are treading and lead them to the glorious highway of progress (*şahrâh-ı nûr-i terakki*); if not compelled, it is their conscientious responsibility.'[102] Notwithstanding that it was only the ulema who could save the degenerated Muslims (*düçâr-ı takahkur olan İslamları*) and lead and raise them to the highest summit of progress (*evc-i a'lâ-yı terakkiye sevk ve is'âd*), they did not appreciate their important and sacred duty, did not act and were even not inclined to act. The ulema were the sole reason why the Muslims vacillated. The tolerance (*müsamahât*) of the ulema was the reason for the decline of Islam. It was due to their tolerance that the number of missionaries had increased in Islamic lands and the 'hearts of the Muslims' were wounded. It would take many years to heal them. Therefore, Süreyya felt he had to inform the 'honourable' ulema of the great role the Protestant missionaries played in Islamic countries and awake them from their 'slumber of negligence' (*hâb-ı gaflet*). The Protestant missionaries' goal was nothing less than to spread Protestantism to all the world but especially in Islamic domains, and according to their 'vain imagination' (*zu'mlarınca*) after ninety years the whole world would adopt Protestantism. The missionaries were active and had spread the 'seeds of Christianity' (*tohum-ı Nasraniyet*) in every corner through their schools. However much these schools were built to train a certain number of missionaries and to extend and consolidate Christian politics (*siyaset-i Nasraniye'yi tahkîm ve tevsî'*), for the sake of formality they were saying that their aim was to educate the Easterners who were deprived of education, protect the religion of the Muslims and their national morality (*ahlâk-ı kavmiye*) from attacks, civilize and enlighten (*temdîn ve tenvîr*) them.[103]

According to Samizade, the scarcity of modern Ottoman schools dragged the Muslims into the traps of the missionaries (*onlara kurmuş oldukları pusulara, tuzaklara doğru sürüklüyor*). Many Muslims, allured by their promises, were leaving their children, who did not even finish primary school and were deprived of Islamic principles and education, in their embrace. He places his discussion of education into the context of Christian 'civilization' and their 'civilizing mission' (*mission civilisatrice*) that he explains as follows with regard to not only Protestant but also Catholic missionaries:

> I wonder with what superstitions the tender brains of those tiny innocents, who are in the care of French nuns called *sœurs*, are filled. Is the alleged intention of the missionaries, who have abandoned their countries and relatives and took pains to come all the way to here, really to offer a humanitarian service (*hizmet-i insaniyet-kârâne*) to the Easterners and the Muslims? Would anyone with a sound mind (*akl-ı selim*) believe this? The missionaries do not inform anyone of their true aims, they solely regard the 'civilizing mission' (*vazife-i temeddüniyye*) as a mere humanitarian service and necessity, and shout at the top of their voice 'We are servants of humanity!' What the missionaries mean by this 'civilization' is such an issue to understand that it can baffle any careful investigator from the East. They do not regard people who are outside Christendom as civilized and therefore conceive a 'civilizing mission' the aim of which is to make the Muslims accept Christianity.[104]

Samizade further contended that there were other Protestants with political motives. They were sending missionaries in the guise of teachers and armed with secret political ideas to Turkey and other Muslim countries for the sake of trade or in search for new territory for the dense population in their respective countries. After they spread their national language and extend their trade, these missionaries isolate the Muslims from their nationality and change it. In their schools, such as the American School in Beirut, every year they instilled into hundreds of Muslim minds whatever they wanted. The students were busy adapting Western decadence and immoralities and did not attach importance to spirituality or religious matters that constitute the essence of a nation or a people. An investigating commission that went every year to inspect the activities of the American School would return praising the institution. In Samizade's opinion, this was a shame, and there had to be a solution to save the Muslims.

Samizade writes that he was talking from experience, as he referred in another article to the efforts of the missionaries.[105] He had spent years among the missionary schools and struggled to find out their 'most sensitive secrets', and he says that he succeeded. Hence, with his 'insider knowledge', readers would read his articles with confidence. The missionaries played their role with perfect earnestness, and their stage was wider and bigger than those of other countries because these countries knew how to outlaw the missionaries and were not in need of their schools, unlike the Muslims. When Samizade stopped at Izmir during one of his travels, he visited to the Protestant College. After the director showed him the around, Samizade was invited for a break in his office. There the director spoke about foreigners and missionaries. He felt that during those days Ottoman public opinion had turned against foreigners; he felt this was wrong giving the example of Japan's brilliant progress and its victories which were owed to the Europeans and Americans. Hence, the Young Turks should accept Japan as a guideline (*numûne-i imtisâl*) and place foreign consultants in each ministry. In short, there should be foreign officials everywhere until the Ottomans became competent in every respect. After this they could tell the foreigners to leave and Turkey's future would be very bright (*Türkiyâ'nın istikbâli pek şaşaadâr olur*). The director also did not understand why the Ottomans wanted to close the missionary schools. This was unfair because the 'poor' (*zavallı*) missionaries had left their countries to toil in these lands and were spending large sums of money for nothing but humanitarian purposes (*hizmet-i insaniyet-kârâne*). 'Such requital to our kindness is indeed not befitting humanism' (*Bizim lütfumuza karşı böyle bir mukabele doğrusu insaniyete yakışmaz*). It was obvious that as soon as Ottoman schools reached an equal level with missionary schools, then the missionaries could be told to leave. But for that present time, it would have been disastrous for the Ottomans if the missionaries left.[106]

Samizade Süreyya further observed that even though Muslims in Syria were 'action and perseverance incarnate' (*faaliyet ve gayretin birer timsal-i mücessemidirler*), their efforts had multiplied since the Revolution, they slowly removed the 'veil of ignorance', many schools were opened, which were the guarantors of the people's future welfare and happiness, these were not able to meet the current needs of the Muslims. Instead, they had to resort to Christian schools, which were in fact 'traps' (*tuzaklar*) and built for political, religious and economic reasons. Samizade was not comparing the progress of Syria's Muslims with the Europeans or other countries, for compared with the latter they 'paled in comparison with them' (*solda sıfır kalır*). He compared Syria's Muslims with those in other countries; wherever one went, there was discord (*nifak*), schism (*tefrika*) and corruption of morals (*fesad-ı ahlak*) but these 'deadly diseases' (*maraz-ı mühlik*) almost did not exist in Syria. Nevertheless, there was unity and cooperation in the Islamic world that manifested itself in the economy, crafts and agriculture. This was especially promoted through the education of Ottoman students in Europe. These would return to their countries and be of service to their people. Samizade strongly hoped that 'they go as Arabs and will return as Arabs; they go as Muslims and will return as Muslims. However, some students who were sent to Europe went as Turks and come back as Frenchmen, or they go as Albanians and come back as Germans.'[107] Instead of being useful, these would cause harm in their countries. These students belonged to those who lost their identity through European influence, which also caused other troubles.

Süreyya further observed that one of the fatal consequences of the foreign schools was to instil in native Christians hatred towards Muslims and aversion towards the government. For this reason, there was no affection and sincere feelings between Christians and Muslims. There had been constant disputes and clashes between them in Beirut during the Hamidian despotism but despite things changing there was still no safety. The sympathy of the Christians towards the government was only outward; inwardly they wished to be under the care of a European state.

This sentiment was instilled in them by the foreign schools. The foreign schools in Syria were like a collection of every nation that had a school there. And each of them had a different programme; the French wanted to teach their language and tie their trade to Syria, the Germans increase and strengthen their influence in Syria, and the Americans had opened schools to spread Protestantism and wanted at the same time to safeguard their economic and political interests. American schools put more efforts to spread their religion than their politics and economics; this was one of the main reasons American missionaries left their country.[108]

In another article titled 'Misyonerler ve Mektepleri' (The missionaries and their schools) Samizade Süreyya discussed the usefulness of missionary schools. In his opinion there were two types of fathers who cared about education.[109] The first sent their children to missionary schools, which they found perfect, and did not care about the real aims of the missionaries. For them education was important, wherever the children received it. The second type of fathers deemed it wrong to leave their children to the embrace of people with 'corrupted ideas' and found that their own (Ottoman) schools were good enough, after all their children would not go to school to become scholars. The first type of father, Süreyya argues, was a bit indifferent and lenient but was right. It is here that Samizade dwells lengthily on the tactics of Protestant missionaries and explains why their schools were better than Ottoman schools and therefore why no one should fear to send his children to them.

Apart from their schools and institutions in the East, Süreyya goes on to say, the missionaries had newspapers and journals in the West. If one were to gather and read all these one would be astonished and concerned: 'If you were somewhat simple-hearted (*safdil*) you would believe that the missionaries constantly harvested the fruits of their ceaseless efforts! The articles sent from various Islamic domains persuade you that the Muslims are leaving their religion and throw themselves into the embrace of the Protestants in multitudes!'[110] If one did not know the real truth (*içyüzü*) about the missionaries and examined their nonsense and fabrications, one would certainly hesitate to send the sons to foreign schools. However, someone who was aware of the situation knew that these writings were baseless and therefore just made up. And if someone asked: 'Why do the missionaries feel compelled to lie?', the answer to this laid in the organization of the missionaries: there were many commissions in America and England who consisted of a vast organization. And there was another commission called Board of Trustees (*hey'et-i mü'temene*) that assumed the financial matters as well as supervision and control. The members were rich and respected persons who provided the money that the missionaries then used for schools, hospitals or whatever was needed to propagate Protestantism. In Samizade's opinion, these missionaries were different from Catholic priests or other clerics in that they were neither fanatical nor ignorant. On the contrary, they had graduated from famed universities in their countries, they were liberal, and learned men some of whom had specialized in philosophy or other sciences. Samizade was informed because he had spent long periods among them. Although he calls them 'learned' he says that whatever they wrote was one hundred per cent contrary to truth.

What is more, their publications were intended to fool people by only talking about successes in order secure money from commissions or other rich people in their countries for establishing new institutions in the East and securing funding. As a result, they published those journals to present to would-be funders the dominance of Christianity over Islam. The Protestants were especially active in Syria but Samizade contends that despite visiting all the provinces of Syria he never met any Muslims who had converted to Protestantism. On the contrary, he found that those who had been tolerant towards the missionaries became fanatical after they entered missionary schools and felt an indescribable hatred towards the missionaries. Yet reading their publications one could believe that not a single Muslim was left in Syria.[111]

In Samizade's opinion all the missionary activities were in vain, their goals were not fulfilled. Yet, despite his negative approach, he also praised those schools because they were better than the Ottoman schools:

> But how could they dare to reveal the deplorable truth? To do this is equal to being left starving! Therefore, all this charlatanry and babbling ... We, however, need to look to the benefits. Their schools are by all means perfect, enough to compete with the ones in the West; the method of teaching and education too. It follows that once we disregard their charlatanry, we do not need to be afraid of the foreign schools. Quite the reverse, we stand to gain very much from them. Whenever our schools attain that perfection, it is natural that we will turn away from missionary schools; but not yet.[112]

Once one acknowledged that someone in foreign schools did not lose his religious beliefs, he could send his son to one of those. 'Let's be sure: our best schools pale in comparison to them!'[113]

Samizade's opinions in this article were criticized by a certain Mehmed Şevket.[114] For him Samizade directed the Muslims, who were experiencing an awakening (*intibâh*), to the 'wrong path'. If intellectuals, who Şevket saw as guides of a nation, led people to the wrong path, then they would be soon dragged to 'a calamitous abyss'. In this sense, by praising missionary schools Samizade was misguiding fathers: 'Pity, what a pity! It's a shame for this nation! We still did not understand the source of these calamities! We are ruined; it's a tragedy because we still hope for help from the priests and the missionaries.' Even if Samizade had good intentions he was wrong, and most people, according to Şevket, did not think like Samizade. Those Muslim fathers who wanted education (*tahsil*) for their children at any rate were fools. They did not know what it meant; it was more than stuffing knowledge into the brains of the children like filling a barrel. Rather, it meant to instil national ideals, Muslim education, patriotism and hate towards the Christians; the children should be aware that their enemies were delighted when they killed the Muslims like monsters.[115]

Mehmed Şevket openly called for Muslims to take revenge on the Christians. He went so far that he encouraged killing them with bombs, and that this should be taught in lessons at schools. His line of reasoning was as follows: every nation has an 'ideal', a 'goal of hope' (*gaye-i emel*), which is taught and instilled at schools. And each nation's goal of hope is different, as it was different for Muslims and Christians and even among the Christian nations. The goal of the foreign nations, 'our enemies', was illustrated with the case of the Bulgarians: their goal was to free the Bulgarians from the Turkish and Muslim yoke and establish Bulgaria, and for this everyone, teachers, writers and poets, did their best to instil this ideal in the people. For thirty years the new generation grew up with hatred towards the Turks and Muslims, even bombs were used to frighten them and Bulgarians gave their lives for the cause. The same for the Greeks: formerly Sultan Mehmed the Conqueror had taken Istanbul from Constantine, and now at the beginning of the twentieth century, Constantine had to take Istanbul back from Mehmed. The Muslim ideal, hence, was to counter the enemies by force as described above; some would think that this was imagination (*hayal*) but in Şevket's opinion many people needed imagination, ones which were realized even more.[116]

Mehmed Şevket continued: was it possible for a missionary priest to propagate the religion of Islam to Muslim children? Samizade wrote that those who had been tolerant in religious affairs became fanatical with regard to Islam after they visited missionary schools and nurtured immense hatred towards the missionaries. This meant for Şevket that in their schools the missionaries committed excesses against Islam and, as a result, the Muslim students nurtured hatred towards them. Samizade thought that Muslim children were being taught about Islam at those schools. Even stranger was the fact that the missionaries wrote in their newspapers that they were infusing the Christian spirit into Muslim children and this way Christianity was expanding day by day, but Samizade replied to this by saying that this was contrary to truth and the missionaries were writing such things in order to secure money from rich Christians in Europe. Şevket adds that if Samizade was right than he was confirming that the missionaries were liars and impostors, and since falseness and imposture were unethical traits everywhere, leaving children in the hands of corrupt people was a crime.

Şevket did not believe that Muslim parents who sent their children to missionary schools betrayed their country. He argues that when Christians declared crusades, the Muslims were astonished how a holy war could be declared in the twentieth century. 'Those people, who forget calamities and tribulations, cannot escape calamities. This is the meaning of "eating": the law of survival is they eat you if you do not eat them.'[117] His advice to the parents:

> O Muslims! Come to your senses. Giving your children to foreign schools is a grave danger (*büyük tehlike*). And if you leave the innocent ones to the care and education of French, Italian, etc. priests, you are doing no good to your faith, and your homeland, nay, you are doing harm because this sacrifice of yours for the purpose of teaching them French, English, or whatever language, will raise a nonbeliever, a homeless, nationless and idealless person.

In Şevket's estimation, it was better to forsake knowledge/science (*ilm*) than leave a person deprived of national education (*milli terbiye*) at a foreign school; a patriot and real Muslim with less knowledge was better than a nationless person with much knowledge.

According to Edhem Nejad, yet another Ottoman writer, educating and raising children, who were aware of their Islamic and Ottoman heritage, was hence of vital concern, and who were better candidates to raise such a generation than girls? There was urgent need for but lack of enough girls' schools in the time period discussed here. The wave of reforms in the Young Turk period allowed for an exchange of ideas among diverse groups – be they political, ethnic or religious. The Young Turks regarded education, secular and moral, as the pivot of reform. To achieve this, the Ministry of Education ventured to reform schools and increased their numbers.[118] Most of the resources were put aside for primary schools but there were not enough teachers. Therefore, 'teacher factories' (*muallim fabrikaları*), i.e., schools for teachers were established that were incessantly working to train teachers for village schools. These were aware of their duties, yet, the education of teachers was not enough. The efforts of the schools for teachers were also not sufficient to contribute to progress (*terakkiyât*):

> Nations who desire strong and solid progress consider, in the first place, their women. It is an unshakeable truth that the progress of nations begins with the women. The education and progress of men alone is fathomless, empty and worthless. The children of a nation, a race and a people, whose women are not educated, are not as easily and well educated as the children of a nation, a race and a people, whose women are educated. The education of a mother is the basic and the most essential education. The wise one who said 'The hand that swings the cradle rules the world' did not say this in vain.

Since the father had the duty to earn a living for the family, he did not have the time for the education of the children. It was incumbent on the mother to care for the moral and secular education. European nations such as England and Germany progressed because of this. The Ottomans, on the other hand, failed in this matter because their mothers were ignorant, and fanatics accused men who advocated the education of women of a impiety. However, Islamic history was full of examples of learned women who had educated many men. What the Ottomans needed were many girls' schools otherwise progress would stop.[119]

Conversely, Edhem Nejad states, the Americans who laboured to spread Protestantism in the East established girls' schools first wherever they went as they recognized the importance of women in fostering the education of children. He argued that the Ottomans, namely the Young Turk Committee of Union and Progress, should open girls' schools in order to influence the education of the children in a similar way.[120]

The dichotomy between Muslim and foreign schools was also expressed by Ahmed Vasfi Zekeriya, another Ottoman intellectual, in the context of the decline of Islam and the superiority of European civilization.[121] He observed that the greatest cause for that decline and stagnancy in the Islamic world was ignorance (*cehalet*). The pitiful state of the Muslims manifested itself in the lethargy and carelessness that had caused divisions between them. Wherever one went, the level of science, society and civilization of the Muslims was lower than that of neighbouring countries. Even though the 'civilized people' of Europe constantly attacked the Islamic world, there was no sign of an awakening, or vigilance among the Muslims. Wretchedness, sloth and inertia were ruling over the people even though the prophet Muhammad had advised his followers that it was a duty to seek knowledge. Neglecting this religious command and not establishing 'perfect' schools all over the Islamic world whose 'lights of science and knowledge' penetrated the farthest corners, the Muslims would be called to account in the hereafter and also remain in a desolate state in this world and not take a step towards progress in a time of international struggle. The abundance of Muslim schools would not be enough, the curriculum needed to be orderly and appropriate so that the students acquired a real moral and social Islamic education. Otherwise, the Islamic world would not benefit from their guidance and enter 'the path of progress'. The Muslim schools, especially the official Ottoman schools, of that time were described as tiring the brains of the students; the teaching was monotonous, fruitless and weary. For this reason, the students were brought up inactive and lazy and of no use to society.

On the other hand, Missionary schools were, according to Zekeriya, infusing their own ideology into young minds and trying to 'make them French or English'. This a grave danger to the Empire yet no one cared . His solution was for Muslim teachers to play a crucial role in transmitting religious and moral knowledge among Muslim youth, encouraging their students to develop ideals such as brotherhood, unity, perseverance and ambition, and to thus do a great service for the future of Islam.

Zekeriya envisioned a full-fledged Islamic school at an appropriate spacious place in Istanbul with libraries, a mosque, an observatory, sports facilities etc., where Muslim students from as far as the frozen deserts of Siberia and the hot deserts of Africa could receive a real Islamic education and be a perfect example of a united Islamic community. Then 'light would reflect from every corner; everything would be wreathed in smiles and signs of life and happiness would be manifest'. The author dreamed of a school in the calibre of Istanbul's missionary Robert College or others; a school named the 'School of Islamic Brotherhood' (*Uhuvvet-i İslâmiyye Mektebi*).[122]

In the estimation of Ahmed Şerif, yet another Ottoman writer, hopes like this were obviously threatened by the efforts of Protestant missionaries to obstruct the revival of Islam, since their goal was to diffuse Protestantism.[123] One of the foremost and active institutions for this goal was the Syrian Protestant College ('The American University of Beirut'), which was like a *külliye* (in the Islamic context a mosque with a complex of social buildings and a school). The Protestant college had a similar structure to a church, to which Ottoman youngsters came from Beirut, Syria and other places in the Ottoman Empire; apparently, there were more Muslim children than non-Muslim. Ahmed Şerif argued that like at other foreign institutions the 'Ottoman upbringing' (*terbiye-i Osmaniyye*) of the children was doubtful. He argues that the Protestant college was abusing the right of freedom of conscience (*hürriyet-i vicdan*): and that despite not wanting to, the

4. The Nusayris under Young Turk Rule (1908–1918)

Muslim pupils were made to attend church. Students' assertion of Islamic identity was punishable with expulsion from the college:

> Poor freedom of conscience, you unlucky sacred right (*bedbaht hakk-ı mukaddes*), even though you are being imposed on us every day, how are you being abused by them! A Muslim child gets slowly used to it until it becomes a habit. Those masses, spiritual views, counsels, sad melodies and the divine voices of the organs; all these are so attractive that they gradually cover the soul like a cloak and leave their traces, like on a gramophone plate, on the pure brain of a child that is receptive to every impression.

In Şerif's opinion, at the foreign schools the Ottoman children were not taught about their country. There were maps in classrooms of America and France, and the students could describe them perfectly but did not know how to go from Beirut to Istanbul. For the missionaries and teachers these were lessons in 'civilization'. The writer continues in a sarcastic style:

> Meet the missionaries and teachers; honey flows from their mouths (*ağızlarından bal akar*). They only speak about civilizing less humane places and adorning them with the light of knowledge (*İnsaniyetten geri kalmış yerleri temdîn ve nûr-ı irfânla tezyîden başka şeylerden bahs etmezler*). Politics? It's impossible, they don't even think about it. But their deeds do not agree with their words. In reality, they are enemies of our Ottoman and Islamic identity. They always fight against this.

In 1908, the Muslim students at the Syrian Protestant College protested against being forced to go to church. Also, after a missionary gave a speech in which he talked against Islam, they were agitated and refused to participate at the mass. This was six months before the school break, and the parents of those students received a letter saying that that their children could continue in 1909 provided they attended church service. Of course, most of them accepted.[124] Even though no Muslim had become a Protestant, many Muslims had forgotten their Islamic and Ottoman identity.[125] This was, at least, the prejudiced opinion of Ahmed Şerif.

Samizade had given the information about the college in Beirut to Ahmed Şerif but apparently, only a summary of it was published.[126] It was a pity for Samizade because Muslims had the right to know everything about that school that 'played an important role in our economic and political life and was dragging our sacred homeland to a fallacious and dangerous mirage by poisoning the pure character of the children of our homeland with promptings that attract Satan'. Even the Ottoman Ministry of Education was not aware of the danger and had no substantial but superficial information about the college. The failure on the part of the Ottoman central administration was, according to him, part of the political situation in which Sultan Abdülaziz had mismanaged the Empire financially and faced an administrative crisis. He refers to the 'Young Ottomans' who went to Europe and published there against the neglectful Ottoman officials; he cites from a long and detailed letter of the Egyptian liberal Prince Mustafa Fazıl Paşa addressed to Abdülaziz.[127] There it was signalled that the Empire was moving towards a whirlpool of destruction and annihilation and that the only solution was liberty and new regulations. Attention was drawn to the fact that Europe was investing in the education of its people and making progress.[128]

To counter the deleterious effects of missionary activity, he proposed a kind of counter-missionary Islamic society, a 'Society of Spiritual Guides' (*Mürşidîn Cemiyeti*). This required people who would commit their lives for it or spend parts of their lives devoted to the spread of Islam. Spiritual guidance (*mürşidlik*) was a special art which members would need to master. A spiritual guide could be a doctor, a farmer, but they needed to be an expert of something as well as have some knowledge of Islam, the method of disputation, the laws of other religions, in sum of religious studies. A spiritual guide who could render all kinds of material and spiritual service, could be successful everywhere. While the Christian missionaries were actively promoting their religion among Muslims all over the world, it was a shame that Muslims were hesitating and not founding similar societies. However, Samizade Süreyya concludes, the Muslim youth who would perform this, those Ottoman youth, who brightened the Ottoman Revolution (of 1908) and left the world speechless, would stage a revolution in the Islamic world with their idea of guidance and open the brightest page in the history of Islam and the Ottoman Empire.[129]

Rashid Rida (1865–1935),[130] the Syrian–Egyptian Islamic reformer and publicist, tried to fulfil these hopes of educating a new generation of conscious and active young Muslim men who would propagate Islam in the first years of Young Turk rule. He tried to set up a missionary institute in Istanbul in 1910 but failed to convince the Ottomans. He was probably inspired by the Ottoman project of proselytizing and settling groups in Anatolia, Iraq or Yemen who had strayed doctrinally or were nomadic.[131] Rida reported in his *al-Manar* (1900),[132] based on what he read in some newspapers, that the Ottoman centre issued an imperial decree and decided to send some religious scholars to districts in Iraq, such as Basra and Karbala, and to guide (*irshad*) the nomadic tribes there. He was thankful that the Ottoman state was alerted to this matter before it passed out of its hands. The Shi'is had previously disseminated preachers and guides to these Arab tribes and others living on the banks of the Tigris and Euphrates, and most of them entered the Shi'i legal school. For this the Shi'i mullah would go to the tribe and mingle with its elder (*sheikh*) 'like water commingles with an intoxicant', make the religious obligations easy for him and induce his desire as to the approval to enjoy many women, which was the highest concern for those elders. The mullah became the elder's intimate friend and adviser at his command. Thus, the mullah could disseminate his doctrine in the tribe as soon as possible. As regards politics, the Shi'i mullah was satisfied when the people understood that the chief of the Shi'ites was the Iranian shah (*shah al-'ajam*) and the chief of the Sunnis was Abdülhamid. Rida added that those Arabs, even though they did not live in Iran, would undoubtedly assist their chief (the Shah) in case of a dispute between him and the chief of the other sect (the Sultan). In a quite discursive way Rida was saying that the Ottomans could combat Shi'ism to a certain extent by choosing missionaries who are selfless and ready to prioritize reform (*islah*) and guidance (*irshad*) over particular interests, but by paying them, all the more since Shi'a proselytes are contended with merely reaching their missionary goals.

Rida had deep anxieties regarding competition not only from new religious groups such as the Baha'is[133] but also from older and 'misguided' Islamic factions such as the Shi'is. Likewise, he was highly aware of the cultural alienation created by mostly Jesuit and Protestant missionary schools within the Muslim populations of the Ottoman Empire. In his view the Muslims were to be blamed for this state of affairs for having allowed their religion to become the plaything of charlatans, and for having neglected their own education at the hands of incompetent ulema. Rida finally brought to life a missionary institute whose double function was to bring to Islam loosely Islamized populations from outside the Ottoman domains, and to correct the beliefs of 'heretical' Muslims from within the Empire's margins. As a result, Rida opened his *Dar ad-Da'wa wa al-Irshad* ('School of Propaganda and Guidance') in Cairo in 1912 on the eve of World War I.[134]

In any case, the Ottoman Islamist journal *Sırat-ı Müstakim* (*Sırâtımüstakīm*) praised his enterprise in 1911. News came from Cairo that Rida intended to set up a school with a programme similar to those of Christian missionaries but with no political aims whatsoever, only with the purpose of conveying religious and moral education. Religious matters would be taught with sufficient classes on secular topics. The journal's view was that this was great news for the Muslims but it would have been better if such a school were established in Istanbul.[135]

It is striking that Ottoman thinkers of the post-Young Turk Revolution (after 1908) – Turks, Arabs, and others – even Islamists or authors who wrote for Islamist journals, appear to be 'orientalist' in their mode of thinking despite their criticism of the West. Even a thorough Islamist like Rashid Rida, who ventured to educate a new generation of conscious and active young Muslim men who would propagate Islam, had tried to 'correct the beliefs' of the rural population in his home country of Syria, who had succumbed to 'superstitions' and 'innovations'. Rida set up a committee to promote rural education, imitating efforts in many places of the Empire. He personally gave lessons to villagers and claimed to have enlightened them. Despite his intention to serve unlettered communities and having spent much effort and time on this, he could not hide his disdain for them. Even the people in his own villages, also his extended family, were living in an 'inferior and benighted' world and 'deeply in need of the moral edification that he and his fellow scholars would bring'.[136] Vast cultural disparities were dividing him from the 'superstitious' and 'ignorant' people, and this disparity between the 'centre' and the 'periphery' prevailed in his time in the form of 'Ottoman orientalism'.

Rashid Rida's efforts did not yield fruit; his school for Muslim missionaries in Cairo was closed at the beginning of the war in 1914. Britain, assuming the role of overlord of Egypt, had previously put pressure on other Islamic institutions. It had arrested and interrogated members of several societies: the society for the protection of orphans (*Himaye-i Eytâm*), for the encouragement of education (*Teşvik-i Maarif*) and one named 'Unity of Islam' (*İttihad-ı İslam*, i.e. Pan-Islam). All three were not political but civil (*medeni*) in their own estimation: while the first one aimed at rescuing poor orphans from being left to Christian orphanages and so losing their

Muslim and national identity, the second organization wanted to prevent Egyptian Muslims from going to missionary schools and increase the number of national schools. 'Unity of Islam' was a religious institution, and its goal was wiping out sectarian differences among the Muslims. In the estimation of *Sırat-ı Müstakim* the British, whose 'strongest political means were mischief and slander (*fesad ve iftira*)', thought that these were revolutionary political actions and needed to be suppressed.[137]

Surprisingly, Sunni and Shi'i religious scholars in Najaf, Iraq, issued a statement of solidarity (*tezamün*) in 1911 in response to Italy's war in Tripoli directed against Muslims, calling for 'unity and alliance' (*ittihad ve ittifak*). Despite the splits in the Muslim community and the existing differing views between the Sunnis and Shi'is, it was necessary to stand side by side against the 'onslaught of the enemies'. The constant attacks by foreign countries (Europe) against the Ottomans and Iran compelled those religious scholars to unite in order to find solutions to protect the Islamic world.[138] Almost all leading Shi'i clerics in Najaf signed a *fatwa* calling for jihad against Italy. This obviously had a strong impact in Iraq, for following its declaration there were protests, the collection of financial contributions for the war against Italy and the formation of Muslim committees for the defence of Libya. The public meetings were attended by Shi'is and Sunnis alike, and there was a wave of strong pro-Sunni feelings among the Shi'is. The Italian invasion was compared to the Crusades and was seen as an opportunity for unity among all Muslims. Likewise, the call for unity and defence against European powers was reinforced when Britain and Russia occupied parts of northern and southern Iran.[139]

'The homeland of Islam is at danger in the final stage,' wrote Mehmed Fahreddin, another Ottoman to his 'sound minded correligionists'. Of what use, he asked, were Islamic duties after the homeland of Islam is destroyed, the chains of bondage put around the Muslims' neck, the Qur'an torn apart and defiled? He thought that the purpose of all Islamic duties was to defend the Islamic homeland by fighting and protecting the Qur'an, the mosques, the schools from being trampled upon by the enemies and keeping the mothers' and daughters' honour safe from them. The greatest fear of the Europeans was the 'Unity of Islam'. For the Muslims, losing the Ottoman Empire meant losing all the other Islamic domains.[140]

Ottoman writers were voicing 'broad apprehensions over a threatened culture and a vanishing way of life'.[141] The Ottomans had been confronting threats from within and outside in every aspect over several decades, and only seen from the field of education, they thought that the missionaries and other foreigners were much more organized, well-funded and successful than themselves. The schooling efforts of the Ottomans were strongly influenced by a sense that the empire was under siege and vulnerable.[142]

4.4. Late Ottoman official perceptions of non-Sunnis: the case of the Beirut province

However much Ottoman Syria was a 'high-profile case' during the reign of Abdülhamid II in which he aimed to bring 'civilization' and education to religious groups outside Sunni Islam and tie them to a centralized state, efforts to this effect did not yield much fruit. Even though the post-Hamidian Young Turk period aimed at bringing about positive changes in society and seemed to have a secular ideology with an egalitarian approach, the view from above, i.e., from the centre towards the periphery, the 'progressive we' and the 'backward others', continued regardless of regime change. This chapter's focus is on the various nuances in the description and perception of non-Sunni religious groups, foremost the Nusayris/ Alawis, in the late-Ottoman regime of knowledge about them that it gained through a 'scientific and civilizational' tour just before the onset of World War I in Ottoman Syria and Palestine.

The event that made the Ottomans most vulnerable and brought about their end was World War I. The Ottomans, on the verge of extinction owing to strong war enemies such as Russia, England and France, were in search of solutions to shape society in order to survive. Azmi Bey,[143] the governor of Beirut, was looking for new ways to collect information during wartime and sent two officials on two inspection tours in Syria and Palestine in 1916 and 1917. The Ottomans had created the province (*vilayet*) of Beirut in 1888 from the coastal areas of the province of Syria as a recognition of the booming city of Beirut.[144] The new province comprised five *sancak*s or prefectures, namely Latakia, Tripoli, Beirut proper, Akka and Nablus/Balqa. The *sancak* of Lebanon, the regions around Beirut had a special status since 1861, and the *sancak* of Jerusalem was half-autonomous since 1872.

The source in question is the annual/yearbook (*salname*)[145] titled *Beyrut Vilayeti* ('The Province of Beirut') which was intended to provide sound information about the geography and population of the province. The two chosen men touring the province for two months were the young and modern Arab officials, Mehmet Behcet (Muhammad Bahjat) and Refik Temimi (Rafiq at-Tamimi).[146] These energetic men were 'model products' of the modern Ottoman state that had given them the opportunity to study in Istanbul, Salonika and Paris. They authored the two-volume work *Beyrut Vilayeti*, in which they wrote every minute detail of their tour.

Volume 1 is about the southern part (*cenub/janub*) comprising Beirut as the capital, and the prefectures (*sancak*) of Akka/Acre and Nablus/Balqa, and volume 2 deals with the northern part (*şimal/shimal*) of the province, with the *sancak* of Latakia and Tripoli (Trablusşam).[147] The two volumes were published in 1917 and 1918, that is, during the climax and towards the end of World War I, just before it extended to Syria and Palestine. The two volumes were published at the same time in Arabic with the title *Wilayat Bayrut*.[148] A third volume was planned but apparently not realized despite its announcement in the introduction of the second volume: 'However much the detailed investigations relating to the districts in general were completed, a very detailed study of Beirut City, the centre of the province, and its publication as a third volume is planned by the exalted provincial government.' There is, however, another volume in Arabic titled *Lubnan: mabahith 'ilmiyya wa ijtima'iyya* ('Lebanon: Scholarly and Social Researches', Beirut 1918) commissioned by Ismail Hakkı Bey, *mutasarrif* of Jabal Lubnan.

The two volumes were conceived to be very detailed and not a 'meaningless register of ranks and officials' like the old yearbooks:[149] 'It contains observations and descriptions with analyses concerning the geography, ethnography, geology, history, antiquities, psychology, morals, sociology, health, religion, language, literature, fine arts, education, agriculture, commerce, public works and industry of its [Beirut Province] districts.'[150] In terms of religious and ethnic groups, volume 1 comprises the Arabs of Syria, Assyrians (*Süryani*), Babis (i.e., the Baha'is)[151] Shi'is (Metawalis), the Druze, Christians, Jews, Samaritans and Bedouins, and volume 2 includes the Turcomans (Türkmen), Isma'ilis and the Nusayris.

The publication was considered a 'scientific and civilizational guide' (*rehber-i ilmî ve medenî*) and its purpose 'to analyse and study the general condition of our country from the point of view of science and civilization (*ilm ve medeniyet nokta-yı nazarından*) in order to properly know our holy homeland'.[152] *Beyrut Vilayeti* is infused with these kinds of observations to instil in the reader the necessity and importance of civilization, progress, enlightenment and science/knowledge as opposed to decline, ignorance and tradition.[153]

Representing the state's power, Behcet and Temimi travelled freely, entered cities and villages, talked to people and asked questions. In the words of a historian, 'The two officials project state power, too. They go wherever they want and interrogate whomever they please, peasants, merchants, notables, and state officials high and low. And they speak the language of power. They rebuke and reprove, advise and advocate, and address their readers in the second person plural – "you!" ...'[154] As much as the authors were proud of being role models of a modern state, proposing scientific and educational approaches and methods to problems, the power of the state had its limits in regions of the province stricken with poverty, famine and ignorance. The two volumes are infused with these kinds of observations about the people, be they Sunni, from non-Muslim or non-Sunni groups. As argued by Avi Rubin, Behcet and Temimi present in their text 'a version of internalized orientalism', and this let them view the Muslim groups in a more negative fashion than, for instance, the Zionist Jews.[155]

Beyrut Vilayeti reveals this kind of worldview of 'civilizing mission' and 'moral superiority' vis-à-vis various ethnic and religious groups. It is a compendium, social encyclopaedia, government information manual for the formation of policy, and record of a voyage. In sum, the two volumes fulfilled an 'enlightenment' nineteenth-century purpose by transmitting many 'facts' to a literate and official class. The bibliographical sources show the same intent and support claims to Western 'scientific thoroughness'. Beside Turkish, the official language of the Empire (7 entries) and Arabic (33), they include writings French (75); English (22); and German (15).[156]

Thus, 'scientific method guides their steps', and the province presents no obstacles to Behcet's and Temimi's 'measured progress'. Yet, as much as the two authors travelled freely and with ease, and did as they wished, at times they felt directionless and perplexed. In some places science and knowledge had their limits. These were places 'beyond the horizon' of the intellectuals. There was no guide whatsoever and no point of reference. There were places not worthy of being recorded in dictionaries and chronicles written before the time of Temimi and Behcet. But even here our two authors created a new kind of subject and a new kind of text, one in which even the most miserable and un-writable of regions and groups could be sited. *BV* is an organized text, not around the deeds of local leaders and learned men, nor their horsemanship and military prowess, but by the self-consciously 'modern' programme of scientific classification and description. Behcet and Temimi name and record each village, rivers, bridges, gardens and the activity or inactivity of the people. Then come the numbers for the district, the distances between places, and the amount and names of the crops of agricultural productivity. Lastly, they list the population, the numbers of the religious groups, in 'correct' numbers because the earlier censuses were incorrect.[157]

4.4.1. Defining religious groups in 'The Province of Beirut'

Education is one of the main problems wherever the authors go, at least in the outback of cities and towns. Usually, only a low percentage of the Muslims could read and write and their schools were badly organized, provided they had a school; girls were not allowed to go to school. At least half of the Christian population could read and write. Reportedly, most of the Christians knew English due to their wish to emigrate. The social world of the Muslims in many towns and villages of the province is depicted negatively. Their shelters were wretched, cut of stone or made from clay, and the interior sections 'cannot reasonably be called rooms'. The floors were dirty. As one of the authors observed:

> ... and one finds amidst this rocky shabbiness a few brick buildings which look like houses. Then the Government Office and the municipality, and the house of the *qaimaqam* ... and would that I knew whether these are houses? or what on earth I should call them?

Final observations at such places were usually the absence of culture and defining marks of community. Sometimes there was no church despite the majority of Christians, and mosques were shabby and without minaret. The Muslims of these 'wretched' villages were 'like small children, without qualities of spiritual perception, bereft of all light and civilization, mere corporeal beings. One looks at their faces and sees emptiness devoid of all meaning, learning, and experience'. The authors add, resorting to occidental rhetoric and stereotypes of 'the East', that one finds a degree of 'unadulterated oriental rusticity'.[158]

According to the two authors, the Christians were different: they were intellectually more advanced and ahead of the Muslims, also in terms of work and social life. Emigration drew their eyes and hearts away from the homeland. Through money from America they renewed their buildings and their villages were ordered. People said that half of these Christians in the Beirut Province lived from payments from their relatives in America. And when these returned, they brought no worthy characteristics but rather idleness and laziness, using their money to guarantee that they do not have to work. Behcet and Temimi also gave a political explanation for both the submissiveness of the Muslims and their low social condition: this wretchedness stemmed from the oppression of the tyrannical 'princes' and leaders. The villagers were excluded from civilization and progress, not because of some psychological quality or immemorial tradition, but by the arbitrary power of the rulers for whom they laboured. They were convinced that the ruin of the spiritual and social landscape was not 'natural' but indeed the consequence of the domination of the leaders.[159]

Going around the Druze community Behcet and Temimi praised their positive traits such as being very hospitable, ethical and refraining from pomp, but they also criticized their internal hierarchy made up of the 'wise' (*'uqqal*), who possessed and knew the secret religious tenets, and the 'ignorants' (*juhhal*) who had a low rank and were deprived of religious knowledge. Based on this the two authors described the Druze regions as being 'heavily ravaged by fanaticism and ignorance'. What is more, for the authors it was a 'shame for the present civilization' that there was not sufficient knowledge about and access to the religion of the Druze despite the fact that they coexisted for so many years with other religions and had exchanges of all sorts, and even though so many inventions and scientific discoveries were made in the twentieth century. Behcet and Temimi hoped that in the future knowledge and sciences of all sorts would spread in their country and that authoritative Druze scholars would explain their religion as a service for the sake of scholarship and science.[160]

Touring in what is now known as the West Bank, they arrived in the town of Salfit that had a Sunni population. All of them were peasants who lived simple lives. While the men worked the fields, the women helped them but they were also busy at home with the children, cooking, etc. The authors observed the wretched condition of the women who struggled and fought with each other but had to be patient with the hard conditions of life.[161] They noted the religiosity of the Salfit people: that they 'struggle in full measure to hold on to religion and to be religious but since they do not really know their religion their holding on to religion is superficial'. Only 15 to 20 per cent of the townspeople would perform their daily prayers; and this number was dwindling, because very few people went to the mosque. What is more, the people 'deem it not necessary to keep their promises and commit perjury; it can be said that dishonesty is a hereditary disorder'. A notable Salfit is quoted as having uttered these words: 'We are liars and commit perjury. Do not believe us even if we swear by God and the Prophet.'[162] Behcet and Temimi even said, based on the people's statements, that the whole of the region of Nablus was a hotbed of dishonesty. Despite all these 'bad traits' and the poverty they observed that there was no theft and killing among the people of Salfit.

4.5. *The Nusayris in the Province of Beirut*

Another group in a desolate situation in the very late Ottoman Empire was the Nusayri/Alawi community.[163] After a long description of their history and religious tenets, Behcet and Temimi described their social structure, which consisted of the secular/tribal chiefs (*mukaddems*), the religious leadership (sheikhs) and the common people. What follows is a summary of their observations, descriptions and opinions.

The authors stated that there were three classes in Nusayri society: 1. The chiefs, 2. The sheikhs, and 3. The common people. Of course, the chiefs were the most esteemed class. The chiefdom in Safita, for instance, that was inherited and specific to certain families had extraordinary influence and authority. There were many family members who were directly tied to the chief, and so was he was the leader of his family and the clan. As in other ethnic and religious groups described in *BV*, the common people were those who their leaders oppressed and abused. It was known that the Nusayri chiefs, who were quite influential, were arbiters in cases of conflict and dispute and therefore active powerful agents. However, if one considered how the tribal chiefs widened their circle of influence by means of endearing themselves to their people through their generosity and kindness, one should not forget how much they were 'smooth-tongued', felt the pulse of others and suited their actions to their personal requirements. It was especially common that some tribal chiefs consulted state officials in order to increase their own influence.

The Nusayris also had a class of sheikhs who were influential and possessed authority in matters of religion. They report that Nusayrism was an esoteric community that had various mysteries and secrecies, and in order to reveal and teach these (to male followers) there was a need for guides. As these guides could naturally only consist of the conscious class, the people of Safita and other places had to respect the sheikhs. Even as the chiefs bestowed on this learned class their favours and tried to please them, the people had to give taxes under the name of alms (*zekat/zakat*); for this reason, this religious class of the Nusayris lived a pleasant life.

The secular and the religious groups joined forces and were in agreement with each other. But there was a class whose way of life only consisted of serving the fame and pomp of those two groups. And despite that this third group was the working class and intrinsic to all the activities in the district, they were villagers without name or fame. It was the peasantry or the *Fellaheen*, the common people, who worked, toiled and were tired but did not get the reward for their labour:

> As is everywhere, the class that is most worthy of examination is no doubt this majority group of common people. This despised class that is outwardly honoured by the secular leaders with favours and generosity is in fact in a deplorable state. If one thinks carefully that half of the district is in the possession of the class of leaders and the other half belongs to all thirty thousand Nusayris, it becomes clear how much of what is due to the majority of the common people, who are shown artificial favours, is usurped by the leaders. The common people can be divided into three groups: the first is occupied with agriculture, the second with sericulture (silk trade), and the third lives with the money that is sent from America. Two thirds of the Nusayris of Safita live from agriculture: one group consists of agricultural labourers on their own fields but the other

group works on the fields of others, especially of their leaders. As to the other third, half of these people are agriculture and sericulture workers and the other half lives from the money that is sent from America. The yearly income from America in the district amounted 250,000 Liras, and this gives an idea about the number that emigrated from Safita. Yet, whereas the Christian invested in their villages to some extent, the Nusayris have spent the money arbitrarily and did not benefit from it.[164]

It was common knowledge that the *mukaddem*s were the greatest administrative leaders and the sheikhs the religious leaders with utmost authority (*salahiyet*). Consequently, ensuring the livelihood and welfare of the *mukaddem*s as well as the sheikhs was the most important duty of the Nusayris. Outwardly, the *mukaddem*s appeared as quite ordinary and simple people. In fact, in the eyes of the Nusayris who were in their employ they were as frightful and intimidating as giants. Even their names were almost as harsh: *Ghazi* [warrior], *Saqr* [hawk, falcon], etc. There were only a few among the *mukaddem*s who could read and write. The education of the sheikhs was also limited. They only had a grasp of the Nusayri religion and did not have any other specialization. The primary duties of the *mukaddem*s were to administer the affairs between the tribe they belonged to and the government, to protect the rights of the tribe, to ascertain the stance of the tribe towards the government and finally to solve disagreements between the tribes and the government and between the tribes themselves. It was therefore necessary to view the *mukaddem*s as formal representatives (*kapı kethüdası*, also 'deputy') and sometimes as 'local princes' (*emir*). Thus, whenever disputes arose between the tribes the *mukaddem*s of the respective tribes came together, exchanged thoughts, made a decision, and eventually their judgement or decree followed.

The tribes chose the *mukaddem*s for lifetime service. Since the position of the *mukaddem* was hereditary from father to son, it could be likened to medieval feudalism (*derebeylik*). In sum, these 'headstrong and stubborn' leaders, these feudal lords of the Nusayris had seized all influence. However, they also highly respected the sheikhs. In fact, the respect they showed towards each other must be considered as the principle of due reciprocity (*mukabele bi'l-misl*) and was nothing but a tactical manoeuvre at the expense of the common Nusayris. The sheikhs constituted the highest social stratum and the spiritual rulers of the Nusayris as centres of authority. When there was a case of murder, pillage, plundering or theft the *mukaddem*s gathered quickly. At times, the people also asked sheikhs for legal opinions (*istiftâ*) or they solved a murder case, for instance by a verdict to pay 18,000 *kuruş* (piasters) as blood money, and other issues were examined by analogy. For this reason, the *mukaddem*s had immense governing authority over the Nusayris.

As the *mukaddem*s who wielded such power earned their income based on the power and wealth of the tribe, the sheikhs, too, received allocations under the name of alms (*zekât*) and the like. The annual income of a *mukaddem*s was 150–200 Liras, and that of a sheikh 100–150 Liras. The *mukaddem*s were not obliged to engage in agriculture and the like but the common Nusayris worked for them.

4. The Nusayris under Young Turk Rule (1908–1918)

They wore silken robes and when they went to the town there were usually two armed Nusayri cavalry men before them and two armed strong men beside them as aide-de-camps. It was of the most established habits of the *mukaddem*s to have a big rifle in their hands and wear a bandoleer. The *mukaddem*s had the power to get what they want through force, intimidation and oppression.

While the Nusayris generally lived in simple houses, the *mukaddem*s, who were always engaged in fighting and violence owing to their tribal life, lived in houses that were rather solid like small castles. Sometimes the *mukaddem*s had to defend their houses, so they filled them with weapons and ammunition, and were surrounded by guards. The reason the *mukaddem*s had so much influence was because, according to our authors, the 'common people were covered with a very thick cloak of ignorance'. They sent their children to schools in Latakia, where they learned the Qur'an and the religious (Islamic) tenets. However, this kind of learning was to preserve appearances, as the children were ultimately brought into the circle of the fundamental principles of Nusayrism once they reached a specific age.

Once grown up, the sons, as did their fathers, slowly started to oppress the tribe members and employed them 'as if they were cows to be milked'. In their view all the people owed their lives to the *mukaddem*s, and thus it was their most obvious and legitimate right to make them live according to their own whims. Some thirty or forty thousand people were thus instruments in the hands of the leaders whose number was not more than fifty.

Among this huge mass of Nusayris were, based on the authors' approximate calculation, 10,000 whose annual income was less than one thousand *kuruş* and 20,000 whose annual income was less than five thousand *kuruş*. This showed how poor the Nusayris were. What is more, it was said that banditry had been increasing in the district due to this poverty, and some of the Nusayris of Jabla made their living through pillaging and theft. They attacked people in the towns and at the coast and seized whatever they found, and if they faced resistance, people were killed after which they retreated to the mountains.

When looting, the Nusayris of Jabla, according to our authors, resorted to the same method: first, they sent guides in the guise of villagers who spied. Then, during the night, these guides showed the way to 100–150 people who then raided. These vandalized and took whatever they found. They laid waste to places by taking all grain and animals. Because of this banditry, the wide and fertile plains at the coast could not be exploited. Some rich people of Jabla were forced under the protection of some *mukaddem*s by paying an annual tribute (*haraç*) or poll-tax. In return, they were given immunity from pillage and theft. In sum, according to the *BV*, social life in Jabla was immersed in deep anarchy. It was impossible to find here the least amount of 'felicity or a trace of humanity'.[165]

When the two authors visited a Nusayri village, the inhabitants were agitated and stood armed with Martini rifles on the roofs of their houses or in front of the doors. Until the people realized that they were travellers the agitation continued. Among the gunmen was a *mukaddem*, and Behcet and Temimi felt the need to visit him and stayed there for a while. They were invited to their houses; the dwelling of one *mukaddem* had two storeys which were certainly not clean:

They are free of such a positive characteristic. We went to the upper floor and stayed for a while.... Since we didn't feel like staying too much here our conversation was rather superficial and short. The statements of the *mukaddem* who talked about the ignorance of the Nusayris were sincere, lively and genuine. We also heard that the children of the *mukaddem* were studying with the village imam in the other room.

We waited for an opportunity in order to enquire why they were always armed. In response those present sighed and said: 'If you only knew how unsafe our lives are. At any time, we are exposed to a fight, a fire or an attack. Our lives are always in such turmoil and will continue to be.'

Behcet and Temimi contented themselves with listening to the complaints of the *mukaddem* and his followers; they concluded that the main reason for the condition of the Nusayris were the *mukaddem*s. After soothing the mukkaddem's temper somewhat, the authors left.[166]

Referring to the population of Sahyun, the authors say that the majority of the inhabitants were Nusayris, and for this reason one could say that Sahyun was a Nusayri district. The Nusayris of Sahyun were divided into several tribes with armed members and allies. In contrast to them, the authors note that there was no dissension among the Sunni tribes. These collaborated against the Nusayris, who were the majority; the Sunnis were united and free from power struggles. Although there were cases of murder and kidnapping of girls among the Sunni tribes, they mostly settled issues and prevented lasting conflicts among themselves. The attitude of the Sunnis towards the Nusayris was deemed worthy of analysis by the authors. It was very difficult to accept that the Sunnis were fond of the Nusayris; since the Sunnis believed that the beliefs of the Nusayris were erroneous, they presumed that they were worlds apart from the Nusayris, more so than with followers of other religions, such as the Christians. For this reason, the Sunnis did not marry their daughters to Nusayris. But it happened that Sunni men married Nusayri girls; it was said that there were Nusayri girls especially in the houses of local power-holders.[167]

Equally, since there was no evidence that the Nusayris were fond of anyone outside their religion, their attitude was the same as that of the Sunnis. The Sunnis and the Nusayris upheld the status quo in a friendly manner: even if the Sunni and Nusayri tribes of Sahyun did not oppress each other, this situation was, according to the authors, due to equilibrium between the two sides. Therefore, despite having been a minority the Sunnis believed that acting in this way was a means to preserve their own power. This feature, which the Sunnis interpreted as 'courage', had frustrated the Nusayris. However, the Nusayris ascribed this balance to the conflicts between their tribes rather than to what the Sunnis perceived as power and expediency. Groups of Nusayris were like enemies fighting each other at the slightest provocation. The authors observed: 'After all, what delight these two ignorant groups take in spilling the blood of each other like tigers? We see that the Sunni tribes exploit this in order to maintain their own existence. Yet, the Nusayris also admit that the Sunnis attach importance to the power of their arms.'

Owing to this equilibrium it seemed that there were no confrontations between Sunnis and Nusayris; however, about one thousand persons from among the Nusayri tribes made a regular living from banditry. Sometimes they formed bands consisting of one hundred men and attacked villages adjacent to the district, especially those at the coast and places in the district of Latakia; they raided, burned, looted and killed anyone who confronted them. Altogether, according to the authors, the Nusayris were being reduced to the lowest abyss imaginable through this practice that was far from 'civilized' and unbecoming even of 'primitive people'. They caused disaster for their paradise-like and 'magnificent' country and the homeland whose worth they did not know. It was time to end this cruelty by calling them to their senses.[168]

The authors also observed that the Nusayris did not attach any social importance to women. The women in the district of Sahyun were victims of harsh male cruelty. One could only feel compassion for these miserable women who constantly worked and walked around without shoes and clean clothes. Of course, they had the right to loudly complain about the violence they faced. Alas, their frail voices were not heard among the severe uproar caused by those who committed crimes. Nevertheless, the 'civilized' authors considered this as the greatest social crime. Of course, these 'creatures', the male Nusayris, armed with rifles, did not realize what they were doing. As concerned the religious system of the Sunnis, they only had imams in the province capital. There were no religious leaders in their villages. The institution of the Nusayri sheikhs, however, was established everywhere. The sheikhs and the secular leaders governed/controlled the people together as they wished.[169]

Behcet and Temimi set out to study Nusayrism with the purpose of 'disclosing' a sect that was worthy of attention. As much as they intended to be 'as unbiased as possible', relying on 'scientific' works such as those written by Westerners and Alawi authors, they often label the Nusayris negatively owing to their religion the core of which they consider as 'abstruse' Nusayri cosmology. They are described as a 'delusional group', they are basically 'fanatical dreamers' (*müfrit hayalperest*); their religious leaders, starting from Muhammad ibn Nusayr, are described as being 'encircled by a halo of superstitions';[170] 'selfishness' or 'egotism' is 'one of the most important fundamentals' of the Nusayris since they regard themselves as the most important people because they originally were celestial and that only they would be resurrected after death;[171] Behcet and Temimi also state that the Nusayris 'are an ignorant crowd ... tumbling about in thick ignorance', who 'embroider the decorations and ornaments of the door and walls of their visionary house of beliefs with strange imageries'. The two authors thought they were 'realistic' in their judgement owing to their 'scientific' and 'progressive' worldview:

> The Nusayris should know that dreamers with this mental state and who destroy the obligations of civilization and the foundations of reciprocal social affection will be dragged into a whirlpool of degradation and misery and drift away from humaneness. And the more they remain far from intellect, logic, science and civilization they will hardly ascend to the celestial spheres but rather fall into the

lowest abyss of despair and destruction and maybe become non-existent. The strong ones are only those who are nominated for going through the struggle of life in this age. But the weak ones, they will be afflicted by death.[172]

For Behcet and Temimi the Nusayris were as much attached to illusions as the Ismailis, the Druze and the Christians because they were worshipping the sky, believed in metempsychosis and were faithful to the trinity, respectively.[173] Attachment to a legendary cosmology and metaphysical concerns and leading a life as primitive peasants had no good effect on the generations of young Nusayris: they were deprived of science and grew up without reasoning and intellect. For these reasons they did not have ordered towns and streets, hygienic conditions of life, schools, factories, and the like. In short, they neither knew nor could make use of the institutions of civilization and knowledge. Cultivating their imaginary life caused the decline of their cognitive powers.[174] Overall, they considered the Nusayris as being far from logical, having no sense of humanity and society and no. What is more, they were neither attached to each other nor to outsiders who they even hated, and in the authors' view important sacred things such as 'homeland' or 'flag' did not mean anything to them.

From the observations of Behcet and Temimi one could get the impression that only Nusayris and similar people were in such a miserable state. However, the two authors also describe Sunni common people, for instance in Babanna in the district of Safita, as being in a similar state as the Nusayris; they were feeble and weary under the domination of the small number of rich Sunnis.[175] The lifestyle of the poor Sunnis of Sahyun was not different from that of the Nusayris. The latter all lived in damaged houses. In these old houses, they had a white carpet called *libâd*, and those who could spread it on the filthy floor felt lucky. They could not escape their wretched condition because they had been living in the houses together with their cattle. The main cause of their lifestyle was ignorance. All but a few were illiterate. Supposedly, the Sunnis were in the same situation.

Most of the ethnic and religious groups described in *Beyrut Vilayeti* are Arabs, and one might think that it was only they in difficult circumstances. But the Türkmen (Turcoman) of Latakia were no exception. Their lifestyle and community was no better than the Arab people; they too were materially and spiritually deprived.[176]

Clearly, Behcet and Temimi were serving the late Ottoman state, which strived to catch up with the modern and 'rational' European Powers: as much as there were problems, in the end the rational imperial administration would solve those, they believed. Despite the hardships and negative experiences of their tour among so many towns and villages during the hottest months of summer, at the end of their tour they were full of hope and envisioned a bright future for a new race of men:

> We have to admit that when we wanted to return from the northernmost point of the Syrian coast to Beirut, our minds were busy with all the bitter truths. We said to ourselves: 'No, no, the future has much light in store for this most beautiful region on earth. . . . The future will be full of light. Let's be sure about this.' . . . All

the way on our monotonous journey... until Beirut... we were thinking of attaining the various future means of civilization and humanitarian institutions, and meet enlightened civilized people with strong minds and steel bodies who finally would have the full right to live. And we were intoxicated with the promise of the choice wine that the fairy of the future would give us to drink abundantly.[177]

All in all, Behcet and Temimi approached and evaluated their impressions and experiences from the perspective of 'Ottoman orientalism': they talked about a 'we', who were modern and rationalistic and the 'other(s)', who were not. Whatever the worldview of *Beyrut Vilayeti* is, it is an entertaining mixture of travelogue and encyclopaedia and a valuable and unexploited source about a province so difficult to administer and yet diverse and rich in its culture. And to this end we can say that the authors of *Beyrut Vilayeti*, as representatives of the late 'modern' and 'rationalistic' Ottoman Empire during the long nineteenth century until the First World War wished to transform the people for the better and were in search of identities in motion.

As a 'community in motion' in search for a new identity, the Nusayris chose to rename themselves. Most studies about them agree that the term 'Alawi' was not

Figure 4.1 Alawite women gleaning

used until after WWI and probably coined and circulated by Muhammad Amin Ghalib at-Tawil, the Ottoman official and author of the *Ta'rikh al-'Alawiyyin*, and given by the French during their mandate in Syria (1920–1946) However, the term 'Alawi' was already used at the end of the nineteenth century. It is interesting to note that in a memorandum about and petitions by the Nusayris from 1892 and 1909 they are called 'the Alawi people from the children of Arabs' (*evlad-ı Arap Alevi taifesi*), 'our Alawi Nusayri people' (*ta'ifatuna an-Nusayriyya al-'Alawiyya*) or 'signed with Alawi people' (*Alevi taifesi imzasıyla*).[178] Moreover, in 1903 Henri Lammens visited a certain Nusayri sheikh Abdullah of the Haydari branch in a village near Antakya and mentions that the latter preferred the name 'Alawi' for his people.[179]

I would describe the issue of the identity of the Alawis and similar groups by calling to attention Heather Sharkey's question about whether all these groups such as the Yezidis, Alawis, Druze or Alevis were Muslims.[180] Her answer to this question is between 'technically yes', 'maybe', 'maybe not', 'not really' and 'sort of'. Even outside observers in the nineteenth century gave different assessments on this issue, and members of these groups appeared to identify themselves with Islam and the Muslims to different degrees. While the question is not easy to answer, it does show the ambivalent approach of the Ottomans to minority faiths.

CONCLUSION

In earlier centuries, the Ottomans carried out efforts to consolidate Ottoman Sunnism in the context of the Qur'anic dictum of 'commanding right and forbidding wrong'. Efforts aimed at correcting the beliefs of Muslims and non-Muslims alike by the Ottoman state and ulema in the eighteenth and nineteenth centuries need to be seen in the context of the centralization of the state and its attempt to 'civilize' people it deemed as being outside the scope of official Ottoman Islam, by which it meant Hanafi-Sunnism. Ottoman governors began to suggest sending Sunni preachers, scholars and later 'missionaries' to these regions to teach the fundamentals of Islam, thereby making these 'disobedient' groups at the peripheries o supportive Muslim allies. The concept of *tashih-i itikad* replaced the more widely used 'commanding the right and forbidding wrong' and became a political tool to 'civilize' those groups they considered to be outside the Sunni fold with an eye towards centralization efforts and, towards the end of the nineteenth century, a desire for pan-Islamic unity.

As early as the late eighteenth century, the Ottomans applied a policy of 'correction of belief(s)' as a measure to 'civilize' what they considered to be heretical groups or disobedient borderland tribes, such as the Circassians. This reached a climax after 1826, with the harsh ban on the Bektaşi order and the attempt to Sunnitize its followers following the centralization policies of Mahmud II. I argue that Mahmud II's efforts at taming the Bektaşis were not out of religious zeal, but imperial anxieties. Mahmud II was concerned with the preservation of order and entrenching his policies of centralization. However, after Mahmud II's death, these efforts declined to the point where the Bektaşi order silently resurfaced pretending to be Sunni Nakşbendis; predominantly after the state had placed the latter in control of many of the former Bektaşi institutions.

During the Tanzimat, the state became rather more tolerant towards 'heterodox' groups. There were attempts to unite the various non-Sunni sects for military purposes. The Ottomans applied the idea of 'correction of belief(s)' in a broader fashion. Ottoman thinkers, recognizing that a significant part of the Ottoman population was composed of different sectarian groups, many of whom were considered to be superficially Muslim, called for a missionary proselytization of these different groups. In this regard, the main Ottoman concern had a primarily military aspect: in its determination to establish and implement standardization policies, the state wanted to unify all the different Ottoman soldiers militarily under the umbrella of Sunni Islam in order to improve their effectiveness. It seems that the Ottoman view of sectarian difference was not completely negative; these groups were rather seen as potential allies if they could be persuaded to positions that were more 'orthodox'. The influence of the Ottoman policy of 'correction of belief(s)' was not strong but the reforms during the Tanzimat as a project of standardization, promised equal rights to all 'citizens'. It allowed the Nusayris/Alawis to make use of Ottoman educational institutions, admitting them to schools, mosques, councils and other institutions, although they faced the enmity of many Sunnis, high and low, and from the Christians who discriminated them as local competitors.

The measure that the state took during the reign of Abdülhamid II in response to the missionary schools was a systematized policy based on a new ideological approach. The policy of Islamism or Pan-Islamism, which was introduced as the official ideology of the state during that time, was initiated to strengthen the loyalty of the Muslim subjects to the state. This policy aimed to strengthen the bond between the state and 'heterodox' Muslim groups, which were outside Sunni Islam and were targeted by Western Christian missionaries. However, according to Islamism the relationship that could be established with these groups could be made by *ihtida*, conversion to Islam, or by adopting the official ideology of the state through 'correction of belief(s)'. The new relations that were to be established with those outside Sunni Islam and with the Nusayris would be made from this ideological perspective.

Then again, by the Abdülhamid II period, following catastrophic military defeats, sectarianism was viewed as an urgent duty that needed to be vigorously suppressed, the 'heretical' groups not just won over. While cooperating with groups who were willing to be won over and drawn closer to the state, other groups were defined as being 'uncivilized' or 'barbarous' and Ottoman state pursued the 'carrot-and-stick' tactics to suppress groups who would not cooperate. And when Protestant missionaries attempted to evangelize groups that were seen as 'heretical' and outside the Sunni community, the state responded by defining these groups as Muslims and marginals, and successfully suppressed many of the Protestant attempts at converting these groups. Sunni education as counter-propaganda was favoured instead of forceful measures.[1]

What was distinctive to the Hamidian period, as opposed to the earlier efforts of Mahmud II, is that the whole policy of reforms was subordinated to a more strongly felt need for 'unity among the Muslim population of the Empire'.[2] With the rule of Abdülhamid II, the concept of 'correction of belief(s)' was applied differently once again, this time in the context of a 'civilizing mission', again for the centralization of the sultan's powers. This was also intended to protect various non-Sunni groups from the conversion campaigns of Christian missionaries. Even if Abdülhamid's strategy of incorporating heretical groups did not really win them over, the government's policy successfully isolated them from the American Protestant missionaries. Protestantism as represented by the ABCFM, became a main ideological enemy for the Ottomans because it regarded Islam as the archenemy and challenged traditional Muslim cohesion and power. Particularly as it seemed to have the ideological potential to win over groups of nominal Muslims or to initiate something like a renaissance of the Alevis, Nusayris and Yezidis.

Behcet and Temimi's solution for the 'backward' people, as expressed in *Beyrut Vilayeti*, was proper education in primary schools. They criticized the Young Turk government, despite its discourse on the 'morality of progress', for failing to provide public education and so boost the provincial peripheries out of their assumed backwardness. Behcet and Temimi approached and evaluated their impressions and experiences from the perspective of an 'Ottoman orientalism'.

Certainly, the identities of the Nusayris, the Alevis, the Yezidis and the like, changed due to the influence of American missionaries on American–Ottoman relations and their identities are therefore a 'story of reciprocal impact',[3] as Heather Sharkey put it. It started with the first missionaries in the Ottoman Empire, Pliny and Fisk, who initiated foundational encounters between the United States and the region that we now call the Middle East. American missionary activities also changed the social history of the Ottomans in that schools, hospitals and other institutions were established and involved many people, be they Jews, Muslims or Christians, orthodox or heterodox groups, Turks, Arabs, Armenians etc. Even though the number of conversions to Protestantism was low all parties involved were affected. It can be argued likewise that 'foundational encounters' between state-sponsored Sunni missionaries and heterodox religious groups led to the identity transformation of the latter. Hitherto unnoticed opportunities provided the Alawis with a new perspective. They also enjoyed a political education, which would lay the basis for future claims for individuals and the community as a whole.

The initial negative attitude of the Ottomans towards the Nusayris changed considerably during the nineteenth century. One of the reasons for that was the increasing intervention of the European Powers in internal Ottoman politics on behalf of religious minorities. It compelled the Ottoman government to acknowledge the Nusayris as a religious community in its own right. Another factor inducing the Ottoman administrative system to get closer to the Nusayris was the expansion of missionary activities of the American Protestants organized by the *American Board of Commissioners for Foreign Missions* (ABCFM) among heterodox Muslim groups. Fearing the infiltration of the Nusayris by these missionaries, Sultan Abdülhamid II took pains to integrate them into the Muslim community and to draw them closer to the official Hanafi School. The construction of mosques and schools (sg. *medrese*) in the Nusayri region was intended to turn the 'heretics' into good and loyal subjects. Despite the fact that official Ottoman documents mention conversions of tens of thousands of heretics to Sunni Islam, the 'civilizing project' of Abdülhamid was not successful in the end. In the same vein, the missionaries, who had been trying to establish a new social order based on the millenarian belief, hardly succeeded in converting 'heterodox' Muslims to their belief. The Nusayris, in turn, underwent a collective transformation process in this period, in the course of which they started to term themselves 'Alawis' (Turk. *Aleviler*, Arab. *'Alawiyyun*).

As I have argued earlier,[4] this early self-designation has, in my opinion, a triple importance. Firstly, it shows that the word 'Alawi' was always used by these people, as Alawi authors emphasize; secondly, it hints at the reformation of the Nusayris, launched by some of their sheikhs in the nineteenth century and their attempt to be accepted as part of Islam; and thirdly, it challenges the claims that the change of the identity and name from 'Nusayri' to 'Alawi' took place around 1920, in the beginning of the French mandate in Syria.[5]

The name 'Alawi' became accepted after World War I with the short-lived 'State of the Alawis' (Arab. *Dawlat al-'Alawiyyin*, French *l'État des Alaouites*)[6] under French mandate in Syria as an autonomous region and later as one of the 'Federation States of Syria'.[7] It known that the Alawis were made into a dominant sect by the French, who were trying to counter Sunni hegemony in Syria.[8] The findings here indicate that the Alawis were already prepared for this role ultimately by the tension between the Ottomans and the Western powers.

NOTES

Acknowledgements

1 *Die Welt des Islams* 52 (2012), pp. 23–50; integrated here in a modified and extended version.
2 Edinburgh University Press 2019; this chapter is also included here in a modified version.

Introduction

1 al-Adhani, Sulayman. *Kitab al-Bakura as-Sulaymaniyya fi Kashf Asrar ad-Diyana an-Nusayriyya*. Beirut, 1863.
2 For the issue, see Stefan Winter, *A History of the 'Alawis: From Medieval Aleppo to the Turkish Republic* (Princeton, 2016), p. 204. Among the most recent publications about Alawi theology are Meir M. Bar-Asher and Arieh Kofsky, *The Nusayri-'Alawi Religion: An Enquiry into Its Theology and Liturgy* (Leiden, 2002); and Yaron Friedman, *The Nusayri-'Alawis: An Introduction to the Religion, History and Identity of the Leading Minority in Syria* (Leiden, 2010).
3 Edward A. Salisbury, 'The Book of Sulaimân's First Ripe Fruit, Disclosing the Mysteries of the Nusairian Religion', *Journal of the American Oriental Society* 8 (1866), pp. 227–308. The *Bakura* is the main source for René Dussaud, *Histoire et religion des Nosairîs* (Paris, 1900).
4 Henry H. Jessup, *Fifty-Three Years in Syria*, 2 vols. (New York, 1910), 1: 255–264, quotes from pp. 255 and 261.
5 See his official biography in the *sicill-i ahval* at the Ottoman Archives, BOA, DH. SAIDd. 113/439, 29 Zi'l-Hicce 1294/4 January 1878. My thanks to Abdulhamit Kırmızı for this reference.
6 An important study that does not use Ottoman sources, is Dick Douwes, 'Knowledge and Oppression: The Nusayriyya in the late Ottoman Period,' in: *Convegno sul tema La Shia nell'impero Ottomano* (Roma: Accademia nazionale dei Lincei, Fondazione Leone Caetani, 1993), pp. 149–169. Otherwise, the following utilize Ottoman archival sources: Selim Deringil, 'The Invention of Tradition as Public Image in the Late Ottoman Empire, 1808 to 1908,' in: *Comparative Studies in Society and History*, Vol. 35, No. 1. (Jan., 1993), pp. 3–29; Stefan Winter, 'La révolte alaouite de 1834 contre l'occupation égyptienne: perceptions alaouites et lecture ottomane', *Oriente Moderno* 79-3 (1999), pp. 61–71; idem, 'The *Nusayris* before the Tanzimat in the Eyes of Ottoman Provincial Administrators, 1804-1834', in: Thomas Philipp/Christoph Schumann (eds.), *From the Syrian Land to the States of Syria and Lebanon* (Ergon: Würzburg, 2004), pp. 100–103. Contributions are by Yvette Talhamy (in Hebrew), *Meridot ha-Nusayrim ('Alawim) be-Surya be-me'a ha-tesha' 'esre* ("The Nusayriyya Uprisings in Syria in the Nineteenth

Century'), Ph.D. thesis, University of Haifa, 2006; idem, 'The *Nusayri* Leader Isma'il Khayr Bey and the Ottomans (1854–58)', in: *Middle Eastern Studies (MES)* 44:6 (November 2008), pp. 895–908; idem, 'American Protestant Missionary Activity among the Nusayris (Alawis) in Syria in the Nineteenth Century', in: *MES*, 44:6 (March 2011), pp. 215–236; idem, 'Conscription among the Nusayris ('Alawis) in the Nineteenth Century', *British Journal of Middle Eastern Studies, (BJMES)* 38:01 (2011), pp. 23–40; idem, 'American Protestant Missionary Activity among the Nusayris (Alawis) in Syria in the Nineteenth Century', in: *Middle Eastern Studies* 47:2 (March 2011), pp. 215–236. See also the Nusayri issue of *Türk Kültürü ve Hacı Bektaş Veli Araştırma Dergisi* (henceforth *TKHBVAD*), Bahar/Spring 2010, no. 54.

Turkish Studies that use Ottoman sources are: İlber Ortaylı, '19. Yüzyılda Heterodox Dinî Gruplar ve Osmanlı İdaresi', in: *İslâm Araştırmaları Dergisi*, I/1 (İstanbul 1996), pp. 63–68, republished in: idem, *Batılılaşma Yolunda* (Merkez Kitaplar: Istanbul 2007), pp. 156–160; idem, 'Alevilik, Nusayrîlik ve Bâbıâli', in: *Tarihî ve Kültürel Boyutlarıyla Türkiye'de Aleviler, Bektaşiler, Nusayrîler* (Ensar Neşriyat: Istanbul, 1999), republished in *Batılılaşma Yolunda*, pp. 161–169; Hakan Mertcan, *Türk Modernleşmesinde Arap Aleviler: Tarih, Kimlik, Siyaset* (3rd edn. Adana, 2015). A study in Arabic with no reference to Ottoman sources are Muhammad Amin Ghalib at-Tawil, *Tarikh al-'Alawiyyin* (Latakia, 1924), p. 443; Turkish translation: Muhammed Emîn Gâlip et-Tavîl, *Arap Alevîlerinin Tarihi: Nusayrîler* (transl. İsmail Özdemir; Istanbul, 2000).

7 See, e.g., Ömer Uluçay, *Arap Aleviliği: Nusayrilik* (Adana, 1996); idem, *Tarih'te Nusayrilik* (Adana, 2011).
8 Dick Douwes, 'Knowledge and Oppression: The Nusayriyya in the late Ottoman Period.'
9 *Conversion and Apostasy in the Late Ottoman Empire* (Cambridge/UK, 2012).
10 Yvette Talhamy, 'American Protestant Missionary Activity among the Nusayris'.
11 See my review of Winter's book in *Der Islam* 96:1 (2019), https://doi.org/10.1515/islam-2019-0022
12 'The Yezidis and the Ottoman State: Modern Power, Military Conscription, and Conversion Policies, 1830-1909', MA Thesis, Boğaziçi University (Istanbul, 2008); "'Heretik' aşiretler ve II. Abdulhamid rejimi: Zorunlu askerlik meselesi ve ihtida siyaseti odağında Yezidiler ve Osmanlı idaresi', in: *Tarih ve Toplum-Yeni Yaklaşımlar* 9 (2009), 87–156; 'Turning the "Heretics" into Loyal Muslim Subjects: Imperial Anxieties, the Politics of Religious Conversion, and the Yezidis in the Hamidian Era' in: *Muslim World* 103 (2013) 1–23; '"Devil Worshippers" Encounter the State: "Heterodox" Identities, State Building, and the Politics of Imperial Integration in the Late Ottoman Empire', in: Ali Sipahi / Dzovinar Derderian / Yaşar Tolga Cora (eds.), *The Ottoman East in the Nineteenth Century: Societies, Identities and Politics* (London, 2016), 133–155.
13 Heather J. Sharkey, *A History of Muslims, Christians, and Jews in the Middle East* (Cambridge, 2017).
14 Since the office of the prime minister in Turkey was abolished on 9 July 2018 and the supreme power was handed to the president, all archives are now under his aegis and thus the name of this archive was changed into *T.C. Cumhurbaşkanlığı Devlet Arşivleri Başkanlığı* (Turkish Presidential State *Archives* of the Republic of Turkey). However, I will use throughout the book the established abbreviation BOA for documents from the Ottoman Archive.
15 Ahmed Cevdet Paşa, *Sosyalistlere Dair Bir Makale*, Atatürk Kitaplığı (Istanbul), MC_Yz_O_0008; latinised text in: Ahmet Zeki İzgöer, 'Ahmet Cevdet Paşa'nın Sosyal ve İktisadî Görüşleri', PhD Thesis (Marmara Üniversitesi: Istanbul 1997) pp. 183–186.

16 Kamal Salibi/Yusuf K. Khoury (eds.), *The Missionary Herald: Reports from Syria 1819-1870*, 5 vols. (Amman, 1995).
17 Salibi/Khoury, *The Missionary Herald*, 5: 253-328; Uygur Kocabaşoğlu, *Kendi Belgeleriyle Anadolu'daki Amerika: 19. Yüzyılda Osmanlı İmparatorluğu'ndaki Amerikan Misyoner Okulları* (Istanbul, 1989), p. 126.
18 Henri Lammens, 'Au pays des Nosairis', in: *Revue de l'Orient chrétien* 4 (1899), pp. 572-590; and in: *Revue de l'Orient chrétien* 5 (1900), pp. 99-117, 303-318, 423-444; 'Les Nosairis Furent – Ils Chrétiens ?', in: *Revue de l'Orient chrétien* 6 (1901), pp. 33-50; 'Une visite au šaih supreme des Nosairis Haidaris', in: *Journal Asiatique* XI:V (1915), pp. 139-159.
19 *Writing Religion: The Making of Turkish Alevi Islam* (Oxford, 2013).
20 Christin Allison, *The Yezidi Oral Tradition in Iraqi Kurdistan* (London, 2001), pp. 40-41.

Chapter 1

1 Ahmet Yaşar Ocak, *Osmanlı Toplumunda Zındıklar ve Mülhidler (15.-17. Yüzyıllar)*, (Istanbul, 1998). The quotation is in Turkish and on the page before the introduction (Önsöz).
2 English translation: Xenophon, *Memorabilia*. Translated and annotated by Amy L. Bonnette (Ithaca/London, 1994), p. 1.
3 İsmail Albayrak, 'The Other' Among Us: The Perception of Khārijī and Ibāḍī Islam in the Muslim Exegetical Traditions', in: *Ankara Üniversitesi İlahiyat Fakültesi Dergisi* 54:1 (2013), pp. 35-63 (here p. 36).
4 Kohlberg, E., 'al-Rāfiḍa', in: *Encyclopaedia of Islam*, Second Edition, edited by: P. Bearman, Th. Bianquis, C.E. Bosworth, E. van Donzel, W.P. Heinrichs. Consulted online on 18 January 2018, http://dx.doi.org/10.1163/1573-3912_islam_SIM_6185.
5 Mehmet Zeki Pakalın, *Osmanlı Tarih Deyimleri ve Terimleri Sözlüğü*, 3 vols. (Istanbul, 1983), 3:2-5, q.v. 'Rafizî'; Mustafa Öz, 'Râfızîler', in: *Diyanet İslam Ansiklopedisi* (DİA), 34:396-397, online: https://islamansiklopedisi.org.tr/rafiziler (accessed 15 January 2020).
6 Yalçın Çakmak, *Sultanın Kızılbaşları*, pp. 95, fn. 148.
7 Ahmet Yaşar Ocak, 'Türk Heterodoksi Tarihinde Zındık, Hâricî, Râfizî, Mülhid ve Ehl-i Bid'at Terimlerine Dair Bazı Düşünceler', in: *İstanbul Üniversitesi Edebiyat Fakültesi Tarih Enstitüsü Dergisi*, no. 12 (1981-82), pp. 507-520; F.C. De Blois, 'Zindīḳ', in: *Encyclopaedia of Islam*, Second Edition, Edited by: P. Bearman, Th. Bianquis, C.E. Bosworth, E. van Donzel, W.P. Heinrichs. Consulted online on 4 April 2019, http://dx.doi.org/10.1163/1573-3912_islam_COM_1389.
8 Unless otherwise indicated, I am using A. J. Arberry translation, *The Koran interpreted* (Oxford, 1964) but sometimes depart from it. I also use *The Quranic Arabic Corpus*, http://corpus.quran.com/
9 See, Ze'ev Maghen, *After Hardship Cometh Ease: The Jews as Backdrop for Muslim Moderation* (Berlin/New York, 2006), p. 55-57.
10 Ibid., p. 4.
11 Ibid., p. 58 and footnote (fn.) 13.
12 Maghen, p. 58; cf. Abu Abdullah al-Qurtubi, *al-Jamiʿ li-Ahkam al-Qur'an* (Beirut, 2006), 24 vols., 8:103.
13 Quoted in Maghen, *After Hardship Cometh Ease*, p. 58, and fn. 14; for the inaccurateness of the term 'extremism', see fn. 23.

14 For an excellent analysis, see Michael Cook's monumental work, *Commanding Right and Forbidding Wrong in Islamic Thought*, published first in 2000 by Cambridge University Press (in this paper I use the 2004 edition) and the abridged version *Forbidding Wrong in Islam* (Cambridge/UK, 2003). See also, Patricia Crone, *God's Rule: Government and Islam* (New York, 2004), pp. 300–303; Gerhard Böwering et al. (eds.), *The Princeton Encyclopedia of Islamic Political Thought* (Princeton, 2013), q.v. 'commanding right and forbidding wrong', pp. 104–105.
15 Bernard Lewis, *The Political Language of Islam* (Chicago, 1991), p. 29, fn. 8, and p. 129.
16 Asma Afsaruddin, 'Maslaha as a Political Concept', in: Mehrzad Boroujerdi (ed.), *Mirror for the Muslim Prince: Islam and the Theory of Statecraft* (New York, 2013), p. 31.
17 Maghen, *After Hardship Cometh Ease*, p. 59.
18 Quoted in ibid. p. 58–59 and fn. 18.
19 Cf. ibid. p. 59. Here the original for 'transgress not' is not *la taghlu* but *la ta'tadu*.
20 Jane Dammen McAuliffe, *Encyclopedia of the Qur'an*, 6 vols. (*EQ*; Leiden, 2001-2006), 3:402, q.v. 'Moderation'.
21 Qurtubi, *al-Jami'*, 7:229.
22 Ibid. 2:434.
23 Whereas the name of this branch of Shi'ism has often been translated as 'extremists' or 'exaggerators', it has been suggested to use 'transgressors', since the word 'extremism' in modern English carries the meaning of terrorism, and 'exaggeration' does not convey the sense of malice implied, i.e., going to harmful excess in belief; see Sean W. Anthony, *The Caliph and the Heretic: Ibn Saba' and the Origins of Shi'ism* (Leiden, 2012), pp. 2–3, n. 1, and idem, 'Ghulāt (extremist Shī'īs)', in: *Encyclopaedia of Islam, THREE*, Edited by: Kate Fleet, Gudrun Krämer, Denis Matringe, John Nawas, Everett Rowson. Consulted online on 17 January 2018, http://dx.doi.org/10.1163/1573-3912_ei3_COM_27473. First published online: 2018; see also Marshall Hodgson, 'Ghulāt', in: *Encyclopaedia of Islam*, Second Edition, Edited by: P. Bearman, Th. Bianquis, C.E. Bosworth, E. van Donzel, W.P. Heinrichs. Consulted online on 18 January 2018, http://dx.doi.org/10.1163/1573-3912_islam_SIM_2517; idem, 'How Did the Early Shī'a become Sectarian?', in: *Journal of the American Oriental Society*, Vol. 75, No. 1 (Jan.–Mar., 1955), pp. 1–13; and Heinz Halm, 'ḠOLĀT', in: *Encyclopædia Iranica*, online at www.iranicaonline.org/articles/golat (accessed 10 October 2018). For a concise summary of *ghulat*, see Ayatollah Ja'far Sobhani, *Doctrines of Shi'i Islam: A Compendium of Imami Beliefs and Practices* (London, 2001), pp. 175–176.
24 Yaron Friedman, *The Nuṣayrī-'Alawīs: An Introduction to the Religion, History and Identity of the Leading Minority in Syria* (Leiden, 2010), pp. 81–84.
25 Sean W. Anthony, 'The Legend of 'Abdallāh ibn Saba' and the Date of Umm al-Kitāb', in: *Journal of the Royal Asiatic Society*, Third Series, Vol. 21, No. 1 (Jan. 2011), pp. 1–30; idem, *The Caliph and the Heretic*.
26 William T. Tucker, *Mahdis and Millenarians: Shī'ite Extremists in Early Muslim Iraq* (Cambridge/UK, 2008), pp. 13–15.
27 Quoted in Meir M. Bar-Asher, 'The Qur'ān Commentary Ascribed to Ḥasan al-'Askarī', in: *The Jerusalem Studies in Arabic and Islam* 24 (2000), pp. 358–379 (here pp. 371–372).
28 Muhammad Baqir al-Majlisi, *Bihar al-Anwar*, vol. 25 (Beirut, 1983), p. 266; my translation.
29 Quoted in Bar-Asher, 'The Qur'ān Commentary', p. 370.
30 Ibid., p. 372.
31 Ayatullah Ibrahim Amini, *Imamate and the Imams*, trans. Hamideh Elahinia (Qom, 2011), online at www.al-islam.org/imamate-and-imams-ayatullah-ibrahim-

amini/chapter-2-ahlul-bayt-quran-and-traditions (accessed 2 March 2016); al-Majlisi, 25:288.
32 Ibid., p. 265; English in Sobhani, *Doctrines of Shi'i Islam*, p. 176. The last sentence is my own translation.
33 Diana Steigerwald, 'Ibn Nuṣayr', in: *Encyclopaedia of Islam, THREE*. Edited by: Kate Fleet, Gudrun Krämer, Denis Matringe, John Nawas, Everett Rowson. Brill Online, 2015. Reference. Universitatsbibliothek Bamberg. 16 December 2015, http://referenceworks.brillonline.com/entries/encyclopaedia-of-islam-3/ibn-nusayr-COM_23483; Matti Moosa, *Extremist Shiites: The Ghulat Sects* (New York, 1988), pp. 259–262.
34 Heinz Halm, 'Nuṣayriyya', in: *Encyclopaedia of Islam*, Second Edition, Edited by: P. Bearman, Th. Bianquis, C.E. Bosworth, E. van Donzel, W.P. Heinrichs. Consulted online on 16 January 2018, http://dx.doi.org/10.1163/1573-3912_islam_COM_0876; Asad Haydar, *al-Imam as-Sadiq wa al-madhahib al-arba'a*, vol. 1 (Beirut, 1969, 3. ed.), p. 235.
35 Quoted in Sobhani, *Doctrines of Shi'i Islam*, p. 175.
36 For al-Majlisi's excommunication of the *ghulat*, see Friedman, *The Nuṣayrī-'Alawīs*, pp. 176–180.
37 Al-Majlisi, 25:346; English in Sobhani, *Doctrines of Shi'i Islam*, p. 176.
38 Mohammad Ali Amir-Moezzi, *The Divine Guide in Early Shi'ism: The Sources of Esotericism in Islam* (New York, 1994), p. 130; for this, see Stefan Winter, *A History of the 'Alawis: From Medieval Aleppo to the Turkish Republic* (Princeton, 2016), pp. 13–14.
39 Moojan Momen, *An Introduction to Shi'a Islam: The History and Doctrines of Twelver Shi'ism* (Oxford, 1985), pp. 67–68.
40 Aslam Farouk-Alli, 'The Genesis of Syria's Alawi Community', in: Michael Kerr/Craig Larkin (eds.), *The Alawis of Syria: War, Faith and Politics of the Levant* (Oxford, 2015), pp. 27–47.
41 Momen, *Shi'a Islam*, pp. 65–66.
42 Ibid., p. 66.
43 Heinz Halm, *Die Islamische Gnosis: Die Extreme Schia und die 'Alawiten* (Zürich/München, 1982), p. 23 ff.; idem, *Die Schia* (Darmstadt, 1988), pp. 24–25.
44 Ibid., p. 21.
45 Halm, *Die Schia*, p. 7, pp. 11–12.
46 Momen, *Shi'a Islam*, pp. 65–68; Halm, *Die Schia*, pp. 21–26.
47 Halm, *Die Islamische Gnosis*, p. 25. A recently published study on *ghulat* is Mushegh Asatryan, *Controversies in Formative Shi'i Islam The Ghulat Muslims and their Beliefs* (London: I. B. Tauris, 2017). See also Tucker 2008 for an analysis of the earliest evolution of the ghulat during the Umayyad dynasty from 661 to 750.
48 Friedman, *The Nuṣayrī-'Alawīs*, pp. 10, 14–15, 16–17, 18–19; Moosa, *Extremist Shiites*, pp. 262–263.
49 Yaron Friedman, 'Al-Ḥusayn ibn Ḥamdân al-Khasîbî. A Historical Biography of the Founder of the Nuṣayrī- 'Alawi Sect', in: *Studia Islamica*, vol. 93 (2001), pp. 91–112.; idem, *The Nuṣayrī-'Alawīs*, S. 17–35.
50 Idem, 'al-Khasîbî', p. 20.
51 Iranian dynasty in the tenth–eleventh centuries; Tilman Nagel, 'Buyids', in: Encyclopaedia Iranica, http://www.iranicaonline.org/articles/buyids (accessed 28.01.2019).
52 Arabic-Shi'i dynasty in Northern Iraq and Syria between 890 and 1003; Hugh N. Kennedy, *The Prophet and the Age of the Caliphates: The Islamic Near East from the 6th to the 11th Century* (Harlow/UK, 2004), chapter 10.
53 Friedman, 'al-Khasîbî', pp. 289–294.

54 Moosa, *Extremist Shiites*, pp. 267-268; Friedman *The Nuṣayrī-'Alawīs*, pp. 40-42; Meir Bar-Asher/Aryeh Kofsky, *The Nuṣayrī-'Alawī Religion*; idem, *Kitab Al-Ma'arif by Abu Sa'id Maymun B. Qasim Al-Tabarani: Critical Edition with an Introduction* (Leuven, 2012).
55 Friedman *The Nuṣayrī-'Alawīs*, pp. 260-261; Arabic Text and commentary: Rudolf Strothmann, 'Festkalender der Nusairier: Grundlegendes Lehrbuch im syrischen Alawitenstaat', in: *Der Islam* (1944-46), vol. 27.
56 Stephan Procházka, 'The Alawis', in: *Oxford Research Encylopedia of Religion* (2015), DOI:10.1093/acrefore/9780199340378.013.85, p. 4 (downloaded PDF).
57 Winter, *A History of the 'Alawis*, pp. 37-41.
58 Ibid., pp. 8, 61-68.
59 Ibid., S. 8.
60 Isma'ili dynasty in North Africa and Syria, 909-1171; see Heinz Halm, *Das Reich des Mahdi: Der Aufstieg der Fatimiden (875-973)* (München, 1991), idem, *Die Kalifen von Kairo: Die Fatimiden in Ägypten (973-1074)* (München, 2003).
61 Winter, *A History of the 'Alawis*, pp. 41-42.
62 Ibid. pp. 54-61, 73, 80, 174 and 269.
63 Ibid., p. 8.
64 Ibid. chapter. 3; Winter, 'The Alawis in the Ottoman Period', in: Kerr/Larkin, *The Alawis of Syria*, pp. 49-62.
65 Winter, *A History of the 'Alawis*, pp. 159-160.
66 Moosa, *Extremist Shiites*, pp. 337-341; Laila Prager, *Die 'Gemeinschaft des Hauses': Religion, Heiratsstrategien und transnationale Identität türkischer Alawi-/Nusairi-Migranten in Deutschland* (Münster, 2010), pp. 67-69; a third and later split is the Murshidiyya; see Patrick Franke, *Göttliche Karriere eines syrischen Hirten: Sulaimān Muršid und die Anfänge der Muršidiyya* (Berlin, 1994) and more recently Dmitry Sevruk, *Die Muršidiyya. Entstehung und innere Entwicklung einer religiösen Sondergemeinschaft in Syrien von den 1920er Jahren bis heute* (Bamberg, 2013).
67 Necati Alkan, '"Fighting for the Nuṣayrī Soul": State, Protestant Missionaries and the 'Alawīs in the Late Ottoman Empire', in: *Die Welt des Islams*, vol. 52:1 (2012), pp. 23-50, (here p. 32).
68 Winter, *A History of the 'Alawis*, chapter 5.
69 Ibid., pp. 181-192.
70 Alkan, '"Fighting for the Nuṣayrī Soul"'.
71 Ibid., pp. 28-30.
72 Procházka, 'The Alawis', p. 4.
73 Necati Alkan, 'Divide and Rule: The Creation of the Alawi State after World War I', in: *Fikrun wa Fann*, Nr. 100, Jubiläumsausgabe '100 Jahre Erster Weltkrieg', Goethe-Institut (2013).
74 Mehmed Behcet (Yazar)/Refik Temimi, *Beyrut Vilayeti*, vol. 2: Şimal Kısmı (Beirut 1918), pp. 403-404.
75 Prager, *Die 'Gemeinschaft des Hauses'*; Erkan Tümkaya, 'Die Entwicklung der türkisch-alawitischen Organisationen und ihre Beziehungen zu den Organisationen der anatolischen Aleviten in Deutschland', in: Wiebke Hohberger/Roy Karadag/Katharina Müller/Christoph Ramm (Hg.): *Grenzräume, Grenzgänge, Entgrenzungen. Junge Perspektiven der Türkeiforschung* (Wiesbaden, 2018), 197–211.
76 Procházka, 'The Alawis', p. 3; Winter, *A 'History of the Alawis*, p. 6.
77 Winter, *A 'History of the Alawis*, p. 43-44.

78 Munir Sharif, *al-Muslimun al-'alawiyyun: man hum wa ayna hum?* (Beirut, 1994), pp. 115–125; Hashim Uthman, *al-'Alawiyyun bayna al-ustura wa al-haqiqa* (Beirut, 1985), pp. 133; Abu Musa al-Hariri, *al-'Alawiyyun an-Nusayriyyun: bahth fi al-'aqida wa at-ta'rikh* (Beirut, 1980), pp. 191–196.
79 Taqi Sharafuddin, *an-Nusayriyya: Dirasa tahliliyya* (n.p., n.d.). pp. 40–48.
80 Ibid., pp. 29–31.
81 Ja'far al-Kanj al-Dandashi, *Madkhal ila al-Madhhab al-'Alawi an-Nusayri* (Irbid, 2000), p. 29.
82 Patrick Franke, *Göttliche Karriere*, pp. 16–18.
83 See, e.g., Janet Wallach, *Desert Queen: The Extraordinary Life of Gertrude Bell: Adventurer, Adviser to Kings, Ally of Lawrence of Arabia* (London, 1996).
84 Gertrude Lowthian Bell, *Syria: The Desert and the Sown* (London, 1907), p. 210, 211; cf. her diary entry dated 13 March 1905: 'The country was full of processions of Nosairiyeh who were going to the funeral feast of a great sheikh. This takes place a few days after the burial. They eat of the meats and each pays money according to his kind, from a lira upwards. This is taken by the family of the holy man - it's as good as insuring one's life to have a great reputation for piety.' at *Getrude Bell Archives*, Newcastle University, http://gertrudebell.ncl.ac.uk/diary_details.php?diary_id=421 (accessed 20 February 2020).
85 Idem, *The Desert and the Sown*, p. 213; cf. her letter dated 15 March 1905, *Getrude Bell Archives*, Newcastle University, http://gertrudebell.ncl.ac.uk/letter_details.php?letter_id=1499, and her diary entry of 15 March 1905, http://gertrudebell.ncl.ac.uk/diary_details.php?diary_id=423 (accessed 20 February 2020).
86 J. M. Balph, 'Among the Nussairyeh', *Olive Trees*, No. 8, August 1912, pp. 180–85 (here 182).
87 Samuel Lyde, *The Asian Mystery: Ansaireeh or Nusairis of Syria* (London, 1860), p. 171.
88 Gudrun Krämer/Sabine Schmidtke, 'Introduction: Religious authority and religious authorities in Muslim societies. A critical overview', in: idem/idem, *Speaking for Islam: Religious Authorities in Muslim Societies* (Leiden, 2006), pp. 1–14.
89 Ibid.
90 T.H. Rigby, 'Weber's Typology of Authority: Difficulty and Some Suggestions', in: *Anthropological Forum*, vol. 1:1 (1963), pp. 2–15.
91 *EQ* 1:189, q.v. 'Authority'.
92 Muhammad ibn Jarir at-Tabari, *Tafsir at-Tabari*, 26 vols. (Cairo, 2001), 7-176-185; al-Qurtubi, *al-Jami'*, 6:428–432.
93 *EQ* 1:189; Oliver Leaman (ed.), *The Qur'an: An Encyclopedia* (London/N.Y., 2006), q.v. 'Ulu'l-Amr', pp. 672-673; for a lengthy discussion of authority in Islam, see Meir J. Kister, 'Social and Religious Concepts of Authority in Islam', in: *Jerusalem Studies in Arabic and Islam* (JSAI), no. 18 (1994), pp. 84–127; see also Moshe Sharon, 'The Development of the Debate around the Legitimacy of Authority in Early Islam', in (JSAI) 5 (1984), pp. 121–141.
94 *EQ* 1:189; Kister, 'Authority in Islam', p. 99.
95 Krämer/Schmidtke, 'Introduction', p. 1.
96 Ibid., pp. 1–2 (emphasis in the original).
97 Ibid., p. 1.
98 For a detailed description, see Hüseyin Türk, *Anadolu'nun Gizli İnancı Nusayrîlik: İnanç Sistemleri ve Kültürel Özellikleri* (Istanbul, 2005), pp. 89–100.
99 For an assessment of the inferior status of Nusayri women by a Protestan missionary, see Wm. Sproull, 'The Fellaha', in: *Herald of Mission News* 1887, pp. 75–77.

100 Halm, *Islamische Gnosis*, pp. 303–315.
101 Franke, *Göttliche Karriere*, pp. 16–18.
102 Ibid., p. 18.
103 See, e.g., David Swartz, 'Bridging the Study of Culture and Religion: Pierre Bourdieu's Political Economy of Symbolic Power', in: *Sociology of Religion*, 57:1, Special Issue: Sociology of Culture and Sociology of Religion (Spring, 1996), pp. 71–85; Joseph Jurt, 'Bourdieus Kapital-Theorie', in: Manfred Max Bergman (Hrsg.): *Bildung, Arbeit, Erwachsenwerden: ein interdisziplinärer Blick auf die Transition im Jugend- und jungen Erwachsenenalter* (Wiesbaden, 2012), pp. 21–41.
104 Franke, 'Die syrischen Alawiten', p. 246.
105 Ibid. p. 256.
106 Online at http://alawi12.tripod.com/wathiqa.htm (17 August 2016)
107 Franke, 'Die syrischen Alawiten', p. 257.
108 See, e.g., BOA, HAT 385/20647; HAT 386/20671 and 20671-A; Stefan Winter, 'The *Nusayris* before the Tanzimat', pp. 100–103.
109 Report of the *Morning Post* of 25 December 1854, in: *Allgemeine Zeitung*, no. 13, 13 Januar 1855, p. 200 (PDF at Google Books).
110 L. J. Rousseau, 'Memoire sur les Ismaelis et les Nosairis de Syrie', in: *Annales des Voyages* 14 (1811), pp. 271–303 (here 300); F. Walpole, *The Ansayrii*, 3 vols. (London, 1851), 3:352; Dick Douwes, 'Knowledge and Oppression: The Nusayriyya in the late Ottoman Period', p. 159.
111 For conscription under Mehmed Ali and the Ottomans, see Yvette Talhamy, 'Conscription among the Nusayris ('Alawis) in the Nineteenth Century'.
112 Yvette Talhamy, 'The Nusayri and Druze Minorities in Syria in the Nineteenth Century: The Revolt against the Egyptian Occupation as a Case Study', in: *MES* 48:6 (2012), pp. 973–995; Stefan Winter, 'La révolte alaouite de 1834'. It is interesting that around the same time the peasants of Palestine also began a rebellion against the Egyptians.
113 Joel Beinin, *Workers and Peasants in the Middle East* (Cambridge/UK, 2001), p. 34.
114 *The Annual Register or a View of the History, Politics, and Literature of the Year* 1835 (London, 1836), p. 498.
115 Ibid., pp. 498–499.
116 *The Museum of Foreign Literature, Science, and Art*, vol. III new series, January to April 1839, whole number volume XXXV (Philadelphia, 1839), p. 331, fn. (PDF at Google Books); for this, see LaVerne Kuhnke, *Lives at Risk: Public Health in Nineteenth-Century Egypt* (Berkeley, 1990), pp. 69–91.
117 *Allgemeine Zeitung*, Ausserordentliche Beilage, nos. 201 & 202, 21 May 1835, p. 805 (report based on the Constantinople correspondent of *The Times*).
118 Yvette Talhamy, *Meridot ha-Nusayrim*, pp. 77–111. I have no copy of Talhamy's thesis in Hebrew, there would also have been a language barrier; I thank her for pointing out the relevant pages and sending me an English summary of her thesis. See also, idem, 'Isma'il Khayr Bey', p. 896.
119 Walpole, *The Ansayrii*, 3:353.
120 Winter, 'The *Nusayris* before the Tanzimat', p. 105.
121 Ibid., pp. 110–11; Mehmed Süreyya, *Sicill-i Osmani*, 6 vols. (Istanbul, 1996), 4:1058–59; Muhammad Amin Ghalib at-Tawil, *Tarikh al-'Alawiyyin* (Latakia, 1924), p. 443; a Turkish translation: Muhammed Emîn Gâlip et-Tavîl, *Arap Alevilerin Tarihi: Nusayrîler* (transl. İsmail Özdemir; Istanbul, 2000), p. 301.
122 Winter, 'The *Nusayris* before the Tanzimat', pp. 110–11.
123 Süreyya, *Sicill-i Osmani*, 3:909.

124 Süreyya, *Sicill-i Osmani*, 5:1648–49; see also Bursalı Mehmed Tahir, *Osmanlı Müellifleri*, vol. 3, (Istanbul, 1342/1924), p. 160.
125 For details, see Yavuz Ercan, 'Seyyid Mehmed Emin Vahid Efendi'nin Fransa Sefaretnamesi', in: *Osmanlı Tarihi Araştırma ve Uygulama Merkezi Dergisi*, Ankara Üniversitesi (1991), no. 2, pp. 73–125.
126 Ahmed Cevdet Paşa, *Ma'rûzât*, ed. Yusuf Halaçoglu (Istanbul, 1980), p. 2.
127 Idem, *Tarih-i Cevdet*, vol. 1 (Dersaadet [Istanbul], 1309/1891-92), pp. 332–334; latinised version: Ahmed Cevdet Paşa, *Târîh-i Cevdet*, vol. 1 (Mehmet İpşirli ed., Ankara, 2018), 357–358. See also İlber Ortaylı, '19. yüzyılda heterodox dinî gruplar ve Osmanlı idaresi', pp. 156–161 and idem, 'Alevîlik, Nusayrîlik ve Bâbıâlî', pp. 161–169.
128 Ahmed Cevdet Paşa, *Sosyalistlere Dair Bir Makale*, manuscript at the Atatürk Kitaplığı (Istanbul), MC_Yz_O_0008; latinised text in: Ahmet Zeki İzgöer, 'Ahmet Cevdet Paşa'nın Sosyal ve İktisadî Görüşleri', PhD Thesis (Marmara Üniversitesi: Istanbul, 1997), pp. 183–186.
129 Another intellectual who calls Mazdakism the Bolshevism of ancient Persia is Ameen Rihani; see his *The Descent of Bolshevism* (Boston/Mass. 1920).
130 Ahmed Cevdet Paşa, *Sosyalistlere Dair Bir Makale*, p. 4.
131 *Huwa alladhi khalaqa lakum ma fi al-ard jami'an*; Cevdet Paşa has *ja'ala* instead of *khalaqa*.
132 Ahmed Cevdet Paşa, *Sosyalistlere Dair Bir Makale*, p. 4.
133 See, e.g., *Hakayık el-Vekayi*, no. 466, 14 Ağustos 1861, p. 1863 (online PDF at Google Books), and the Arabic newspaper *al-Jinan*, Haziran/June 1870, pp. 323, 324, 325 (online PDF at Google Books).
134 Douwes, 'Knowledge and Oppression', p. 160.
135 BOA, MD. 160/73-1, mentioned by Mesut Aydıner, 'Sinek Sözüyle İş Yapan Pâdişahın Hâli Ya Da Karaman Valisi Darendeli Sarı Abdurrahman Paşa İsyanı', in: *Selçuk Üniversitesi Sosyal Bilimler Enstitüsü Dergisi*, no. 16 (2006), p. 789, n. 16.
136 Consul (Dr. Wilhelm) Seewald to Graf (Gyula) Andrássy, Beirut, 7 Juni 1877, letter no. 66, in: *Actenstücke aus dem Correspondenzen des Kais. und Kön. gemeinsamen Ministeriums Äussern über orientalische Angelegenheiten* (vom 7. April 1877 bis 3. November 1878), Wien 1878, p. 44 (online PDF at Google Books).
137 Eric Hobsbawm, *Bandits* (New York 1969; revised edition 1981), see also idem, *Primitive Rebels* (Manchester,1959); Fernand Braudel, *The Mediterranean and the Mediterranean World in the Age of Philip II*, vol. 2 (Los Angeles etc., 1995; translated from the French by Siân Reynolds), pp. 734–756.
138 Douwes, 'Knowledge and Oppression', p. 161.
139 Winter, 'The *Nusayris* before the Tanzimat', pp. 103–104.
140 Dick Douwes, *The Ottomans in Syria: A History of Justice and Oppression* (London, 2000), 142; Winter, *A History of the 'Alawis*, p. 70.
141 Douwes, *The Ottomans in Syria*, pp. 142–43.
142 Ibid., p. 143.
143 BOA, Y.PRK.MF. 2/57, 5 Cemaziyelevvel 1310/24 November 1892, no. 1, p. 3.
144 Same file, no. 1, p. 2.
145 Douwes, *The Ottomans in Syria*, p. 164; at-Tawil, *Tarikh al-'Alawiyyin*, 398–99; idem, *Arap Alevilerin Tarihi*, 312–13.
146 Murat Çelikdemir, 'Maarif Müdürü Halil Kemal Bey ve Antakya Nusayrileri hakkında Layihası', in: Ahmet Gündüz et al., *Hatay (Anavatana Katılışının 80. Yıl Armağanı)* (Istanbul, 2019), pp. 261–283; Erol Karcı, 'Suriye Maarif Müdürü Halil Kemal Bey'in Antakya Nusayrilerine dair bir Layihası', in: Erdem Ünlen/H. Aytuğ Tokur (eds.),

Anavatana Katılışının 80. Yılında Hatay Uluslararası Sempozyumu (Ankara 2020), pp. 411–428.
147 BOA, Y.PRK.MF. 2/57, 5 Cemaziyelevvel 1310/24 November 1892, nos. 1 and 2.

Chapter 2

1. Isabel Burton, *The Inner Life of Syria, Palestine, and the Holy Land: From My Private Journal*, 2. vols. (London, 1875), 1:180.
2. Ibid., 1:105–06; cf. William Thomson, *The Land and the Book* (New York, 1861), p. 168.
3. Consul (Dr. Wilhelm) Seewald to Graf (Gyula) Andrássy, Beirut, 7 Juni 1877, letter no. 66, in: *Actenstücke*.
4. Kocabaşoğlu, *Anadolu'daki Amerika*, pp. 9–14.
5. The wars between the USA, Sweden and the Barbary (Berber) States – Tunis, Algiers and Tripoli (or Maghreb) – that were legally in Ottoman possession; Michael Oren, *Power, Faith and Fantasy: America in the Middle East, 1776 to the Present* (Norton: New York 2007), pp. 17–40. For a brief overview of the relations between the USA and the Ottoman Empire in the nineteenth century, see Hans-Lukas Kieser, *Nearest East: American Millennialism and Mission to the Middle East* (Philadelphia, 2010), pp. 35–37.
6. Oren, *America in the Middle East*, pp. 116–118; Kocabaşoğlu, *Anadolu'daki Amerika*, p. 10; Çağrı Erhan, 'Ottoman Official Attitudes Towards American Missionaries', in: *The Turkish Yearbook*, no. XXX (2000), pp. 191–212 (here 192).
7. Joseph L. Grabill, *Protestant Diplomacy and the Near East: Missionary Influence on American Policy, 1810-1927* (Minneapolis, 1971), p. 39; Oren, *America in the Middle East*, pp. 118–121.
8. Grabill, *Protestant Diplomacy*, pp. 14–15.
9. Erhan, 'Ottoman Official Attitudes', p. 195.
10. Oren, *America in the Middle East*, pp. 308–309.
11. Ibid., pp. 80–97.
12. Ibid., p. 85.
13. Timothy Marr, '"Drying up the Euphrates": Muslims, Millennialism, and Early American Missionary Enterprise', in: Abbas Amanat and Magnus T. Bernhardsson (eds.), *U.S.-Middle East: Historical Encounters, a Critical Survey* (Gainesville/FL, 2007), pp. 60–76 (here p. 62); see also, Timothy Marr, *The Cultural Roots of American Islamicism* (Cambridge/UK, 2006).
14. Hans-Lukas Kieser, 'Some Remarks on Alevi Responses to the Missionaries in Eastern Anatolia (19th-20th cc.)', in: Eleanor H. Tejirian/Reeva Spector Simon (eds.), *Altruism and Imperialism. Western Cultural and Religious Missions to the Middle East (19th-20th cc.)*, (New York, 2002), pp. 120–142 (here p. 120). See also Kieser, *Nearest East*.
15. See, e.g., Joseph Tracy, *History of the American Board of Commissioners for Foreign Missions. Compiled Chiefly from the Published and Unpublished Documents of the Board* (2nd ed., New York 1842); Samuel C. Bartlett, *Sketches of the Missions of the American Board* (Boston, 1872); both *online at archive.org*; see also Hami Gümüş İnan, *American Missionaries in the Ottoman Empire: A Conceptual Metaphor Analysis of Missionary Narrative, 1820-1898* (Bielefeld, 2017), ch. 1, pp. 17–46; Devrim Ümit, 'The American Protestant Missionary Network in Ottoman Turkey, 1876-1914', in: *International Journal of Humanities and Social Science*, vol. 6:1 (April 2014), pp. 16–51, online at www.ijhssnet.com/journal/index/2460 (accessed 26 December 2017); Heather J. Sharkey, 'American Missionaries in Ottoman Lands: Foundational Encounters' (2010),

Retrieved from http://repository.upenn.edu/nelc_papers/19 (accessed 26 December 2017).
16 Bayard Dodge, 'American Educational and Missionary Efforts in the Nineteenth and Early Twentieth Centuries', in: *Annals of the American Academy of Political and Social Science*, vol. 401, America and the Middle East (May 1972), pp. 15–22; Ussama Makdisi, 'Reclaiming the Land of the Bible: Missionaries, Secularism, and Evangelical Modernity', in: *The American Historical Review*, 102:3 (June 1997), pp. 680–713.
17 Daniel Oliver Morton (ed.), *Memoir of Rev. Levi Parsons* (Poultney, Vt., 1824); (PDF online at Google Books).
18 Alvan Bond (ed.), *Memoir of the Rev. Pliny Fisk, A.M., late missionary to Palestine* (Boston, 1828).
19 William Goodell, *Forty Years in the Turkish Empire* (New York, 1876), pp. 73–74; Kocabaşoğlu, *Anadolu'daki Amerika*, pp. 29–37; Oren, *America in the Middle East*, pp. 80–83, 87–88, 90–93; Kieser, *Nearest East*, pp. 37–43; Talhamy, 'American Protestan Missionary Acitivity'.
20 Oren, *America in the Middle East*, p. 88.
21 Kieser, *Nearest East*, p. 40.
22 Hans-Lukas Kieser, 'Muslim Heterodoxy and Protestant Utopia: The Interactions between Alevis and Missionaries in Ottoman Anatolia', in: *WI* 41 (2001), pp. 89–111 (here p. 92); idem, 'Mission as Factor of Change in Turkey (nineteenth to first half of twentieth century)', in: *Islam and Christian–Muslim Relations* 13 (2002), pp. 391–410 (here p. 393).
23 On the issue of conversion and apostasy in the late Ottoman Empire, see Selim Deringil, '"There Is No Compulsion in Religion": On Conversion and Apostasy in the Late Ottoman Empire: 1839-1856', in: *Comparative Studies in Society and History* 42 (2000), pp. 547–575; idem, *Conversion and Apostasy in the Late Ottoman Empire* (Cambridge/UK, 2012).
24 Salibi/Khoury, *The Missionary Herald*, 1:15.
25 Ibid.
26 Ussama Makdisi, *Artillery of Heaven: American Missionaries and the Failed Conversion of the Middle East* (Ithaca/London, 2008), p. 67.
27 Ibid.
28 Salibi/Khoury, *The Missionary Herald*, 2:195 (1830).
29 Makdisi, *Artilerry of Heaven*, p. 67.
30 *Memoirs of Rev. Levi Parsons*, p. 343; Kieser, *Nearest East*, p. 42.
31 Gümüş, *American Missionaries*, p. 80.
32 Makdisi, *Artillery of Heaven*, p. 67.
33 For a history of the missions in Syria and Palestine until 1854, see Harvey Newcomb, *Cyclopedia of Missions* (New York, 1854), pp. 733–743; about Protestant missions in Syria and Palestine, see Julius Richter, *A History of Protestant Missions in the Near East* (New York, 1910), pp. 181–278, and idem, *Evangelische Missionskunde* (Leipzig/Erlangen, 1920), pp. 322–326; see also A. J. McFarland, *Eight Decades in Syria* (Topeka, Kan., 1937); here I used the previously published in installments in the journal *The Covenanter Witness*, nos. 15:26–18:13, 25 December 1925 – 31 March 1937, online at www.rparchives.org/cov_witness.html; another experienced Presbyterian missionary was Henry H. Jessup, *Fifty-Three Years in Syria* (2 vols.). For an analysis of the first decades of American Protestant missionary efforts: Christine B. Lindner, 'Negotiating the Field: American Protestant Missionaries in Ottoman Syria, 1823 to 1860' (PhD Thesis, University of Edinburgh, 2009). For a broader Analysis: Uta Zeuge, *Die Mission*

des American Board in Syrien im 19. Jahrhundert: Implikationen eines transkulturellen Dialogs (Stuttgart, 2016); English transl. by Elizabeth Janik: *The Mission of the American Board in Syria: Implications of a transcultural dialogue* (Stuttgart, 2017).
34 Salibi/Khoury, *The Missionary Herald*, 2:149 (1829).
35 Ibid. 2:438 (1835).
36 Joseph K. Greene, *Leavening the Levant* (Boston, 1916); Kieser, 'Mission as Factor of Change in Turkey', pp. 392–393.
37 Roderic H. Davison, 'Tanẓīmāt', in: *Encyclopaedia of Islam*, Second Edition, Edited by: P. Bearman, Th. Bianquis, C.E. Bosworth, E. van Donzel, W.P. Heinrichs. Consulted online on 14 January 2015, http://dx.doi.org/10.1163/1573-3912_islam_COM_1174.
38 Several works on the Tanzimat written in the 1960s hold that it was due to Western/European influence of all kinds showed the way for non-Western lands to modernisation; this then dominant but now outdated view holds that failure to emulate European political, economic and social development denoted backwardness for Islamic lands; see İsmail Hakkı Uzunçarşılı, *Osmanlı Devletinin İlmiye Teşkilâtı* (Ankara, 1988); Enver Ziya Karal (vols. 5–8), *Osmanlı Tarihi* (Ankara, 1961-1983); Niyazi Berkes, *The Development of Secularism in Turkey* (Montreal, 1964); Bernard Lewis, *The Emergence of Modern Turkey* (Oxford, 1961); Standord J. Shaw and Ezel Kural Shaw, *History of the Ottoman Empire*, 2 vols. (Cambridge: Cambridge University Press, 1977), see vol. 2 passim. For recent revisionist studies about Ottoman reformism, see, e.g., Frederick Anscombe, 'Islam and the Age of Reform', in: *Past and Present*, 208 (2010), pp. 159–189; Olivier Bouquet, 'Is it Time to Stop Speaking About Ottoman Modernization?', in: Marc Aymes et al (eds.), *Order and Compromise: Government Practices in Turkey from the Late Ottoman Empire to the Early 21st Century* (Leiden, 2015), pp. 45–67.
39 Butrus Abu-Manneh, 'The Islamic Roots of the Gülhane Rescript', in: *Die Welt des Islams* 34 (1994), pp. 173–203; see also idem, 'The Naqshbandiyya-Mujaddidiyya in the Ottoman Lands in the Early 19th Century,' in: *Die Welt des Islams*, 22:4/1 (1982), pp. 1–36; see further idem, 'The Naqshbandi-Mujaddidi and the Bektashi Orders in 1826,' in: idem, *Studies on Islam and the Ottoman Empire in the 19th Century (1826-1876)* (Istanbul, 2001), pp. 59–71.
40 The year 1876 was labelled as 'the year of the three Sultans'; Roderic Davison, *Reform in the Ottoman Empire: 1856–1876* (Princeton: Princeton University Press, 1963), chapter IX. See also Florian Riedler, *Opposition and Legitimacy in the Ottoman Empire: Conspiracies and political cultures* (London, 2011), chapter 4.
41 'Translation of the Firmân of His Imperial Majesty Sultân 'Abd-el-Mejîd, Granted in Favor of His Protestant Subjects', in: *Journal of the American Oriental Society*, 3 (1853), pp. 218–220; Grabill, *Protestant Diplomacy*, p. 14; Kieser, *Nearest East*, p. 47.
42 BOA, İ.HR. 72/3473, 15 Muharrem 1266/1 December 1849.
43 For the issue, see Özgür Yıldız, *Anadolu'da Amerikan Misyonerleri* (Istanbul, 2015), pp. 34–35.
44 Hans-Lukas Kieser, *Der verpasste Friede: Mission, Ethnie und Staat in den Ostprovinzen der Türkei, 1839-1938* (Zürich 2000), p. 62; idem., *Iskalanmış Barış: Doğu Vilayetlerinde Misyonerlik Etnik Kimlik ve Devlet 1839-1938* (transl. Atilla Dirim, Istanbul, 2005), pp. 93–94; Gábor Agoston and Bruce Masters, *Encyclopedia of the Ottoman Empire* (New York, 2009), pp. 385–386.
45 Kieser, *Nearest East*, p. 53.
46 Markus Dressler, 'Alevīs', in: *Encyclopaedia of Islam*, THREE, Edited by: Kate Fleet, Gudrun Krämer, Denis Matringe, John Nawas, Everett Rowson. Consulted online on 18 January 2018, http://dx.doi.org/10.1163/1573-3912_ei3_COM_0167.

47 For a critique of the term 'heterodox' with regard to the Alevis, see Janina Karolewsksi, 'What is Heterodox About Alevism? The Development of Anti-Alevi Discrimination and Resentment', in: *Die Welt des Islams* 48 (2008), pp. 434–456; Robert Langer/Udo Simon, 'The Dynamics of Orthodoxy and Heterodoxy. Dealing with Divergence in Muslim Discourses and Islamic Studies', in: ibid. 48 (2008), pp. 273–288.
48 Kieser, *Nearest East*, p. 52.
49 Ibid.
50 Ibid., pp. 52–53. See also, Çakmak, *Sultan'ın Kızılbaşları*, chapter 3.
51 Kieser, *Nearest East*, p. 54.
52 Ibid., p. 55.
53 Çakmak, *Sultan'ın Kızılbaşları*, pp. 148–149.
54 Ibid., 149–156; Abdulhamit Kırmızı, 'Şikâyât Tezâyüd Etmekte: Memduh Bey'in Sivas Valiliği'nde Ermeni Politikası (1889-1892)', in: *Osmanlılar Döneminde Sivas Sempozyumu Bildirileri (21-25 Mayıs 2007)*, 1. cilt (Sivas, 2007), pp. 363–376.
55 Hans-Lukas Kieser, 'Muslim Heterodoxy', pp. 96–97; Edip Gölbaşı, "Heretik' aşiretler', p. 108.
56 Cf. Çakmak, *Sultan'ın Kızılbaşları*, chapter 2.
57 Richter, *A History of Protestant Missions*, p. 181.
58 Ibid., pp. 182–185.
59 Ibid., 187–189; see also, M. Valentine Chirol, 'French Diplomacy in Syria, past and present', in: *The Fortnightly Review*, 31 (1882), pp. 427–438.
60 Richter, *A History of Protestant Missions*, pp. 195–196; Salibi/Khoury, 5: 78–79, 114–115.
61 Richter, ibid., pp. 192–193.
62 Yvette Talhamy, 'The Nusayri and Druze Minorities'.
63 *The Religious Monitor and Evangelical Repository* (Philadelphia, 1841-1842), p. 332 (PDF at Google Books).
64 Jessup, *Fifty-Three Years in Syria*, 1: 350–353.
65 Richter, *A History of Protestant Missions*, pp. 192–193.
66 Samer Traboulsi, 'Converting the Druzes: The American Missionaries' Road Map to Nowhere', in: Nadia Maria El-Cheikh, Lina Choueiri and Bilal Orfali (eds.), *One Hundred and Fifty* (Beirut, 2016), pp. 25–41. See also, Henry Easson, letter of 15 February 1888, in: *Herald of Mission News*, 1888, p. 76.
67 Salibi/Khoury, *The Missionary Herald*, 2:292 (1831).
68 Lyde, *The Asian Mystery*, pp. 208–210.
69 Salibi/Khoury, ibid., 2:316 (1832).
70 Ibid., 3:65 (1836).
71 Salibi/Khoury, *The Missionary Herald*, 3:260f.; cf. pp. 267f. (1841).
72 Ibid., 3:269.
73 Mounted police or soldier.
74 A stranger admitted to protection as though a member of the family/tribe.
75 Diary entry dated 18 March 1905, *Getrude Bell Archives*, Newcastle University, http://gertrudebell.ncl.ac.uk/diary_details.php?diary_id=427 (accessed 20 February 2020).
76 Salibi/Khoury, *The Missionary Herald*, 3:276 (1841); in 3:317 the number for Nusayris and Isma'ilis in Syria is given as 200,000; cf. John Wortabet, *Researches into the Religions of Syria* (London, 1860), p. ix.
77 Written in 1847, in: Salibi/Khoury, Salibi/Khoury, *The Missionary Herald*, 4:6.
78 Ibid.

79 James Dennis, *A Sketch of the Syria Mission* (New York, 1872), p. 5; Arthur J. Brown, *Report of a Visitation of the Syria Mission of the Presbyterian Board of Foreign Missions* (USA, 1902), p. 23; Grabill, *Protestant Diplomacy*.
80 Brown, *Syria Mission*, p. 18; for a discussion, see Moosa, *Extremist Shiites*, pp. 405–406.
81 Salibi/Khoury, *The Missionary Herald*, 4:18–19 (1847).
82 Rufus Anderson, *History of the Mission of the American Board of Commissioners for Foreign Missions to the Oriental Churches*, 2 vols. (Boston, 1872), 1:viii.
83 Ibid.
84 Salibi/Khoury, *The Missionary Herald*, 1:45.
85 For an evaluation, see Zeuge-Buberl, *Die Mission des American Board in Syrien*, pp. 34–35.
86 Quoted in ibid., p. 35.
87 Salibi/Khoury, *The Missionary Herald*, 5:182.
88 Richter, *A History of Protestant Missions in the Near East*, p. 214; Douwes, 'Knowledge and Oppression', p. 166.
89 *Minutes of the Synod of the Reformed Presbyterian Church*, July & August 1861 (new series vol. VII, No. 7 & 8), p. 238; online at Reformed Presbyterian History Archives (RPHA), www.rparchives.org/synod.html
90 Samuel Lyde, *The Anseyreeh and Ismaeleeh: A Visit to the Secret Sects of Northern Syria with a View to the Establishment of Schools* (London, 1853) and *The Asian Mystery*.
91 *The Covenanter* (July & August 1862), p. 338; vol. 17 online at RPHA, www.rparchives.org/covenanter.html; James McKinnis Balph, *Fifty Years of Mission Work in Syria* (Latakia, 1913), p. 38.
92 'Register of Baptisms in Syria', *Our Banner*, No. 10, October 1875, p. 403.
93 Balph, *Fifty Years*, see photo on the frontipiece; see also pp. 47–50.
94 Daoud's story was not recounted in Lyde's book but published in 1899 and 1900 after his death by Rev. Henry Easson in the Reformed Presbyterian journal *Olive Trees* (online at RPHA, www.rparchives.org/olive.html), based on unpublished notes of Lyde, missionary letters and a personal reminiscence by Daoud. See *Olive Trees*, no. 8, August 1899, pp. 253–257; no. 9, September 1899, pp. 279–282; no. 10, October 1899, pp. 315–319; no. 11, November 1899, pp. 345–350; no. 12, December 1899, pp. 378–380; no. 6, June 1900, pp. 178–181. See also, Balph, *Fifty Years*, p. 52, 56, 58, 62, 87, 98–100; Marjorie Allen Sanderson, *A Syrian Mosaic* (Pittsburgh, Pa., 1976), pp. 5–6, 16–22.
95 *Olive Trees*, June 1900, p. 181.
96 BOA, İ.HR. 266/15960, no. 1, 10 Muharrem 1292/16 February 1875.
97 Kahramanmaraş in present Turkey.
98 If this is the second Tanzimat Edict then it should be 1856.
99 BOA, İ.HR. 266/15960, no. 1.
100 For a detailed summary based on British archival records and those of the Evangelical Alliance, see Gerhard Lindemann, *Für Frömmigkeit in Freiheit: die Geschichte der Evangelischen Allianz im Zeitalter des Liberalismus (1846–1879)* (Berlin, 2011), pp. 868–902. The British archival records that refer to this are FO 881/2618, esp. pp. 136–165; for a discussion of the issue, see also Türkyılmaz, 'Anxieties of Conversion', pp. 209–215.
101 For the term, see Candan Badem, *The Ottoman Crimean War (1853-1856)* (Leiden, 2010), p. 50.

102 Aleih, Syria, 19 September 1873, inclosure No.1, in: *Turkey, No. 5 (1875): Correspondence Respecting Cases of Religious Persecution in Turkey. Presented to both Houses of Parliament by Command of Her Majesty, London 1875*, House of Commons Parliamentary Papers Online, at https://parlipapers.proquest.com/parlipapers/docview/t70.d75.1875-051731?accountid=8485 (accessed 7 November 2017); henceforth *Turkey, No. 5* (1875). See also ibid., pp. 79–80, *Our Banner*, June 1874, pp. 205–208, and Balph, *Fifty Years*, p. 52. The first paragraph of the letter was extracted and presented to the Sublime Porte with its Ottoman Turkish translation; BOA, HR.TO. 248/38. It is odd that the term 'Ansariyeh' in the English letter was translated as 'Ensariye' in spite of the Ottomans' usual use of the term 'Nusayriye', and the name Jedeed was translated as 'Did'.
103 *Our Banner*, 15 June 1874, pp. 206–207; see also *The Missionary Herald*, February 1875, p. 59.
104 Rev. William Wright, letter of 11 November 1873, in: *Evangelical Christendom*, vol. 15 (new series), 1 January 1874 issue, London 1874, p. 32.
105 Letter dated 19 November 1873, *The Reformed Presbyterian and Covenanter*, vol. XII, no. 2, p. 60.
106 Ottoman Turkish translation of a letter by the British Embassy at Istanbul, BOA, HR.TO. 251/27.
107 For the issue, see Mehmet Hacısalihoğlu, 'Inclusion and Exclusion: Conscription in the Ottoman Empire', in: *Journal of Modern European History* 5:2 (2007), pp. 264–286.
108 Letter dated 26 August 1874, in: *The Reformed Presbyterian and Covenanter*, December 1874, pp. 401–402; see also the German (Berlin) journal *Magazin für die Literatur des Auslandes* ('Journal for Foreign Literature'), no. 16, 18 April 1874, pp. 239–240, about freedom of religion in 'Turkey', mentioning the case of 'Daud Suleiman' (p. 240); PDF at Google Books.
109 *Reformed Presbyterian and Covenanter*, no. 13/7, July 1875, p. 238; *Our Banner*, June 1875, p. 246.
110 *Our Banner*, February 1875, p. 76 and 117.
111 *Our Banner*, August 1875, pp. 336–337; emphasis in the text.
112 Ibid. p. 338.
113 *Reformed Presbyterian and Covenanter*, no. 13/7, July 1875, p. 251.
114 BOA, HR.MKT. 83/45.
115 U.K. Parliamentary Papers, 19th Century House of Commons Hansard Sessional Papers, https://parlipapers.proquest.com/parlipapers/docview/t71.d76.cds3v0225p0-0027?accountid=8485 (accessed 7 November 2017).
116 *Evangelical Christendom*, vol. 15 (new series), issue of 1 July 1874, London 1874, p. 219; emphasis in the text. See also Jessup, *Fifty-Three Years in Syria* 2: 436–437.
117 Ibid.
118 *Turkey, No. 5* (1875), pp. 112, 113, 115.
119 *Evangelical Christendom*, 1 March 1875, vol. 16 (1875), p. 65.
120 The German language Viennese Christian journal *Der Pilger* (Familienblatt für alle Stände), No. 6, 21 February 1875, p. 65.
121 *The Manchester Guardian*, 3 August 1875, p. 8.
122 Mr Boker to Mr Fish, Legation of the United States, Constantinople, 9 March 1875; letter in: *Executive documents printed by order of the House of Representatives. 1875-76*, Vol. II (Washington, D.C.: U.S. Government Printing Office, 1875-1876), p. 1294; online at http://digital.library.wisc.edu/1711.dl/FRUS.FRUS187576v02 (Accessed 30 January 2018).

123 *Our Banner*, nos. 6 & 7 (June & July 1880), p. 221.
124 *Olive Trees*, no. 11, November 1899, pp. 349; Balph, *Fifty Years*, p. 62; Sanderson, *A Syrian Mosaic*, p. 21.
125 *Minutes of the Synod of the Reformed Presbyterian Church*, July & August 1881 (vol. XIX, No. 7 & 8), p. 228.
126 *Olive Trees*, June 1900, p. 181.
127 Sanderson, *A Syrian Mosaic*, p. 22
128 Balph, *Fifty Years*, p. 87.
129 Ibid., p. 100.
130 *Olive Trees*, August 1912, p. 184.
131 Cf. Türkyılmaz, 'Anxieties of Conversion', p. 210.
132 *Olive Trees*, June 1900, p. 179; Henry Easson is quoting a letter by Miss Wylie, dated 30 May 1893.
133 *Herald of Mission News*, 1890; quoted in Kathryn A. Medill, 'David Metheny, Missionary Doctor: Work and Trouble at the Mersine Mission 1890-1897' (MA Thesis, Geneva College 2011), pp. 15–16.
134 For a biographical sketch, see Owen F. Thompson, *Sketches of the Ministers of the Reformed Presbyterian Church of North America from 1880 to 1930* (Blanchard/Iowa, n.d.), pp. 232-235; online at http://www.rparchives.org/rp-ministers.html, and Jessup, *Fifty-Three Years in Syria* 2:536, 627-628. For the details of his mission in Mersin, see Medill, 'David Metheny'. The author is a descendant of David Metheny and uses published and unpublished family papers in her thesis; private communication, 8 December 2015.
135 For a contemporary account, see Edwin Munsell Bliss, *Turkey and the Armenian Atrocities* (Philadelphia, 1896), esp. Chapter 17.
136 Bilâl N. Şimşir, 'Washington'daki Osmanlı Elçisi Alexandre Mavroyeni Bey ve Ermeni Gailesi (1887-1896)', in: *Ermeni Araştırmaları Dergisi*, Ermeni Araştırmaları Enstitüsü, Ankara, Aralık 2001-Ocak-Şubat 2002, Sayı 4, pp. 32–54.
137 D. Emre Amasyalı, 'Missionary Influence and Nationalist Reactions: The Case of Armenian Ottomans', in: *Nationalities Papers* 43:9 (2020), pp. 1–19, doi:10.1017/nps.2020.12.
138 Zahra is given as Zahara, and Safiya as Sophia in missionary reports.
139 BOA, BEO. 314/23496.
140 BOA, Y.MTV. 87/44, 6 Teşrin-i Sâni 1309.
141 BOA, MKT.MHM. 700/5; this is a large file of various reports from the province of Adana and Mersin to the Sublime Porte and vice versa. Another large file from 1894 about Metheny is HR.H. 348/15, 13 January 1894. See also BEO, 314/23496.
142 BOA, A.MKT.MHM, 700/5 and Y.PRK.MF. 3/11.
143 Letter of 9 Cemaziyelahir 1311/18 December 1893 in A.MKT.MHM, 700/5.
144 HR.H. 348/15, no. 3.
145 A.MKT.MHM, 700/5, 15 Kanun-i-Sâni 1309.
146 A.MKT.MHM, 700/5, 7 Şaban 1311/13 February 1894.
147 Whereas this name appears as Daraf in Ottoman reports; the correct name should be Daras; see Medill, 'David Metheny', pp. 56–57.
148 A.MKT.MHM, 700/5, 27 Şaban 1311.
149 'Treaty between the United States of America and the Ottoman Empire: Commerce and navigation', proclaimed February 4, 1832, online at https://archive.org/details/ldpd_11015515_000 (accessed 9 October 2018).
150 A.MKT.MHM, 700/5, 12 May 1894.

151 HR.H. 348/15, no. 29.
152 Ibid.
153 29 April 1894, A.MKT.MHM, 700/5.
154 8 Mai 1894, A.MKT.MHM, 700/5.
155 For a study based only on Ottoman archival sources and without the evaluation of the missionary view, see Ercan Uyanık, 'II. Abdülhamit ile Amerikan Protestan Misyonerlerinin Eğitim Mücadelesi: Amerika'ya Kaçırılan Nusayri Kızları', in: *Kebikeç*, 37 (2014), pp. 35–56.
156 *Our Banner*, February 1890, p. 52.
157 Telj or Telji would be the Syrian colloquial variant. Sometimes the name appears as 'Teljy' or 'Teljie'; see Herald of Mission News, 1888, p. 75 and 95, and Herald of Mission News, 1894, p. 170. Once her real name Nacide/Najida is misspelled as 'Tadjidi'; in Herald of Mission News, May 1894, p. 111. Even though Ottoman reports usually give her name as Nacide, it also appears as Telc but the compilation on the Nusayris in Ottoman Archival documents replaced it(!) with Nacide in the latinised version; see Bilgili, et al. (eds.), *OABNN*, pp. 236–237.
158 Letter 6 August 1886, *Reformed Presbyterian and Covenanter* (1886), p. 430; see also the letter of Miss Sterrett dated 7 January 1888, in *Herald of Mission News* 1888, p. 75.
159 *Herald of Mission News*, 1887, p. 82–83.
160 As described by Mary Metheny in *Herald of Mission News*, letter of 22 January 1890, pp. 56–57 (in the volume consisting of the years 1889-1891 at http://rparchives.org/mission_news.html, nos. 1–12 of the year 1890); *Herald of Mission News*, May 1894, pp. 107–110, 170–175; Mrs. [Mary] Metheny, 'Mission Difficulties in Turkey', in: *Quarterly Register*, vol. 3, November 1893, no. 8, pp. 135–136; Medill, 'David Metheny', pp. 21–22, 57–58. The account published in the *Presbyterian Journal* in 1890, and republished elsewhere, such as in *Our Banner*, February 1890, pp. 52–53, was seen as 'full of absurd mistakes'; see *Herald of Mission News* 1890, p. 59.
161 Cf. Medill, 'David Metheny', pp. 53–54.
162 Ibid., pp. 57–58.
163 *Herald of Mission News*, May 1894, p. 110; Medill, 'David Metheny', p. 56.
164 BOA, HR.SFR.3. 422/83.
165 Ibid., pp. 1–2.
166 Ibid., p. 3.
167 Letter of David Metheny, dated 26 March 1894, in: *Herald of Mission News*, July-August 1894, pp. 169–170.
168 Letter of David Metheny, dated 13 April 1894, in: ibid., pp. 170–171.
169 I was not able to find the report at the Ottoman Archives.
170 Ibid. February 1895, pp. 31–32.
171 Letter of David Metheny, dated 26 March 1894, in: ibid. July–August 1894, pp. 170–171.
172 Ibid., July-August 1894, pp. 170.
173 The letter to the Evangelical Alliance is dated 26 April 1894 (London), in ibid. July & August 1894, p. 172.
174 *Herald of Mission News*, May 1894, pp. 171–173.
175 *Herald of Mission News*, March 1895, pp. 52–54.
176 Letter of Mary Metheny, 15 July 1893, in: ibid. September 1893, p. 190, emphasis in the text.
177 *Herald of Mission News*, April 1895, p. 75; Medill, 'David Metheny', p. 68.
178 See also, *Reformed Presbyterian and Covenanter*, April 1894, p. 111.

179 *Herald of Mission News*, April 1895, p. 75
180 Letter of 13 December 1894; published in *Christian Nation*, vol. 22, 23 January 1895, p. 7. Her letter was translated into Turkish and is in the file BOA, A. MKT. MHM. 700/5. Bilgili et al., *OABNN*, p. 277, transliterated her name wrongly as Jeni B. Rotsi.
181 Samuel Sullivan Cox, *Diversions of a Diplomat in Turkey* (New York, 1893), pp. 592–593.
182 *Christian Nation*, vol. 23, 21 August 1895, p. 3.
183 Ibid., 27 November 1895; Medill, 'David Metheny', pp. 67, 70–72, 80.
184 Letter of Mary Metheny, *Christian Nation*, 25 December 1895, p. 5.
185 'Missions and Gunboats' in: *The Independent*, 6 June 1895, p. 19; see also, 'Gunboats to the Rescue', in: *The Congregationalist*, 20 June 1895, p. 969. See also, BOA, HR.SYS. 64/38, 25 October 1895, HR.SYS. 65/5, 9 December 1895, and HR.SYS. 65/45, 25 April 1896.
186 *Herald of Mission News*, February 1895, pp. 30–31.
187 Ibid. June & July 1897, pp. 138–139.
188 Ibid.
189 After 1897 the *Herald of Mission News* was renamed *Olive Trees*.
190 *Olive Trees*, March 1898, p. 70.
191 Ibid., July 1898, pp. 209–210.
192 Ibid., June 1898, p. 172.
193 Ibid., July 1899.
194 Ibid., September 1900, pp. 284–285.
195 Ibid., May 1902, p. 135.
196 Ibid., January 1905, p. 7.
197 For her photograph, see *Herald of Mission News*, May 1892, p. 96, and May 1894, p. 108.
198 Applications, Box 09, www.gallaudet.edu/archives-and-deaf-collections/genealogy-resources/pennsylvania-school-for-the-deaf-applications/psd-apps-i; I am grateful to Christopher Shea for sending a digital copy; private communication, 13 November 2015.
199 See also, *The Philadelphia Inquirer*, 27 June 1900, p. 5.
200 *Olive Trees*, December 1900, p. 379.
201 Ibid., September 1901, p. 292.
202 *Herald of Mission News*, May 1894, p. 109.
203 See www.findagrave.com/memorial/146499625/telgie-price; Carol Hoff, who created this grave entry of Telgie and her husband, kindly sent to me copies of the death certificates extant at the Pennsylvania Department of Health, and copies of the obituaries of her and her family from the local newspaper *Easton Express*; private communications, 21 November 2015.
204 Nazan Maksudyan, *Orphans and Destitute Children in the Late Ottoman Empire* (New York, 2014), pp. 10–11.
205 Ibid., pp. 11–12.
206 BOA, A.MKT.MHM. 702/29, 14 Şaban 1317/18 December 1899, cited by Maksudyan, *Orphans and Destitute Children*, p. 137.
207 Ibid.

Chapter 3

1 H. Erdem Çıpa, *The Making of Selim: Succession, Legitimacy, and Memory in the Early Modern Ottoman World* (Indiana, 2017); Feridun M. Emecen, *Yavuz Sultan Selim* (Istanbul, 2013).

2 Roger M. Savory and Ahmet T. Karamustafa, "ESMĀʿĪL I ṢAFAWĪ," in: *Encyclopædia Iranica* online, http://www.iranicaonline.org/articles/esmail-i-safawi (accessed 6 April 2017).
3 Karen Barkey, *Empire of Difference: The Ottomans in Comparative Perspective* (Cambridge, 2008), pp. 103–106.
4 Ibid., 161–162, for the concept of *nizam-ı âlem*, see Gottfried Hagen, 'Legitimacy and World Order', in: Hakan T. Karateke and Maurus Reinkowski (eds.), *Legitimizing the Order: The Ottoman Rhetoric of State Power* (Leiden, 2005), pp. 55–83.
5 Guy Burak, 'Faith, law and empire in the Ottoman "age of confessionalization" (fifteenth–seventeenth centuries): the case of "renewal of faith", in: *Mediterranean Historical Review* 28:1 (2013), pp. 1–23 (here pp. 6–9).
6 İbrahim Peçevi, *Tarih-i Peçevi*, 2 vols. (Istanbul, 1283/1866), 1:311–312; in the latinized and modern Turkish version, Bekir Sıtkı Baykal (ed.), *Peçevi Tarihi*, 2 vols. (Ankara, 1981), 1:220–221.
7 *Tarih-i Peçevi*, 1:337–340 and *Peçevi Tarihi*, 1:239–241; Metin Atmaca, 'Osmanlı Zihin Dünyasında Bir Doğu Ülkesi: Diyar-ı Acem Yahut İran', in: *Muhafazakâr Düşünce* 11:43 (2015), pp. 97–112 (here pp. 100–101). For the purpose of the Ottoman polemic against the Safawis from the political point of view, see Elke Eberhard, *Osmanische Polemik gegen die Safawiden im 16. Jahrhundert nach arabischen Manuskripten* (Freiburg i. Br., 1970), pp. 155–162.
8 Ahmet Yaşar Ocak, *Türkler, Türkiye ve İslâm: Yaklaşım, Yöntem ve Yorum Denemeleri* (Istanbul, 2000, 3rd ed.), pp. 41–43, 82–83. See further, Abdurrahman Atçıl, 'The Safavid Threat and Juristic Authority in the Ottoman Empire during the 16th Century', in: *International Journal of Middle East Studies* 49 (2017), pp. 295–314.
9 Rıza Yıldırım, 'Turkomans between two empires: the origins of the Qızılbash identity in Anatolia (1447–1514)', PhD Thesis, Bilkent University (Ankara, 2008), p. 609.
10 E. Ekin Tuşalp Atiyas, 'The "Sunna-Minded Trends"', in: Marinos Sariyannis, *History of Ottoman Political Thought up to the Early Nineteenth Century* (Leiden, 2019), pp. 233–278.
11 See also Kaya Şahin, *Empire and Power in the Reign of Süleyman. Narrating the Sixteenth-Century Ottoman World* (Cambridge/UK 2017) esp. pp. 205–213.
12 Kasim Kufrevî, 'Birgewī', in: *Encyclopaedia of Islam*, Second Edition, Edited by: P. Bearman, Th. Bianquis, C.E. Bosworth, E. van Donzel, W.P. Heinrichs. Consulted online on 15 January 2016, http://dx.doi.org/10.1163/1573-3912_islam_SIM_1434; Emrullah Yüksel, 'Birgivî', in: *DİA* 6:191–194, online https://islamansiklopedisi.org.tr/birgivi (15 January 2020).
13 Istanbul, 1316/1898; for the contents, see, Osman Karadeniz, 'Tarîkat-ı Muhammediyye', in: Mehmet Şeker (ed.), *İmam Birgivî* (Ankara, 1994), pp. 115–123; Emrullah Yüksel, 'Müslüman Türk Âlimi olarak İmâm Birgivi'nin Osmanlı Döneminde ve Günümüz Türkiyesinde Yeri', in ibid., pp. 32–37; and Huriye Martı, 'et-Tarîkatü'l-Muhammediye', in: *DİA* 40:106–108, online https://islamansiklopedisi.org.tr/et-tarikatul-muhammediyye (15 January 2020); for detailed elaborations, see Cook, *Commanding Right*, pp. 323–330; Katharina Ivanyi, *Virtue, Piety and the Law: A Study of Birgivī Meḥmed Efendī's* al-Ṭariqa al-muḥammadiyya. Leiden: Brill, 2020.
14 Birgivi, *aṭ-Ṭariqa al-Muḥammadiyya*, p. 17 ff.
15 See also the English translation by Tosun Bayrak, *The Path of Muhammad: A Book on Islamic Morals and Ethics–Imam Birgivi, a 16th Century Islamic Mystic* (Indiana, 2005); p. 85 ff.
16 Ivanyi, 'Virtue, Piety and the Law', p. 83.

17 Ivanyi, 'Virtue, Piety and the Law', p. 26.
18 The most recent work is Nir Shafir, 'Moral Revolutions: The Politics of Piety in the Ottoman Empire Reimagined." in: *Comparative Studies in Society and History* 61:3 (2019), pp. 595–623. Older and more recent studies are: Necati Öztürk, 'Islamic Orthodoxy among the Ottomans in the Seventeenth Century with Special Reference to the Qadizade Movement', PhD Thesis, University of Edinburgh (Edinburgh, 1981); Madeline C. Zilfi, *The Politics of Piety: The Ottoman Ulema 1600–1800* (Bibliotheca Islamica: Chicago 1988); idem, 'The Kadizadelis: Discordant Revivalism in Seventeenth Century Istanbul', in: *Journal of Near Eastern Studies* 45:42 (October 1986), pp. 251–269; Semiramis Çavuşoğlu, 'The Ḳāḍīzādeli movement: An attempt of şerī'at-minded reform in the Ottoman Empire', PhD Thesis, Princeton University (Princeton, 1990); Simeon Evstatiev, 'The Qāḍīzādeli Movement and the Revival of takfīr in the Ottoman Age', in: Camilla Adang et al., *Accusations of unbelief in Islam: a diachronic perspective on takfīr* (Leiden, 2016), pp. 213–243; Mustapha Sheikh, *Ottoman Puritanism and its Discontents: Ahmad al-Rumi al-Aqhisari and the Qadizadelis* (Oxford, 2016); see further James Muhammad Dawud Currie, 'Kadizadeli Ottoman Scholarship, Muḥammad ibn ʿAbd al-Wahhāb, and the Rise of the Saudi State', in: *Journal of Islamic Studies* 26:3 (September 2015), pp. 265–288.
19 Suraiya Faroqhi, *Kultur und Alltag im Osmanischen Reich: Vom Mittelalter bis zum Anfang des 20. Jahrhunderts* (München, 1995), pp. 78–79.
20 Marc Baer, *Honored by the Glory of Islam: Conversion and Conquest in Ottoman Europe* (Oxford, 2008), p. 81.
21 Ibid., pp. 63–68, 105–119; for the conversion of Jews and Christians and their holy places, see pp. 81–104 and 121–138; see also Ocak, *Türkler, Türkiye ve İslâm*, pp. 84–85.
22 Hagen, 'Legitimacy and World Order', p. 78; Cook, Commanding Right, pp. 312–313.
23 Hüseyin Yılmaz, 'Containing Sultanic Authority: Constitutionalism in the Ottoman Empire before Modernity', in: *Journal of Ottoman Studies/Osmanlı Araştırmaları* 45 (2015), pp. 231–264.
24 Amit Bein, *Ottoman Ulema, Turkish Republic: Agents of Change and Guardians of Tradition* (Stanford, 2011). On the ilmiye institution in the Ottoman Empire, see İsmail Hakkı Uzunçarşılı, *Osmanlı Devletinin İlmiye Teşkilâtı*.
25 Birgit Schäbler, 'Civilizing Others: Global Modernity and the Local Boundaries (French/German/Ottoman and Arab) of Savagery', in: idem and Leif Stenberg (eds.), *Globalization and the Muslim World: Culture, Religion, and Modernity* (Syracuse/NY, 2004), pp. 3–31 (here pp. 17–18); Ruhi Güler, 'Tanzimattan II. Meşrutiyete *Medeniyet* Anlayışının Evrimi', PhD Thesis, Marmara Üniversitesi (Istanbul, 2006); A. Kevin Reinhart, 'Civilization and its Discussants: Medeniyet and the Turkish Conversion to Modernism', in: Denis Washburn and A. Kevin Reinhart (eds.), *Converting Cultures: Religion, Ideology and Transformations of Modernity* (Leiden, 2007), pp. 267–290; see also Ekmeleddin İhsanoğlu (ed.), *Osmanlı Devleti ve Medeniyeti Tarihi*, 2 vols. (Istanbul, 1994–1997), 2:201–202. For a wider general outlook for civilization, see Brett Bowden, 'Civilization and Its Consequences', in: *Oxford Handbooks Online* (February 2016); idem, 'In the Name of Civilization: War, Conquest, and Colonialism', in: *Pléyade* 23, enero-junio 2019, pp. 73–100.
26 See, e.g., Selim Deringil, *The Well-Protected Domains: Ideology and the Legitimation of Power in the Ottoman Empire, 1876–1909* (London, 1998), p. 19, 41, 73, 102, 103.
27 Sariyannis, *A History of Ottoman Political Thought*, pp. 84, 386, 392.

28 I was not able to find information about this creed, unless Lutfi wrongly attributed it to Zoroastrianism.
29 Süreyya, *Sicill-i Osmani*, 2:516–517; Zübeyde Güneş Yağcı, 'Ferah Ali Paşa'nın Soğucak Muhafızlığı (1781–1785)' PhD Thesis, Ondokuz Mayız Üniversitesi (Samsun, 1998).
30 Ahmed Lûtfî Efendi, *Vak'anüvis Ahmed Lutfî Tarihi*, 8 vols. (Istanbul, 1999), 1:170; see also, Kadir I. Natho, *Circassian History* (New Jersey, 2009), p. 137.
31 Yılmaz Kurt, 'Muṣṭafā Nūrī', *Historians of the Ottoman Empire*, www.ottomanhistorians.uchicago.edu; eds. C. Kafadar, H. Karateke, C. Fleischer (accessed 17 February 2017).
32 Mustafa Nuri Paşa, *Netāyicü'l-Vukū'āt: Kurumlarıyla Osmanlı Tarihi I-IV*, ed. Yılmaz Kurt (Ankara, 2008), p. 414.
33 Yağcı, 'Ferah Ali Paşa'nın Soğucak Muhafızlığı', pp. 27–29, 39.
34 H. Bowen, 'Aḥmad Djewdet Pas̲h̲a', in: *Encyclopaedia of Islam*, Second Edition, Edited by: P. Bearman, Th. Bianquis, C.E. Bosworth, E. van Donzel, W.P. Heinrichs. Consulted online on 15 January 2016, http://dx.doi.org/10.1163/1573-3912_islam_SIM_0406.
35 Ahmed Cevdet Paşa, *Tezâkir 1–12*, ed. Cavid Baysun (Ankara, 1953), p. 95; quoted in Abdullah Saydam, 'Soykırımdan Kaçış: Cebel-i Elsineden Memâlik-i Mahrûsa'ya' in: Mehmet Hacısalihoğlu (ed.), *1864 Kafkas Tehciri: Kafkasya'da Rus Kolonizasyonu, Savaş ve Sürgün* (Istanbul, 2014), pp. 71–115 (here p. 74).
36 *Tarih-i Cevdet*, 12 vols. (new ed., Matbaa-i Osmaniye: Istanbul 1309/1891–1892), 3:160.
37 Cf. Deringil, *The Well-Protected Domains*, p. 170.
38 Süreyya, *Sicill-i Osmani*, 2:636.
39 *Vak'anüvis Ahmed Lutfî Tarihi*, 1:170.
40 BOA, HAT 1103/44569H, quoted in: Murat Dursun Tosun, 'Çeçenzade Hasan Paşa'nın Abaza ve Çerkes Kabileleri ile İlişkileri', online at https://muratdursuntosun.wordpress.com/2014/04/03/cecenzade-haci-hasan-pasanin-abaza-ve-cerkes-kabileleri-ile-iliskileri/ (accessed 21 December 2016). See also BOA, C.DH. 199/9935, no. 1, 21 Rebiülevvel 1243/12 October 1827 for *mecusi* Circassians leaving the *mecus adeti olan şası bid'ati* and accepting Islam and the authority of the Ottoman state.
41 *Blackwood's Edinburgh Magazine*, no. 297, vol. 48, July 1840, p. 86; emphasis in text; see also, Walter Richmond, *The Northwest Caucasus: Past, Present, Future* (London, 2008), p. 60.
42 FFor instance, Shaw/Shaw, *History of the Ottoman Empire* 2:1.
43 Baki Tezcan, 'The New Order and the Fate of the Old – The Historiographical Construction of an Ottoman Ancien Régime in the Nineteenth Century', in: Peter Bang and Christopher Bayly (eds.), *Tributary Empires in Global History* (Basingstoke, 2011), pp. 74–95 (here pp. 76–77); idem, *The Second Empire: Political and Social Transformation in the Early Modern World* (Cambridge/UK, 2010), pp. 191–226. For a similar ground-breaking research about radical social and political changes in the Ottoman Empire '[d]uring the age of revolutions between 1760 and 1820', see Ali Yaycıoğlu, *Partners of the Empire: The Crisis of the Ottoman Order in the Age of Revolutions* (Stanford, 2016); the quotation is from p. 1.
44 The idea of 'fine tuning' in imperial structures comes from Faruk Birtek; see Deringil, *The Well-Protected Domains*, p. x; 10, fn. 50.
45 Ibid., pp. 8–10.
46 Thierry Zarcone, 'Bektaşiyye', in: *Encyclopaedia of Islam*, THREE (EI³), Edited by: Kate Fleet, Gudrun Krämer, Denis Matringe, John Nawas, Everett Rowson. Consulted online on 9 March 2017, http://dx.doi.org/10.1163/1573-3912_ei3_COM_24010.
47 Ahmet Yaşar Ocak, 'Balım Sultan', in: *DİA* online at https://islamansiklopedisi.org.tr/balim-sultan (15 January 2020).

48 Thierry Zarcone, 'Bektaş, Hacı', in: *Encyclopaedia of Islam*, THREE, Edited by: Kate Fleet, Gudrun Krämer, Denis Matringe, John Nawas, Everett Rowson. Consulted online on 9 March 2017, http://dx.doi.org/10.1163/1573-3912_ei3_COM_24009.
49 Markus Dressler, 'Alevīs', in: ibid.
50 See Karolewsksi, 'What is Heterodox About Alevism?'.
51 For an in-depth study about who can be called a 'Bektaşi' in the Ottoman Empire/ Turkey, see Rıza Yıldırım, 'Bektaşi kime derler? Bektaşi kavramının kapsamı ve sınırları üzerine tarihsel bir analiz denemesi', in: *TKHBVAD* 55 (2010), pp. 23–58.
52 Ibid., p. 37; Thierry Zarcone, 'Bektaşiyye'; Suraiya Faroqhi, 'Conflict, Accomodation and Long-Term Survival: The Bektashi Order and the Ottoman State', in: *Revue des Études Islamiques LX (1992), numéro spécial: Bektachiyya* (eds. Alexandre Popovic, Gilles Veinstein), pp. 167–184, (here pp. 177–178); Muharrem Varol, *Islahat, Siyaset, Tarikat: Bektaşiliğin Ilgası Sonrasında Osmanlı Devleti'nin Tarikat Politikaları* (Istanbul, 2013), pp. 29–30.
53 An important study of Bektaşism in the nineteenth century is: A. Yılmaz Soyyer, *19. Yüzyılda Bektaşîlik* (Istanbul, 2012).
54 Shaw/Shaw, *History of the Ottoman Empire* 2:19.
55 Mehmet İpşirli, 'Kadızâde Mehmed Tâhir', in: *DİA* 24:97–98, online (15 January 2020).
56 Kieser, *Nearest East*, p. 36.
57 Virginia H. Aksan, *Ottoman Wars 1700–1870: An Empire Besieged* (London, 2007), pp. 306–325; Christine M. Philliou, *Biography of an Empire: Governing Ottomans in an Age of Revolution* (Berkeley etc. 2010), pp. 74–81.
58 Cahit Haksever, 'Osmanlı'nın Son Döneminde Islahat ve Tarikatlar: Bektâşîlik ve Nakşbendîlik Örneği', n: *EKEV Akademi Dergisi*, 13/38 (2009), pp. 39–60 (here 40).
59 Şamil Mutlu (ed.), *Yeniçeri Ocağının Kaldırılışı ve II. Mahmud'un Edirne Seyahati: Mehmed Daniş Bey ve Eserleri* (Istanbul, 1994), pp. 24–25; Sipahi Çataltepe, *19. Yüzyıl Başlarında Avrupa Dengesi ve Nizam-ı Cedit Ordusu* (Istanbul, 1997), pp. 245–246; Fahri Maden, 'Yeniçerilik-Bektaşilik İlişkileri ve Yeniçeri İsyanlarında Bektaşiler', in: *Türk Kültürü ve Hacı Bektaş Velî Araştırma Dergisi* 73 (2015), pp. 173–202 (here 186).
60 *Takvim-i Vekâyi*, no. 68, 21 Cemâziyelevvel 1249 (6 October 1833); İlber Ortaylı, 'Tarikatlar ve Tanzimat Dönemi Osmanlı Yönetimi', in: *OTAM Dergisi* (Ankara Üniversitesi), 6 (1995), pp. 281–287; Edhem Eldem, 'Yeniçeri Mezartaşları Kitabı Vesilesiyle Yeniçeri Taşları ve Tarih Üzerine', in: *Toplumsal Tarih*, 188 (Ağustos 2009), pp. 2–13.
61 *Ocakları'nın külliyyen ref'ine ve rû-yı arzdan Yeniçerilik nâmının eseri bile kalmayup, cenâb-ı hâlık-i heft-asmân levh-i mahfuzundan dahi gerek Ocağın ve gerek Yeniçerilik nâmın hakk etdüğüne iştibâh yokdur*; Mutlu, *Yeniçeri Ocağının Kaldırılışı*, p. 54; this volume contains the latinized text of *Neticetü'l-Vekayi'*, pp. 41–80. The 'Preserved Tablet' (*lawh mahfuz*) occurs in Qur'an 85:22.
62 Gülay Tulasoğlu, 'Türk-Sünnî Kimlik İnşasının II. Mahmud Dönemindeki Kökenleri Üzerine', in: Yalçın Çakmak/İmran Gürtaş (eds.), *Kızılbaşlık, Alevilik, Bektaşilik: Tarih-Kimlik-İnanç-Rituel* (Istanbul, 2015), pp. 165–183 (here pp. 169–170). See further Çakmak, *Sultanın Kızılbaşları*, chapter 1.
63 Ziya Yılmazer, 'Esad Efendi, Sahaflar Şeyhizâde', in: *DİA*, online at https://islamansiklopedisi.org.tr/esad-efendi-sahaflar-seyhizade (15 January 2020).
64 Sahaflar Şeyhizâde Esad Efendi, *Üss-i Zafer* (Istanbul 1243/1828); for an elaboration, see Tobias Heinzelmann, 'Die Auflösung der Janitscharentruppen und ihre historischen Zusammenhänge: Sahhaflarşeyhizade Mehmed Esad Efendis Üss-i Zafer', in: *Asiatische Studien: Zeitschrift der Schweizerischen Asiengesellschaft* 54:3 (2000), pp. 653–675.

65 Heinzelmann, 'Die Auflösung der Janitscharentruppen', p. 654.
66 For the revolts of the Janissaries throughout Ottoman history, see Gülay Yılmaz, 'İstemezük', in: Mehmet Ö. Alkan, *Osmanlı'dan Günümüze Darbeler* (Istanbul 2017), pp. 1–15.
67 Esad Efendi, *Üss-i Zafer*, pp. 177–178, Heinzelmann, 'Die Auflösung der Janitscharentruppen', p. 656; see also Erika Glassen, 'Krisenbewusstsein und Heilserwartung in der islamischen Welt zu Beginn der Neuzeit', in: Ulrich Haarmann et al. (ed.), *Die islamische Welt zwischen Mittelalter und Neuzeit: Festschrift für Hans Robert Roemer zum 65. Geburtstag* (Beirut/Wiesbaden, 1979), pp. 167–179; see also Butrus Abu-Manneh, 'The Naqshbandiyya-Mujaddidiyya in the Ottoman Lands in the Early 19th Century', in: *Die Welt des Islams*, New Series, 22:1/4 (1982), pp. 1–36.
68 He had various posts as an Ottoman official, including as minister of the interior; Zekeriya Kurşun, 'Mehmed Memduh Paşa', in: *DİA*, online at https://islamansiklopedisi.org.tr/mehmed-memduh-pasa (15 January 2020).
69 The verse is actually *fa-'azzazna-huma bi-thalith*, 'We strengthened the two with a third'.
70 Already Şeyh Galib (1757–1799), an Ottoman poet belonging to the Mevlevi Sufi Order and a contemporary of Selim III, called the sultan *müceddid* and compared his efforts to that of the Muslim redeemer Mehdi, who would renew the world on the day of judgment; Cem Dilçin, 'Şeyh Galip'in Şiirlerinde III. Selim ve Nizam-ı Cedit', in: *Türkoloji Dergisi*, 11/1 (1993), pp. 209–219. For the sacredness of sultans, see Hakan T. Karateke, 'Opium for the Subjects?: Religiosity as a Legitimizing Factor for the Ottoman Sultan', in: idem and Maurus Reinkowski (eds.), *Legitimizing the Order: the Ottoman Rhetoric of State Power* (Leiden, 2005), pp. 111–129; on Selim III, see p. 115.
71 Mehmed Memduh, *Tasvîr-i Ahvâl Tenvîr-i İstikbâl* (Izmir 1327/1909), pp. 43–44; latinized modern Turkish edition in: Mehmed Memduh and Ahmet Nezih Galitekin (ed.), *Tanzimat'tan Meşrutiyet'e*, vol. 2 (Istanbul, 1995), pp. 137–138.
72 Cornell Fleischer, 'The Lawgiver as Messiah: The Making of the Imperial Image in the Reign of Süleymân', in: Gilles Veinstein (ed.), *Soliman le magnifique et son temps* (Paris, 1992), pp. 159–177; Çıpa, *The Making of Selim*, p. 161; Tijana Krstic, *Contested Conversions to Islam: Narratives of Religious Change in the Early Modern Ottoman Empire* (Stanford, 2011), p. 81.
73 Krstic, *Contested Conversions*, p. 76.
74 Hamid Algar and K.A. Nizami, 'Nak͟shbandiyya', in: *Encyclopaedia of Islam*, Second Edition, Edited by: P. Bearman, Th. Bianquis, C.E. Bosworth, E. van Donzel, W.P. Heinrichs. Consulted online on 15 January 2020, http://dx.doi.org/10.1163/1573-3912_islam_COM_0843; for the Nakşbendis in the Ottoman Empire and Turkey, see ibid.
75 BOA, HAT. 290/17351, 29 Zilhicce 1242/24 July 1827. Üss-i Zafer, pp. 208–209; *Tarih-i Cevdet*, 12: 181–182; Mesut Ayar, *Bektaşilik'te Son Nefes: Yeniçeriliğin Kaldırılmasından Sonra Bektaşilik* (Istanbul, 2009); pp. 38–40; Varol, *Islahat, Siyaset, Tarikat*, pp. 45–47.
76 *Vak'anüvis Ahmed Lutfî Tarihi*, 1:110.
77 'Mahmoud est un Alexandre terrible. Le moindre signe menaçant de son visage arrêterait, comme une muraille, les efforts de cent mille Yadjoudj'; A. P. Caussin de Perceval (transl.), *Précis historique de la destruction du corps des Janissaires par le sultan Mahmoud, en 1826* (Paris, 1833), pp. 6–7.
78 Ayar, *Bektaşilik'te Son Nefes*, p. 39.
79 BOA, HAT 290/17351; Ayar, *Bektaşilik'te Son Nefes*, pp. 36–37 and 134/n. 92; Soyyer, *19. Yüzyılda Bektaşîlik*, p. 70.
80 BOA, HAT 290/17351; Ayar, *Bektaşilik'te Son Nefes*, p. 134.

81 Cf. Baer, *Honored by the Glory of Islam*, p. 6 and 13.
82 Butrus Abu-Manneh, 'The Naqshbandiyya-Mujaddidiyya in the Ottoman Lands in the Early 19th Century', p. 13; for the relation between the Müceddidi-Nakşbendis and the Bektaşis, see ibid. and idem, 'The Naqshbandi-Mujaddidi and the Bektashi Orders in 1826', in: idem, *Studies on Islam and the Ottoman Empire in the 19th Century (1826–1876)* (Istanbul, 2001), pp. 59–71.
83 Abu-Manneh, 'The Islamic Roots of the Gülhane Rescript'.
84 Christopher Bayly, *The Birth of the Modern World 1780–1914* (Oxford, 2004), chapter 9, 'Empires of Religion'; Abdulhamit Kırmızı, '19. Yüzyılı Laiksizleştirmek: Osmanlı-Türk Laikleşme Anlatısının Sorunları', in: *Cogito*, 94 (2019), pp. 1–17.
85 BOA, C.DH. 125/6218, 29 Ramazan 1241/7 May 1826; BOA, HAT 290/17351, 29 Zilhicce 1242/24 July 1827; BOA, C.ZB., 17/843, 21 Cemaziyelâhir 1243/9 January 1828; BOA, C.ZB., 34/1680, 9 Zilkâde 1255/14 January 1840; BOA, HAT 512/25094-D, E, F, and G, 25 Rebîülevvel 1249/12 August 1233; *Üss-i Zafer*, pp. 211–212; *Vak'anüvis Ahmed Lutfî Tarihi*, 1:151; Fahri Maden, *Bektaşî Tekkelerinin Kapatılması (1826) ve Bektaşiliğin Yasaklı Yılları* (Ankara, 2013), p. 99; Varol, *Islahat, Siyaset, Tarikat*, pp. 45–47.
86 Esad Efendi, *Üss-i Zafer*, pp. 213–221; Fahri Maden, 'Hacı Bektaş Veli Tekkesi'nde Nakşî Şeyhler ve Sırrı Paşa'nın Lâyıhası'. *Türk Kültürü ve Hacı Bektaş Veli Araştırma Dergisi* 59 (2011), pp. 159–180 (here p. 160).
87 This is one of the early uses of the term 'Alevi' in the nineteenth century in the Ottoman context; cf. Markus Dressler, *Writing Religion: The Making of Turkish Alevi Islam* (Oxford, 2015), pp. 2–3. For another mention of 'Alevi' in 1871, see below.
88 BOA, C.ADL, 29/1734, 29 Safer 1242/2 October 1826; BOA, HAT, 290/17386, 29 Zilhicce 1241/4 August 1826; BOA, Mühimme-i Asakir Defteri, nr. 26, 29 Rebîülevvel 1244/9 October 1828, pp. 89–90, 108–110, 192–194; Esad Efendi, *Üss-i Zafer*, pp. 213–221; Maden, 'Sırrı Paşa'nın Layıhası', p. 175/n. 1; idem, *Bektaşî Tekkelerinin Kapatılması*, pp. 170–171.
89 Ayar, *Bektaşilik'te Son Nefes*, p. 42; Soyyer, *19. Yüzyılda Bektaşîlik*, pp. 67 and 72.
90 Ayar, *Bektaşilik'te Son Nefes*, pp. 43–44.
91 BOA, C.ZB. 17/843, 21 Cemaziyelâhir 1243/ 9 January 1828.
92 BOA, HAT 512/25094-E, 25 Rebiülevvel 1249/12 August 1833; BOA, HAT 512/25094-E, 25 Rebiülevvel 1249/12 August 1833; BOA, HAT 512/25094-G, 27 Rebiülevvel 1249/14 August 1833; cf. full text in Ayar, *Bektaşilik'te Son Nefes*, pp. 147–148. See also Sibel Kavaklı, '929/A Numaralı Nefy Defterinin (1826/1833) Transkripsiyon ve Değerlendirilmesi', MA Thesis, (Gaziosmanpaşa Üniversitesi: Tokat, 2005), p. 581.
93 Maden, *Bektaşî Tekkelerinin Kapatılması*, p. 99.
94 Yaycıoğlu, *Partners of the Empire*, p. 2.
95 Kadir Üstün, 'Rethinking Vaka-i Hayriyye (Auspicious Event): Elimination of the Janissaries on the Path of Modernization', PhD Thesis, Bilkent University (Ankara, 2002), p. 41.
96 BOA, DH.MKT. 1487/38, 8 Cemaziyelahir 1305/21 February 1888; DH.MKT. 1975/31, 25 Zilhicce 1309/20 July 1892; DH. MKT. 1983/15, 11 Muharrem 1310/5 August 1892.
97 Maden, *Bektaşî Tekkelerinin Kapatılması*, pp. 196–197.
98 Ibid., pp. 197–200.
99 Ibid., pp. 210–211.
100 Ibid., pp. 214–215.

101 This was published in several issues of *Hakayık el-Vekayi*, e.g., no. 545, 15 Safer 1289/23 April 1872; it could be the *Velayetname* (or *Vilayetname*) published in 1288/1871 by a certain Ahmed Muhtar Efendi, see the digital library of the Atatürk Kitaplığı at http://ataturkkitapligi.ibb.gov.tr/yordambt/yordam.php?sayfaOturumAc#; for the Velayetname of Hacı Bektaş in general, see Ahmet Yaşar Ocak, 'Hacı Bektaş Vilayetnamesi', in: *DİA*, online at https://islamansiklopedisi.org.tr/haci-bektas-vilayetnamesi (accessed 2 February 2020).
102 Maden, *Bektaşî Tekkelerinin Kapatılması*, p. 214.
103 Maurus Reinkowski, 'Hapless Imperialists and Resentful Nationalists: Trajectories of Radicalization in the Late Ottoman Empire', in: idem/Gregor Thum (eds.), *Helpless Imperialists: Imperial Failure and Radicalization* (Göttingen, 2013), p. 55.
104 Ibid.
105 Ibid., pp. 55–56.
106 Selim Deringil, 'The Struggle against Shiism in Hamidian Iraq: A Study in Ottoman Counter Propaganda', in: *Die Welt des Islams*, New Series, Bd. 30, Nr. 1/4 (1990), pp. 45–62; Yitzhak Nakash, 'The Conversion of Iraq's Tribes to Shiism', in: *International Journal of Middle East Studies* 26:3 (August 1994), 443–463; Meir Litvak, *Shi'i Scholars of Nineteenth-Century Iraq: The ulema' of Najaf and Karbala'* (Cambridge/UK, 1998), pp. 128–134, pp. 140–142; Gökhan Çetinsaya, 'The Caliph and Mujtahids: Ottoman Policy towards the Shiite Community of Iraq in the Late Nineteenth Century', in: *MES* 41:4 (July 2005), 561–574; Faruk Yaslıçimen, 'Saving the Minds and Loyalties of Subjects: Ottoman Education Policy Against the Spread of Shiism in Iraq During the Time of Abdülhamid II', in: *Dîvân: Disiplinlerarası Çalışmalar Dergisi* 21:41 (2016/2), pp. 63–108.
107 Kieser, *Nearest East*, p. 36.
108 Bayly, *The Birth of the Modern World*, p. 325.
109 Enver Ziya Karal, *Osmanlı Tarihi: Islahat Fermanı Devri*, vol. 7 (Ankara, 2003), pp. 282–283; see also, Abu-Manneh, 'The Sultan and the Bureaucracy: The Anti-Tanzimat Concepts of Mahmud Nedim Paşa', in: *International Journal of Middle East Studies* 11 (1990), pp. 257–274 (here pp. 268–269).
110 Deringil, *The Well-Protected Domains*, pp. 68–92; İlber Ortaylı, '19. yüzyılda heterodox dinî gruplar ve Osmanlı idaresi', pp. 156–161 and idem, 'Alevîlik, Nusayrîlik ve Bâbıâlî', pp. 161–169.
111 For Sunni orthodox trends in the Tanzimat Period, see the following two studies by Butrus Abu-Manneh: 'The Naqshbandiyya-Mujaddidiyya in Istanbul in the Early Tanzimat Period', and 'The Porte and the Sunni-Orthodox Trend in the Later Ottoman Period', in: idem, *Studies on Islam and the Ottoman Empire in the 19th Century (1826–1876)* (Istanbul, 2001), pp. 99–114 and 125–140.
112 BOA, BEO.AYN.d (Haleb Ayniyat Defteri), 867, pp. 138, 141, 144, 149, 156 and 190, in: *OABNN*, p. 71–75.
113 BOA, BEO.AYN.d (Haleb Ayniyat Defteri), 867, ibid., p. 144.
114 Ibid., p. 149.
115 Ibid., p. 156.
116 Ibid., p. 190.
117 Selahattin Tozlu, 'Osmanlı Arşiv Belgelerinde Antakya ve İskenderun Nusayrîleri (19. Yüzyıl)', in: *Türk Kültürü ve Hacı Bektaş Velî Araştırma Dergisi* 54 (2010), pp. 79–110 (here pp. 86–89).
118 *Hakayık el-Vekayi*, no. 416, 6 Ramazan 1288/18 November 1871, pp. 2–3; this is part of an installment published before and after this issue. I was not able to find the name of the author.

119 It is interesting to note that this is one example of the use of the term 'Alevi' for 'Kızılbaş' in the late Ottoman period, despite Dressler's assertion that 'it is important to emphasize that in the late Ottoman period there was as of yet no necessary connection between the terms Alevi and Kızılbaş established'; Dressler, *Writing Religion*, p. 3. Another much earlier example from the early sixteenth century is when an official Ottoman chronicler called the Bektaşi poet Hayretî as belonging to the 'Alevi school/sect (*alevi mezheb*)'; Hanna Sohrweide, 'Der Sieg der Safaviden in Persien und seine Rückwirkungen auf die Schiiten Anatoliens im 16. Jahrhundert', in: *Der Islam* 41 (1965), pp. 95–223 (here p. 164, n. 437) and Mustafa Tatcı, 'Hayretî', in: *DİA*, online at https://islamansiklopedisi.org.tr/hayreti (15 January 2020). For a discussion of the use of 'Alevi' in late nineteenth-century Ottoman dictionaries and encyclopedias, see Johannes Zimmermann, 'Aleviten in osmanischen Wörterbüchern und Enzyklopädien des späten 19. Jahrhunderts', in: Robert Langer et al. (eds.), *Ocak und Dedelik: Institutionen religiösen Spezialistentums bei den Aleviten* (Frankfurt am Main, 2013), pp. 179–204.

120 For the use of *ittihad-ı kulûb* among the soldiers during the reign of Mahmud II, see Esad Efendi, *Üss-i Zafer* (latinised), pp. 11 and 46, and *ittifak-ı kulûb* on p. 99 and Esad Efendi's chronicle *Vakʻa-Nüvîs Esʻad Efendi Tarihi* (latinised), ed. Ziya Yılmazer (Istanbul, 2000), p. 574; cf. Abu-Manneh, 'The Sultan and the Bureaucracy', pp. 262, 267.

121 Ali Akyıldız, 'Mehmed Ârif Bey', in: *DİA*, online at https://islamansiklopedisi.org.tr/mehmed-arif-bey (15 January 2020).

122 Mehmed Arif, *Başımıza Gelenler* (Kahire/Cairo: Maarif Matbaası, 1321/1903), pp. 393–395; latinized modern Turkish edition: *Başımıza Gelenler*, 3 vols., ed. M. Ertuğrul Düzdağ (Istanbul, İrfan Matbaası, 1973), 3:784–787, drawn to my attention by Veysel Şimşek.

123 This word comes from *çırağ puf*, which means 'the candle is blown' (see *Steingass Persian Dictionary*, *charāgh-rā puf kardan*, 'To puff out the candle', – *mum söndü* in Turkish – and refers to the fabricated Alevi ritual of 'extinguishing the light ceremony' where they are supposedly involved in incestuous sex orgies in the dark; for *mum söndü* and its use to vilify non-Sunni groups, see Moosa, *Extremist Shiites*, pp. 136–138; Karolewski, 'What is Heterodox About Alevism?', pp. 442–443, 447–448; Bella Tendler Krieger, 'New Evidence for the Survival of Sexually Libertine Rites among some Nuṣayrī- ʻAlawīs of the Nineteenth Century,' in: Behnam Sadeghi et al. (eds.), *Islamic Cultures, Islamic Contexts: Essays in Honor of Professor Patricia Crone* (Leiden, 2015), pp. 565–596 (here pp. 573–574, esp. fn. 27).

124 While the word means 'stupid, rascal, babbler' etc., it is was used in some places in Anatolia such as Adana and Niğde for nominal Muslims and the Alevis; see the dictionary for colloquial Turkish, *Türkiye Türkçesi Ağızları Sözlüğü*, at the online dictionary of the Türk Dil Kurumu (TDK, Turkish Language Association) at www.tdk.gov.tr. Recently the TDK had to defend itself for listing *vazalak* in its dictionaries due to the accusation in social media and newspapers that it was belittling the Alevis; see "Vazalak' Sözü ile İlgili Açıklama', 21.01.2018, at http://tdk.gov.tr/index.php?option=com_content&view=article&id=963&Itemid=75 (accessed 26 March 2019).

125 Or Sofu, Sofu/Sûfiyân Süreği, a name given to the Alevis; see Baha Said/İsmail Görkem (ed.), *Türkiye'de Alevi-Bektaşi, Ahi ve Nusayri zümreleri* (Ankara, 2000), pp. 123–138; Birol Azar, 'Benzerlik ve Farklılıklar Ekseninde Alevî-Bektaşî İnançları Üzerine Bir Değerlendirme', in: *Fırat Üniversitesi İlahiyat Fakültesi Dergisi* 10:2 (2005), pp. 81–87 (here p. 83).

126 See hadith no. 892 in Mehmed Arif, *Binbir Hadis-i Şerif* (Kahire/Cairo: Maarif Matbaası, 1319/1901), pp. 397–415; on p. 402 he mentions the terms Kızılbaş, Sufiler/Sofular, Sofu/Sufi Süreği, Çerapof, Vazalak, Türk and Türkmen for the Bektaşis/Alevis. However, in the latinized modern Turkish version all these terms are omitted, probably due to political correctness; see Mehmet Arif/Ahmet Kahraman (ed.), *Binbir Hadis* (Istanbul, n.d.), 2 vols., 2:423.

127 Stephen Duguid, 'The Politics of Unity: Hamidian Policy in Eastern Anatolia', in: *MES* 9:2 (May, 1973), pp. 139–155; Jacob M. Landau, *The Politics of Pan-Islam: Ideology and Organization* (Oxford, 1990), pp. 9–79; Kemal H. Karpat, *The Politicization of Islam: Reconstructing Identity, State, Faith, and Community in the Late Ottoman State* (Oxford, 2001).

128 Cihangir Gündoğdu/Vural Genç, *Dersim'de Osmanlı Siyaseti: İzâle-i Vahşet, Tashîh-i İtikâd ve Tasfiye-i Ezhân* (Kitap Yayınevi: Istanbul 2013), pp. 11–13; cf. Deringil, *The Well-Protected Domains*, p. 102.

129 Abdullah Uçman, 'Şemseddin Sâmi', in: *DİA*, online at https://islamansiklopedisi.org.tr/semseddin-sami (accessed 29 June 2021).

130 Isa Blumi, *Rethinking the Late Ottoman Empire: A Comparative Social and Political History of Albania and Yemen 1878–1918* (Istanbul 2003), pp. 32–33.

131 For him, see İz, Fahir, 'Ḥasan Bedr al-Dīn', in: *Encyclopaedia of Islam*, Second Edition, Edited by: P. Bearman, Th. Bianquis, C.E. Bosworth, E. van Donzel, W.P. Heinrichs. Online abgerufen am 28 June 2021, http://dx.doi.org/10.1163/1573-3912_islam_SIM_8606, and Necati Alkan, 'The Young Turks and the Baha'is in Palestine', in: Yuval Ben-Bassat and Eyal Ginio, *Late Ottoman Palestine: The Period of Young Turk Rule* (London, 2011), pp. 259–278 (here 265–269).

132 Quoted in George Walter Gawrych, *The Crescent and the Eagle: Ottoman Rule, Islam and the Albanians, 1874–1913* (London, 2006), pp. 178–179.

133 Ibid., pp. 187–188.

134 Faika Çelik, '"Community in Motion": Gypsies in Ottoman Imperial State Policy, Public Morality, and the Sharia Court of Üsküdar (1530s-1585s)' (PhD Thesis, McGill University: Montreal, 2013); on pp. 396–411 Çelik discusses the memorandum of an Ottoman teacher by name of Sadi in Siroz (Serres) and other attached documents from which the Ottoman terms above are taken (Çelik rendered *cahile* wrongly as *cehale*): BOA, Y.MTV. 47/180, 24 Cemaziyelâhir 1308/4 February 1891; idem, '"Civilizing Mission" in the Late Ottoman Discourse: The Case of Gypsies', in: *Oriente Moderno*, no. 93:2 (2013), pp. 577–597.

135 Gündoğdu/Genç, *Dersim'de Osmanlı Siyaseti*, pp. 13–15.

136 Türkyılmaz, 'Anxieties of Conversion', pp. 267–268.

137 He was the author of *Hiss-i İnkılâb yahud Sultan Abdülazizin hal'i ile Sultan Murad-i hamisin cülusu* (Istanbul, 1326/1910), a detailed account of the deposition of Sultan Abdülaziz; translated into English by Robert Devereux, 'Süleyman Paşa's "The Feeling of the Revolution"', in: *MES* 15:1 (Jan. 1979), pp. 3–35.

138 BOA, YEE 9/34 (previous classification, as used by Deringil and Çetinsaya below, is YEE 14/1188/126/9), 9 Ramazan 1309/7 April 1892. For the whole issue, see Selim Deringil, 'Legitimacy Structures in the Ottoman State: The Reign of Abdulhamid II (1876–1909)', in: *International Journal of Middle East Studies* 23:3 (August 1991), pp. 345–359 (here pp. 348–349); idem, 'The Struggle against Shiism in Hamidian Iraq', pp. 53–54; idem, *The Well-Protected Domains*, p. 49; Gökhan Çetinsaya, *Ottoman Administration of Iraq, 1890–1908* (London, 2006), pp. 108–109; for a summary and the style of the petition, see Erol Özbilgen, *Osmanlının Balkanlardan Çekilişi*:

Süleyman Hüsnü Paşa ve Dönemi (Istanbul, 2006), pp. 264–267; for Süleyman Hüsnü's petition and other petitions from and about Iraq, see Halil İbrahim Güngör, 'II. Abdülhamid Dönemi'nde Irak'la İlgili Hazırlanan Layihalar', MA Thesis, Dumlupınar Üniversitesi (Kütahya, 2009).

139 Followers of the ancient religion of Sabianism usually traced to John the Baptist; see T. Fahd, 'Ṣābi'a', in: *Encyclopaedia of Islam*, Second Edition, Edited by: P. Bearman, Th. Bianquis, C.E. Bosworth, E. van Donzel, W.P. Heinrichs. Consulted online on 15 March 2016, http://dx.doi.org/10.1163/1573-3912_islam_COM_0953; for the neglected topic of the Sabians of Iraq in the late Ottoman period, see Selda Güner, 'Irak Sâbiîlerine Dair Bir Asayiş Dosyası (1873–1898)', in: *Cumhuriyet Tarihi Araştırmaları Dergisi*, 9:18 (Güz 2013), pp. 3–28.

140 BOA, YEE 9/34, p. 1: 'İşte bu taksimat devletin mezheb ve lisan-ı resmiyesine intisabı olan fırkaların akalliyet mikdarını ve muhalif gürühun ağlabiyet nüfusunu nazarlarda pek vazıh olarak tebyin eder'; quoted in Deringil, *The Well-Protected Domains*, p. 49.

141 For the Babis and Baha'is in the Ottoman Empire, see Necati Alkan, *Dissent and Heterodoxy in the Late Ottoman Empire: Reformers, Babis and Baha'is* (Istanbul, 2008).

142 BOA, YEE 9/34, p. 1.

143 Deringil misread this as *dâi-ul-hak-misyoner*; see 'The Struggle against Shiism in Hamidian Iraq', p. 53; idem, 'Legitimacy Structures in the Ottoman State', p. 349.

144 Cf. *da'iy*ᵃⁿ *ila Allah* ('calling unto God') in Qur'an 33:46, and *da'i Allah* ('God's caller/summoner') in 46:31 and 32.

145 BOA, YEE 9/34, p. 3.

146 Deringil, 'The Struggle against Shiism in Hamidian Iraq', p. 53.

147 BOA, Y.A. HUS. 260/130, 28 Şevval 1309/25 May 1892, mentioned in: Faruk Yaslıçimen, 'Sunnism versus Shi'ism? Rise of the Shi'i Politics and of the Ottoman Apprehension in Late Nineteenth Century Iraq', M.A. Thesis, Bilkent University (Ankara, 2008), pp. 69–70, 72, 115–116, and 120–121; the author kindly shared a copy of the document.

148 Yaslıçimen, 'Sunnism versus Shi'ism?', pp. 119–120; see also, Gökhan Çetinsaya, 'The Caliph and Mujtahids', pp. 561–574.

149 BOA, Y.A. HUS. 260/130, p. 1.

150 Ibid., p. 2.

151 BOA, YEE 9/34, p. 4; quoted in Deringil, 'The Struggle against Shiism in Hamidian Iraq', p. 53.

152 Ibid., p. 54.

153 Idem *Well-Protected Domains*, pp. 75–84.

154 BOA, Y.MTV. 231/79, nos. 1 and 2; cf. ibid., pp. 75–76.

155 Deringil, *Well-Protected Domains*, p. 82, quoting from BOA, Y.MTV 53/108, 2 Zilkade 1308/9 June 1891.

156 Mehmet İpşirli and Kemal Beydilli, 'İbrâhim Efendi, Haydarîzâde', in: *DİA* 21:297–298, online at https://islamansiklopedisi.org.tr/ibrahim-efendi-haydarizade (accessed 4 February 2021).

157 BOA, DH.İ.UM 19/1, 14 Cemaziyelevvel 1338/4 February 1920. These kinds of efforts were under the aegis of the *Darü'l-Hikmeti'l-İslamiyye* ('House of Islamic Wisdom'). It was established in 1918 and was active until 1922 (during the occupation of Istanbul by the Allied Forces after WWI and the Kemalist War of Independence), with the aim of settling some newly emerging religious issues in the

Islamic world for the rejection of anti-Islamic movements that were also active in the Ottoman lands, within the framework of Islamic principles. Among those appointed were Haydarizade, Mehmed Şemsettin (Günaltay, discussed below), Bediüzzaman Said Nursi (founder of the later İslamist Nurcu movement) and Mehmed Akif (Ersoy; poet, writer and author of the Turkish national anthem); see Sadık Albayrak, 'Dârü'l-Hikmeti'l-İslâmiyye', in: *DİA*, online at https://islamansiklopedisi.org.tr/ibrahim-efendi-haydarizade (accessed 4 February 2021), and 'Dârü'l-Hikmeti'l-İslâmiyye Hakkında', in: *Sebilürreşad*, no. 17/421–422, online at (accessed 9 February 2021).

158 James Grehan, *Twilight of the Saints: Everyday Religion in Ottoman Syria and Palestine* (Oxford, 2014), p. 21.
159 *Olive Trees*, December 1898, p. 381. Henry Martyn, who is mentioned here, was a prominent English missionary among Muslims in India and Iran whose legacy inspired later missionaries; see Martyn, Henry (1781–1812), www.bu.edu/missiology/missionary-biography/l-m/martyn-henry-1781-1812/ (25 February 2019).
160 BOA, Y.MTV. 68/90.
161 BOA, DH.MKT. 2012/117; for an Ottoman 'colonial' exposé about the Yezidis, see Mustafa Nuri Paşa's *Abede-i İblis* ('The Devil Worshippers'), (Istanbul, 1328/1910); translated into German and annotated by Theodor Menzel, Die Teufelsanbeter oder ein Blick auf die widerspenstige Sekte der Jeziden: Ein Beitrag zur Kenntnis der Jeziden', in: Hugo Grothe, *Meine Vorderasienexpedition 1906 und 1907: Die fachwissenschaftlichen Ergebnisse*, vol. 1.1. (Leipzig, 1911), pp. 90–211.
162 BOA, Y.A. HUS. 260/130, 28 Şevval 1309/25 May 1892, the above report of Ahmed Cevad Paşa.
163 BOA, ŞD. 2280/40, 29 Zilhicce 1310/14 July 1893.
164 BOA, İ.MMS. 113/4821, 29 Şevval 1307/18 June 1890.
165 BOA, BEO 2250/168719, 22 Şevval 1321/11 January 1904.
166 BOA, DH.MKT 74/10, 8 Muharrem 1311/22 July 1893.
167 BOA, Y.PRK.BŞK 19/27, 27 Muharrem 1308/12 September 1890, and DH. MKT. 1555/58, 12 Safer 1306/18 October 1888.
168 BOA, Y.PRK.KOM. 7/59, 3 Zilkâde 1307/21 June 1890.
169 BOA, Y.A.RES 51/9, 22 Ramazan 1307/12 May 1890.
170 BOA, Y.A.RES. 60/27, 17 Safer 1310/10 September 1892.
171 Christine Allison, *The Yezidi oral tradition in Iraqi Kurdistan* (Richmond/UK, 2001), p. 36.
172 Ussama Makdisi, 'Ottoman Orientalism', in: *The American Historical Review*, Vol. 107, No. 3 (June 2002), pp. 768–796; for the conversion campaigns, see Selim Deringil, *The Well-Protected Domains*, pp. 68–92; Selçuk Akşin Somel, 'Osmanlı Modernleşme Döneminde Periferik Nüfus Grupları', in: *Toplum ve Bilim* 83 (Kış 1999/2000), pp. 178–201; see further Christoph Herzog/Raoul Motika, 'Orientalism 'alla turca': Late 19th / Early 20th Century Ottoman Voyages into the Muslim 'Outback'', in: *Die Welt des Islams*, New Series, 40:2: Ottoman Travels and Travel Accounts from an Earlier Age of Globalization (Juli, 2000), pp. 139–195. See also, Mustafa Serdar Palabıyık, 'Travel, civilization and the east: Ottoman travellers' perception of 'the east' in the late Ottoman Empire', PhD Thesis, ODTÜ (Ankara, 2010).
173 Selim Deringil, '"They Live in a State of Nomadism and Savagery": The Late Ottoman. Empire and the Post-Colonial Debate', in: *Comparative Studies in Society and History*, Vol. 45, No. 2 (Apr., 2003), pp. 311–342 (here p. 312).
174 Palabıyık, 'Travel, Civilization and the East: Ottoman Travellers', pp. 10–11.

175 Selim Deringil, '"They Live in a State of Nomadism and Savagery"', p. 312; Abdulhamit Kırmızı, 'Going round the province for progress and prosperity: inspection tours and reports by late Ottoman governors', in: *Studies in Travel Writing*, 16:4, 387–401 (here p. 388).
176 Kırmızı, 'Going round the province', p. 390–396; Deringil, *The Well-Protected Domains*, p. 77.
177 John Curry, 'Some Reflections on the Fluidity of Orthodoxy and Heterodoxy in an Ottoman Sunni Context', in: Erginbaş, *Ottoman Sunnism*, pp. 191–210 (here, pp. 207–208).
178 Blumi, *Rethinking the Late Ottoman Empire*.
179 For the political atmosphere of Turkish nationalism and the context of Günaltay's writings, see Umut Uzer, *An Intellectual History of Turkish Nationalism: Between Turkish Ethnicity and Islamic Identity* (Salt Lake City, 2016), esp. pp. 102, 142, 160 and 163–164.
180 Mehmed Şemseddin, *Hurafâtdan Hakikate* (Istanbul, 1332/1916), pp. 183–184; in Latin letters and modern Turkish, Ahmet Gökbel (ed.), *Hurafeler ve İslam Gerçeği* (Istanbul, 1993).
181 Mehmed Şemseddin, *Hurafâtdan Hakikate*, pp. 183–184; see also, Hakan Feyzullah Karpuzcu, 'Late Ottoman Modernist/Rationalist Discourses on Islam: Superstition, Sufism and Şemseddin Günaltay', MA Thesis, Sabancı University (Istanbul, 2008), esp. pp. 123–126.
182 Mehmed Şemseddin, *Hurafâtdan Hakikate*, p. 207
183 Ibid., pp. 209–211.
184 Ibid., p. 209.
185 Ibid., p. 211.
186 Ibid., 213.
187 Ibid., pp. 204–205.
188 Madelung, W. and M. G. S. Hodgson, 'Ibāḥa', in: *Encyclopaedia of Islam*, Second Edition, Edited by: P. Bearman, Th. Bianquis, C.E. Bosworth, E. van Donzel, W.P. Heinrichs. Consulted online on 15 January 2020, http://dx.doi.org/10.1163/1573-3912_islam_SIM_3016.
189 Mehmed Şemseddin, *Hurafâtdan Hakikate*, pp. 203–204.
190 Ibid., p. 205.
191 *Preussisches Handelsarchiv* (Berlin), no. 50, 13 December 1878, p. 576 (PDF at Google Books).
192 Julius Richter, *A History of Protestant Missions*, p. 214; Dick Douwes, 'Knowledge and Oppression', p. 166.
193 The Circassian Ziyâeddin Mehmed Efendi; *Sicill-i Osmani*, 5:1717.
194 *Herald of Mission News*, vol. 1892–93, p. 26.
195 A.L. Tibawi, *American Interests in Syria* (Oxford, 1966), p. 262; Deringil, *The Well-Protected Domains*, p. 83.
196 Jens Hanssen, *Fin de siècle Beirut: The Making of an Otoman Provincial* Capital (Oxford, 2005), pp. 68–69.
197 BOA, Y.PRK.AZN 4/57, 10 Eylül 1306 Rumi.
198 Yakup Karataş, 'Sultan II. Abdülhamid'in Eğitim Politikalarının Mali Bir Veçhesi: Evkâf-ı Münderisenin Maarife Terki', in: *A.Ü. Türkiyat Araştırmaları Enstitüsü Dergisi*, 57 (2016), pp. 1839–1867.
199 Cf. Sacit Uğuz, 'II. Abdülhamid'in kapsayıcı eğitim politikasına bir örnek: Lazkiye Nusayrileri ve Hamidiye Mektepleri' in: *Current Research in Social Sciences* 5:1 (2019), pp. 9–27.

200 Ismail Kemal Bey Vlora or Ismail Qemali (1844–1919), is considered as the founding father of modern Albania and served as its first prime minister from 1912 to 1914.
201 Ismail Kemal Bey/Sommerville Story (ed.), *The Memoirs of Ismail Kemal Bey* (London, 1920), pp. 199–200.
202 Hanssen, *Fin de siècle Beirut*, p. 68.
203 Benjamin Fortna, *Imperial classroom: Islam, the State, and Education in the Late Ottoman Empire* (Oxford, 2002), pp. 50–60; Makdisi, p. 208.
204 Deringil, *The Well-Protected Domains*, pp. 101–102; Ebubekir Ceylan, 'Carrot or Strick? Ottoman Tribal Policy in Baghdad, 1831–1876', in: *International Journal of Contemporary Iraqi Studies*, 3:2 (2009), pp. 169–186.
205 Deringil, 'The Invention of Tradition'; Selçuk Akşin Somel, *The Modernization of Public Education in the Ottoman Empire 1839–1908* (Leiden, 2001), pp. 222–223. For the conversion policies among the Yezidis, see, e.g., Edip Gölbaşı, 'The Yezidis and the Ottoman State: Modern Power, Military Conscription, and Conversion Policies, 1830–1909', MA Thesis, Boğaziçi University (Istanbul, 2008) and idem, "Heretik' aşiretler ve II. Abdülhamid rejimi'.
206 Faruk Yaslıçimen, 'Sunnism versus Shi'ism? Rise of the Shi'i politics and of the Ottoman Apprehension in Late Nineteenth Century Iraq', MA Thesis (Bilkent University, Ankara 2008), p. 106, based on BOA, İ.DH. 1237/96880, 14 Zilkâde 1308/20 June 1891 and Y.EE. 10/69, 11 Safer 1312/13 August 1894. I prefer my translation of *cebren tashih-i itikad kâideten mümkün olmadığı cihetle*, to Yaslıçimen's rendering 'enforcement for the correction of faith is not allowed'.
207 BOA, İ.MMS. 114/4687, 13 Haziran 1306/26 June 1891, quoted in Deringil, 'The Invention of Tradition', p. 15; about the 'reeducation' of the Alawis, see Winter, *A History of the Alawis*, pp. 220–238.
208 Also, Arap İzzet Holo Paşa, an Ottoman official of Kurdish origin who was *mutasarrıf* (local governor) of several places in Syria; see Mehmed Süreyya, *Sicill-i Osmani*, 2:676; called 'the black box of Abdülhamid', recently his memoirs were published: *Abdülhamid'in Kara Kutusu: Arap İzzet Holo Paşa'nın Günlükleri* (Istanbul 2019).
209 For Isma'il and Hawash, see Talhamy, 'The Nusayri Leader Isma'il Khayr Bey'.
210 at-Tawil, *Tarikh al-'Alawiyyin*, pp. 454–455; et-Tavîl, *Arap Alevilerin Tarihi*, pp. 308–309; cf. Türkyılmaz, 'Anxieties of Conversion', pp. 217–218.
211 at-Tawil, *Tarikh al-'Alawiyyin*, pp. 454–456 and et-Tavîl, *Arap Alevilerin Tarihi*, pp. 309–310.
212 Ibid., pp. 456–457 and ibid., pp. 310–311; cf. Ömer Uluçay, *Tarihte Nusayrilik* (Adana, 2001), pp. 56–59; see also Moosa, *Extremist Shiites*, pp. 278–279.
213 A Protestant Pietist movement from South Germany, members of which migrated to the Holy Land to prepare the imminent return of Christ; see Alex Carmel, *Die Siedlungen der württembergischen Templer in Palästina 1868–1918* (Stuttgart, 1997); Jakob Eisler, 'Die württembergischen Templer', in: *Württembergische Kirchengeschichte online*, at www.wkgo.de/themen/die-wuerttembergischen-templer (accessed 9 October 2018).
214 Letter of Friedrich Lange (a Templer teacher), dated 30 May 1880, published on 24 June 1880 in the Templer weekly journal *Süddeutsche Warte*; in: Alex Carmel, *Palästina-Chronik 1853 bis 1882: Deutsche Zeitungsberichte vom Krimkrieg bis zur ersten jüdischen Einwanderungswelle* (Ulm, 1978), pp. 324–325.
215 For details of Midhat Paşa as governor of Syria, see Midhat Paşa's memoirs *Tabsira-i Ibret*, 2 vols. in one (Istanbul, 1325/1907, (2nd volume *Mir'ât-ı Hayret*) 1:207–227; Ali Haydar Midhat, *The Life of Midhat Paşa* (London, 1903), pp. 178–195; Najib Saliba,

'The Achievements of Midhat Paşa as Governor of the Province of Syria, 1878–1880,' in: *International Journal of Middle East Studies* 9 (1979), pp. 307–323; and Butrus Abu-Manneh, 'The Genesis of Midhat Paşa's Governorship in Syria 1878–1880,' in: Thomas Philipp and Birgit Schäbler (eds.), *The Syrian Land: Processes of Integration and Fragmentation in Bilād al-Shām from the 18th to the 20th Century* (Stuttgart, 1998), pp. 251–267.

216 At-Tawil, *Tarikh al-'Alawiyyin*, pp. 456–457; et-Tavîl, *Arap Alevilerin Tarihi*, p. 311. In fact, Midhat Paşa sent several petitions regarding reforms in Syria to Abdülhamid; see, Midhat Paşa, *Suriye Lâyihası*, ed. Hüseyin Tosun (Istanbul, 1324/1906), latinized and with introduction by Fethi Gedikli, 'Midhat Paşa'nın Suriye Layihası,' in: *Dîvân*, no. 2 (1999), pp. 169–189; see also BOA, Y.EE. 79/67, 12 Muharrem 1296/6 January 1879; BOA, Y.EE. 79/68, 4 Safer 1296/28 January 1879; and BOA, Y.EE. 79/92, 10 Receb 1297/18 June 1880. Cf. Selçuk Günay, 'II. Abdülhamid Döneminde Suriye ve Lübnan'da Arap Ayrılıkçı Hareketlerinin Başlaması ve Devletin Tedbirleri,' in: *Ankara Üniversitesi Dil ve Tarih-Coğrafya Fakültesi Tarih Bölümü Tarih Araştırmaları Dergisi* 28/17 (1992), pp. 85–108 (here pp. 95–96), online at http://dergiler.ankara.edu.tr (accessed 3 May 2010).

217 Alkan, 'Fighting for the Nuṣayrī Soul,' pp. 45–46; see further Winter, *A History of the Alawis*, pp. 238–244.

218 Fatih is, of course, the title of the Ottoman sultan Mehmed II, who had conquered Constantinople in 1453.

219 BOA, İ.MMS. 113/4821, no. 7, 29 Şevval 1306/18 June 1890; see also BOA, DH.MKT. 1823/38, 21 Şaban 1308/31 March 1891. The same was to be carried out for the Nusayris in Antakya and its environs; see BOA, DH.MKT. 1958/80, 12 Zîlkâde 1309/8 June 1892; BOA, DH.MKT. 2049/13, 18 Receb 1310/5 February 1893; BOA, DH.MKT. 31/9, 11 Rebîülâhir 1311/22 October 1893.

220 Deringil, *The Well-Protected Domains*, p. 84.

221 Türkyılmaz, 'Anxieties of Conversion,' pp. 18, 216–223.

222 Winter, *A History of the 'Alawis*, p. 229; BOA, DH.TMIK.S. 26/31, 1 Rebîülâhir 1317/9 August 1899. Other references to Hüdai are BOA, DH.TMIK.M. 76/19, 29 Cemaziyelevvel 1317/5 October 1899; ŞD. 214/58, 25 Muharrem 1314/6 July 1896; MF.MKT. 755/34, 15 Şevval 1321/4 January 1904; and İ.MF. 4/7, 11 Safer 1314/22 July 1896.

223 Mehmed Ali Ayni, *Hatıralar* (Istanbul 2009), pp. 95–96, emphasis mine. *Murtada/Murtaza* is a title and means 'one with whom God is pleased' and *Haydar-ı Kerrar* is another epiphet meaning 'the lion that fights and attacks repeatedly'.

224 BOA, MF.MKT. 77/10, 1 Şaban 1312/28 January 1895, and MF.MKT. 246/56, 1 Şaban 1312/28 January 1895, state that primary *(ibtidai)* schools were abandoned.

225 Muhammad Farid Wajdi, *Da'irat al-ma'arif li-qarn al-'ashrun*, 10 vols. (Beirut, 1971), s.v. 'Nuṣayriyya' (quoting an article from the Egyptian newspaper *al-Ahram*), 10:249–253 (here p. 252); Moosa, *Extremist Shiites*, p. 279; Douwes, 'Knowledge and Oppression,' p. 168.

226 J. M. Balph, 'Among the Nussairyeh,' p. 182.

227 Martin Kramer, *Arab Awakening and Islamic Revival* (New Brunswick/London, 2008), p. 191.

228 BOA, İ.MF.2/1311/R-1, 8 Ramazan 1311/15 March 1894; BOA, DH.MKT 866/56, 18 Ramazan 1822/26 November 1904. For 'mass conversions' in Latakia, see BOA, İ.DH. 1306/1311/M-10, 12 Muharrem 1312/16 July 1894.

229 Douwes, 'Knowledge and Oppression,' p. 167.

230 Naim Ürkmez and Aydın Efe, 'Osmanlı Arşiv Belgelerinde Nusayrîler Hakkında Genel Bilgiler', in: *Türk Kültürü ve Hacı Bektaş Velî Araştırma Dergisi* 54 (2010), pp. 127–134 (here p. 130); Tozlu, 'Antakya ve İskenderun Nusayrîleri', p. 88.
231 BOA, Y.PRK.MF. 2/57, 5 Cemaziyelevvel 1310/24 November 1892.
232 BOA, BEO.AYN.D, 867:138, 23 Zilkade 1286/12 February 1285.
233 BOA, BEO.AYN.D, 867:141, 16 Zilhicce 1286/ 19 March 1870; Tozlu, 'Antakya ve İskenderun Nusayrîleri', p. 83.
234 For this technical term that occurs once in the Qur'an, see A. J.Wensinck, 'Mamlūk', in: *Encyclopaedia of Islam*, First Edition (1913–1936), edited by M. Th. Houtsma, T.W. Arnold, R. Basset, R. Hartmann. Consulted online on 14 October 2021, http://dx.doi.org/10.1163/2214-871X_ei1_SIM_4513.
235 BOA, DH.MKT. 31/9, 11 Rebîülâhir 1311/16 April 1893; Tozlu, 'Antakya ve İskenderun Nusayrîleri', pp. 91–92.
236 Deringil, *The Well-Protected Domains*, pp. 83–84; Somel, *The Modernization of Public Education*, p. 223; Ali Karaca, *Anadolu ıslahatı ve Ahmet Şakir Paşa* (Istanbul, 1993), p. 127.
237 Türkyılmaz, 'Anxieties of Conversion', pp. 162–163.
238 Henry Lammens, 'Voyage au pays des Nosairis', in: *Revue de l'Orient chrétien* 5 (1900), pp. 99–117 (here p. 110); my translation.
239 Ibid., fn. 1.
240 Behcet/Temimi, *Beyrut Vilayeti*, 2:403.
241 Apart from the above cited BOA, Y.PRK.MF. 2/57, 5 Cemaziyelevvel 1310/24 November 1892, no. 1, p. 1, which is a memorandum by Halil Kemal, who was the director of education in Syria, the following are petitions by Alawis: BOA, DH.MKT. 2739/90, 25 Muharram 1327/16 February 1909, and BOA, DH.MKT. 2792/76, 27 Şubat 1324/12 March 1909.
242 E.g. in Antakya; BOA, DH.EUM.EMN. 80/21, 20 Receb 1332/14 June 1914.

Chapter 4

1 Bedros Der Matossian, *Shattered Dreams of Revolution: From Liberty to Violence in the Late Ottoman Empire* (Stanford, 2014), p. 21.
2 For an overview of the Young Turk period, see M. Şükrü Hanioğlu, *A Brief History of the Late Ottoman Empire* (Princeton, 2008), chapter 6, and for a very detailed study of the Revolution, see idem, *Preparation for a Revolution: The Young Turks 1902–1908* (Oxford, 2001).
3 Hikmet Bayur, 'İkinci Meşrutiyet Devri Üzerinde Bazı Düşünceler', in: *Belleten* 23:90 (Nisan 1959), pp. 267–285 (here p. 267).
4 Hanioğlu, *A Brief History of the Late Ottoman Empire*, p. 148.
5 Ibid., p. 151.
6 Der Matossian, *Shattered Dreams of Revolution*, p. 21.
7 Ibid., p. 7.
8 For an extensive treatment of the relationship between the American Protestant missionaries and the Young Turks, see Kieser, *Nearest East*, chapter 3 about 'Missionary America and Young Turkey'.
9 *Reformed Presbyterian Standard*, 8 October 1908, p. 10.
10 Ibid., 27 August 1908, p. 5.
11 Kieser, *Nearest East*, p. 67.

12 Qur'an 61:13, it should be 'help from God and a nigh victory' (Arberry).
13 Proverbs 9:10 (N.A.)
14 *Reformed Presbyterian Standard*, 8 October 1908, p. 11; cf. Der Matossian, *Shattered Dreams of Revolution*, p. 28.
15 Hanioğlu, *A Brief History of the Late Ottoman Empire*, pp. 148–149, 150–153.
16 Michelle U. Campos, *Ottoman Brothers: Muslims, Christians and Jews in Early Twentieth-Century Palestine* (Stanford, 2011), p. 74.
17 According to the Ottoman Rumi calendar it occurred on 31 March 1909; 13 April 1909 Gregorian calendar.
18 For post-revolutionary developments after 1908, see Noémi Lévy-Aksu and François Georgeon, *The Young Turk Revolution and the Ottoman Empire: The Aftermath of 1908* (London, 2017); for the 31 March Incident, see chapter 8 by Erik-Jan Zürcher, '31 Mart: A Fundamentalist Uprising in Istanbul in April 1909?'.
19 *Reformed Presbyterian Standard*, 8 October 1908, p. 5.
20 Ibid., 13 August 1908, p. 3.
21 Ibid.
22 Ibid.
23 *Olive Trees*, November 1908, p. 248.
24 *Reformed Presbyterian Standard*, 27 August 1908, p. 5.
25 *Olive Trees*, January 1909, p. 5.
26 Ibid. November 1908, p. 248.
27 Ibid., June 1908, pp. 134 and 143: cf. *Minutes of the Synod* 1908, p. 64.
28 *Olive Trees*, March 1909, 58.
29 Ibid., April 1909, p. 78.
30 Ibid., June 1909, p. 131; *Christian Nation*, 23 June 1909, p. 9; *Minutes of the Synod* 1909, p. 61.
31 *Olive Trees*, July 1909, p. 155.
32 Ibid., October 1909, p. 222.
33 *Reformed Presbyterian Standard*, 25 March 1909, p. 5.
34 BOA, Y.EE. 43/103, 6 Rebiülahir 1327/27 April 1909.
35 *Olive Trees*, July 1909, p. 152.
36 Suadia or Suadea, as written by Westerners, is Suwaydiya or the modern Samandağ near Antakya and was an important seaport in ancient times. For Protestant mission work there, see *The Christian Nation*, vol. 48, 8 April 1908, pp. 14–15.
37 *Olive Trees*, March 1910, p. 56.
38 Ibid., January 1910, p. 8.
39 Ibid., April 1910, p. 77.
40 Ibid., June 1910, p. 133.
41 Ibid., p. 143.
42 Ibid., March 1910, p. 58.
43 Ibid., June 1910, p. 144.
44 Ibid., July 1910, p. 148.
45 Ibid., November 1910, p. 249.
46 *Christian Nation*, 7 June 1911, p. 16.
47 *Olive Trees*, June 1908, p. 136; ibid., July 1908, p. 149.
48 *Christian Nation*, 7 June 1911, p. 16.
49 Since 1971 Boğaziçi (Bosporus) University.
50 *Olive Trees*, February 1910, pp. 26–27.
51 Ibid., p. 25.

52 BOA, MF.İBT. 320/32, 2 Cemaziyelevvel 1329/1 May 1911.
53 BOA, MF.İBT. 358/19, 12 Nisan 1327/25 April 1911.
54 *Olive Trees*, September 1911, p. 198.
55 Ibid., October 1911, p. 222.
56 Ibid., October 1912, p. 239.
57 *Christian Nation*, 15 July 1908, p. 7; emphasis in text.
58 J. M. Balph, 'Among the Nussairyeh', p. 184.
59 Matthew 21:16; cf. Psalm 8:2.
60 *Christian Nation*, 19 April 1911, p. 6.
61 Ibid., p. 7.
62 *Olive Trees*, January 1912, pp. 6–7.
63 Ibid., March 1912, p. 55.
64 Ibid., June 1912, p. 134.
65 Ibid., July 1912, pp. 150–151; cf. *Christian Nation*, 28 June 1911, p. 9.
66 *Olive Trees*, July 1912, p. 153.
67 Matthew 9:37–38, American Standard Version. (N.A.)
68 *Olive Trees*, July 1912, p. 154.
69 Ibid., p. 155.
70 Ibid., p. 156.
71 Ibid., December 1911, p. 269.
72 Ibid., December 1912, pp. 275, 276.
73 Ibid., p. 276.
74 Ibid., March 1913, p. 54.
75 Ibid., April 1913, p. 80.
76 Ibid., August 1913, pp. 175, 199.
77 Ibid., January 1914, p. 8.
78 Ibid., July 1914, p. 162.
79 Ibid., September 1914, p. 201.
80 *Olive Trees*, April 1915, pp. 103–104.
81 Ibid., September 1915, p. 223; see also ibid., April 1915, pp. 93–95.
82 Ibid., May 1915, p. 127.
83 Ibid., July 1915, p. 163.
84 Ibid., p. 164.
85 Ibid., p. 165.
86 Ibid., August 1915, p. 193.
87 Ibid., p. 203
88 Ibid., November 1915, p. 256.
89 Ibid., January 1916, p. 15.
90 Ibid., March 1916, pp. 82–83.
91 Ibid., p. 73.
92 See, e.g., various issues of *Olive Trees* from 1916.
93 Ibid., July 1917, p. 152.
94 Ibid., p. 154, 155.
95 Kieser, *Nearest East*, p. 64.
96 'İstanbul Hakiki Ulemâsı ile Dârülfünûn İlâhiyât Şubesi ve Medresetü'l-Vâizîn'in Genç ve Fedâkâr Talebelerinin Nazargâh-ı Dikkatlerine', in: *Sebîlü'r-Reşâd* 11:281, 3 Rebiülevvel 1332/29 Ocak 1914, p. 334–335.
97 A mostly Armenian-populated town near Latakia in north-western Syria, close to the Turkish border.

98 These are excerpts from the *Kitab al-Dustur*, second and third chapter respectively; see al-Adhani, *Bakura*, pp. 7–34; Edward A. Salisbury, *The Book of Sulaimân's First Ripe Fruit*, pp. 227–308; Dussaud, *Histoire et religion des Nosairîs*, pp. 181–198 and 161–179.
99 M. Ali Münir, 'İnhitâtât-ı İctimâiyye', in: *Sırat-ı Müstakim* 3:60, 13 Şevval 1327/28 October 1909, p. 113.
100 Ibid., 3:58, p. 86.
101 Samizade Süreyya, 'Memalik-i İslamiyede Protestan Müslümanları', in: *Tearüf-i Müslimîn* 1:11, 12 Ağustos 1326/25 August 1910, pp. 177–179. For biographies of Süreyya, see www.biyografi.net/kisiayrinti.asp?kisiid=1934 (accessed 29 April 2021).
102 Ibid., p. 177.
103 Ibid., pp. 177–178.
104 Ibid., p. 178; cf. Güler, 'Tanzimattan II. Meşrutiyete "Medeniyet" Anlayışını Evrimi, Marmara Üniversitesi', p. 235.
105 Samizade Süreyya, 'Misyonerler ve Sa'y u Gayreti', *Tearüf-i Müslimîn* 1:22, 17 Kasım 1910, pp. 348–350.
106 Ibid., p. 349.
107 Samizade Süreyya, 'Suriye Ahvali Hakkında – 1', in: *Tearüf-i Müslimîn* 2:27, 16 Kanun-i Evvel 1326/29 December 1910, pp. 47–48.
108 Samizade Süreyya, 'Suriye Ahvali Hakkında – 2', in: *Tearüf-i Müslimîn* 2:28, 4 Muharrem 1329/5 January 1911, pp. 57–58 (here p. 57).
109 Samizade Süreyya, 'Misyonerler ve Mektepleri', in: *İslam Dünyası* 2:2, 2 Nisan 1914, pp. 19–22.
110 Ibid., p. 19.
111 Ibid., pp. 20–21.
112 Ibid., p. 21.
113 Ibid., p. 22.
114 Mehmed Şevket, 'Tenkidât: 'Misyonerler ve Mektebleri' makalesine cevab', in: *İslam Dünyası* 2:3, 16 Nisan 1914, pp. 41–46. Unfortunately, I could not ascertain his identity since there are several authors by the same name.
115 Ibid., p. 42.
116 Ibid., p. 44.
117 Ibid., p. 45.
118 Edhem Nejad, 'Neden muallime yetiştirilmiyor?', in: *Sırat-ı Müstakim* 6:155, 28 Şaban 1329/24 Ağustos 1911, pp. 390–391.
119 Ibid., p. 390–391.
120 Ibid., p. 391.
121 See, e.g., Ahmed Vasfi Zekeriya, 'Müslümanlar nasıl mekteblere muhtaçtır?', in: *Sırat-ı Müstakim* 6:137, 20 Rebîülâhir 1327/11 May 1909, pp. 105–107.
122 Ibid., pp. 106–107.
123 Ahmed Şerif, 'Beyrut'da maârif-i ecnebiyye te'sîrât ve netâyici', in: *Sırat-ı Müstakim* 6:139, 5 Cemaziyelevvel 1327/4 Mayıs 1911, pp. 135–136.
124 Idem, 'Hamiş' (postscript to the article above), ibid. 127–128.
125 Ahmed Şerif, 'Beyrut'da maârif-i ecnebiyye te'sîrât ve netâyici', p. 135.
126 Samizade Süreyya, 'Beyrut'da Amerikan Protestan Mektebi', in: *Sırat-ı Müstakim*, 6:144, 11 Cemaziyelâhir 1327/8 Haziran 1911, pp. 218–220.
127 This is his famous *Paris'den bir mektub* (Dersaadet/Istanbul 1326/1908); latinised version in: Mehmet Kaplan et al., *Yeni Türk Edebiyatı Antolojisi*, vol. 2 (Istanbul, 1993), pp. 1–11.

128 Samizade Süreyya, 'Beyrut'da Amerikan Protestan Mektebi', pp. 219–220.
129 Ibid.
130 Muhammad Rashid Rida, s.v. Ende, W., 'Ras͟hīd Riḍā', in: *Encyclopaedia of Islam*, Second Edition, Edited by: P. Bearman, Th. Bianquis, C.E. Bosworth, E. van Donzel, W.P. Heinrichs. Consulted online on 1 February 2019, http://dx.doi.org/10.1163/1573-3912_islam_SIM_6240; Charles C. Adams, *Islam and Modernism in Egypt: A Study of the Modern Reform Movement Inaugurated by Muhammad 'Abduh* (London, 1933), pp. 177–204.
131 For Yemen, see Thomas Kuehn, *Empire, Islam, and Politics of Difference: Ottoman Rule in Yemen, 1849–1919* (Leiden, 2011).
132 *al-Manar*, vol. 2, no. 43, 5 Ramadan 1317/6 January 1900, pp. 687–688. My thanks to Dyala Hamzah for these references. PDF versions at https://archive.org/details/almanaralmanar (1 February 2019); for al-Manar, see Florian Zemmin, *Modernity in Islamic Tradition: The Concept of 'Society' in the Journal al-Manar* (Cairo, 1898–1940), (Berlin/Boston 2018), chapter 5, pp. 138–176.
133 A dispute between Rida and his mentor Muhammad 'Abduh erupted about the role and significance of the Baha'is in Egypt; see Juan Cole, 'Muhammad 'Abduh and Rashid Rida: A Dialogue on the Baha'i Faith', in: *World Order*, 15:3–4 (Spring/Summer 1981), pp. 7–16, online at www.h-net.org/~bahai/diglib/articles/A-E/cole/abduh/abduh.htm (accessed 3 February 2019); idem, 'Rashid Rida on the Baha'i Faith: A Utilitarian Theory of The Spread of Religions', in: *Arab Studies Quarterly* 5:3 (1983), pp. 276–291.
134 Dyala Hamzah, 'Proselytism and reform. Muhammad Rashid Rida, al-Manar and Dar al-da'wa wa-l-irshad', paper read at *Missionaries as experts: religious networks, knowledge of the field and public action in the Middle East (19th–21st century)* – IFEA & Orient Institut, Istanbul, 26–27 October 2018, MissMo Workshop, https://missmo.hypotheses.org/306; see also, Adams, Islam and Modernism in Egypt, pp. 195–198.
135 'Mısır'da Da'vet ve İrşâd Meselesi', in: *Sırat-ı Müstakim* 6:144, 11 Cemaziyelâhir 1327/8 Haziran 1911, p. 223. Rida published several articles in this same journal, the first including the constitution and curriculum of his school: 7:170 and 171; see also 'Mısır'da Te'sîs Olunan "Ed-Da'vetü ve'l-İrşâd" Usûl-i Tedrîsi', in 7:177, 178, 179, 180, 181 and 182. Online PDF of *Sırat-ı Müstakim* (from volume 8 on named *Sebilürreşad*), at the online library of the Bağcılar municipality in Istanbul, www.bagcilar.bel.tr/siratimustakim (accessed 29 April 2021).
136 Grehan, *Twilight of the Saints*, p. 20.
137 'Mısır: İslam Cemiyetlerini Tazyik', in: *Sırat-ı Müstakim* 6:150, 23 Recep 1327/20 Temmuz 1911, p. 319.
138 'Hadisât-ı Hâzıraya Karşı Ehl-i İslam Arasında Âsâr-ı Tezamün', in: ibid. 7:170, 16 Zilhicce 1329/7 Aralık 1911, pp. 224–225.
139 Yitzhak Nakash, *The Shi'is of Iraq* (Princeton, 1994), pp. 59–60.
140 Mehmed Fahreddin, 'Aklı Başında Din Kardeşlerime', in: *Sırat-ı Müstakim* 7:170, 25 Teşrinisani 1327/28 November 1911, pp. 225–226.
141 Fortna, *Imperial Classroom*, p. 44.
142 Ibid., p. 47.
143 Azmi Samurkaş (d. 1944); Taner Tunç, 'Mehmet Behcet Yazar'ın Hayatı ve Eserleri Üzerine Bir İnceleme', M.A. Thesis (Celal Bayar Üniversitesi: Manisa 2014), p. 154.
144 Hanssen, *Fin de Siècle Beirut*, pp. 4–5, 51–52.
145 See Ágoston/Masters, *Encyclopedia of the Ottoman Empire*, pp. 501–502. Salnames were official yearbooks or annual reports by the Ottoman government from 1847

until 1918. Among *salname*s were state yearbooks (*devlet salnamesi*) and provincial yearbooks (*vilayet salnamesi*). Through these the state could assess the conditions of the provinces and determine resources. *Salname*s were also registers of Ottoman sultans and history, they provided state and province budgets, listed the names of officials in charge, of religious dignitaries and foreign ambassadors and consuls, provided distances between cities, villages, and statistics of the population.

146 Their biographies are at the beginning of volume 1.
147 Mehmed Behcet (Yazar)/Refik Temimi, *Beyrut Vilayeti*, vol. 1: Cenub Kısmı (Vilayet Matbaası: Beirut 1917); vol. 2: Şimal Kısmı (Vilayet Matbaası: Beirut 1918); henceforth I will refer to Beyrut Vilayeti as *BV*.
148 Beirut 1917/1918; reprint Beirut 1979; henceforth *WB*.
149 *BV* 1, *mukaddime* (foreword).
150 *BV* 1 & 2, epigraph: *Livalarına aid müşahedât ve tavsifât ile coğrafya, etnografya, jeoloji, tarih, âsâr-ı atika, ahvâl-ı ruhiyye, ahlakiyye, ictimaiyye, sıhhiyye, din, lisan, edebiyat, sanayi-i nefîse, maarif, ziraat, ticaret, nâfia ve sanayi tedkîkâtını hâvidir.*
151 Alkan, *Dissent and Heterodoxy*, pp. 146–150.
152 *BV* 1, *mukaddime* (Preface); WB 1:5.
153 For assessments of *Beyrut Vilayeti/Wilayat Bayrut*, see Michael Gilsenan, *Lords of the Lebanese Marches: Violence and Narrative in an Arab Society* (Berkeley/LA 1996), pp. 69–76; Avi Rubin, 'East, West, Ottomans and Zionists: Internalized Orientalism at the Turn of the Twentieth Century,' in: Nedret Kuran-Burçoğlu/Susan Gilson Miller (eds.), *Representations of the 'other/s' in the Mediterranean World and their Impact on the Region* (Istanbul, 2005), pp. 149–166; Hanssen, *Fin de Siècle Beirut*, pp. 80–81; Cyrus Schayegh, *The Middle East and the Making of the Modern World* (Cambridge/Mass., 2017), pp. 92–95; see further, Tunç, 'Mehmet Behcet Yazar'ın Hayatı ve Eserleri Üzerine Bir İnceleme', pp. 154–157.
154 Schayegh, *The Middle East*, p. 93.
155 Rubin, 'East, West, Ottomans and Zionists', p. 150.
156 Gilsenan, *Lords of the Lebanese Marches*, p. 70
157 Ibid.
158 Ibid., pp. 70–74.
159 Ibid., p. 74
160 *BV* 1:19.
161 Ibid., 1:94–95.
162 Ibid., 1:98
163 *BV*, pp. 2:120–161, 415–436 and 508–513, etc. In Latin letters: Selahattin Tozlu and Naim Ürkmez, *Nusayrîler: Tarih, İnanç, Edebiyat ve Kaynakça* (Istanbul, 2018).
164 *BV* 2:403–405
165 *BV* 2:502–505.
166 *BV* 2:509–510.
167 The Egyptian periodical *al-Manar* reported in 1898 about the selling of Nusayri girls as slaves; see *al-Manar*, vol. 1, pp. 379–380.
168 *BV* 2:523–526.
169 Ibid., 2:526–528
170 Ibid., 2:124.
171 Ibid., 2:134.
172 Ibid., 2:419.
173 Ibid.
174 Ibid., 2:421.

175 Ibid., 2:520 ff.
176 Ibid., 2:570–571
177 *BV* 2:578.
178 BOA, Y.PRK.MF. 2/57, DH.MKT. 2739/90 and DH.MKT. 2792/76.
179 Henri Lammens, 'Une visite au šaih supreme des Nosairis Haidaris', *Journal Asiatique* XI:V (1915), pp. 139–159.
180 Sharkey, *A History of Muslims Christians, and Jews*, p. 220.

Conclusion

1 Cf. Curry, 'Some Reflections on the Fluidity of Orthodoxy and Heterodoxy.
2 Duguid, 'The Politics of Unity', p. 139.
3 Sharkey, 'American Missionaries in Ottoman Lands', p. 1.
4 Alkan. '"Fighting for the Nuṣayrī Soul"'.
5 For discussions, see at-Tawil, *Tarikh al-'Alawiyyin*, pp. 448–49; Muhammad Kurd Ali, *Khitat ash-Sham*, 6 vols. (Damascus, 1928), 6:265–68; Moosa, *Extremist Shiites*, p. 280; Daniel Pipes, *Greater Syria: The History of an Ambition* (Oxford, 1990), p. 159; Kais M. Firro, 'The 'Alawīs in Modern Syria: From Nuṣayrīya to Islam via 'Alawīya', *Der Islam* 82 (2005), pp. 1–31 (here pp. 9–12); Yvette Talhamy, 'The Fatwas and the Nusayri/Alawis of Syria', in: *MES* 46:2 (2010), pp. 175–194 (here p. 185); idem, 'The Syrian Muslim Brothers and the Syrian-Iranian Relationship', in: *Middle East Journal* 63:4 (Autumn 2009), pp. 561–580 (here p. 562); Gisela Procházka-Eisl and Stephan Procházka, *The Plain of Saints and Prophets: The Nusayri-Alawi Community of Cilicia (Southern Turkey) and its Sacred Places* (Wiesbaden, 2010), pp. 19–23, esp. 19–20.
6 Philip S. Khoury, *Syria and the French Mandate. The Politics of Arab Nationalism, 1920–1945* (London, 1987); Fabrice Balanche, *La région alaouite et le pouvoir syrien* (Paris, 2006).
7 Procházka-Eisl/Procházka, *The Plain of Saints and Prophets*, p. 20.
8 For this, see Necati Alkan, 'Divide and Rule: The Creation of the Alawi State after World War I', *Fikrun wa Fann* (Art and Thought), no. 100: 100 Years First World War (a publication of the Goethe Institut). Also in German, Arabic and Persian translation.

BIBLIOGRAPHY

Archival Sources

1. Başbakanlık Osmanlı Arşivi (BOA, Ottoman Archives, Istanbul)

A. MKT. MHM, 700/5, from 9 Cemaziyelevvel 1311/18 November 1893 to 22 Zîlhicce 1312/16 June 1895.
A. MKT. MHM. 702/29, 14 Şaban 1317/18 December 1899.
BEO. 314/23496, 9 Cemaziyelevvel 1311/18 November 1893.
BEO. 2250/168719, 22 Şevval 1321/11 January 1904.
BEO. AYN.d (Haleb Ayniyat Defteri), 867, pp. 138, 141, 144, 149, 156 and 190.
BEO. AYN.D, 867:138, 23 Zilkade 1286/12 February 1285.
BEO. AYN.D, 867:141, 16 Zilhicce 1286/ 19 March 1870.
C. ADL. 29/1734, 29 Safer 1242/2 October 1826.
C. DH. 125/6218, 29 Ramazan 1241/7 May 1826.
C. DH. 199/9935, no. 1, 21 Rebîülevvel 1243/12 October 1827.
C. ZB. 17/843, 21 Cemaziyelâhir 1243/9 January 1828.
C. ZB. 34/1680, 9 Zîlkâde 1255/14 January 1840.
DH. EUM .EMN. 80/21, 20 Receb 1332/14 June 1914.
DH. İ. UM. 19/1, 14 Cemaziyelevvel 1338/4 February 1920.
DH. MKT. 31/9, 11 Rebîülâhir 1311/22 October 1893.
DH. MKT. 74/10, 8 Muharrem 1311/22 July 1893.
DH. MKT 866/56, 18 Ramazan 1822/26 November 1904.
DH. MKT. 1487/38, 8 Cemaziyelahir 1305/21 February 1888.
DH. MKT. 1555/58, 12 Safer 1306/18 October 1888.
DH. MKT. 1823/38, 21 Şaban 1308/31 March 1891.
DH. MKT. 1958/80, 12 Zîlkâde 1309/8 June 1892.
DH. MKT. 1975/31, 25 Zîlhicce 1309/20 July 1892.
DH. MKT. 1983/15, 11 Muharrem 1310/5 August 1892.
DH. MKT. 2012/117, 28 Rebîülevvel 1310/20 October 1892.
DH. MKT. 2049/13, 18 Receb 1310/5 February 1893.
DH. MKT. 2739/90, 25 Muharram 1327/16 February 1909.
DH. MKT. 2792/76, 27 Şubat 1324/12 March 1909.
DH. SAIDd. 113/439, 29 Zî'l-Hicce 1294/4 January 1878.
DH. TMIK. M. 76/19, 29 Cemaziyelevvel 1317/5 October 1899.
BOA, DH. TMIK. S. 26/31, 1 Rebîülâhir 1317/9 August 1899.
HAT. 290/17351, 29 Zîlhicce 1242/27 July 1827.
HAT. 290/17386, 29 Zîlhicce 1241/4 August 1826.
HAT. 385/20647, 9 Şevval 1237/29 June 1822.
HAT. 386/20671, 29 Zîlhicce 1237/16 September 1822.

HAT. 386/20671-A, 29 Zîlhicce 1237/16 September 1822.
HAT. 512/25094-D, E, F, and G, 25 Rebîülevvel 1249/12 August 1833.
HAT. 1103/44569H, 25 Rebîülâhir 1242/26 November 1826.
HR. H. 348/15, 13 January 1894.
HR. MKT. 83/45, 6 Cemaziyelahir 1292/9 July 1875.
HR. SFR. 422/83, 23 July 1894.
HR.SYS. 64/38, 25 October 1895.
HR. SYS. 65/5, 9 December 1895.
HR. SYS. 65/45, 25 April 1896.
HR. TH. 59/47, 21 November 1885.
HR. TH. 64/5, 8 June 1886.
HR. TO. 248/38, 19 September 1873.
HR. TO. 251/27, 12 March 1876.
İ.DH. 1237/96880, 14 Zilkâde 1308/20 June 1891.
İ. DH. 1306/1311/M-10, 12 Muharrem 1312/16 July 1894.
İ. HR. 72/3473, 15 Muharrem 1266/1 December 1849.
İ. HR. 266/15960, no. 1, 10 Muharrem 1292/16 February 1875.
İ. MF.2/1311/R-1, 8 Ramazan 1311/15 March 1894.
İ. MF. 4/7, 11 Safer 1314/22 July 1896.
İ. MMS. 113/4821, 29 Şevval 1307/18 June 1890.
İ. MMS. 114/4687, 13 Haziran 1306/26 June 1891
MD. 160/73-1, 10 Cemaziyelâhir 1171/19 February 1758.
MF. İBT. 320/32, 2 Cemaziyelevvel 1329/1 May 1911.
MF. İBT. 358/19, 12 Nisan 1327/25 April 1911.
MF. MKT. 77/10, 1 Şaban 1312/28 January 1895.
MF. MKT. 246/56, 1 Şaban 1312/28 January 1895.
MF. MKT. 755/34, 15 Şevval 1321/4 January 1904.
Mühimme-i Asakir Defteri, nr. 26, 29 Rebîülevvel 1244/9 October 1828.
ŞD. 214/58, 25 Muharrem 1314/6 July 1896.
ŞD. 2280/40, 29 Zîlhicce 1310/14 July 1893.
Y. A. HUS. 260/130, 28 Şevval 1309/25 May 1892.
Y. A. HUS. 374/103, 26 Safer 1315/27 July 1897.
Y. A. RES. 51/9, 22 Ramazan 1307/12 May 1890.
Y. A. RES. 60/27, 17 Safer 1310/10 September 1892.
Y. EE. 7/17, no date (ca. 1890-91).
Y. EE. 9/34, 9 Ramazan 1309/7 April 1892.
Y. EE. 10/69, 11 Safer 1312/13 August 1894.
Y. EE. 43/103, 6 Rebîülahir 1327/27 April 1909.
Y. EE. 79/67, 12 Muharrem 1296/6 January 1879.
Y. EE. 79/68, 4 Safer 1296/28 January 1879.
Y. EE. 79/92, 10 Receb 1297/18 June 1880.
Y. MTV. 47/180, 24 Cemaziyelâhir 1308/4 February 1891.
Y. MTV 53/108, 2 Zilkade 1308/9 June 1891.
Y. MTV. 68/90, 19 Rebîülevvel 1310/11 October 1892.
Y. MTV, 87/44, 6 Teşrin-i Sâni 1309/18 November 1893.
Y. MTV. 231/79, 14 Rebîülevvel 1320/1 July 1902.
Y. PRK. AZN 4/57, 7 Safer 1308/22 September 1890 (10 Eylül 1306 Rumi).
Y. PRK. BŞK. 19/27, 27 Muharrem 1308/12 September 1890.

Y. PRK. KOM. 7/59, 3 Zîlkâde 1307/21 June 1890.
Y. PRK. MF. 2/57, 5 Cemaziyelevvel 1310/24 November 1892.
Y. PRK. MF. 3/11, 2 Receb 1311/9 January 1894.
Y. PRK. MK. 4/80, 27 Şevval 1306/26 June 1889.

2. *British National Archives (London)*

FO 881/2618

3. *Foreign Relations of the United States (online)*

Executive documents printed by order of the House of Representatives. 1875–76, Vol. II (Washington, D.C.: U.S. Government Printing Office, 1875–1876), p. 1294; at http://digital.library.wisc.edu/1711.dl/FRUS.FRUS187576v02 (accessed 30 January 2018).

4. *Gallaudet University (Pennsylvania)*

Applications, Box 09

5. *Gertrude Bell Archives (Newcastle University/UK), digital: http://gertrudebell.ncl.ac.uk*

6. *Reformed Presbyterian History Archives, digital: http://rparchives.org*

7. *UK Parliamentary Papers Online*

19th Century House of Commons Hansard Sessional Papers, https://parlipapers.proquest.com/parlipapers/docview/t71.d76.cds3v0225p0-0027?accountid=8485 (accessed 7 November 2017).

Turkey, No. 5 (1875): Correspondence Respecting Cases of Religious Persecution in Turkey. Presented to both Houses of Parliament by Command of Her Majesty, London 1875, at https://parlipapers.proquest.com/parlipapers/docview/t70.d75.1875-051731?accountid=8485 (accessed 7 November 2017)

Newspapers and Journals

1. Ottoman

al-Manar
Hakayık el-Vekayi'
Sebîlürreşâd (Sebîlü'r-Reşâd)
Sırâtımüstakîm (Sırât-ı Müstakîm)
Tearuf-i Müslimîn

2. Western

Christian Nation
Covenanter, The
Covenanter Witness, The
Congregationalist, The
Herald of Mission News
Independent, The
Magazin für die Literatur des Auslandes
The Manchester Guardian
Minutes of the Synod of the Reformed Presbyterian Church
Olive Trees
Our Banner
Quarterly Register
Philadelphia Inquirer
Der Pilger (Familienblatt für alle Stände)
Reformed Presbyterian and Covenanter
Reformed Presbyterian Standard

Unpublished Sources

Ahmed Cevdet Paşa. *Sosyalistlere Dair Bir Makale*, MC_Yz_O_0008. Atatürk Kitaplığı (Istanbul)

Published Sources

Actenstücke aus dem Correspondenzen des Kais. und Kön. gemeinsamen Ministeriums Äussern über orientalische Angelegenheiten (vom 7. April 1877 bis 3. November 1878), Wien 1878.
al-Adhani, Sulayman. *Kitab al-Bakura as-Sulaymaniyya fi Kashf Asrar ad-Diyana an-Nusayriyya*. Beirut, n.d.
Ahmed Cevdet Paşa. *Tarih-i Cevdet*, 12 vols. (Dersaadet [Istanbul]: Matbaa-yı Osmaniye, 1309/1891-92.
Ahmed Cevdet Paşa. *Tezâkir 1-12*, edited by Cavid Baysun. Ankara: Türk Tarih Kurumu, 1953.
Ahmed Cevdet Paşa. *Ma'rûzât*, edited by Yusuf Halaçoglu. Istanbul: Çağrı Yayınları, 1980.
Ahmed Cevdet Paşa, *Târîh-i Cevdet*, vol. 1, edited by Mehmet İpşirli. Ankara: Türk Tarih Kurumu, 2018.
Ahmed Lûtfî Efendi. *Vak'anüvis Ahmed Lutfî Tarihi*, 8 vols. Istanbul: Yapı Kredi, 1999.
Bilgili, Ali Sinan, et al. (eds.), *Osmanlı Arşiv Belgelerinde Nusayrîler ve Nusayrîlik (1745–1920)*. Ankara, Gazi Üniversitesi, 2010.
Birgivi, Mehmed Efendi. *at-Tariqa al-Muhammadiyya*. Istanbul, 1316/1898.
Esad Efendi (Sahaflar Şeyhizâde). *Vak'a-Nüvîs Es'ad Efendi Tarihi*, edited by Ziya Yılmazer. Istanbul: OSAV, 2000.
Esad Efendi (Sahaflar Şeyhizâde). *Üss-i Zafer (Yeniçeriliğin Kaldırılmasına Dair)*, edited by Mehmet Arslan. Istanbul: Kitabevi, 2005.
Mehmed Arif. *Binbir Hadis*. Kahire/Cairo: Maarif Matbaası, 1329/1901.

Mehmed Arif. *Başımıza Gelenler*. Kahire/Cairo: Maarif Matbaası, 1321/1903.
Mehmed Arif. *Başımıza Gelenler*. 3 vols., edited by M. Ertuğrul Düzdağ. Istanbul: İrfan Matbaası, 1973.
Mehmed Behcet (Yazar) and Refik Temimi. *Beyrut Vilayeti*. vol. 1: Cenub Kısmı. Beirut: Vilayet Matbaası, 1335/1917; vol. 2: Şimal Kısmı. Beirut: Vilayet Matbaası, 1336/1918.
Mehmed Memduh. *Tasvîr-i Ahvâl Tenvîr-i İstikbâl*. Izmir 1327/1909.
Mehmed Memduh. *Tanzimat'tan Meşrutiyet'e*. vol. 2., edited by Ahmet Nezih Galitekin. Istanbul: Nehir, 1995.
Midhat, Ali Haydar. *The Life of Midhat Paşa*. London: J. Murray, 1903.
Midhat Paşa. *Tabsira-i Ibret*, vol. 1, and *Mir'ât-ı Hayret*, vol. 2. Istanbul, 1325/1907.
Midhat Paşa. *Suriye Lâyihası*, edited by Hüseyin Tosun. Istanbul, 1324/1906.
Muhammad Bahjat and Rafiq al-Tamimi. *Wilayat Bayrut*. 2 vols. reprint Dar Lahd Khatir: Beirut 1979.
Mustafa Fazıl Paşa. *Paris'den bir mektub*. Dersaadet/Istanbul, 1326/1908.
Mustafa Nuri Paşa. *Abede-i İblis*. Istanbul: Matbaa-i İctihad, 1328/1910.
Mustafa Nuri Paşa. *Netâyicü'l-Vukū'ât: Kurumlarıyla Osmanlı Tarihi I-IV*, edited by Yılmaz Kurt. Ankara: Birleşik, 2008.
Peçevi, İbrahim. *Tarih-i Peçevi*, 2 vols. Istanbul, 1283/1866.
Peçevi, İbrahim. *Peçevi Tarihi*, edited by Bekir Sıtkı Baykal. 2 vols. Ankara, 1981.
Salibi, Kamal and Yusuf K. Khoury (eds.). *The Missionary Herald: Reports from Syria 1819-1870*. 5 vols. Amman: Royal Institute for Inter-Faith Studies, 1997.
Süleyman Hüsnü Paşa. *Hiss-i İnkılâb yahud Sultan Abdülazizin hal'i ile Sultan Murad-i hamisin cülusu*. Istanbul, 1326/1910.
'Translation of the Firmân of His Imperial Majesty Sultân 'Abd-el-Mejîd, Granted in Favor of His Protestant Subjects'. *Journal of the American Oriental Society* 3 (1853): 218–220.
'Treaty between the United States of America and the Ottoman Empire: Commerce and navigation', proclaimed February 4, 1832, online at https://archive.org/details/ldpd_11015515_000 (accessed 9 October 2018).
Walpole, Frederick. *The Ansayrii*, 3 vols. London: Richard Bentley, 1851.

Articles in Ottoman Journals and Newspapers

'Hadisat-ı Hazıraya Karşı Ehl-i İslam Arasında Asar-ı Tezamun'. *Sırât-ı Müstakîm* 7:170, 16 Zilhicce 1329/7 Aralık 1911: 224–225.
'İstanbul Hakiki Uleması ile Darulfunun İlahiyat Şubesi ve Medresetu'l-Vaizin'in Genc ve Fedakar Talebelerinin Nazargah-ı Dikkatlerine'. *Sebîlu'r-Reşâd* 11:281, 3 Rebiulevvel 1332/29 Ocak 1914: 334–335.
'Mısır'da Da'vet ve İrşad Meselesi'. *Sırât-ı Müstakîm* 6:144, 11 Cemaziyelahir 1327/8 Haziran 1911: 223.
'Mısır: İslam Cemiyetlerini Tazyik'. *Sırât-ı Müstakîm* 6:150, 23 Recep 1327/20 Temmuz 1911: 319.
Ahmed Şerif. 'Beyrut'da maarif-i ecnebiyye te'sirat ve netayici'. *Sırât-ı Müstakîm* 6:139, 5 Cemaziyelevvel 1327/4 Mayıs 1911: 135–136.
Ahmed Vasfi Zekeriya. 'Muslumanlar nasıl mekteblere muhtactır? *Sırât-ı Müstakîm* 6:137, 20 Rebiulahir 1327/11 May 1909: 105–107.
Edhem Nejad. 'Neden muallime yetiştirilmiyor?' *Sırât-ı Müstakîm* 6:155, 28 Şaban 1329/24 Ağustos 1911: 390–391.

M. Ali Munir. 'İnhitatat-ı İctimaiyye'. *Sırât-ı Müstakîm* 3:60, 13 Şevval 1327/28 October 1909: 113.
Mehmed Fahreddin. 'Aklı Başında Din Kardeşlerime'. *Sırât-ı Müstakîm* 7:170, 25 Teşrinisani 1327/28 November 1911:ü225-226.
Mehmed Şevket. 'Tenkidat: 'Misyonerler ve Mektebleri' makalesine cevab'. *İslam Dünyası* 2:3, 16 Nisan 1914: 41-46.
Samizade Süreyya. 'Memalik-i İslamiyede Protestan Müslümanları'. *Tearuf-i Muslimin* 1:11, 12 Ağustos 1326/25 August 1910: 177-179.
Samizade Süreyya. 'Misyonerler ve Sa'y u Gayreti'. *Tearuf-i Muslimin* 1:22, 17 Kasım 1910: 348-350.
Samizade Süreyya. 'Suriye Ahvali Hakkında – 1'. *Tearuf-i Muslimin* 2:27, 16 Kanun-i Evvel 1326/29 December 1910: 47-48.
Samizade Süreyya. 'Suriye Ahvali Hakkında – 2'. *Tearuf-i Muslimin* 2:28, 4 Muharrem 1329/5 January 1911: 57-58.
Samizade Süreyya. 'Beyrut'da Amerikan Protestan Mektebi'. *Sırât-ı Müstakim*, 6:144, 11 Cemaziyelahir 1327/8 Haziran 1911, pp. 218-220.
Samizade Süreyya. 'Misyonerler ve Mektepleri'. *İslam Dünyası* 2:2, 2 Nisan 1914: 19-22.

Secondary Literature

Abu-Manneh, Butrus. 'The Naqshbandiyya-Mujaddidiyya in the Ottoman Lands in the Early 19th Century'. *Die Welt des Islams* 22:4/1 (1982): 1-36.
Abu-Manneh, Butrus. 'The Sultan and the Bureaucracy: The Anti-Tanzimat Concepts of Mahmud Nedim Paşa'. *International Journal of Middle East Studies* 11 (1990): 257-274.
Abu-Manneh, Butrus. 'The Islamic Roots of the Gülhane Rescript'. *Die Welt des Islams* 34 (1994): 173-203.
Abu-Manneh, Butrus. 'The Genesis of Midhat Paşa's Governorship in Syria 1878-1880'. In *The Syrian Land: Processes of Integration and Fragmentation in Bilād al-Shām from the 18th to the 20th Century* edited by Thomas Philipp and Birgit Schäbler, 251-267. Stuttgart: Franz Steiner, 1998.
Abu-Manneh, Butrus. 'The Naqshbandiyya-Mujaddidiyya in Istanbul in the Early Tanzimat Period'. In *Studies on Islam and the Ottoman Empire in the 19th Century (1826-1876)*. Idem, 99-114. Istanbul: Isis Press, 2001.
Abu-Manneh, Butrus. 'The Porte and the Sunni-Orthodox Trend in the Later Ottoman Period'. In *Studies on Islam and the Ottoman Empire in the 19th Century (1826-1876)*. Idem, 125-140. Istanbul: Isis Press, 2001.
Abu-Manneh, Butrus. *Studies on Islam and the Ottoman Empire in the 19th Century (1826-1876)*. Istanbul: Isis Press, 2001.
Adams, Charles C. *Islam and Modernism in Egypt: A Study of the Modern Reform Movement Inaugurated by Muhammad 'Abduh*. London: Oxford University Press, 1933.
Afsaruddin, Asma. 'Maslaha as a Political Concept'. In *Mirror for the Muslim Prince: Islam and the Theory of Statecraft*, edited by Mehrzad Boroujerdi, 16-44. New York: Syracuse University Press, 2013.
Agoston, Gábor, and Bruce Masters. *Encyclopedia of the Ottoman Empire*. New York: Facts On File, 2009.
Aksan, Virginia H. *Ottoman Wars 1700-1870: An Empire Besieged*. London: Routledge, 2007.

Akyıldız, Ali. 'Mehmed Ârif Bey', in: *DİA*, online at https://islamansiklopedisi.org.tr/mehmed-arif-bey (15 January 2020).
Albayrak, İsmail. 'The Other' Among Us: The Perception of Khārijī and Ibāḍī Islam in the Muslim Exegetical Traditions'. *Ankara Üniversitesi İlahiyat Fakültesi Dergisi* 54:1 (2013): 35-63.
Albayrak, Sadık. "Dârü'l-Hikmeti'l-İslâmiyye", *DİA (Diyanet İslam Ansiklopedisi)*, online at https://islamansiklopedisi.org.tr/ibrahim-efendi-haydarizade (accessed 4 February 2021).
Algar Hamid, and K.A. Nizami, 'Naḳshbandiyya', in: *Encyclopaedia of Islam*, Second Edition, Edited by: P. Bearman, Th. Bianquis, C.E. Bosworth, E. van Donzel, W.P. Heinrichs. Consulted online on 15 January 2020 <http://dx.doi.org/10.1163/1573-3912_islam_COM_0843>
Alkan, Necati. *Dissent and Heterodoxy in the Late Ottoman Empire: Reformers, Babis and Baha'is*. Istanbul: Isis Press, 2008.
Alkan, Necati. 'The Young Turks and the Baha'is in Palestine'. In *Late Ottoman Palestine: The Period of Young Turk Rule*, edited by Yuval Ben-Bassat and Eyal Ginio, 259-278. London; I. B. Tauris, 2011.
Alkan, Necati. 'Fighting for the Nuṣayrī Soul: State, Protestant Missionaries and the 'Alawīs in the Late Ottoman Empire'. In *Die Welt des Islams* 52 (2012): 23-50.
Alkan, Necati. 'Divide and Rule: The Creation of the Alawi State after World War I'. *Fikrun wa Fann* 100, Jubiläumsausgabe '100 Jahre Erster Weltkrieg', Goethe-Institut (2013).
Alkan, Necati. 'The Ottoman Policy of "Correction of Belief(s)"'. In *Ottoman Sunnism: New Perspectives*, edited by Vefa Erginbaş, 166-192. Edinburgh: Edinburgh University Press, 2019.
Allison, Christin. *The Yezidi Oral Tradition in Iraqi Kurdistan*. London: Routledge, 2001.
Amanat, Abbas, and Magnus T. Bernhardsson (eds.) *U.S.-Middle East: Historical Encounters, a Critical Survey*. Gainesville/FL, 2007.
Amasyalı, D. Emre. 'Missionary Influence and Nationalist Reactions: The Case of Armenian Ottomans'. *Nationalities Papers* 43:9 (2020): 1-19.
Amini, Ayatullah Ibrahim. *Imamate and the Imams*, translated by Hamideh Elahinia (Qom, 2011), online at http://www.al-islam.org/imamate-and-imams-ayatullah-ibrahim-amini/chapter-2-ahlul-bayt-quran-and-traditions (accessed 2 March 2016).
Amir-Moezzi, Mohammad Ali. *The Divine Guide in Early Shi'ism: The Sources of Esotericism in Islam*. New York: State University of New York Press, 1994.
Anderson, Rufus. *History of the Mission of the American Board of Commissioners for Foreign Missions to the Oriental Churches*, 2 vols. Boston: Congregational Publishing Society, 1872.
Anscombe, Frederick. 'Islam and the Age of Reform'. *Past and Present* 208 (2010): 159-189.
Anthony, Sean W. 'The Legend of ʿAbdallāh ibn Sabaʾ and the Date of Umm al-Kitāb', in: *Journal of the Royal Asiatic Society*, Third Series, 21:1 (Jan. 2011): 1-30.
Anthony, Sean W. *The Caliph and the Heretic: Ibn Saba' and the Origins of Shi'ism*. Leiden: Brill, 2012.
Anthony, Sean W. 'Ghulāt (extremist Shīʿīs)', in: Encyclopaedia of Islam, THREE, Edited by: Kate Fleet, Gudrun Krämer, Denis Matringe, John Nawas, Everett Rowson. Consulted online on 17 January 2018 <http://dx.doi.org/10.1163/1573-3912_ei3_COM_27473> First published online: 2018.
Arap İzzet Holo Paşa. *Abdülhamid'in Kara Kutusu: Arap İzzet Holo Paşa'nın Günlükleri*, edited by Pınar Güven. Istanbul: Türkiye İş Bankası, 2019.
Arberry, A. J., translator, *The Koran interpreted*. Oxford: Oxford University Press, 1964.
Asatryan, Mushegh. *Controversies in Formative Shi'i Islam The Ghulat Muslims and their Beliefs*. London: I. B. Tauris, 2017.

Atçıl, Abdurrahman. 'The Safavid Threat and Juristic Authority in the Ottoman Empire during the 16th Century', in: *International Journal of Middle East Studies* 49 (2017): 295-314.

Atmaca, Metin. 'Osmanlı Zihin Dünyasında Bir Doğu Ülkesi: Diyar-ı Acem Yahut İran'. *Muhafazakâr Düşünce* 11:43 (2015): 97-112.

Ayar, Mesut. *Bektaşilik'te Son Nefes: Yeniçeriliğin Kaldırılmasından Sonra Bektaşilik*. Istanbul: Giza, 2009.

Aydıner, Mesut. 'Sinek Sözüyle İş Yapan Pâdişahın Hâli Ya Da Karaman Valisi Darendeli Sarı Abdurrahman Paşa İsyanı'. *Selçuk Üniversitesi Sosyal Bilimler Enstitüsü Dergisi* 16 (2006): 785-799.

Aymes, Marc, et al (eds.), *Order and Compromise: Government Practices in Turkey from the Late Ottoman Empire to the Early 21st Century*. Leiden: Brill, 2015.

Ayni, Mehmed Ali. *Hatıralar*. Istanbul: Yeditepe, 2009.

Azar, Birol. 'Benzerlik ve Farklılıklar Ekseninde Alevî-Bektaşî İnançları Üzerine Bir Değerlendirme'. *Fırat Üniversitesi İlahiyat Fakültesi Dergisi* 10:2 (2005): 81-87.

Badem, Candan. *The Ottoman Crimean War (1853-1856)*. Leiden: Brill, 2010.

Baer, Marc. *Honored by the Glory of Islam: Conversion and Conquest in Ottoman Europe*. Oxford: Oxford University Press, 2008.

Baha Said. *Türkiye'de Alevi-Bektaşi, Ahi ve Nusayri zümreleri*, edited by İsmail Görkem. Ankara: Kültür Bakanlığı, 2000.

Balanche, Fabrice. *La région alaouite et le pouvoir syrien*. Paris: Karthala, 2006.

Balph, James McKinnis. 'Among the Nussairyeh', *Olive Trees* 8, August 1912: 180-85.

Balph, James McKinnis. *Fifty Years of Mission Work in Syria*. Latakia, 1913.

Bang, Peter, and Christopher Bayly (eds.), *Tributary Empires in Global History*. Basingstoke: Palgrave Macmillan, 2011.

Bar-Asher, Meir M. 'The Qur'ān Commentary Ascribed to Ḥasan al-'Askarī'. *The Jerusalem Studies in Arabic and Islam* 24 (2000): 358-379.

Bar-Asher, Meir M., and Arieh Kofsky. *The Nusayri-'Alawi Religion: An Enquiry into Its Theology and Liturgy*. Leiden: Brill, 2002.

Bar-Asher, Meir M., and Arieh Kofsky. *Kitab Al-Ma'arif by Abu Sa'id Maymun B. Qasim Al-Tabarani: Critical Edition with an Introduction*. Leuven: Peeters, 2012.

Barkey, Karen. *Empire of Difference: The Ottomans in Comparative Perspective*. Cambridge: Cambridge University Press, 2008.

Bartlett, Samuel C. *Sketches of the Missions of the American Board*. Boston: The Board, 1872.

Bayly, Christopher. *The Birth of the Modern World 1780-1914*. Oxford: Blackwell, 2004.

Bayrak, Tosun (transl.) *The Path of Muhammad: A Book on Islamic Morals and Ethics - Imam Birgivi, a 16th Century Islamic Mystic*. Indiana: World Wisdom, 2005.

Bayur, Hikmet. 'İkinci Meşrutiyet Devri Üzerinde Bazı Düşünceler'. *Belleten* 23:90 (Nisan 1959): 267-285.

Bein, Amit. *Ottoman Ulema, Turkish Republic: Agents of Change and Guardians of Tradition*. Stanford. Stanford University Press, 2011.

Beinin, Joel. *Workers and Peasants in the Middle East*. Cambridge/UK; Cambridge University Press, 2001.

Bell, Gertrude Lowthian. *Syria: The Desert and the Sown*. London: William Heinemann, 1907.

Berkes, Niyazi. *The Development of Secularism in Turkey* (Montreal: McGill University Press, 1964.

Beydilli Kemal. "Süleyman Hüsnü Paşa". *DİA*, online at https://islamansiklopedisi.org.tr/suleyman-husnu-pasa (accessed 18 July 2021).
Biyografi.net. "Süreyya Sami Berkem", https://www.biyografi.net/kisiyazdir.asp?kisiid=1934 (29 April 2021).
Bliss, Edwin Munsell. *Turkey and the Armenian Atrocities* (Philadelphia: Edgewood Pub., 1896.
De Blois, F.C. 'Zindīḳ', in: *Encyclopaedia of Islam*, Second Edition, Edited by: P. Bearman, Th. Bianquis, C.E. Bosworth, E. van Donzel, W.P. Heinrichs. Consulted online on 04 April 2019 <http://dx.doi.org/10.1163/1573-3912_islam_COM_1389>
Blumi, Isa. *Rethinking the Late Ottoman Empire: A Comparative Social and Political History of Albania and Yemen 1878–1918*. Istanbul: Isis Press, 2003.
Bond, Alvan (ed.), *Memoir of the Rev. Pliny Fisk, A.M., late missionary to Palestine* (Boston: Crocker & Brewster, 1828).
Boroujerdi, Mehrzad (ed.) *Mirror for the Muslim Prince: Islam and the Theory of Statecraft*. New York: Syracuse University Press, 2013.
Bouquet, Olivier. 'Is it Time to Stop Speaking About Ottoman Modernization?' In *Order and Compromise: Government Practices in Turkey from the Late Ottoman Empire to the Early 21st Century*, edited by Marc Aymes et al, 45–67. Leiden: Brill, 2015.
Bowden, Brett. 'Civilization and Its Consequences', in: *Oxford Handbooks Online* (February 2016), DOI:10.1093/oxfordhb/9780199935307.013.30
Bowden, Brett. 'In the Name of Civilization: War, Conquest, and Colonialism', in: *Pléyade* 23, enero-junio 2019, pp. 73–100, online https://scielo.conicyt.cl/scielo.php?script=sci_arttext&pid=S0719-36962019000100073 (accessed 26 September 2020).
Bowen, H. 'Aḥmad Djewdet Pasha', in: *Encyclopaedia of Islam*, Second Edition, Edited by: P. Bearman, Th. Bianquis, C.E. Bosworth, E. van Donzel, W.P. Heinrichs. Consulted online on 15 January 2016 <http://dx.doi.org/10.1163/1573-3912_islam_SIM_0406>
Böwering, Gerhard, et al. (eds.), *The Princeton Encyclopedia of Islamic Political Thought*. Princeton: Princeton University Press, 2013.
Braudel, Fernand. *The Mediterranean and the Mediterranean World in the Age of Philip II*, vol. 2, translated from the French by Siân Reynolds. Los Angeles etc., 1995.
Brown, Arthur J. *Report of a Visitation of the Syria Mission of the Presbyterian Board of Foreign Missions*. USA: *Presbyterian Board of Foreign Missions*, 1902.
Burak, Guy. 'Faith, law and empire in the Ottoman "age of confessionalization" (fifteenth–seventeenth centuries): the case of "renewal of faith", in: *Mediterranean Historical Review* 28:1 (2013): 1–23.
Burak, Guy. *The Second Formation of Islamic Law: The Ḥanafī School in the Early Modern Ottoman Empire*. Cambridge: Cambridge University Press 2015.
Bursalı Mehmed Tahir, *Osmanlı Müellifleri*, 3 vols. Istanbul, 1333–1342/1915–1924.
Burton, Isabel. *The Inner Life of Syria, Palestine, and the Holy Land: From My Private Journal*, 2. vols. London: Henry S. King & Co, 1875.
Campos, Michelle U. *Ottoman Brothers: Muslims, Christians and Jews in Early Twentieth-Century Palestine*. Stanford: Stanford University Press, 2011.
Carmel, Alex. *Palästina-Chronik 1853 bis 1882: Deutsche Zeitungsberichte vom Krimkrieg bis zur ersten jüdischen Einwanderungswelle*. Ulm: Armin Vaas, 1978.
Carmel, Alex. *Die Siedlungen der württembergischen Templer in Palästina 1868–1918*. Stuttgart: Kohlhammer, 1997.
Caussin de Perceval, Armand-Pierre, transl. [Assad Efendi]. *Précis historique de la destruction du corps des Janissaires par le sultan Mahmoud, en 1826*. Paris: F. Didot, 1833.

Chirol, M. Valentine. 'French Diplomacy in Syria, past and present'. *The Fortnightly Review* 31 (1882): 427–438.
Cole, Juan. 'Muhammad 'Abduh and Rashid Rida: A Dialogue on the Baha'i Faith'. *World Order* 15:3–4 (Spring/Summer 1981): 7–16.
Cole, Juan. 'Rashid Rida on the Baha'i Faith: A Utilitarian Theory of The Spread of Religions'. *Arab Studies Quarterly* 5:3 (1983): 276–291.
Cook, Michael. *Commanding Right and Forbidding Wrong in Islamic Thought*. Cambridge: Cambridge University Press, 2001/2004.
Cook, Michael. *Forbidding Wrong in Islam: An Introduction*. Cambridge: Cambridge University Press, 2003.
Cox, Samuel Sullivan. *Diversions of a Diplomat in Turkey*. New York: C. L. Webster and Co., 1893.
Crone, Patricia. *God's Rule: Government and Islam*. New York: Columbia University Press, 2004.
Currie, James Muhammad Dawud. 'Kadizadeli Ottoman Scholarship, Muḥammad ibn ʿAbd al-Wahhāb, and the Rise of the Saudi State'. *Journal of Islamic Studies* 26:3 (September 2015): 265–288.
Curry, John. 'Some Reflections on the Fluidity of Orthodoxy and Heterodoxy in an Ottoman Sunni Context', in: *Ottoman Sunnism: New Perspectives*, edited by Vefa Erginbaş, 191–210. Edinburgh: Edinburgh University Press, 2019.
Çakmak, Yalçın. *Sultanın Kızılbaşları: II. Abdülhamid Dönemi Alevi Algısı ve Siyaseti*. Istanbul: İletişim, 2019.
Çataltepe, Sipahi. *19. Yüzyıl Başlarında Avrupa Dengesi ve Nizam-ı Cedit Ordusu*. Istanbul: Göçebe, 1997.
Çavuşoğlu, Semiramis. 'The Ḳāḍīzādeli movement: An attempt of şerīʿat-minded reform in the Ottoman Empire'. PhD Thesis. Princeton: Princeton University, 1990.
Çelik, Faika. '"Civilizing Mission" in the Late Ottoman Discourse: The Case of Gypsies'. *Oriente Moderno* 93:2 (2013): 577–597.
Çelik, Faika. '"Community in Motion": Gypsies in Ottoman Imperial State Policy, Public Morality, and the Sharia Court of Üsküdar (1530s-1585s)' PhD Thesis. Montreal: McGill University, 2013.
Çelikdemir, Murat. 'Maarif Müdürü Halil Kemal Bey ve Antakya Nusayrileri hakkında Layihası'. In *Hatay (Anavatana Katılışının 80. Yıl Armağanı)*, edited by Ahmet Gündüz et al., 261–283. Istanbul: Hiper, 2019.
Çetinsaya, Gökhan. 'The Caliph and Mujtahids: Ottoman Policy towards the Shiite Community of Iraq in the Late Nineteenth Century'. *Middle Eastern Studies* 41:4 (2005): 561–574.
Çetinsaya, Gökhan. *Ottoman Administration of Iraq*. London: Routledge, 2006.
Çıpa, H. Erdem. *The Making of Selim: Succession, Legitimacy, and Memory in the Early Modern Ottoman World*. Indiana: Indiana University Press, 2017.
al-Dandashi, Ja'far al-Kanj. *Madkhal ila al-Madhhab al-'Alawi an-Nusayri*. Irbid: ar-Ruzna, 2000.
Davison, Roderic. *Reform in the Ottoman Empire, 1856–1876*. Princeton: Princeton University Press, 1963.
Davison, Roderic H. 'Tanzīmāt', in: *Encyclopaedia of Islam*, Second Edition, Edited by: P. Bearman, Th. Bianquis, C.E. Bosworth, E. van Donzel, W.P. Heinrichs. Consulted online on 14 January 2015 <http://dx.doi.org/10.1163/1573-3912_islam_COM_1174>
Dennis, James. *A Sketch of the Syria Mission*. New York: Edward O. Jenkins, 1872.

Deringil, Selim. 'The Struggle against Shiism in Hamidian Iraq: A Study in Ottoman Counter Propaganda'. *Die Welt des Islams*, New Series, 30:1/4 (1990): 45–62.
Deringil, Selim. 'Legitimacy Structures in the Ottoman State: The Reign of Abdulhamid II (1876–1909)'. *International Journal of Middle Eastern Studies* 23:3 (1991): 345–359.
Deringil, Selim. 'The Invention of Tradition as Public Image in the Late Ottoman Empire, 1808 to 1908'. *Comparative Studies in Society and History* 35:1 (1993): 3–29.
Deringil, Selim. *The Well-Protected Domains: Ideology and the Legitimation of Power in the Ottoman Empire, 1876–1909*. London: I. B. Tauris, 1998.
Deringil, Selim. '"There Is No Compulsion in Religion": On Conversion and Apostasy in the Late Ottoman Empire: 1839–1856'. *Comparative Studies in Society and History* 42 (2000): 547–575.
Deringil, Selim. '"They Live in a State of Nomadism and Savagery': The Late Ottoman. Empire and the Post-Colonial Debate". *Comparative Studies in Society and History* 45:2 (2003): 311–342.
Deringil, Selim. *Conversion and Apostasy in the Late Ottoman Empire*. Cambridge/UK: Cambridge University Press, 2012).
Der Matossian, Bedros. *Shattered Dreams of Revolution: From Liberty to Violence in the Late Ottoman Empire* (Stanford: Stanford University Press, 2014.
Devereux, Robert. *The First Ottoman Constitutional Period: A Study of the Midhat Constitution and Parliament* (Baltimore: John Hopkins University Press, 1963).
Devereux, Robert. 'Süleyman Paşa's "The Feeling of the Revolution"'. *Middle Eastern Studies* 15:1 (1979): 3–35.
Dilçin, Cem. 'Şeyh Galip'in Şiirlerinde III. Selim ve Nizam-ı Cedit'. *Türkoloji Dergisi* 11/1 (1993): 209–219.
Dodge, Bayard. 'American Educational and Missionary Efforts in the Nineteenth and Early Twentieth Centuries'. *Annals of the American Academy of Political and Social Science* vol. 401, America and the Middle East (May 1972): 15–22.
Douwes, Dick. 'Knowledge and Oppression: The Nusayriyya in the late Ottoman Period'. In: *Convegno sul tema La Shia nell'impero Ottomano*. Roma: Accademia nazionale dei Lincei, Fondazione Leone Caetani, 1993: 149–169.
Douwes, Dick. *The Ottomans in Syria: A History of Justice and Oppression*. London: I. B. Tauris, 2000.
Dressler, Markus. "Alevīs", in: Encyclopaedia of Islam, THREE, Edited by: Kate Fleet, Gudrun Krämer, Denis Matringe, John Nawas, Everett Rowson. Online abgerufen am 09 March 2017 http://dx.doi.org/10.1163/1573-3912_ei3_COM_0167
Dressler, Markus. *Writing Religion: The Making of Turkish Alevi Islam*. Oxford: Oxford University Press, 2013.
Duguid, Stephen. 'The Politics of Unity: Hamidian Policy in Eastern Anatolia'. *Middle Eastern Studies* 9:2 (1973): 139–155.
Dussaud, René. *Histoire et religion des Nosairîs*. Paris: É. Bouillon, 1900.
Eldem, Edhem. 'Yeniçeri Mezartaşları Kitabı Vesilesiyle Yeniçeri Taşları ve Tarih Üzerine'. *Toplumsal Tarih* 188 (Ağustos 2009): 2–13.
Eberhard, Elke. *Osmanische Polemik gegen die Safawiden im 16. Jahrhundert nach arabischen Manuskripten* (Freiburg i. Br.: Klaus Schwarz, 1970.
Eisler, Jakob. 'Die württembergischen Templer', in: *Württembergische Kirchengeschichte online*, at https://www.wkgo.de/themen/die-wuerttembergischen-templer (accessed 9 October 2018).
Emecen, Feridun M. *Yavuz Sultan Selim*. Istanbul: Yitik Hazine, 2013.

Ende, Werner. 'Rashīd Riḍā'. *Encyclopaedia of Islam*, Second Edition, Edited by: P. Bearman, Th. Bianquis, C.E. Bosworth, E. van Donzel, W.P. Heinrichs. Consulted online on 01 February 2019 <http://dx.doi.org/10.1163/1573-3912_islam_SIM_6240>

Ercan, Yavuz. 'Seyyid Mehmed Emin Vahid Efendi'nin Fransa Sefaretnamesi'. *Osmanlı Tarihi Araştırma ve Uygulama Merkezi Dergisi*, Ankara Üniversitesi, no. 2 (1991): 73-125.

Erginbaş, Vefa (ed.). *Ottoman Sunnism: New Perspectives* (Edinburgh: Edinburgh University Press, 2019).

Erhan, Çağrı. 'Ottoman Official Attitudes Towards American Missionaries'. *The Turkish Yearbook*, no. XXX (2000): 191-212.

Evstatiev, Simeon. 'The Qāḍīzādeli Movement and the Revival of takfīr in the Ottoman Age'. In *Accusations of unbelief in Islam: a diachronic perspective on takfīr*, edited by Camilla Adang et al., 213-243. Leiden: Brill, 2016).

Fahd, T. 'Ṣābiʾa', in: *Encyclopaedia of Islam*, Second Edition, Edited by: P. Bearman, Th. Bianquis, C.E. Bosworth, E. van Donzel, W.P. Heinrichs. Consulted online on 15 March 2016 <http://dx.doi.org/10.1163/1573-3912_islam_COM_0953>

Faroqhi, Suraiya. "Conflict, Accomodation and Long-Term Survival: The Bektashi Order and the Ottoman State", *Revue des Études Islamiques LX (1992), numéro spécial: Bektachiyya*, edited by Alexandre Popovic, Gilles Veinstein, 167-184.

Faroqhi, Suraiya. *Kultur und Alltag im Osmanischen Reich: Vom Mittelalter bis zum Anfang des 20. Jahrhunderts*. München: Beck, 1995).

Farouk-Alli, Aslam. 'The Genesis of Syria's Alawi Community'. In *The Alawis of Syria: War, Faith and Politics of the Levant*, edited by Michael Kerr and Craig Larkin, 27-47. Oxford: Oxford University Press, 2015.

Firro, Kais M. 'The ʿAlawīs in Modern Syria: From Nuṣayrīya to Islam via ʿAlawīya'. *Der Islam* 82 (2005): 1-31.

Fleischer, Cornell. 'The Lawgiver as Messiah: The Making of the Imperial Image in the Reign of Süleymân'. In *Soliman le magnifique et son temps*, edited by Gilles Veinstein, 159-177. Paris, 1992.

Fortna, Benjamin. *Imperial classroom: Islam, the State, and Education in the Late Ottoman Empire*. Oxford, 2002.

Franke, Patrick. *Göttliche Karriere eines syrischen Hirten: Sulaimān Muršid und die Anfänge der Muršidiyya*. Berlin: Klaus Schwarz, 1994.

Franke, Patrick. 'Die syrischen Alawiten in der westlichen Forschung: einige kritische Anmerkungen'. In *Sprache, Mythen und Mythizismen: Festschrift für Walter Beltz*, edited by A. Drost-Abgarjan and J. Tubach, 219-270. Halle/Saale: Hallesche Beiträge zur Orientwissenschaft, 2004.

Friedman, Yaron. 'Al-Ḥusayn ibn Ḥamdân al-Khasîbî. A Historical Biography of the Founder of the Nuṣayrî-ʿAlawi Sect'. *Studia Islamica* 93 (2001): 91-112.

Friedman, Yaron. *The Nusayri-ʿAlawis: An Introduction to the Religion, History and Identity of the Leading Minority in Syria*. Leiden: Brill, 2010.

Gedikli, Fethi. 'Midhat Paşa'nın Suriye Layihası'. *Dîvân*, no. 2 (1999): 169-189.

Gilsenan, Michael. *Lords of the Lebanese Marches: Violence and Narrative in an Arab Society*. Berkeley/LA: University of California Press, 1996.

Glassen, Erika. 'Krisenbewusstsein und Heilserwartung in der islamischen Welt zu Beginn der Neuzeit'. In *Die islamische Welt zwischen Mittelalter und Neuzeit: Festschrift für Hans Robert Roemer zum 65. Geburtstag*, edited by Ulrich Haarmann et al., 167-179. Beirut/Wiesbaden: Orient Institut/Franz Steiner, 1979.

Goodell, William. *Forty Years in the Turkish Empire*. New York: Robert Carter & Brothers, 1876.
Gölbaşı, Edip. "The Yezidis and the Ottoman State: Modern Power, Military Conscription, and Conversion Policies, 1830–1909". MA Thesis. Istanbul: Boğaziçi University, 2008.
Gölbaşı, Edip. "'Heretik' aşiretler ve II. Abdulhamid rejimi: Zorunlu askerlik meselesi ve ihtida siyaseti odağında Yezidiler ve Osmanlı idaresi". *Tarih ve Toplum-Yeni Yaklaşımlar* 9 (2009), 87–156.
Gölbaşı, Edip. "Turning the 'Heretics' into Loyal Muslim Subjects: Imperial Anxieties, the Politics of Religious Conversion, and the Yezidis in the Hamidian Era". *Muslim World* 103 (2013), 1–23.
Gölbaşı, Edip. "'Devil Worshippers' Encounter the State: 'Heterodox' Identities, State Building, and the Politics of Imperial Integration in the Late Ottoman Empire". In *The Ottoman East in the Nineteenth Century: Societies, Identities and Politics*, edited by Ali Sipahi, Dzovinar Derderian and Yaşar Tolga Cora, 133–155. London: I. B. Tauris, 2016.
Grabill, Joseph L. *Protestant Diplomacy and the Near East: Missionary Influence on American Policy, 1810–1927*. Minneapolis: University of Minnesota Press, 1971.
Greene, Joseph K. *Leavening the Levant*. Boston: The Pilgrim Press, 1916.
Grehan, James. *Twilight of the Saints: Everyday Religion in Ottoman Syria and Palestine*. Oxford: Oxford University Press, 2014.
Grothe, Hugo. *Meine Vorderasienexpedition 1906 und 1907: Die fachwissenschaftlichen Ergebnisse*, vol. 1.1.: 90–211. Leipzig: Karl W. Hiersemann, 1911.
Güler, Ruhi. 'Tanzimattan II. Meşrutiyete *Medeniyet* Anlayışının Evrimi'. PhD Thesis. Istanbul: Marmara Üniversitesi, 2006.
Günay, Selçuk. 'II. Abdülhamid Döneminde Suriye ve Lübnan'da Arap Ayrılıkçı Hareketlerinin Başlaması ve Devletin Tedbirleri'. *Ankara Üniversitesi Dil ve Tarih-Coğrafya Fakültesi Tarih Bölümü Tarih Araştırmaları Dergisi* 28/17 (1992): 85–108.
Günaltay, Mehmed Şemseddin. *Hurafâtdan Hakikate*. Istanbul: Tevsi-i Tibaat Matbaası, 1332/1916.
Günaltay, Mehmed Şemseddin. *Hurafeler ve İslam Gerçeği*, edited by Ahmet Gökbel. 2nd edn. Istanbul: Marifet, 1997.
Gündoğdu, Cihangir, and Vural Genç. *Dersim'de Osmanlı Siyaseti: İzâle-i Vahşet, Tashîh-i İtikâd ve Tasfiye-i Ezhân*. Istanbul: Kitap Yayınevi, 2013.
Güner, Selda. "Irak Sâbiîlerine Dair Bir Asayiş Dosyası (1873–1898)". *Cumhuriyet Tarihi Araştırmaları Dergisi*, 9:18 (2013): 3–28.
Güneş Yağcı, Zübeyde; "Ferah Ali Paşa'nın Soğucak Muhafızlığı (1781–1785)". PhD Thesis. Samsun: Ondokuz Mayız Üniversitesi, 1998.
Güngör, Halil İbrahim. 'II. Abdülhamid Dönemi'nde Irak'la İlgili Hazırlanan Layihalar'. M.A. Thesis.Kütahya: Dumlupınar Üniversitesi, 2009.
Haarmann, Ulrich, et al. (ed.): *Die islamische Welt zwischen Mittelalter und Neuzeit: Festschrift für Hans Robert Roemer zum 65. Geburtstag* (Beirut/Wiesbaden: Franz Steiner, 1979.
Hacısalihoğlu, Mehmet. 'Inclusion and Exclusion: Conscription in the Ottoman Empire'. *Journal of Modern European History* 5:2 (2007): 264–286.
Hacısalihoğlu, Mehmet (ed.) *1864 Kafkas Tehciri: Kafkasya'da Rus Kolonizasyonu, Savaş ve Sürgün*. Istanbul: BALKAR & IRCICA, 2014.
Hagen, Gottfried. 'Legitimacy and World Order'. In *Legitimizing the Order: The Ottoman Rhetoric of State Power*, edited by Hakan T. Karateke/Maurus Reinkowski (eds.), 55–83. Leiden: Brill, 2005.

Haksever, Cahit. 'Osmanlı'nın Son Döneminde Islahat ve Tarikatlar: Bektâşîlik ve Nakşbendîlik Örneği'. *EKEV Akademi Dergisi* 13/38 (2009): 39-60.

Halm, Heinz. *Die Islamische Gnosis: Die Extreme Schia und die 'Alawiten*. Zürich/München: Artemis, 1982.

Halm, Heinz. *Die Schia*. Darmstadt: Wissenschaftliche Buchgesellschaft, 1988.

Halm, Heinz. *Das Reich des Mahdi: Der Aufstieg der Fatimiden (875-973)*. München: Beck, 1991.

Halm, Heinz. *Die Kalifen von Kairo: Die Fatimiden in Ägypten (973-1074)*. München: Beck, 2003.

Halm, Heinz. 'ĠOLĀT', in: *Encyclopædia Iranica*, online at http://www.iranicaonline.org/articles/golat (accessed 10 October 2018).

Halm, Heinz. 'Nuṣayriyya', in: *Encyclopaedia of Islam*, Second Edition, Edited by: P. Bearman, Th. Bianquis, C.E. Bosworth, E. van Donzel, W.P. Heinrichs. Consulted online on 16 January 2018 <http://dx.doi.org/10.1163/1573-3912_islam_COM_0876>

Hamzah, Dyala. 'Proselytism and reform. Muhammad Rashid Rida, al-Manar and Dar al-da'wa wa-l-irshad', paper read at *Missionaries as experts: religious networks, knowledge of the field and public action in the Middle East (19th - 21st century)* - IFEA & Orient Institut, Istanbul, 26-27 October 2018, MissMo Workshop, https://missmo.hypotheses.org/306.

Hanioğlu, M. Şükrü. *Preparation for a Revolution: The Young Turks 1902-1908*. Oxford: Oxford University Press, 2001.

Hanioğlu, M. Şükrü. *A Brief History of the Late Ottoman Empire*. Princeton: Princeton University Press, 2008.

Hanssen, Jens. *Fin de siècle Beirut: The Making of an Otoman Provincial Capital*. Oxford: Oxford University Press, 2005.

al-Hariri, Abu Musa. *al-'Alawiyyun an-Nusayriyyun: bahth fi al-'aqida wa at-ta'rikh*. Beirut, 1980.

Haydar, Asad. *al-Imam as-Sadiq wa al-madhahib al-arba'a*. vol. 1. 3rd edn. Beirut, 1969.

Heinzelmann, Tobias. 'Die Auflösung der Janitscharentruppen und ihre historischen Zusammenhänge: Sahhaflarşeyhizade Mehmed Esad Efendis Üss-i Zafer'. *Asiatische Studien: Zeitschrift der Schweizerischen Asiengesellschaft* 54:3 (2000): 653-675.

Hermann, Denis. "SHAYKHISM". *Encyclopædia Iranica*, online edition 2017, http://www.iranicaonline.org/articles/shaykhism (accessed on 16 April 2021).

Herzog, Christoph, and Raoul Motika. "Orientalism 'alla turca': Late 19th / Early 20th Century Ottoman Voyages into the Muslim 'Outback'". *Die Welt des Islams*, New Series, 40:2 (2000): 139-195.

Hobsbawm, Eric. *Primitive Rebels*. New York: Norton, rev. edn. 1965 (1959).

Hobsbawm, Eric. *Bandits*. New York: Pantheon Books, rev. edn. 1981 (1969).

Hodgson, Marshall. 'How Did the Early Shi'a become Sectarian?', in: *Journal of the American Oriental Society* 75:1 (Jan.-Mar., 1955): 1-13.

Hodgson, Marshall. 'Ghulāt'. *Encyclopaedia of Islam*, Second Edition, Edited by: P. Bearman, Th. Bianquis, C.E. Bosworth, E. van Donzel, W.P. Heinrichs. Consulted online on 18 January 2018 <http://dx.doi.org/10.1163/1573-3912_islam_SIM_2517>

İhsanoğlu, Ekmeleddin (ed.) *Osmanlı Devleti ve Medeniyeti Tarihi*. 2 vols. Istanbul: IRCICA, 1994-1997.

İnan Gümüş, Hami. *American Missionaries in the Ottoman Empire: A Conceptual Metaphor Analysis of Missionary Narrative, 1820-1898*. Bielefeld: Transcript, 2017.

İpşirli, Mehmed, and Kemal Beydilli. "İbrâhim Efendi, Haydarîzâde". *DİA*, online at https://islamansiklopedisi.org.tr/ibrahim-efendi-haydarizade (accessed 10 February 2021).
Ismail Kemal Bey (Vlora). *The Memoirs of Ismail Kemal Bey*, edited by Sommerville Story. London: Constable, 1920.
Ivanyi, Katharina. *Virtue, Piety and the Law: A Study of Birgivī Meḥmed Efendī's al-Ṭarīqa al-muḥammadiyya*. Leiden: Brill, 2020.
İz, Fahir. 'Ḥasan Bedr al-Dīn', in: *Encyclopaedia of Islam*, Second Edition, Edited by: P. Bearman, Th. Bianquis, C.E. Bosworth, E. van Donzel, W.P. Heinrichs. Consulted online on 28 June 2021, http://dx.doi.org/10.1163/1573-3912_islam_SIM_8606
İzgöer, Ahmet Zeki. 'Ahmet Cevdet Paşa'nın Sosyal ve İktisadî Görüşleri'. PhD Thesis. Istanbul: Marmara Üniversitesi, 1997.
Jessup, Henry H. *Fifty-Three Years in Syria*, 2 vols. New York: Fleming H. Revell, 1910.
Jurt, Joseph. 'Bourdieus Kapital-Theorie'. In: *Bildung, Arbeit, Erwachsenwerden: ein interdisziplinärer Blick auf die Transition im Jugend- und jungen Erwachsenenalter*, edited by Manfred Max Bergman, 21–41. Wiesbaden: Springer, 2012.
Karaca, Ali. *Anadolu ıslahatı ve Ahmet Şakir Paşa*. Istanbul: Eren, 1993.
Karadeniz, Osman. 'Tarîkat-ı Muhammediyye'. In *İmam Birgivî*, edited by Mehmet Şeker, 115–123. Ankara: Türkiye Diyanet Vakfı, 1994.
Karal, Enver Ziya. *Osmanlı Tarihi*. vols. 5–8. Ankara: Türk Tarih Kurumu, 1961–1983.
Karal, Enver Ziya. *Osmanlı Tarihi: Islahat Fermanı Devri*. vol. 7. Ankara, 2003.
Karataş, Yakup. 'Sultan II. Abdülhamid'in Eğitim Politikalarının Mali Bir Veçhesi: Evkâf-ı Münderisenin Maarife Terki'. *A.Ü. Türkiyat Araştırmaları Enstitüsü Dergisi* 57 (2016): 1839–1867.
Karateke, Hakan T. 'Opium for the Subjects?: Religiosity as a Legitimizing Factor for the Ottoman Sultan'. In *Legitimizing the Order: the Ottoman Rhetoric of State Power*, edited by idem and Maurus Reinkowski, 111–129. Leiden: Brill, 2005.
Karateke, Hakan T. and Maurus Reinkowski (eds.). *Legitimizing the Order: The Ottoman Rhetoric of State Power*. Leiden: Brill, 2005.
Karcı, Erol. 'Suriye Maarif Müdürü Halil Kemal Bey'in Antakya Nusayrilerine dair bir Layihası'. In *Anavatana Katılışının 80. Yılında Hatay Uluslararası Sempozyumu*, edited by Erdem Ünlen and H. Aytuğ Tokur, 411–428. Ankara: Atatürk Araştırma Merkezi, 2020.
Karpuzcu, Hakan Feyzullah. 'Late Ottoman Modernist/Rationalist Discourses on Islam: Superstition, Sufism and Şemseddin Günaltay'. M.A. Thesis. Istanbul: Sabancı University, 2008.
Karolewsksi, Janina. 'What is Heterodox About Alevism? The Development of Anti-Alevi Discrimination and Resentment'. *Die Welt des Islams* 48 (2008); 434–456.
Karpat, Kemal H. *The Politicization of Islam: Reconstructing Identity, State, Faith, and Community in the Late Ottoman State*. Oxford: Oxford University Press, 2001.
Kavaklı, Sibel. '929/A Numaralı Nefy Defterinin (1826/1833) Transkripsiyon ve Değerlendirilmesi', M.A. Thesis. Tokat: Gaziosmanpaşa Üniversitesi, 2005.
Kennedy, Hugh N. *The Prophet and the Age of the Caliphates: The Islamic Near East from the 6th to the 11th Century*. 2nd edn. Harlow/UK: Pearson/Longman, 2004.
Kerr, Michael and Craig Larkin (eds.) *The Alawis of Syria: War, Faith and Politics of the Levant*. Oxford: Oxford University Press, 2015.
Khoury, Philip S. *Syria and the French Mandate. The Politics of Arab Nationalism, 1920–1945* (London: I. B. Tauris, 1987.
Kieser, Hans-Lukas. *Der verpasste Friede: Mission, Ethnie und Staat in den Ostprovinzen der Türkei, 1839–1938*. Zürich: Chronos, 2000.

Kieser, Hans-Lukas. *Iskalanmış Barış: Doğu Vilayetlerinde Misyonerlik Etnik Kimlik ve Devlet 1839–1938*, translated by Atilla Dirim. Istanbul; İletişim, 2005.

Kieser, Hans-Lukas. 'Muslim Heterodoxy and Protestant Utopia: The Interactions between Alevis and Missionaries in Ottoman Anatolia'. *Die Welt des Islams* 41 (2001): 89–111.

Kieser, Hans-Lukas. 'Mission as Factor of Change in Turkey (nineteenth to first half of twentieth century)', in: *Islam and Christian–Muslim Relations* 13 (2002): 391–410.

Kieser, Hans-Lukas. "Some Remarks on Alevi Responses to the Missionaries in Eastern Anatolia (19th-20th cc.)." In *Altruism and Imperialism. Western Cultural and Religious Missions to the Middle East (19th-20th cc.)*, edited by Tejirian, Eleanor H. and Reeva Spector Simon, 120–142. New York: Columbia University, 2002.

Kieser, Hans-Lukas. *Nearest East: American Millennialism and Mission to the Middle East*. Philadelphia: Temple University Press, 2010.

Kister, Meir J. 'Social and Religious Concepts of Authority in Islam'. *Jerusalem Studies in Arabic and Islam* 18 (1994): 84–127.

Kırmızı, Abdulhamit. 'Şikâyât Tezâyüd Etmekte: Memduh Bey'in Sivas Valiliği'nde Ermeni Politikası (1889–1892)'. *Osmanlılar Döneminde Sivas Sempozyumu Bildirileri (21–25 Mayıs 2007)*, 1. cilt (Sivas: Sivas Valiliği, 2007): 363–376.

Kırmızı, Abdulhamit. "Going round the province for progress and prosperity: inspection tours and reports by late Ottoman governors". *Studies in Travel Writing* 16:4 (2012): 387–401.

Kırmızı, Abdulhamit. '19. Yüzyılı Laiksizleştirmek: Osmanlı-Türk Laikleşme Anlatısının Sorunları'. *Cogito* 94 (2019): 1–17.

Kocabaşoğlu, Uygur. *Kendi Belgeleriyle Anadolu'daki Amerika: 19. Yüzyılda Osmanlı İmparatorluğu'ndaki Amerikan Misyoner Okulları*. Istanbul: Arba, 1989.

Kohlberg, Ethan. "al-Rāfiḍa", in: *Encyclopaedia of Islam*, Second Edition, Edited by: P. Bearman, Th. Bianquis, C.E. Bosworth, E. van Donzel, W.P. Heinrichs. Consulted online on 18 January 2018 http://dx.doi.org/10.1163/1573-3912_islam_SIM_6185

Kramer, Martin. *Arab Awakening and Islamic Revival*. New Brunswick/London: Transaction Publishers, 2008.

Krämer, Gudrun, and Sabine Schmidtke (eds.) *Speaking for Islam: Religious Authorities in Muslim Societies*. Leiden; Brill, 2006.

Krstic, Tijana. *Contested Conversions to Islam: Narratives of Religious Change in the Early Modern Ottoman Empire*. Stanford: Stanford University Press, 2011.

Kuehn, Thomas. *Empire, Islam, and Politics of Difference: Ottoman Rule in Yemen, 1849–1919*. Leiden: Brill, 2011.

Kufrevî, Kasim. 'Birgewî'. *Encyclopaedia of Islam*, Second Edition, Edited by: P. Bearman, Th. Bianquis, C.E. Bosworth, E. van Donzel, W.P. Heinrichs. Consulted online on 15 January 2016 <http://dx.doi.org/10.1163/1573-3912_islam_SIM_1434>

Kuhnke, LaVerne. *Lives at Risk: Public Health in Nineteenth-Century Egypt*. Berkeley, etc.: University of California Press, 1990.

Kurşun, Zekeriya. 'Mehmed Memduh Paşa', in: *DİA*, online at https://islamansiklopedisi.org.tr/mehmed-memduh-pasa (15 January 2020).

Kurt, Yılmaz. 'Muṣṭafā Nūrī', *Historians of the Ottoman Empire*, http://www.ottomanhistorians.uchicago.edu, edited by C. Kafadar, H. Karateke, C. Fleischer (accessed: 17 February 2017).

Kurt, İsmail, and Seyid Ali Tuz. *Tarihi ve Kulturel Boyutlarıyla Turkiye'de Aleviler, Bektaşiler, Nusayriler*. Istanbul: Ensar Neşriyat, 1999.

Lammens, Henri. 'Au pays des Nosairis'. *Revue de l'Orient chrétien* 4 (1899): 572–590; *Revue de l'Orient chrétien* 5 (1900): 99–117, 303–318, and 423–444.

Lammens, Henri. 'Les Nosairis Furent - Ils *Chrétiens* ?' *Revue de l'Orient chrétien* 6 (1901): 33–50.
Lammens, Henri: 'Une visite au šaih supreme des Nosairis Haidaris'. *Journal Asiatique* XI:V (1915): 139–159.
Landau, Jacob M. *The Politics of Pan-Islam: Ideology and Organization*. Oxford: Oxford University Press, 1990.
Langer, Robert, and Udo Simon. 'The Dynamics of Orthodoxy and Heterodoxy. Dealing with Divergence in Muslim Discourses and Islamic Studies', *Die Welt des Islams* 48 (2008): 273–288.
Leaman, Oliver (ed.) *The Qur'an: An Encyclopedia*. London: Routledge, 2006.
Lévy-Aksu, Noémi, and François Georgeon. *The Young Turk Revolution and the Ottoman Empire: The Aftermath of 1908*. London: I. B. Tauris, 2017.
Lewis, Bernard. *The Emergence of Modern Turkey*. Oxford: Oxford University Press, 1961.
Lewis, Bernard. *The Political Language of Islam*. Chicago: University of Chicago Press, 1991.
Lindemann, Gerhard. *Für Frömmigkeit in Freiheit: die Geschichte der Evangelischen Allianz im Zeitalter des Liberalismus (1846 - 1879)*. Berlin: LIT Verlag, 2011.
Lindner, Christine B. 'Negotiating the Field: American Protestant Missionaries in Ottoman Syria, 1823 to 1860'. PhD Thesis. Edinburgh: University of Edinburgh, 2009.
Litvak, Meir. *Shi'i Scholars of Nineteenth-Century Iraq: The ulema' of Najaf and Karbala*. Cambridge: Cambridge University Press, 1998.
Lyde, Samuel. *The Anseyreeh and Ismaeleeh: A Visit to the Secret Sects of Northern Syria with a View to the Establishment of Schools*. London: Hurst and Blackett, 1853.
Lyde, Samuel. *The Asian Mystery illustrated in the history, religion, and present state of the Ansaireeh or Nusairis of Syria*. London: Longman, 1860.
Madelung, W. and M. G. S. Hodgson, 'Ibāḥa', in: *Encyclopaedia of Islam*, Second Edition, Edited by: P. Bearman, Th. Bianquis, C.E. Bosworth, E. van Donzel, W.P. Heinrichs. Consulted online on 15 January 2020 <http://dx.doi.org/10.1163/1573-3912_islam_SIM_3016>
Maden, Fahri. 'Hacı Bektaş Veli Tekkesi'nde Nakşî Şeyhler ve Sırrı Paşa'nın Lâyıhası'. *Türk Kültürü ve Hacı Bektaş Velî Araştırma Dergisi* 59 (2011): 159–180.
Maden, Fahri. *Bektaşî Tekkelerinin Kapatılması (1826) ve Bektaşiliğin Yasaklı Yılları*. Ankara: Türk Tarih Kurumu, 2013.
Maden, Fahri. 'Yeniçerilik-Bektaşilik İlişkileri ve Yeniçeri İsyanlarında Bektaşiler', *Türk Kültürü ve Hacı Bektaş Velî Araştırma Dergisi* 73 (2015): 173–202.
Magazin für die Literatur des Auslandes, no. 16 (Berlin), 18 April 1874.
McFarland, A. J. *Eight Decades in Syria*. Topeka/Kan., 1937.
Maghen, Ze'ev. *After Hardship Cometh Ease: The Jews as Backdrop for Muslim Moderation*. Berlin/New York: De Gruyter, 2006.
al-Majlisi, Muhammad Baqir. *Bihar al-Anwar*. vol. 25. Beirut, Dar Ihya' at-Turath al-'Arabi, 1983.
Makdisi, Ussama. "Reclaiming the Land of the Bible: Missionaries, Secularism, and Evangelical Modernity". *The American Historical Review* 102:3 (1997): 680–713.
Makdisi, Ussama. "Ottoman Orientalism", *The American Historical Review* 107:3 (2002), 768–796.
Makdisi, Ussama. *Artillery of Heaven: American Missionaries and the Failed Conversion of the Middle East*. Ithaca/London: Cornell University Press, 2008.
Maksudyan, Nazan. *Orphans and Destitute Children in the Late Ottoman Empire*. New York: Syracuse University Press, 2014.
Marr, Timothy. '"Drying up the Euphrates": Muslims, Millennialism, and Early American Missionary Enterprise'. In *U.S.-Middle East: Historical Encounters, a Critical Survey*,

edited by Abbas Amanat and Magnus T. Bernhardsson, 60–76. Gainesville/Fl.: University Press of Florida, 2007.
Marr, Timothy. *The Cultural Roots of American Islamicism* (Cambridge: Cambridge University Press, 2006).
Martı, Huriye. 'et-Tarîkatü'l-Muhammediye', in: *DİA*, online https://islamansiklopedisi.org.tr/et-tarikatul-muhammediyye (15 January 2020).
McAuliffe, Jane Dammen. *Encyclopedia of the Qur'an*, 6 vols. Leiden: Brill, 2001–2006.
Medill, Kathryn A. 'David Metheny, Missionary Doctor: Work and Trouble at the Mersine Mission 1890–1897'. M.A. Thesis. Pennsylvania: Geneva College, 2011.
Menzel, Theodor. "Die Teufelsanbeter oder ein Blick auf die widerspenstige Sekte der Jeziden: Ein Beitrag zur Kenntnis der Jeziden". In Hugo Grothe, *Meine Vorderasienexpedition 1906 und 1907: Die fachwissenschaftlichen Ergebnisse*, vol. 1.1.: 90–211. Leipzig: Karl W. Hiersemann, 1911.
Mertcan, Hakan. *Türk Modernleşmesinde Arap Aleviler: Tarih, Kimlik, Siyaset* (3rd edn. Adana: Karahan, 2015.
Momen, Moojan. *An Introduction to Shi'i Islam*. Oxford: George Ronald, 1985.
Moosa, Matti. *Extremist Shiites: The Ghulat Sects*. New York: Syracuse University Press, 1988.
Morton, Daniel Oliver (ed.). *Memoir of Rev. Levi Parsons*. Poultney/Vt.: , 1824.
Mutlu, Şamil (ed.) *Yeniçeri Ocağının Kaldırılışı ve II. Mahmud'un Edirne Seyahati: Mehmed Daniş Bey ve Eserleri*. Istanbul: Edebiyat Fakültesi Basımevi, 1994.
Nagel, Tilman. 'Buyids', in: *Encyclopædia Iranica*, http://www.iranicaonline.org/articles/buyids (accessed 28.01.2019)
Nakash, Yitzhak. "The Conversion of Iraq's Tribes to Shiism". *International Journal of Middle East Studies* 26:3 (1994): 443–463.
Nakash, Yitzhak. *The Shi'is of Iraq*. Princeton: Princeton University Press, 1994.
Natho, Kadir I. *Circassian History*. New Jersey: Xlibris, 2009.
Newcomb, Harvey. *Cyclopedia of Missions*. New York: Scribner, 1854.
Ocak, Ahmet Yaşar. 'Türk Heterodoksi Tarihinde Zındık, Hâricî, Râfizî, Mülhid ve Ehl-i Bid'at Terimlerine Dair Bazı Düşünceler'. *İstanbul Üniversitesi Edebiyat Fakültesi Tarih Enstitüsü Dergisi* 12 (1981–82): 507–520.
Ocak, Ahmet Yaşar. *Osmanlı Toplumunda Zındıklar ve Mülhidler (15.-17. Yüzyıllar)*. Istanbul: Tarih Vakfı, 1998.
Ocak, Ahmet Yaşar. 'Balım Sultan'. *DİA*, online at https://islamansiklopedisi.org.tr/balim-sultan (15 January 2020).
Ocak, Ahmet Yaşar. 'Hacı Bektaş Vilayetnamesi', in: *DİA*, online at https://islamansiklopedisi.org.tr/haci-bektas-vilayetnamesi (accessed 2 February 2020).
Ocak, Ahmet Yaşar. *Türkler, Türkiye ve İslâm: Yaklaşım, Yöntem ve Yorum Denemeleri*. Istanbul: İletişim, 2000.
Oren, Michael. *Power, Faith and Fantasy: America in the Middle East, 1776 to the Present*. New York: Norton, 2007.
Ortaylı, İlber. 'Tarikatlar ve Tanzimat Dönemi Osmanlı Yönetimi'. *OTAM Dergisi* (Ankara Üniversitesi), no. 6 (1995): 281–287.
Ortaylı, İlber. "19. Yüzyılda Heterodox Dinî Gruplar ve Osmanlı İdaresi". *İslâm Araştırmaları Dergisi*, I/1. Istanbul 1996: 63–68.
Ortaylı, İlber. "Alevilik, Nusayrîlik ve Bâbıâli". *Tarihî ve Kültürel Boyutlarıyla Türkiye'de Alevîler, Bektaşiler, Nusayrîler*, edited by İsmail Kurt and Seyid Ali Tuz, 161–169. Istanbul: Ensar Neşriyat, 1999.
Ortaylı, İlber. *Batılılaşma Yolunda*. Istanbul: Merkez Kitaplar, 2007.

Öz, Mustafa. "Râfızîler". *DİA*, online at https://islamansiklopedisi.org.tr/rafiziler (accessed 15 January 2020).
Özbilgen, Erol. *Osmanlının Balkanlardan Çekilişi: Süleyman Hüsnü Paşa ve Dönemi*. Istanbul: İz, 2006.
Öztürk, Necati. 'Islamic Orthodoxy among the Ottomans in the Seventeenth Century with Special Reference to the Qadizade Movement'. PhD Thesis. Edinburgh: University of Edinburgh, 1981.
Pakalın, Mehmet Zeki. *Tarih Deyimleri ve Terimleri Sözlüğü*, 3 vols. Istanbul: Milli Eğitim, 1971–1972.
Palabıyık, Mustafa Serdar. "Travel, civilization and the east: Ottoman travellers' perception of 'the east' in the late Ottoman Empire". PhD Thesis. Ankara: ODTÜ, 2010.
Pipes, Daniel. *Greater Syria: The History of an Ambition*. Oxford: Oxford University Press, 1990.
Philliou, Christine M. *Biography of an Empire: Governing Ottomans in an Age of Revolution*. Berkeley etc.: University of California Press, 2010.
Prager, Laila. *Die 'Gemeinschaft des Hauses': Religion, Heiratsstrategien und transnationale Identität türkischer Alawi-/Nusairi-Migranten in Deutschland*. Münster: LIT Verlag, 2010.
Procházka, Stephan. 'The Alawis'. *Oxford Research Encyclopedia of Religion* (2015), DOI:10.1093/acrefore/9780199340378.013.85, p. 4 (downloaded PDF).
Procházka-Eisl, Gisela, and Stephan Procházka. *The Plain of Saints and Prophets: The Nusayri-Alawi Community of Cilicia (Southern Turkey) and its Sacred Places*. Wiesbaden: Harrasowitz, 2010.
al-Qurtubi, Abu Abdullah. *al-Jami' li-Ahkam al-Qur'an*. 24 vols. Beirut: al-Resalah, 2006.
Reinhart, Kevin. 'Civilization and its Discussants: Medeniyet and the Turkish Conversion to Modernism'. In *Converting Cultures: Religion, Ideology and Transformations of Modernity*, edited by Denis Washburn/A. Kevin Reinhart, 267–290. Leiden: Brill, 2007.
Reinkowski, Maurus. 'Hapless Imperialists and Resentful Nationalists: Trajectories of Radicalization in the Late Ottoman Empire'. In *Helpless Imperialists: Imperial Failure and Radicalization*, edited by idem/Gregor Thum, 47–65. Göttingen: Vandenhoeck & Ruprecht, 2013.
Reinkowski, Maurus, and Gregor Thum (eds.), *Helpless Imperialists: Imperial Failure and Radicalization*. Göttingen: Vandenhoeck & Ruprecht, 2013.
Richmond, Walter. *The Northwest Caucasus: Past, Present, Future*. London: Routledge, 2008.
Richter, Julius. *A History of Protestant Missions in the Near East*. New York: Revell, 1910.
Richter, Julius. *Evangelische Missionskunde* (Leipzig/Erlangen: A. Deichert'sche Verlagsbuchhandlung, 1920.
Riedler, Florian. *Opposition and Legitimacy in the Ottoman Empire: Conspiracies and political cultures*. London: Routledge, 2011.
Rigby, T. H. 'Weber's Typology of Authority: Difficulty and Some Suggestions'. *Anthropological Forum* 1:1 (1963): 2–15.
Rihani, Ameen. *The Descent of Bolshevism*. Boston/Mass.: The Stratford Co., 1920.
Rousseau, L. J. 'Memoire sur les Ismaelis et les Nosairis de Syrie'. *Annales des Voyages* 14 (1811): 271–303.
Rubin, Avi. "East, West, Ottomans and Zionists: Internalized Orientalism at the Turn of the Twentieth Century". In: *Representations of the "other/s" in the Mediterranean World and their Impact on the Region*, edited by Nedret Kuran-Burçoğlu and Susan Gilson Miller, 149–166. Istanbul: Isis Press, 2005.

Sadeghi, Behnam, et al. (eds.). *Islamic Cultures, Islamic Contexts: Essays in Honor of Professor Patricia Crone*. Leiden: Brill, 2015.

Saliba, Najib. 'The Achievements of Midhat Paşa as Governor of the Province of Syria, 1878–1880'. *International Journal of Middle East Studies* 9 (1979): 307–323.

Salisbury, Edward A. 'The Book of Sulaimân's First Ripe Fruit, Disclosing the Mysteries of the Nusairian Religion'. *Journal of the American Oriental Society* 8 (1866): 227–308.

Sanderson, Marjorie Allen. *A Syrian Mosaic* (Pittsburgh/Pa.: Board of Education and Publication of the Reformed Presbyterian Church of North America, 1976.

Sariyannis, Marinos. *History of Ottoman Political Thought up to the Early Nineteenth Century*. Leiden: Brill, 2019.

Savory, Roger M., and Ahmet T. Karamustafa. 'ESMĀʿĪL I ṢAFAWĪ'. *Encyclopædia Iranica* online, http://www.iranicaonline.org/articles/esmail-i-safawi (accessed 6 April 2017).

Saydam, Abdullah. 'Soykırımdan Kaçış: Cebel-i Elsineden Memâlik-i Mahrûsa'ya'. In *1864 Kafkas Tehciri: Kafkasya'da Rus Kolonizasyonu, Savaş ve Sürgün*, edized by Mehmet Hacısalihoğlu, 71–115. Istanbul: BALKAR & IRCICA, 2014.

Schäbler, Birgit. 'Civilizing Others: Global Modernity and the Local Boundaries (French/German/Ottoman and Arab) of Savagery'. In *Globalization and the Muslim World: Culture, Religion, and Modernity*, edited by idem and Leif Stenberg, 3–31. Syracuse: Syracuse University Press, 2004.

Schäbler, Birgit, and Leif Stenberg. *Globalization and the Muslim World: Culture, Religion, and Modernity*. Syracuse: Syracuse University Press, 2004.

Schayegh, Cyrus. *The Middle East and the Making of the Modern World*. Cambridge/Mass.: Harvard University Press, 2017.

Sevruk, Dmitry. *Die Muršidiyya: Entstehung und innere Entwicklung einer religiösen Sondergemeinschaft in Syrien von den 1920er Jahren bis heute*. Bamberg: Bamberg University Press, 2013.

Shafir, Nir. 'Moral Revolutions: The Politics of Piety in the Ottoman Empire Reimagined.' *Comparative Studies in Society and History* 61:3 (2019): 595–623.

Sharafuddin, Taqi. *an-Nusayriyya: Dirasa tahliliyya* (n.p., n.d.).

Sharif, Munir. *al-Muslimun al-ʿalawiyyun: man hum wa ayna hum?* Beirut: Muʾassasa al-Bulagh, 1994.

Sharkey, Heather J. "American Missionaries in Ottoman Lands: Foundational Encounters" (2010), Retrieved from http://repository.upenn.edu/nelc_papers/19 (accessed 26 December 2017).

Sharkey, Heather J. *A History of Muslims, Christians, and Jews in the Middle East*. Cambridge: Cambridge University Press, 2017.

Sharon, Moshe. 'The Development of the Debate around the Legitimacy of Authority in Early Islam'. *Jerusalem Studies in Arabic and Islam* 5 (1984): 121–141.

Shaw, Standord J., and Ezel Kural Shaw. *History of the Ottoman Empire and Modern Turkey*, 2. vols. (Cambridge: Cambridge University Press, 1977.

Sheikh, Mustapha. *Ottoman Puritanism and its Discontents: Ahmad al-Rumi al-Aqhisari and the Qadizadelis*. Oxford: Oxford University Press, 2016.

Sobhani, Ayatollah Jaʿfar. *Doctrines of Shiʿi Islam: A Compendium of Imami Beliefs and Practices*. Translated and edited by Reza Shah-Kazemi. London: I. B. Tauris/Institute of Ismaili Studies, 2001.

Sohrweide, Hanna. "Der Sieg der Safaviden in Persien und seine Rückwirkung auf die Schiiten Anatoliens im 16. Jahrhundert". *Der Islam* 41 (1965): 95–223.

Somel, Selçuk Akşin. "Osmanlı Modernleşme Döneminde Periferik Nüfus Grupları". *Toplum ve Bilim* 83 (Kış 1999/2000), 178–201.

Somel, Selçuk Akşin. *The Modernization of Public Education in the Ottoman Empire 1839–1908*. Leiden: Brill, 2001.
Soyyer, A. Yılmaz. *19. Yüzyılda Bektaşîlik*. Istanbul: Frida, 2012.
Sproull, Wm. 'The Fellaha'. *Herald of Mission News* 1887: 75–77.
Steigerwald, Diana, 'Ibn Nuṣayr'. *Encyclopaedia of Islam, THREE*. Edited by: Kate Fleet, Gudrun Krämer, Denis Matringe, John Nawas, Everett Rowson. Brill Online, 2015. Reference. Universitatsbibliothek Bamberg. 16 December 2015 <http://referenceworks.brillonline.com/entries/encyclopaedia-of-islam-3/ibn-nusayr-COM_23483>
Strothmann, Rudolf. 'Festkalender der Nusairier: Grundlegendes Lehrbuch im syrischen Alawitenstaat'. *Der Islam* (1944–46), vol. 27.
Süreyya, Mehmed. *Sicill-i Osmani*, 6 vols. Istanbul: Tarih Vakfı, 1996.
Swartz, David. 'Bridging the Study of Culture and Religion: Pierre Bourdieu's Political Economy of Symbolic Power'. *Sociology of Religion* 57:1. Special Issue: Sociology of Culture and Sociology of Religion (Spring, 1996); 71–85.
Şahin, Kaya. *Empire and Power in the Reign of Süleyman. Narrating the Sixteenth-Century Ottoman World*. Cambridge: Cambridge University Press, 2017.
Şimşir, Bilâl N. 'Washington'daki Osmanlı Elçisi Alexandre Mavroyeni Bey ve Ermeni Gailesi (1887–1896)'. *Ermeni Araştırmaları Dergisi*. Ankara: Ermeni Araştırmaları Enstitüsü, Aralık 2001-Ocak-Şubat 2002, Sayı 4: 32–54.
at-Tabari, Muhammad ibn Jarir. *Tafsir at-Tabari*, 26 vols. Cairo, 2001.
Talhamy, Yvette. *Meridot ha-Nusayrim ('Alawim) be-Surya be-me'a ha-tesha' 'esre*. Ph.D. thesis. Haife: University of Haifa, 2006.
Talhamy, Yvette. 'The Nusayri Leader Isma'il Khayr Bey and the Ottomans (1854–58)'. *Middle Eastern Studies* 44:6 (November 2008): 895–908.
Talhamy, Yvette. 'The Syrian Muslim Brothers and the Syrian-Iranian Relationship', in: *Middle East Journal* 63:4 (Autumn 2009): 561–580.
Talhamy, Yvette. 'The Fatwas and the Nusayri/Alawis of Syria', in: *Middle Eastern Studies* 46:2 (2010): 175–194.
Talhamy, Yvette. 'American Protestant Missionary Activity among the Nusayris (Alawis) in Syria in the Nineteenth Century'. In: *Middle Eastern Studies* 44:6 (March 2011): 215–236.
Talhamy, Yvette. 'Conscription among the Nusayris ('Alawis) in the Nineteenth Century'. *British Journal of Middle Eastern Studies* 38:01 (2011): 23–40.
Talhamy, Yvette. 'American Protestant Missionary Activity among the Nusayris (Alawis) in Syria in the Nineteenth Century', in: *Middle Eastern Studies* 47:2 (March 2011): 215–236.
Talhamy, Yvette. 'The Nusayri and Druze Minorities in Syria in the Nineteenth Century: The Revolt against the Egyptian Occupation as a Case Study'. *Middle Eastern Studies* 48:6 (2012): 973–995
Tatcı, Mustafa. "Hayretî". *DİA*. online: https://islamansiklopedisi.org.tr/hayreti (accessed 15 January 2020).
et-Tavîl, Muhammed Emîn Gâlip. *Arap Alevîlerinin Tarihi: Nusayrîler*. Translated by İsmail Özdemir. Istanbul: Chiviyazıları, 2000.
at-Tawil, Muhammad Amin Ghalib. *Tarikh al-'Alawiyyin*. Latakia: Matba'a at-Taraqqi, 1924.
Tejirian, Eleanor H., and Reeva Spector Simon, eds. *Conflict, Conquest, and Conversion: Two Thousand Years of Christian Missions in the Middle East*. New York: Columbia University Press, 2012.
Tendler Krieger, Bella. 'New Evidence for the Survival of Sexually Libertine Rites among some Nuṣayrī- 'Alawīs of the Nineteenth Century'. In *Islamic Cultures, Islamic Contexts*:

Essays in Honor of Professor Patricia Crone edited by Behnam Sadeghi et al., 565–596. Leiden: Brill, 2015.

Terzioğlu, Derin: "Where Ilm-i Hal Meets Catechism: Islamic Manuals of Religious Instruction in the Ottoman Empire in the Age of Confessionalization", *Past & Present* 220:1 (2013): 79–114.

Tezcan, Baki. *The Second Empire: Political and Social Transformation in the Early Modern World*. Cambridge: Cambridge University Press, 2010.

Tezcan, Baki. 'The New Order and the Fate of the Old – The Historiographical Construction of an Ottoman Ancien Régime in the Nineteenth Century'. In *Tributary Empires in Global History*, edited by Peter Bang and Christopher Bayly, 74–95. Basingstoke: Palgrave Macmillan, 2011.

Tibawi, A. L. *American Interests in Syria*. Oxford: Clarendon Press, 1966.

The Annual Register or a View of the History, Politics, and Literature of the Year 1835. London, 1836.

The Museum of Foreign Literature, Science, and Art, vol. III new series, January to April 1839, whole number volume XXXV. Philadelphia, 1839.

The Religious Monitor and Evangelical Repository. Philadelphia, 1841–1842.

Thomson, William. *The Land and the Book*. New York, 1861.

Thompson, Owen F. *Sketches of the Ministers of the Reformed Presbyterian Church of North America from 1880 to 1930*. Blanchard/Iowa, n.d.

Tosun, Murat Dursun. 'Çeçenzade Hasan Paşa'nın Abaza ve Çerkes Kabileleri ile İlişkileri', online at https://muratdursuntosun.wordpress.com/2014/04/03/cecenzade-haci-hasan-pasanin-abaza-ve-cerkes-kabileleri-ile-iliskileri/ (accessed 21 December 2016).

Tozlu, Selahattin. 'Osmanlı Arşiv Belgelerinde Antakya ve İskenderun Nusayrîleri (19. Yüzyıl)'. *Türk Kültürü ve Hacı Bektaş Velî Araştırma Dergisi* 54 (2010): 79–110.

Tozlu, Selahattin, and Naim Ürkmez: *Nusayrîler: Tarih, İnanç, Edebiyat ve Kaynakça*. Istanbul: Kitabevi, 2018.

Traboulsi, Samer. 'Converting the Druzes: The American Missionaries' Road Map to Nowhere'. In *One Hundred and Fifty*, edited by Nadia Maria El-Cheikh, Lina Choueiri, and Bilal Orfali, 25–41. Beirut: AUB Press, 2016.

Tracy, Joseph. *History of the American Board of Commissioners for Foreign Missions: Compiled Chiefly from the Published and Unpublished Documents of the Board*. 2nd ed., New York: M. W. Dodd, 1842.

Tucker, William T. *Mahdis and Millenarians: Shī'ite Extremists in Early Muslim Iraq*. Cambridge/UK: Cambridge University Press, 2008.

Tulasoğlu, Gülay. 'Türk-Sünnî Kimlik İnşasının II. Mahmud Dönemindeki Kökenleri Üzerine'. In *Kızılbaşlık, Alevilik, Bektaşilik: Tarih-Kimlik-İnanç-Ritüel*, edited by Yalçın Çakmak/İmran Gürtaş, 165–183. Istanbul: İletişim, 2015.

Tunç, Taner. 'Mehmet Behcet Yazar'ın Hayatı ve Eserleri Üzerine Bir İnceleme', M. A. Thesis. Manisa: Celal Bayar Üniversitesi, 2014.

Tuşalp Atiyas, E. Ekin. 'The 'Sunna-Minded Trends'', in: Marinos Sariyannis, *History of Ottoman Political Thought up to the Early Nineteenth Century*. Leiden: Brill, 2019. 233–278.

Tümkaya, Erkan. 'Die Entwicklung der türkisch-alawitischen Organisationen und ihre Beziehungen zu den Organisationen der anatolischen Aleviten in Deutschland'. In: *Grenzräume, Grenzgänge, Entgrenzungen. Junge Perspektiven der Türkeiforschung*, edited by Wiebke Hohberger, Roy Karadag, Katharina Müller, Christoph Ramm, 197–211. Wiesbaden: Springer, 2018.

Türk, Hüseyin. *Anadolu'nun Gizli İnancı Nusayrîlik: İnanç Sistemleri ve Kültürel Özellikleri.* Istanbul: Kaknüs, 2005.
Türkyılmaz, Zeynep: "Anxieties of Conversion: Missionaries, State and Heterodox communities in the Late Ottoman Empire". PhD Thesis. UCLA, 2009.
Uğuz, Sacit. 'II. Abdülhamid'in kapsayıcı eğitim politikasına bir örnek: Lazkiye Nusayrileri ve Hamidiye Mektepleri'. *Current Research in Social Sciences* 5:1 (2019): 9–27.
Uluçay, Ömer. *Arap Aleviliği: Nusayrilik.* Adana: Gözde, 1996.
Uluçay, Ömer. *Tarih'te Nusayrilik.* Adana: Gözde, 2001.
Uthman, Hashim. *al-'Alawiyyun bayna al-ustura wa al-haqiqa.* Beirut: al-'Alami, 1985.
Uyanık, Ercan. 'II. Abdülhamit ile Amerikan Protestan Misyonerlerinin Eğitim Mücadelesi: Amerika'ya Kaçırılan Nusayri Kızları'. *Kebikeç* 37 (2014): 35–56.
Uzer, Umut. *An Intellectual History of Turkish Nationalism: Between Turkish Ethnicity and Islamic Identity.* Salt Lake City: University of Utah Press, 2016.
Uzunçarşılı, İsmail Hakkı. *Osmanlı Devletinin İlmiye Teşkilâtı.* Ankara: Türk Tarih Kurumu, 1988.
Ümit, Devrim. "The American Protestant Missionary Network in Ottoman Turkey, 1876–1914". *International Journal of Humanities and Social Science,* 6:1 (2014): 16–51.
Ürkmez, Naim, and Aydın Efe. 'Osmanlı Arşiv Belgelerinde Nusayrîler Hakkında Genel Bilgiler'. *Türk Kültürü ve Hacı Bektaş Velî Araştırma Dergisi* 54 (2010) : 127–134.
Üstün, Kadir. 'Rethinking Vaka-i Hayriyye (Auspicious Event): Elimination of the Janissaries on the Path of Modernization', PhD Thesis. Ankara: Bilkent University, 2002.
Varol, Muharrem: *Islahat, Siyaset, Tarikat: Bektaşiliğin Ilgası Sonrasında Osmanlı Devleti'nin Tarikat Politikaları.* Istanbul: Dergah, 2013.
Wajdi, Muhammad Farid. *Da'irat al-ma'arif li-qarn al-'ashrun.* 10 vols. Beirut, 1971.
Wallach, Janet. *Desert Queen: The Extraordinary Life of Gertrude Bell: Adventurer, Adviser to Kings, Ally of Lawrence of Arabia.* London: Anchor, 1996.
Washburn, Denis, and A. Kevin Reinhart (eds.) *Converting Cultures: Religion, Ideology and Transformations of Modernity.* Leiden: Brill, 2007.
Winter, Stefan. 'La révolte alaouite de 1834 contre l'occupation égyptienne: perceptions alaouites et lecture ottomane'. *Oriente Moderno* 79:3 (1999): 61–71.
Winter, Stefan. 'The *Nusayris* before the Tanzimat in the Eyes of Ottoman Provincial Administrators, 1804–1834'. In: *From the Syrian Land to the States of Syria and Lebanon.* Edited by Thomas Philipp/Christoph Schumann, 97–112. Ergon: Würzburg, 2004.
Winter, Stefan. 'The Alawis in the Ottoman Period'. In *The Alawis of Syria: War, Faith and Politics of the Levant,* edited by Michael Kerr and Craig Larkin, 49–62. Oxford: Oxford University Press, 2015.
Winter, Stefan. *A History of the 'Alawis: From Medieval Aleppo to the Turkish Republic.* Princeton: Princeton University Press, 2016.
Wortabet, John. *Researches into the Religions of Syria.* London: Jame Nisbet, 1860.
Xenophon. *Memorabilia.* Translated and annotated by Amy L. Bonnette. Ithaca/London: Cornell University Press, 1994.
Yaslıçimen, Faruk. 'Sunnism versus Shi'ism? Rise of the Shi'i Politics and of the Ottoman Apprehension in Late Nineteenth Century Iraq'. M.A. Thesis. Ankara: Bilkent University, 2008.
Yaslıçimen, Faruk. "Saving the Minds and Loyalties of Subjects: Ottoman Education Policy Against the Spread of Shiism in Iraq During the Time of Abdülhamid II". *Dîvân: Disiplinlerarası Çalışmalar Dergisi* 21:41 (2016): 63–108.

Yaycıoğlu, Ali. *Partners of the Empire: The Crisis of the Ottoman Order in the Age of Revolutions*. Stanford: Stanford University Press, 2016.
Yılmaz, Gülay. 'İstemezük'. In *Osmanlı'dan Günümüze Darbeler*, edited by Mehmet Ö. Alkan, 1-15. Istanbul: Tarih Vakfı, 2017.
Yılmazer, Ziya. 'Esad Efendi, Sahaflar Şeyhizâde'. *DİA*, online at https://islamansiklopedisi.org.tr/esad-efendi-sahaflar-seyhizade (15 January 2020).
Yıldırım, Rıza. 'Turkomans between two empires: the origins of the Qızılbash identity in Anatolia (1447-1514)', PhD Thesis. Ankara: Bilkent University, 2008.
Yıldırım, Rıza. "Bektaşi kime derler? Bektaşi kavramının kapsamı ve sınırları üzerine tarihsel bir analiz denemesi". *Türk Kültürü ve Hacı Bektaş-ı Veli Araştırma Derneği* 55 (2010): 23-58.
Yıldız, Özgür. *Anadolu'da Amerikan Misyonerleri*. Istanbul: Yeditepe, 2015.
Yılmaz, Hüseyin. 'Containing Sultanic Authority: Constitutionalism in the Ottoman Empire before Modernity'. *Journal of Ottoman Studies/Osmanlı Araştırmaları* 45 (2015): 231-264.
Yüksel, Emrullah. 'Müslüman Türk Âlimi olarak İmâm Birgivî'nin Osmanlı Döneminde ve Günümüz Türkiyesinde Yeri'. In *İmam Birgivî*, edited by Mehmet Şeker, 32-37. Ankara: Türkiye Diyanet Vakfı, 1994.
Yüksel, Emrullah. 'Birgivî', in: *DİA*, online https://islamansiklopedisi.org.tr/birgivi (15 January 2020).
Zarcone, Thierry. "Bektaş, Hacı", in: *Encyclopaedia of Islam*, THREE, Edited by: Kate Fleet, Gudrun Krämer, Denis Matringe, John Nawas, Everett Rowson. Consulted online on 09 March 2017 http://dx.doi.org/10.1163/1573-3912_ei3_COM_24009
Zarcone, Thierry. "Bektaşiyye", in: *Encyclopaedia of Islam*, THREE (EI³), Edited by: Kate Fleet, Gudrun Krämer, Denis Matringe, John Nawas, Everett Rowson. Consulted online on 09 March 2017 http://dx.doi.org/10.1163/1573-3912_ei3_COM_24010
Zemmin, Florian. *Modernity in Islamic Tradition: The Concept of 'Society' in the Journal al-Manar (Cairo, 1898-1940)*. Berlin/Boston: De Gruyter, 2018.
Zeuge, Uta. *Die Mission des American Board in Syrien im 19. Jahrhundert: Implikationen eines transkulturellen Dialogs*. Stuttgart; Franz Steiner, 2016.
Zeuge, Uta. *The Mission of the American Board in Syria: Implications of a transcultural dialogue*, translated by Elizabeth Janik. Stuttgart: Franz Steiner, 2017.
Zilfi, Madeline C. *The Politics of Piety: The Ottoman Ulema 1600-1800* (Chicago: Bibliotheca Islamica, 1988).
Zilfi, Madeline C. 'The Kadizadelis: Discordant Revivalism in Seventeenth Century Istanbul'. *Journal of Near Eastern Studies* 45:42 (October 1986): 251-269
Zimmermann, Johannes. "Aleviten in osmanischen Wörterbüchern und Enzyklopädien des späten 19. Jahrhunderts". In *Ocak und Dedelik: Institutionen religiösen Spezialistentums bei den Aleviten*, edited by Robert Langer et al., 179-204. Frankfurt am Main: Peter Lang, 2013.
Zürcher, Erik-31 Mart: A Fundamentalist Uprising in Istanbul in April 1909? *The Young Turk Revolution and the Ottoman Empire: The Aftermath of 1908*, edited by Lévy-Aksu, Noémi, and François Georgeon, 196-211. London: I. B. Tauris, 2017.

INDEX

ABCFM (American Board of Commissioners for Foreign Missions) 11, 40, 43, 44, 48–51, 53, 79, 81, 131, 133, 160, 161

Abdülaziz (Ottoman Sultan) 9, 46, 47, 61, 93, 96, 97, 100, 107, 111, 143–144

Abdülhamid II (Ottoman Sultan) 3, 5, 7, 8, 9, 12, 24, 40, 47, 48–49, 54, 73, 79, 81, 85, 86, 93, 94. 99, 103, 105, 107, 108–109, 110, 111, 113–114, 116, 117, 118, 119, 120–121, 122, 123, 126, 144, 146–147, 160, 161

Abdülmecid (Ottoman Sultan) 9, 46, 89, 93, 96

Abkhaz 8, 84, 85

Adana 1, 26, 39, 52, 64–67, 70, 73, 74, 75, 125, 130, 131

al-Adhani, Sulayman 1, 11

Ahmed Cevad Paşa 101

Ahmed Cevdet Paşa 10, 37–38, 85, 91, 93

Ahmed Lutfi 84, 85, 89

Ahmed Şerif 142–143

Ahmed Vasfi Zekeriya 141–142

Akka 112, 147

Alawi/Nusayri mountains (Jabal al-Ansariyya/Nusayriyya) 3, 4, 7, 22, 23, 26, 27, 28, 33, 34, 36, 37, 38. 73, 74, 104, 108, 110, 114, 131, 153

Alawis/Alawites *passim*

Alawism/Nusayrism 1, 2, 5, 8, 19, 20, 21, 22, 33, 54, 106, 151, 153, 155

Albania/Albanians 35, 99, 137

Alemdar Mustafa Paşa 87

Aleppo 21, 22, 35, 37, 40, 96, 115, 116, 126

Alevis/Alevism 2, 4, 5, 6, 7, 8, 9, 10, 12, 16, 34, 37, 38, 40, 45, 47–49, 81, 86, 91, 97, 102, 105, 106, 158, 161

Ali ibn Abi Talib (Imam) 13, 19, 20, 21, 37, 47, 86, 97, 114, 134

Aliyullahis/Ali-ilahî 101, 106

America/USA 8, 11, 27, 40, 41–44, 50, 51, 54, 56, 57, 59, 62–76, 81, 94, 121, 129, 131, 132, 133, 138, 143, 149, 151, 152, 161

Anatolia 1, 2, 3, 8, 9, 37, 40, 43, 47, 48, 49, 53, 63, 76, 81, 82, 86, 87, 90, 94, 97, 98, 99, 100, 102, 103, 105, 106, 123, 144

Antakya/Antioch 24, 26, 31, 34, 36, 37, 39, 40, 45, 95, 96, 114, 115, 116, 125, 126, 158

apostasy 3, 30, 39, 40, 44, 78, 127

Armenians 5, 40, 47, 48–49, 50, 53, 61, 63, 64, 65, 75–76, 81, 101, 107, 117, 127, 128, 129, 133–134, 161

al-Askari, Hasan (Imam) 19, 21

Assyrians (Süryani) 12, 53, 148

Ayni, Mehmed Ali 114

Ayyubids (Sunni dynasty) 22, 27

al-Azhar University 103

Azmi Bey 147

Babanna 156

Babis/Baha'is 101, 148

Balkans 9, 40, 49, 64, 79, 81, 87, 94, 99, 100, 130

Baybars (Mamluk sultan) 22

Bedri (Hasan Bedreddin) Pasha 99–100

Beirut 1, 2, 11, 22, 38, 42, 50, 57, 58, 60, 74, 75, 94, 109, 120, 123, 134, 135, 136, 137, 142, 143, 146–157

Bektaşis 2, 6, 8, 9, 16, 81, 86–94, 98, 101, 159

Bell, Gertrude 28–29, 52

Birgi 90

Birgivî, Mehmed Efendi 83

Bolshevism 171 n.129

Bourdieu, Pierre 29, 32

Britain/England 25, 56, 57

Burton, Isabel 41, 42, 49

Buyids (Shi'i dynasty) 21

Caucasus 8, 84, 85, 96
Cilicia 1, 24, 26, 40, 63, 73, 122, 125, 131
Circassians 8, 84–85, 159
civilization 8, 12, 62, 84–85, 99–100, 104, 105, 134, 135, 136, 141–142, 143, 146, 147, 148, 149, 150, 156
civilizing mission 8, 12, 86, 104, 105, 108, 110, 136, 148, 160 (chapter 3: 81–116)
Cleveland, Grover (twice US president) 66, 67, 70, 75
commanding right and forbidding wrong 18, 82, 83, 84, 159
Committee of Union and Progress (CUP) 117, 118, 133, 141
conscription 4, 5, 6, 9, 12, 24, 35, 46, 50, 58, 59, 61, 62, 111, 116, 130
conversion 3, 4, 5, 7, 8, 9, 12, 40, 41, 43, 44, 48, 50, 51, 56, 59, 61, 64, 69, 78, 82–86, 90, 96, 101, 110, 114, 116, 120, 127, 160
correction/rectification of the belief(s) 2, 5, 8, 79, 81–116, 159, 160
Crimea 34, 85
Crypto-Christians 2, 4
Çukurova 26, 39

Daoud 10, 41, 54–63, 78, 81, 176 n.94
Dodds, Jennie B. 75, 76
Druze 2, 6, 7, 9, 10, 11, 27, 28, 35, 37, 42, 45, 47, 49–51, 94, 97, 101, 106, 107, 109, 123, 126, 135, 148, 150, 156, 158

Easson, Henry 176 n.94, 178 n.132
Edhem Nejad 141
Eldridge, George Jackson (British consul-general) 57
Elliot, Henry (British ambassador) 57, 59, 61–62
Esad Efendi 88, 90, 92, 93
Evangelical Alliance (Britain) 60–61, 72, 74

Fatimids (Shi'i dynasty) 22, 23
fellah/fellaheen/fellahin ('peasants') 27–28, 36, 77, 122–125, 127, 128, 129, 130, 131, 151
Ferah Ali Paşa 84–85
fine tuning 8, 81, 86, 94, 96, 104
Fisk, Pliny 43–45, 161

France/the French 10, 25, 37, 47, 56, 61, 74, 94, 105, 123, 136, 137, 138, 140, 142, 143, 147, 158, 162
Freemasons 10, 37
French Revolution 117, 119

ghulat/gulât ('exaggerators') 19–21, 38, 106, 166 n.23
ghuluw(w) ('transgression') 17–21
Greeks/Greece 8, 34, 36, 42, 50, 56, 73, 107, 128, 131, 140
Günaltay, Mehmet Şemsettin 105–106
Gypsies 100

Hacı Bektaş Veli 9, 86, 90, 93
Haifa 112
Hakkı (Ottoman official) 108–109
Hamdanids (Shi'i dynasty) 22, 23
Hamood (first baptised Nusayri man) 55, 56
Hanafi Sunnism 3, 7, 8, 9, 34, 79, 84, 96, 98, 101, 102, 103, 108, 110, 113, 159, 161
Hasan Paşa, Çeçenzade 85
Hatay 1, 24, 25, 26, 31
Hawash Bey 111
Haydariyya (Alawi subsect) 24, 31, 33, 114, 158
heresy/heretics 3, 5, 6, 7, 8, 10, 13, 15–16, 23, 24, 26, 30, 34, 37, 40, 45, 48, 81, 82, 84, 86–88, 89, 90, 91, 92, 95, 97, 98–99, 100, 101, 102, 103, 104, 106, 107, 108, 110, 145, 159, 160, 161
heterodoxy 1, 2, 3, 4, 7, 11, 12, 21, 24, 31, 34, 40, 41, 45, 47, 81, 82, 86, 101, 110, 159, 160, 161
Holo (Arap İzzet) Paşa 111
Hüdai (Nusayris) 113–114
al-Husayn, Ali (Imam, Zaynu'l-Abidin) 19

Ibn Nusayr, Muhammad 19, 20, 21, 155
Ibn Saba' 19
Ibn Taymiyya 23
Ibraheem Mohammed/Yusuph, see Ibrahim b. Mahmud
Ibrahim b. Mahmud (Telgie's father) 64, 65, 66, 67, 69, 71, 76, 77
Ibrahim Paşa (governor of Syria) 35, 36, 50
ihtida (conversion to Islam) 10, 86, 160

initiation, Alawi 28, 31–32
Iraq *passim*
Isbar, Muhammad Ali 33
Iskenderun/Alexandretta 25, 26, 130
Islam *passim*
Isma'il Khayr Bey 4, 111
Isma'ilis 10, 16, 23, 27, 37, 50, 97, 106, 135, 148
Ismail Hakkı Bey (mutasarrif) 147
Ismail Kemal Bey (Vlora) 109–110
Istanbul *passim*

Jabla/Jabala/Jableh 22, 25, 26, 153
Janissaries/*Yeniçeri* 2, 9, 36, 81, 85, 86, 87–90, 92
Jessup, Henry H. 1, 50
Jesus Christ 17–18, 19, 42, 44, 47, 48, 53, 55, 63, 76, 77, 103, 126, 127, 128, 130, 131, 132, 133
Jews/Judaism 2, 6, 8, 16, 17–18, 19, 20, 34, 35, 40, 42, 43, 44, 45, 53, 83, 120, 126, 148, 161

Kadızade Mehmed Efendi 83
Kalaziyya (Alawi subsect) 24, 31, 33
Kamil Paşa (Ottoman prime minister) 73
Kara Mehmed Paşa (Kara Cehennem) 36–37
Khalaify, Selim (Nusayri convert) 57, 58
Khalid, Sheikh 90
Khalidiyya (Mujaddidi-Naqshbandi suborder) 90
al-Khasibi, al-Husayn Ibn Hamdan 21–22
Kızılbaş 4, 5–6, 7, 9, 10, 12, 37, 47, 48, 49, 82, 87, 97, 98, 102, 104
Kurds 8, 12, 35, 49, 81, 96, 97, 99, 100, 101, 105

Lammens, Henri 11, 116, 158
Latakia/Lazkiye *passim*
Latin America 105
League of Nations 25
Lebanon 11, 25, 27, 33, 34, 42, 45, 50, 73, 97, 112, 130, 147
Levant 45
Lyde, Samuel 54–55, 58

M. Ali Münir 134–135
Mahmud II (Ottoman Sultan) *passim*

al-Majlisi 19
makarr-ı ulema ('abode of the ulema') 90, 91
Makhloof, Suleiman Hassan, *see* Daoud
Mamluks (Sunni dynasty) 22, 27
Manichaeism 20
Maraş 50, 56, 57, 60, 61, 75, 176 n.97
Mariam (first baptised Nusayri woman) 54, 55
Maronites 42, 50, 123, 128
Mathews, G.D. 72
Mazdakism 10, 20, 37–38, 171 n.129
medeniyet ('civilization') 84, 100, 103, 148
Mehmed/Muhammad Ali Paşa 3, 24, 35, 36
Mehmed Arif 98–99, 106
Mehmed Behcet 116, 147–157, 161
Mehmed Emin Vahid Efendi 37
Mehmed Memduh Paşa 49, 89
Mehmed Şevket 139–141
Mehmed Tahir (Şeyhülislam) 87
Mehmed Ziya Bey 108, 110–111, 113, 114
Mersin 1, 26, 39, 41, 63, 65, 66, 67, 68, 72, 73, 74, 75, 77, 125, 129, 130, 132
Metawalis (Shi'is of Lebanon) 45, 97, 135, 148
Metheny, David 59–60, 63–77, 119, 125
Midhat Paşa 11, 46, 47, 111–113
millet 34, 39, 40, 47, 48, 85, 106
missionaries *passim*
Mount Lebanon 42, 50, 112, 147
Muhammad, Prophet 16, 18, 20, 21, 30, 31, 33, 48, 56, 83, 88, 106, 142
müceddid/mujaddid 88–89
Mujaddidiyya (Naqshbandiyya) 46, 90
muqaddam/mukaddem 28, 29, 111, 151, 152–154
Mustafa (converted Muslim in Maraş) 56, 61
Mustafa Nuri Paşa 84, 85, 191 n.161
Müteferrika, Ibrahim 84

Nakşbendi/Naqshbandiyya 46, 89, 90, 93
Nasuhi Paşa (governor of Adana) 65, 66, 67, 70, 74
non-Sunnis *passim*
Nusayris *passim*

orientalism, Ottoman 11, 104, 145, 148, 157, 161
Ottoman Empire/State *passim*
Ottomans *passim*

Paganism 8, 12, 16, 22, 40, 45, 51, 53, 59, 63, 71, 102, 108, 127, 131
Palestine 8, 25, 35, 43, 44, 45, 53, 103, 105, 107, 112, 147
Pan-Islam (*İttihad-ı İslam*) 79, 99, 145, 159, 160
Parsons, Levi 43–45, 133
Protestantism *passim*
Protestants *passim*

rafida/rawafid (Arab. 'rejecters') 16
râfizî/revâfiz (Turk. 'rejecters', 'heretics') 16, 34, 97, 102, 106
Rashid Rida 144–145
Refik Temimi 116, 147–157, 161
Richter, Julius 49, 50
ar-Rida, Ali ibn Musa (Imam) 19
Robert College (Istanbul) 125, 142
RPCNA (*Reformed Presbyterian Church of North America*) 11, 40, 62, 63, 68, 69, 72, 73
Rüstem Paşa (Ottoman ambassador in London) 72

Sabbataians (Dönme) 2
Sabians 101, 106
as-Sadiq, Ja'far (Imam) 19
Safavid Dynasty (Iran) 49, 82, 88, 98
Safita 26, 50, 151–152, 156
Safiye/Safiya/Sophia (sister of Telgie) 64, 69, 76–77
Salfit 150
Samaritans 148
Samizade Süreyya 135–139, 143–144
Second Awakening 43
Second Coming (Christ) 42, 43
Selim I (Ottoman Sultan) 23, 82
Selim III (Ottoman Sultan) 37, 85, 87, 89, 185 n.70
Şemseddin Sami (Frasheri) 99
Şeyhülislam (Ottoman grand mufti) 84, 87, 89, 91, 92, 93, 102
Shabbatai Zwi 2
Shah Isma'il I 82

Sheikh Mufid 19
sheikhs, Alawi 24, 28–29, 31–33, 52, 55, 96, 124, 128, 131, 134, 152, 158, 169 n.84
Shi'is/Shi'a (Twelver) 1, 8, 13, 16, 19, 20, 21, 22, 23, 27, 29, 30, 31, 33, 34, 38, 40, 47, 81, 82, 86, 95, 97, 98, 101, 103, 105, 110, 144, 145, 146, 148
as-Sinjari, Makzun 22
Socialism 10, 37
Socrates 15
Sterett, Evadna 63
Sterett, Mary 76, 77
Süleyman Hüsnü Paşa 100–102
Süleyman I ('Kanuni', Ottoman Sultan) 82
Sunnis *passim*
Sunnitization 3, 91, 95, 159
Syria *passim*
Syrian Protestant College (Beirut) 142, 143

at-Tabarani, Abu Sa'id 22
at-Tabari, Muhammad ibn Jarir (early Muslim chronicler) 18, 30
Tahmasb I (Iranian Safavid Shah) 82
Tanzimat ('reforms') 3, 9, 24, 36, 37, 38, 46–47, 57, 86, 89, 90, 94, 95, 99, 100, 159, 160
Tarsus 1, 39, 41, 52, 68, 70, 74, 76–77, 122–123, 124
tashih al-i'tiqad 82, 83, 90
tashih-i itikad/akaid, see correction of the belief(s)
at-Tawil, Muhammad Amin Ghalib 1, 11, 111, 112, 113, 158
Telgie Ibrahim 10, 41, 63–79, 81
temeddün ('civilization') 84, 136
Templers, German 112–113
Terrell, A.W. (US Minister in Istanbul) 70–75
tribes, Alawi/Nusayri 9, 23, 24, 27–28, 34, 36, 38, 41, 154, 155
Tripoli (Trablusgarb, Libya) 128, 146
Tripoli (Trablusşam, Lebanon) 4, 37, 50, 58, 130, 147, 172 n.5
Turcomans (Türkmen) 133, 148, 156, 189 n.126

ulema 47, 82, 83, 84, 85, 86, 87, 88, 90, 91, 92, 101, 133, 134, 135, 145, 159

Umayyad (early Islamic dynasty) 21
Uthman, Hashim 33
'Uzayr/Ezra 17, 19

Wahhabis 16, 88, 97, 101
Weber, Max 29, 30, 31

Xenophon 15

Yezidis 5, 6, 7, 8, 9, 11, 12, 34, 40, 47, 49, 81, 96, 97, 101, 103–104, 161, 191 n.161

Young Turks 8, 9–10, 12, 47, 116, 117–158, 161
Yusuf Jadid (Yusef Jadeed) 54, 55

Zehra/Zahra/Zahara (sister of Telgie) 64, 69, 76–77
Zionists 148
Zoroastrianism 12, 16, 19, 20, 21, 84, 85, 106, 183 n.28
Zühdi Paşa (Ottoman minister of education) 64

www.ingramcontent.com/pod-product-compliance
Lightning Source LLC
Chambersburg PA
CBHW062148300426
44115CB00012BA/2044